TRAN...

MY DAYS IN THE UNDERWORLD

Agni Sreedhar is publisher and editor of the Kannada tabloid *Agni*. He recounted his experiences in the underworld in the bestselling *Dadagiriya Dinagalu*, which won the Karnataka State Sahitya Akademi Award. He has six other works to his credit, all of which have run into multiple editions. He also writes extensively on quantum philosophy and his book *In the Path of Modern Mages*, based on his personal experiences, is considered a classic in Kannada.

A film based on his life, *Aa Dinagalu*, which he scripted with award-winning playwright Girish Karnad, received critical acclaim. His other films, *Slum Bala*, *Kallara Santhe* and *Edegarike*, also received popular and critical acclaim. *Thamassu*, on communal intolerance, which he scripted and directed, received the Karnataka State Award for Best Story.

He is also actively involved in social causes and is at the forefront of the agitation against mining in Karnataka.

MY DAYS IN THE UNDERWORLD

Rise of the Bangalore Mafia

Agni Sreedhar

TRANQUEBAR

TRANQUEBAR PRESS
An imprint of westland ltd

61 Silverline, Alapakkam Main Road, Maduravoyal, Chennai 600095
No. 38/10 (New No.5), Raghava Nagar, New Timber Yard Layout, Bangalore 560 026
93, 1st floor, Sham Lal Road, Daryaganj, New Delhi 110002

First published in India by TRANQUBAR, on imprint of westland ltd 2013

10 9 8 7 6 5 4 3 2 1

ISBN 978-93-83260-34-8

Typeset in Sabon Roman by SÜRYA, New Delhi

Printed at HT Media Ltd., Noida

DEDICATED

... to all the boys who travelled with me on this journey

Introduction

Most people have a distorted image of the underworld. To a large extent the media propagates this distortion by glorifying and glamorising the life of crime.

I lived this life for twenty years. This is my attempt to demystify Bangalore's criminal networks. It is an effort at presenting the true nature of this city's substratum to the reading public.

I began by writing about my experiences in my weekly Kannada tabloid *Agni* in 1999. The column ran for four years and the readers' response was overwhelming. On public demand it was published in three volumes and became a bestseller. It won critical acclaim and was conferred the Karnataka Sahitya Academy award.

When I started compiling my recollections, I called it a search.

There was a time in my life when strange eyes followed me at all times. Invisible ears listened to every word I uttered. I could not simply dismiss this as the daily throb of this beast that lies under the city—the monster that I helped make.

There was a world of difference between what lay within me and that which existed without. The harshness, fear, torture, deceit and scheming realm of lawlessness posed a challenge to my conscience. I had to get out of it but I did not know how. Writing, to some extent, meant release. Writing changed me and helped me to unravel what I'd done. It also created strange conflicts in me. Cold-blooded criminals began to look helpless, and the line between the two worlds—under and 'over'—became thin. I began to feel as though we were on a journey. How could I change the world around me? Was it even remotely possible? Contemplating such questions, I bided my time.

Realisation dawned on me. It was not the world that needed to change, but I. The world is fine, with a comfortable mix of this and that. What was topsy-turvy was within me. I needed to transform. I had travelled too far into the crime world. I could not see the road to recovery. I had to make great efforts to get on the right path. But just as I found a road I was drawn to another point of no return. People who promised to show me the path led me away from it. It was a tough fight. I finally found my way, found myself.

I am happy that my book is now available in English translation. Thanks to V.G. Jaideep and Prathibha Nandakumar, without whom it would have been impossible.

Thanks to the publishers, Westland.

I dedicate this book to all those who travelled with me. And to those who stood by me.

Bangalore   AGNI SREEDHAR

PART I

One

It was the summer of 1974 when I came to Bangalore. I was fresh out of college from Kanakapura, an hour's drive from the state capital, and had decided to study law here before eventually entering the civil services.

It was morning when I got off at the bus station in Majestic, and though I had been to Bangalore before, the city never ceased to overwhelm—around me were scores of buses, bringing in people from all corners of Karnataka; people like me. And outside, the crowds flowed; knots of men and women headed purposefully somewhere. This city I was stepping into was entirely different from the town I grew up in. Though a mere fifty kilometres away, Kanakapura was small and dull: it had no parks, one movie theatre, one good hotel and one small river that was dry most of the time.

As soon as I got off the bus, I made my way through the crowds and headed for the Vokkaligara Sangha Hostel. This establishment, run for members of Karnataka's dominant Vokkaliga community, was part of a larger educational institution, which would later expand into one of the largest in the state, offering courses in medicine and engineering. I had enrolled into the Vokkaligara Sangha Law College and turned out to be quite good at my studies, usually wrapping my head around complicated legal arguments much before the lecturer had finished explaining them.

At the hostel, I headed for my room. It was small—three cots, three tables and barely enough room to move around. I unpacked my books: about fifty by prominent Kannada litterateurs; my three favourite writers, Camus, Kafka and Sartre; and, of course, *The Godfather*. My roommates, Venugopal and Muddahanume Gowda, seemed completely in awe of this library unfolding before their eyes. Both were in their second year and would go on to have successful careers as officers of the bar: years later, accused as a criminal, I would stand in the dock before Gowda, who was then a magistrate. Worse still, when he decided to resign and contest elections from Kunigal, I campaigned for him, along with the politician S. Ramesh, much to Gowda's consternation. Gowda went on to become a member of the legislative assembly from the Kunigal constituency. Venugopal was a public prosecutor for a significant portion of his professional life and now serves as a senior civil lawyer.

But my roommates' success came much later; while at college, the two looked at me with respect—for my interest in literature and inherent grasp of the English language—and they believed my gumption would take me places, despite the apparent disadvantages of my small-town upbringing.

The study of law was a leisurely activity when I was in college. Classes would end at ten in the morning and the rest of the day was spent in idle banter and gossip. When conversation wasn't centred on girls, it would veer towards crime and rowdies and the two names that featured constantly in our conversations were M.P. Jayaraj and K.M. Nagraj—two of the most powerful figures in Bangalore. Every college was aligned with one of these two men, their affiliates or someone with a criminal persuasion. It was especially crucial for students contesting college elections to be seen as protégés of these overlords, and victory hinged on the number of rowdies providing their patronage to a particular candidate. At the time, three institutions—Vokkaligara Sangha, R.C. College and the Government Arts and Science (or more popularly, Gas) College—were the Petri dishes for what would later emerge as Bangalore's underground. It was in these three colleges that the nexus between politics, crime and the student body took root.

K.M. Nagraj had a two-fold agenda. He fostered rowdies and students with a view to gain political mileage. A leader of the Indira Brigade, the Congress party's youth wing, Nagraj had determined very early on that forging links with the underworld and student bodies would serve his political career well. Needless to say, Nagraj had powerful patrons, among them Dayanada Sagar, who would go on to create one of Karnataka's largest educational institutions. Nagraj's days were spent in a state of constant struggle—to garner the support of as many rowdies as possible, to wield power over as many colleges as possible, to gain control over south Bangalore, and in intricate political machinations.

M.P. Jayaraj was the polar opposite of Nagraj. He existed for one reason alone: to be the number one player in the city's underworld. He entered and lived a life of crime purely for the sake of villainy. Propped up by M.D. Natraj, the son-in-law of the then chief minister Devaraj Urs, Jayaraj was the de facto head of the Indira Brigade and consequently sat at the centre of a power struggle between Nagraj and Natraj. When he was not embroiled in the workings of the underworld, Jayaraj ran a rag called *Garibi Hatao* (Eradicate Poverty), cleaving to the Socialist mantra parroted by the then prime minister Indira Gandhi. Headquartered in the seedy and overpopulated Tigalara Pet, *Garibi Hatao* was nothing if not sensationalist, and mainly targeted a corrupt and inept police force.

If Jayaraj and Nagraj were paterfamilias to two large, complex and divisive tribes consisting of goons, students, politicians and sundry hangers-on, Razor Vasu and Mohammaden Block Ali (named for his origins in the Muslim quarter of south Bangalore) were the twin avuncular enforcers of a parallel justice system; one that was presided over by Jayaraj. No one could reliably claim to have actually seen either Vasu or Ali, and no one would have been able to identify either man on a street. However, that didn't stop anyone even remotely associated with the underworld from claiming deep and abiding ties with Vasu, Ali, or more ambitiously, both of them. Each had a following that was legion and each had scores of urban legends ascribed to him: Vasu's razor was unerring in its accuracy, Ali was as strong as a lion and could easily take on a gang of a hundred men, both were over six feet tall, they were inseparable and had an unquenchable thirst for women. The big rumour was that Jayaraj gave them each an astronomical weekly allowance of eleven thousand rupees.

At the time, I would visit Jnana Bharathi (Bangalore University) twice a week. Kalegowda Nagwara, a Kannada lecturer at the university, was a relative of mine and I would take with me books that we could discuss. Frequently, the well-known Dalit poet Siddalingiah, the critic D.R. Nagraj and the present secretary of the Sahitya Academy, Agrahara Krishnamurthy, who were then studying for their Master's degree in Kannada, would join us. Discussions were fairly eclectic, ranging from elaborate arguments about the books I had brought along to the city's underworld. There were serious debates about grassroots issues as well as an expression of deep-seated respect for those who had brought in a significant amount of change in society using violence. I was a natural raconteur and my stories, peppered with imaginary incidents and embellished with urban legend, would invariably be about the two dominant rowdies at the time: Razor Vasu and Mohammaden Block Ali.

Naturally, as was the trend at the time, the Marxist revolutionary Ernesto 'Che' Guevara figured prominently in our conversations; we were deeply fascinated with his approach to change and society. Curiously, the American gangster Patty Hearst was also someone we held respect for, and indeed, some of us were so taken with her life that a student with Leftist leanings even wrote a play about her and staged it at Ravindra Kalakshetra near Town Hall.

It was a time of deep unrest, both personal and political, and we felt an attack on crude and money-grabbing capitalists was long overdue. It was a time for active rebellion and for action. It was at this time that I, along with two friends, Ramesh and Sujay, plotted my first act of violence.

It was a Sunday and the three of us were in a hostel run by the Jain community. We were a few beers down and talking of Hearst, bemoaning the lack of a leader of her stature. We then decided that we, too, could form a gang like Hearst and launch an attack on 'capitalist slave-drivers'. At the time, it mattered little that both Ramesh and Sujay came from very wealthy families and, in a sense, represented the enemy we were plotting to attack. We decided who our target would be—a businessman everyone called 'Shetty'. He lived in a large mansion opposite East West School, near Krishna Rao Park in south Bangalore. Ramesh described the man: he owned three cars, was miserly, uncaring and would do just about anything for money. To us, Shetty embodied exploitation and oppression. We decided to launch an attack on his house that same night.

When we set out, the city was absolutely still and the streets were empty. We reached Shetty's house at eleven o'clock and sat on a stone bench near Krishna Rao Park, waiting for people in the house to retire for the night. At half past eleven, when all the lights in the house had been turned off, we decided to move in. The only source of illumination was a lamppost on the road. Sujay, who was a marksman of sorts, picked up a stone and took out that one remaining light. The street was not in complete darkness. We walked up to the gate and, making sure there were no dogs inside, jumped into the compound. We made our way to the front door and bolted it. We then picked up every pot we could find in the garden and threw it into the street outside. We then jumped over the gate and stood at a distance of about twenty metres from the house. A small stockpile of stones was quickly accumulated and we launched the projectiles at the house. Each one found its mark. Glass shattered so loudly in the still of the night that we leapt back towards the park in fear. Soon, shouts of 'thief, thief' rent the air and the lights in the house came on. The balcony door upstairs opened and a man in a dhoti and vest came out gingerly and looked over the parapet. A woman, perhaps his wife, joined him and soon there were about eight people on the balcony, all staring out in fear. They conversed loudly in Telugu and after a few moments went back inside. After about ten minutes, we decided to renew our attack. This time, we weren't as scared as we were earlier. After we were done, we sauntered back to the park and crouched behind a bush.

Shetty came out, screaming expletives in Telugu. He swore and swore and we were delighted. Then, Shetty's son came out, peered at the park for a moment and went back in. By then, we had decided that we weren't going to back down. We picked up three large stones and launched one final offensive against Shetty and his house. The house was quiet, but the lights were still on. We waited in the park.

Soon, a police vehicle came clattering through the night. Many years later, when I would gain notoriety in the underworld, even a hint of such a vehicle approaching would have me on the run, but not then. Then, we had nothing to fear. We were revolutionaries. We had attacked the house of the oppressor. Surely, the police would commend us, we thought.

The Basavanagudi police station is situated inside Krishna Rao Park, and in all likelihood the police vehicle had arrived from this location. About five constables got out and went into Shetty's house. We remained crouched behind the bush. Soon, the policemen walked towards the park with two torches held aloft. This was patently ridiculous. There we were, three teenagers in a twenty-five-acre park and all they could throw at us were five cops with two pathetic torches? But still, we were scared, and after a hastily whispered, 'Let's run', bolted towards B.P. Wadia Road on the other side of the park. The constables gave rigorous chase and one even threw his lathi at us. But we were younger, faster and scared.

We quickly made our way to Gandhi Bazaar, a few hundred metres from the park, and by the time we got there, were much calmer. We walked down Govindayya Road and came upon a parked Fiat. Ramesh said if we could get in, he would hotwire the car. We picked up three large stones, and from a distance of about twenty feet, launched at the front windshield with all the power we could muster. What we didn't know then, was that if you throw a large stone at a car's windshield, it won't implode, it will shatter outwards. And in the explosion, a large shard of glass pierced Sujay's forehead and he passed out cold.

Lights had come on in a couple of houses so we picked up Sujay and started heading towards the hostel. But Sujay, although seething from the pain, wouldn't have any of it. 'Let's smash the windows of all the cars in this city. Let's not go back to the room until we've done this,' he screamed. We told him he needed to rest and put him at ease with the promise that all the cars in the city would still be around after he recovered. Only then would he let us head back to the hostel.

The next morning we took Sujay to a doctor to sew up the gaping wound on his forehead. That was our last attempt at vandalism. But it was by no means our last crack at launching a revolution.

At the time, Professor Nanjundaswamy, who would go on to head the Raitha Sangha, which launched several agitations against large corporations like the seeds industry giant Monsanto, and Kentucky Fried Chicken, was a prominent leader in the Samajwadi Party in Karnataka. He had issued a stern warning to the then government-run luxury hotel Ashoka for setting tariffs that were beyond the reach of the common man. He goaded us to do something about it, to launch a protest and force the hotel to lower their rates to be on par with other such establishments in the city.

One day, a gang of about twenty of us decided to take the professor up on his challenge. We marched up to the hotel, having decided that we would eat all we could and pay a rate that a meal of equivalent proportions would cost at a far cheaper establishment like the Kamat Hotel located not too far away. If the police was called, we would offer ourselves up for arrest as a mark of protest. At least, that was the plan.

We ate that day like we had never eaten before, all the while talking loudly, guffawing and making a general nuisance of ourselves. But the staff put up with our behaviour: this was a luxury hotel and they didn't have a choice. After we were done, coffee was ordered. I decided to ask for a glass of Bournvita, thinking that after this day I wouldn't be allowed anywhere near a luxury hotel. The bill was over a thousand rupees, but we had carried with us the rate card from Kamat Hotel, and according to that document, all we owed the hotel was a hundred and eighty-six rupees. We scratched out the amount written on the bill, put in what we thought was the fair price and sent it back to the cashier with a hundred and eighty-six rupees.

They descended on us: the waiters, the cashier and the manager. We were yelled at and abused. Everyone at the restaurant turned to stare. That was exactly what we wanted. Now, if they would only summon the police. The manager launched into a tirade. 'If you can't afford a five-star hotel, then go to Kamat,' he yelled. But this was our revolution. Our act of civil disobedience. We told him we would come back to his restaurant every day and pay as we deemed fit.

Finally, someone rang the police and soon an inspector walked into the restaurant. When the situation had been explained to him, he stomped up to us and demanded to know what was going on. We told him what our intentions were and that we would not budge. We were warned that we would be arrested; that was exactly our intention, we shot back. 'What sort of a revolution are you gunning for? Not paying a restaurant bill,' the inspector mumbled as he headed back to talk to the manager. A few minutes later, we were informed that an arrest wasn't necessary and that if we had a grouse with the government we should take it up with the chief minister at his office, Balabrooie, a few minutes' walk from Hotel Ashoka. We were dejected. We hadn't been arrested.

We never went back to that restaurant.

Two

The Vokkaligara Sangha Hostel was divided into two groups: one from Mandya, a city about a hundred kilometres south of Bangalore, and the other from Kolar, a city roughly the same distance to the east of the city. The first comprised students from Mandya, Hassan and Mysore. The other group was populated by young men from Kolar, Chintamani and Doddaballapur. Though the Mandya group had the numbers, the Kolar gang had the muscle. The two were on tentatively amicable terms through the year, but when student body elections came around, regionalism superseded these tenuous bonds.

Like the groups, the physical structure of the hostel was divided in two: the old block and the new block. The old block housed about fifty rooms and the new block had eighty. The old block, where the law and postgraduate students stayed, was the power centre. The new block was for graduates and undergraduate students.

My roommates and I owed allegiance to the Mandya group as Venugopal was from Hassan and Gowda, from Kunigal in Channapatna, a small town halfway between Mysore and Bangalore. Though Venugopal and Gowda stayed away from the group's activities, I wanted to be a part of all the action. I sought out one of the boys from the Mandya gang, a student called Venkatappa, who had come to Bangalore from Channapatna. He had a long-standing grudge against Mune Gowda, a boy from Hoskote, and at a time when a blow-out between the groups seemed imminent, we decided to single out Mune Gowda and take him on. We met at my friend Rangaswamy's room in the new block (I lived in the hostel's old block) and decided to launch a well-planned attack.

This was how it would play out: Venkatappa would pick a fight with Mune Gowda and while they were in the heat of things, two of us—a boy named Krishnamurthy and I—would join in and beat him senseless. At that moment, Rangaswamy and a few others would run in, intervene and stop the fight.

It was a Sunday when the plan was set in motion.

Mune Gowda stepped out of the hostel and Venkatappa was waiting for him.

'This has gone a little too far. You've become too big for your own good,' Venkatappa said, standing head to head with Mune Gowda.

'What are you going to do about it?' Gowda shot back, refusing to budge.

Krishnamurthy and I, approaching him from the back, lunged. I didn't stop to think for a moment. I landed punch after punch on Mune Gowda, who only yelled, 'What do you think you're doing? This is none of your business. Go away.'

I hadn't a clue about how to handle myself in a fight back then, and though I had toughened up considerably at the gym, was still too thin. And I hadn't the slightest expectation that Mune Gowda, a boy far thinner than me, would actually fight and fight back with ferocity. Gowda, who had rolled with the punches all this while, hit back hard. He kicked Venkatappa, turned to me and punched me as forcefully as he could. He then pushed at me with such venom that I fell back on the staircase behind me and knocked my head on the railing. I collapsed. Krishnamurthy rushed at Mune Gowda, held him in a vice and signalled to me to strike from behind. But I was too tired and besides, the others, led by Rangaswamy, had arrived to intervene and stop the fight. It was over as soon as it had begun.

That short, otherwise insignificant, incident would soon lead into one of the ugliest brawls the hostel had ever seen, setting off a chain of events that would result in my meeting some of the most dangerous men that lived in Bangalore at the time. It would lead to the purchase of my first weapon and, eventually, take me to the doors of K.M. Nagraj, leader of the Indira Brigade and the man who sought to control all of south Bangalore.

After the fight, I was furious with Venkatappa. I accosted him and asked him why he had stood silent while Mune Gowda continued to beat me senseless. He said he had no idea Gowda would retaliate in the manner he did, and suggested that we plan a second attack soon.

But Mune Gowda sensed we were up to something and decided to send a few of his minions to try and rattle me in any way possible. The boy designated to this task was short and tough and would follow me at a distance, always with an air of menace and the promise of an impending attack. One day, when my roommate Gowda and I were waiting for a bus to go to City Market, the boy decided he would test the waters. He approached us with determination and brushed by so close that I was sure he would attack me.

My companion, who had worked out the reason for this animosity, was stern with me. 'Why do you invite all these problems? Why can't you just keep to yourself?' he asked.

I didn't argue. Instead, I decided to go back to Venkatappa and seek his counsel. 'Don't worry. I'll introduce you to a man who will take care of things. Once he gets involved no one will bother you,' he said.

Right behind the hostel where I lived was the seedy and sprawling area called Parvatipura Extension. This neighbourhood was a maze of narrow lanes and alleys, and was home to moneylenders, loan sharks and auto-rickshaw dealers. It also enclosed a slum where all the local thugs hung out, and had a strong Muslim population. One day Venkatappa called in a boy from this area and introduced him to me. 'This is Shivu. Dairy Shivu. All of Parvatipura shudders at the mention of his name,' he said.

I wasn't terribly impressed. Dairy Shivu, who'd turned to thuggery as a kid, took his name from his day job: he was the boy knocking on every door in the area at four in the morning to deliver milk. I didn't think Shivu measured up even to the puny minion Mune Gowda had employed to keep tabs on me and I said as much to him.

'Sir, just you wait and see what I am capable of,' Shivu shot back, cocky and confident.

I turned to Venkatappa and suggested he get a hold of Mohammaden Block Ali or Razor Vasu, not this thin lad.

'You shouldn't go to people like that for such small matters. Shivu will take care of things,' he replied.

It was late one evening, not long after our meeting, that Shivu came to me, dragging Mune Gowda's minion by the collar. 'Sir, is this the boy who has been following you and who tried to attack you?' he asked. Yes, I answered. 'You can do whatever you want with him. Here,' he offered.

I was scared, so I asked the boy why he wanted to attack me.

His name was Murthy and he used to drive an auto-rickshaw before becoming a hired goon. He said he had no specific allegiances and, for a small sum, would beat up anyone that needed a little intimidation. Mune Gowda had paid him to tail Venkatappa and me. He looked straight into my eyes and said to Shivu, 'I tried to head-butt him once, but missed my chance.'

At this, Shivu flew into a rage. 'If you had done any such thing, the shape of your face would have been altered forever,' he screamed.

Visibly chastened, Murthy looked at me and muttered, 'Now that Shiv *anna* has spoken, I won't trouble you further.'

On his way out, Shivu waved a casual blessing in my direction. 'If anyone troubles you anymore, just tell them you know Dairy Shivu and that will be that.'

I still wasn't fully convinced that Shivu's benevolent presence would serve as adequate protection, so I began to hound Venkatappa to get us in touch with someone with more clout. This is something that I wonder about to this day: this was not my battle, it was Venkatappa's. I have no idea why I decided to walk into a situation that was as complicated as it was dangerous.

Venkatappa finally caved and decided to take me to meet P.M. Ashok, a prominent man in the Indira Brigade. Ashok's parents were career politicians and had close ties with the chief minister, Devaraj Urs.

Ashok's house was milling with young, mean-looking men— I realised later that it always did. After he'd heard our story, Ashok said the man for the job was Appaji and introduced us to him. Appaji was a short, handsome young man from Sunkenahalli, near Hanumanthanagar, one of the areas of south Bangalore that saw early development. He had a reputation as a brave and sharp fellow and he sat us down to plan our second offensive against Mune Gowda.

The hostel usually had fewer students milling around on Sundays, and Gowda tended to keep to his room, drinking into the night. We decided to storm his quarters, and with logs of firewood as weapons, break his knees. Appaji suggested that we bring along as many boys from the new block in the hostel as possible. At the time I claimed some authority on the subject of physical combat and pitched in with my thoughts on how to overpower Mune Gowda. Appaji stared at me for a minute and whisked out a switchblade. He pressed a button at the side and flashed its 'tongue'—as the sharp blade was known amongst his circles—at us. 'You don't know the first thing about Appaji,' he said. 'You will find out when we fight.'

That was the first time I had seen a knife in a rowdy's hand.

The next day, I accompanied Venkatappa to Majestic, near the city railway station, where we bought two switchblades and a couple of showy knives from a Sikh. Then, after we returned to the hostel, we began to train for the attack. Three boys from Channapatna—Shankar, Prabhu and Lingappa— legends from various fights of the previous year, were entrusted with the task of prepping us. Shankar warned us that Mune Gowda would almost certainly try and get back at us later, so it would serve us well to make sure he didn't get a chance to retaliate. To ensure this, we had to reach out to some very powerful people. That's where Prabhu came in. He knew K.M. Nagraj and promised to set up a meeting.

The moment I met Nagraj, I knew he was all charm. Muscular and effusive, he held you with his clear, penetrating eyes, and despite the distracting little goatee that sprouted from his chin, managed to draw you into the conversation of the moment. He greeted Prabhu with warmth and waved us to sit down. I tried veering the conversation toward the Indira Brigade, but he didn't seem keen to hear what I thought. He merely suggested that we involve ourselves in college politics and that we go to him 'for any assistance'. There wasn't anything we wanted from him at that point, but with that one meeting I had progressed from the rather limited protection that Dairy Shivu offered to the far more powerful connections that P.M. Ashok enjoyed to the overwhelming dominance K.M. Nagraj had over the city at the time.

We began preparations in the afternoon the following Sunday. The firewood had been stocked in a room next to Mune Gowda's. Appaji had brought along three boys with him and said he would wait with them in a park opposite the hostel till everything was ready. We were directed to stand at the entrance to the hostel and get involved only if Mune Gowda or his boys attacked; Appaji and his boys would conduct the actual assault. Word came in that Gowda was holed up in his room, and while I waited at the entrance, for a fleeting moment I was overcome by doubt. But the time was near and we had switched off all the lights in the hostel. There was no going back now.

At that moment a vehicle careened into the hostel compound from the direction of Sanjay Theatre nearby. Appaji, who had been looking intently towards the hostel, yelled to his boys. 'Come on!' he shouted and disappeared in the direction of the old block. Venkatappa and I stood there, left to defend ourselves. The vehicle was a police jeep. Four constables and a sub-inspector got out and demanded to know what we were doing.

We told them we had no other place to be.

'Did you make the phone call? How come we were informed that there would be a fight here?' one of them asked.

'Maybe they wanted to test how efficient our police force is,' we replied.

'So, there's no trouble here?'

I shook my head, irritated. 'If there were trouble, would we be standing around like this?' I asked.

'Idiots,' one of them muttered and left.

We looked everywhere for Appaji that night, but he was gone. We never found out who had made the call—we assumed it was someone from the Mandya group. If we had gone ahead with the attack, it would have been the official beginning of my life in crime. Everyone at the hostel, Muddahanume Gowda the most vocal among them, said I was headed for ruin. He was convinced I had to be anywhere but the hostel. I decided to move out with three boys—Vasant, Shankar and Nanjayya. We rented a house in Azadnagar, near Chamrajpet, and for the first couple of months stayed out of any kind of trouble. It seemed as if things were finally settling down.

But one day, an agitated Shankar rushed into the house. Barely intelligible, he told us about a near-fatal attack he'd just escaped from.

Shankar had been asked to accompany K.M. Nagraj, Revanna (who would go on to win the state assembly elections with a Congress ticket) and a minor politician Anand Kumar to the Vokkaligara Sangha College to chalk out plans for the forthcoming elections. Nagraj asked Shankar to get into the car with him, but Shankar said he would follow them with a friend on his motorcycle. As the group reached the busy Chamrajpet area, M.P. Jayaraj, accompanied by about twenty boys, attacked Nagraj's car with swords and metal rods. Nagraj was driving at the time, and the group managed to escape unhurt. 'If Nagraj wasn't driving, he wouldn't have lived, and if I had been in the car, they would have finished me with a single swipe of a sword,' Shankar said. No one slept that night.

Nagraj was a powerful and important man. Surely, an attack as brazen as this one wouldn't go unpunished. Through the night we talked of the bloodbath that was to come.

But nothing happened.

We went to Anand Kumar's room in a hostel in Chamrajpet to meet Nagraj. Anand lived there with another boy, Renu, with whom I had become close. The room was packed and you could feel the tension, but Nagraj was calm. He told everyone to settle down and said that though he hadn't expected Jayaraj to go to such extreme measures, we were to do nothing. The police are looking for him, he said.

But I had to know why Jayaraj harboured such a deep and enduring grudge against Nagraj, so I went up to my friend Renu and asked him. When I learnt the reason, I was shocked. The person who was the basis of the rift between the two men was one of the most revered figures in the state: the Kannada actor Dr Rajkumar.

Two reasons provoked the rivalry, Renu explained. First, the actor had refused Devaraj Urs' request that he perform at an entertainment programme the Congress party had organised. The second was a song from Rajkumar's runaway hit *Sampattige Saval* (A Challenge to Wealth), which translated as: *No matter who shouts in protest/No matter who rises up in arms/I will remain unperturbed*. The song was widely believed to be composed in defiance of Urs and his government. Renu told me that the chief minister had directed his son-in-law Natraj to rein in Rajkumar, and that it didn't matter what means were used to achieve this end. Natraj's Indira Brigade, led by Jayaraj, set about ravaging the theatre that was screening Rajkumar's film, and when a sub-inspector of police, arrest warrant in hand, went to bring in Jayaraj, Urs personally reprimanded him.

Nagraj, who till then had no cause to split with Natraj, was forced to take sides when Urs decided to take on Rajkumar. Renu told me that one of the most prominent actors in the Kannada film industry, Vajramuni, who was related to Nagraj, had voiced strong support for Rajkumar and Nagraj had to stand by the senior actor. Jayaraj and his men stood firmly by Natraj. And thus was born the battle between the two.

Jayaraj had obviously decided to up the ante with the attack on Nagraj's car. Nagraj decided not to retaliate after the offensive, and Jayaraj and his men launched one last raid. They attacked his house and severely beat up the police personnel charged with guarding it. Though he escaped, it would be Nagraj's last few days as the man who controlled south Bangalore. Weakened by a lack of support, he withdrew from the Indira Brigade, and eventually, from public gaze.

Natraj was now established as the 'minister for crime' in his father-in-law Devaraj Urs' shadow cabinet, and became the most powerful man in the city's underworld. Jayaraj, who had stood by him through the crisis, emerged as the most dangerous man in the city.

Three

While Natraj and his henchman Jayaraj carved Bangalore into fiefdoms and distinct polarities began to form in the city's underworld, I was engaged in far more prosaic pursuits.

In the house opposite ours lived the editor of the popular Kannada weekly *Sudha*. He had three children of whom the second, Swapna, was incredibly beautiful. She intrigued me endlessly—she was a rebel of sorts and had recently run away to Goa to live with a bunch of hippies. When she returned we got talking and I thoroughly enjoyed being in her company. Swapna would tell me stories about her time in Goa, and I would recount tales about writers and rowdies.

Among the many people who visited Swapna was a curious, tall man everyone called Vasuki. He stooped a little when he walked and had a peculiar mark on his cheek. He always wore his shirt buttoned to the top. I thought he looked like a medical representative: waiting patiently at a clinic to make an impression on the doctor and hopefully push his company's pharmaceuticals. I was trying to win over Swapna at the time and didn't at all care for the fact that Vasuki visited her every day. We would cross paths occasionally and I would look into his eyes, making it evident that I had every intention of smashing his face in, given the chance. For months this went on, until I discovered who Vasuki really was.

One day, as usual, a minor scuffle broke out between a bunch of boys in the area and my friends over Swapna. The girl, as was her wont, went straight to Vasuki and asked him to intervene. He did so with alacrity and with immediate effect.

Later, with the violence quelled and the mob dispersed, I sat in front of him and decided to state my case. 'I can fight my own fights, you know,' I said, and as with all such statements of valour, embellished by recounting the number of fights I had been in and the sort of people I knew.

Vasuki looked at me for a long time, his light eyes constantly shifting colour. He stood up. 'Do you know who I am?' he whispered, reaching for his waist. 'Razor Vasu,' he bristled, pulling out the instrument that gave him that name. I saw a flash of steel as he swiped the blade across my cheek. I looked at the blade, fully expecting to see my blood on it, but it was clean. I sat there, shocked. Vasu moved across the room and sat down. He had had a couple of drinks but his eyes were focused on me. I had never seen a man resemble an animal more than Razor Vasu did that day. He sat there for a while, clearly angry at how presumptuous and cocky I had been. I begged forgiveness and hoped against hope that Swapna or one of her brothers would walk into the room and rescue me.

Suddenly Vasuki let out an expansive guffaw, startling me. 'Are you scared?' he asked, his voice now soft. I felt for the phantom laceration on my cheek and looked up. 'What would it say about my abilities if I actually slashed your face? You are not an enemy. You're a student. I wouldn't do that to you,' he said.

Over the next forty minutes, Vasu and I became the best of friends. And over the next few months, I would spend all my time with this tall, violent and mysterious man whom the gangster Jayaraj reputedly kept at his service with a weekly allowance of eleven thousand rupees. Vasu became my first real friend in the city's underworld and would direct my first resolute step into a life of crime.

Very quickly I became intimately acquainted with Vasu's life and his work. He would engage an auto-rickshaw, paying the driver whatever he deemed fit, and with me at his side, would set about his work.

Over the next few months I witnessed a botched attempt at

stealing a scooter and a couple of extremely successful extortion jobs. Sometimes, during these acts of petty crime, Vasu would betray his upbringing, switching to impeccable English or turning up in a well-tailored suit—his mother, it turned out, was the principal of a prestigious convent-run school in town and his father a medical officer at a large business house. At other times, the man who had betrayed his family by dropping out of school and taking to crime would offer up a side to him that alarmed and disgusted me.

One day, while we sat at a café in the Lalbagh gardens in south Bangalore, he brought up his third primary area of operations in crime: preying on the young couples that sought refuge from cramped houses and conservative parents in the large botanical gardens.

'You mean you steal jewellery off all these young girls?' I asked.

He laughed and shook his head. 'That's for all those petty thieves. I do it for far more enjoyable reasons. I do it for the girls.'

He meant rape.

I was very angry with him and asked what he would do if someone did that to him.

'Murder,' he seethed.

'Then why do you do this to the girls, Vasu?'

'I don't know. It's their fate, I guess,' he said, throwing up his hands.

For days I was upset and Vasu sensed this. He walked up to me and said, 'Why are you so angry? You are such a wet-behind-the-ears rascal. All this is normal.'

A few days after this conversation, Vasu pulled up at my house in an auto-rickshaw and asked me to get in. He was wearing what looked like an expensive suit. We drove to Brigade Road, in the heart of Bangalore's business district, and met a man called Roberts. For boys like me, a trip to Brigade Road usually meant a small romantic adventure, presenting a chance to literally rub shoulders with all the pretty girls walking up and down the busy street. This time, however, we were on Brigade Road for a very different reason. We were here to steal a scooter. The attempt ended in disaster, with the owner of the scooter landing up at the very moment my new friend was hoisting it off its stand. Vasu, looking oddly like a dolled-up gangster from the movies, hared it down Brigade Road, two constables in rigorous pursuit, while Roberts and I stood and stared. Vasu managed to outrun the cops.

As the days went by, he would include me in several such projects. I agreed to go along, but I never actually took part in his crimes.

In those months, my ideals lost a fair share of their sheen. I had elevated people like Vasu to the status of revolutionaries, only to realise that he, like many of the others, was in it to make a few quick bucks. The tall, tragic Vasu, around whom I'd constructed all sorts of legends, was, albeit dangerous, a regular thug.

But my days as a witness, even an observer, weren't to last. Soon, I would find myself in the thick of things, and Vasu would have to bring to bear all that violence inside him to bail me out of trouble.

I had a pretty stringent fitness regime at the time and would work out at a gym every morning. I decided to change this routine and began exercising in the evening, after which I would go to a park near Hanumanthanagar, in Gavipuram Guttahalli, where the city's famous cave temple is located.

The area, though an integral part of Bangalore, resembled a village more than a city. The families that lived here, mostly belonging to the Naidu community from Andhra Pradesh and the local Vokkaliga group, were very conservative. The park I exercised in, much like the people who lived in Hanumanthanagar, was nondescript.

Here, I would work out some more and spend time in contemplation on a stone bench. One day, I was at the park, talking to a man, when he pointed to a car parked at the end of the road and said the men inside had been staring at me for a while now. I looked up and realised the car, an Ambassador, had been parked at the exact same spot the day before.

Before he could ask what the matter was, I ran. I had to escape. I leaped over the fence and made for Guttahalli, away from the car. The automobile roared to life and began to gain on me. I made straight for Vasu's house and pounded on his door, screaming his name. Luckily, Vasu was at home. He peered out of the window and in a trice knew there was something wrong.

He opened the door, a machete in his hand. I ran in saying, 'Those people. They're after me.'

Vasu was out of the door before I knew it and screaming, 'Teri maa ki . . .' with his weapon held aloft. He spat at the car and the men inside spared no haste. They sped back in the direction from which they'd come.

Vasu ran after them, spewing curses.

He returned a few minutes later. He was shaking with rage and one look at his eyes told me that if he had caught up with the car, he would have hacked its occupants to bits.

Once inside, he sat down. His wife Radhika, scared witless, looked at his face and choked back whatever it was she was going to say. For about ten minutes, no one uttered a word.

After a while, Vasu got up and put on his shirt. 'Where to at this time?' Radhika asked.

'I'll be back very soon. Don't worry about anything,' he said, picking up the machete and sheathing it in the folds of a newspaper. We got into an auto-rickshaw and drove to a bar in Hanumanthanagar. Vasu went in and returned with a short, stout man he introduced to me as Venkatesh. The three of us went to my house and sat down to talk about what had just happened.

'I recognised one of the boys in that car. He's a lowlife ruffian called Gunnees. He hangs around Guttahalli Circle. If we get hold of him, we'll know who is behind all this,' Vasu said.

Venkatesh agreed, and despite Vasu's instructions, I decided to join them. We went to Guttahalli and stopped near Uma Theatre. I was asked to wait in the auto-rickshaw and to leave if things turned ugly.

The two of them walked up to a bunch of boys who were gathered at Guttahalli Circle. I peered out of the auto-rickshaw to look, but couldn't really tell what was happening, so I got out, walked up to a bakery, bought myself a Mangold and sipped the drink while I waited. The auto-rickshaw driver, meanwhile, had made off, sensing trouble.

As I watched, Vasu launched into one of the boys and head-butted him with such ferocity that the young fellow collapsed in a heap. Venkatesh went after another boy and hit him with great force. The others quickly dispersed and bunkered-up at a nearby shop from where they launched soda bottle missiles at Vasu and Venkatesh. Every shop owner in the area downed his shutter, and in a few minutes, the boys who had launched a counter-attack found reinforcements. The group now hurled stones at Vasu and Venkatesh, who had by then decided to retreat. They ran past me, barely noticing my presence. The boys charged after them, but were too slow. The two made off in the direction of the theatre and I could hear their assailants saying they would be prepared for Venkatesh and Vasu's return.

By the time I got home, the two were inside.

'This is not a fight we can fight alone, I must go see him tomorrow,' Vasu said, to no one in particular.

'Who?' I asked.

After a few seconds of silence, Vasu said, 'Ali, my guru.'

I knew then that this was far more serious and personal for Vasu than I had imagined. He would never have sought Mohammaden Block Ali's help for what was in essence a petty quarrel.

The next day, we went to Ali's house. He was as tall as Vasu—over six feet—and burly. Vasu had often talked of Ali—his legendary prowess during fights and his ability to escape each one unscathed. Ali, for his part, was quiet and self-assured. He patiently heard out Vasu and made it clear to us that this whole Guttahalli fracas was a minor incident and all it needed by way of resolution was a night alone with the boys who carried out the attack. 'We just need to go there one of these nights and take out their hands and legs,' he said. He pointed at two of his aides, Iftikar, a dead ringer for the actor Dharmendra, and a diminutive man, Riyaz. They would accompany us, he said, and told us to meet them at Hotel Pilot, in front of Vijaya College, a few days later.

It was evening when we went there. Two auto-rickshaws and an Ambassador were parked outside the hotel. The car was filled with swords, knives, metal rods and machetes. The auto-rickshaw carried empty soda bottles. The 'back-up' team, which would be deployed only if the men in the car couldn't handle the Guttahalli gang, would sit in the rickshaw. Vasu insisted that I stay back, but Ali intervened. 'Let him come along,' he said. Vasu warned me to keep my distance.

We left at around nine in the night. As soon as we got to Guttahalli Circle, I got off and went to a bakery nearby and ordered a glass of warm badam milk. The others went about looking for the boys who had attacked Vasu.

They found them in front of a military hotel—a cheap restaurant that typically serves ragi balls and mutton chops—and determining that surprise was on their side, spilled out of the car, weapons in hand. This was perhaps indicative of the way Ali fought in these skirmishes. He used surprise and his expansive vocal range to good effect. The attackers would emerge out of vehicles with their swords held high and would scream in the most gruesome manner, scaring the victims out of their senses.

Ali charged at the boys and swiped at them with the blunt edge of his sword, intending to injure, not impale. Vasu, who was more deeply invested in this venture, attacked with rage. Iftikar and Riyaz had little to do but stand and watch. Occasionally, they would corral an escaping victim and head-butt him back into the thick of things. In a couple of minutes the boys had all disappeared and the ones that remained lay about moaning in pain. Ali didn't stop. Accompanied by Vasu, he swaggered around the street, sword still high in the air. From where I stood, they looked like two kings, surveying their kingdoms; or at least that road.

We headed to Gandharva Bar at South End Circle where we drank beer and reviewed the attack, lamenting the lack of valour in the Guttahalli camp. Vasu dropped me home at one in the morning. That night, I dreamt of swords.

Those swords would become entrenched in my life, but they wouldn't be borne by Vasu and Ali, both of whom would very soon disappear from my life. They would belong to a man called Kotwal Ramachandra, the man responsible for a grievous attack on my brother and the reason for my entry into the underworld.

But before I get to Kotwal, I have to recount two important events that occurred in the interim—my association with the writer P. Lankesh and my first attempt at murder.

Four

After the attack on the Guttahalli gang, Ali's grip over the city began to slacken. He had made the mistake of taking up arms against Ramakrishna Adiga, the new inspector at Basavanagudi police station, who didn't take too kindly at having a razor flashed at him by a rowdy. So one night Adiga set his constables the task of systematically beating the fight out of him. Broken, Ali gave up his life in the underworld for a sedentary job as a worker at Hindustan Machine Tools. Vasu, who was convinced that Ali's decision was a slight on their partnership, took to drink and became increasingly difficult to control. I went to live in Basavanagudi with a friend, Hiremath. Vasu didn't bother to visit.

It was the height of the Emergency then, and I was twenty-one. Indira Gandhi had halted elections and suspended civil liberties and was ruling the nation by decree. Several leaders of the Opposition were in prison and the judiciary and the press had little or no freedom to function. That was when I met a writer called Lankesh. We would take long walks every day and discuss the atrocities carried out by the regime. Lankesh, who was casting for his film *Anurupa* at the time, would go on to launch one of the most caustic and controversial tabloids the state had ever seen, and would help define the contours of modernist Kannada literature.

He gave me an important role in his film and asked if I knew someone who would play a thug in it. I suggested Mohammaden Block Ali, whom he met and hired. Ali's brother Geelani was

also picked to play a part. We shot a large section of the film at
B.M.S. College and when it was done, I decided to go to Delhi
to prepare for the civil services exam. By the time I returned,
after having completed the exam, six months had passed and
Lankesh's film, *Pallavi*, which he had made a year earlier, in
1976, had just won him a National Award for direction.

A year passed and I continued to hang around Lankesh,
looking for parts in his films. At the time, his daughter, Gowri,
was studying for her state-level exams at Vijaya High School.
She frequently complained to me about being tormented by a
boy who she said sent her letters and stalked her. I dismissed it
as harmless till, one day, the boy followed her home. I asked
her not to go to school the next day.

The next morning, I took along a boy called Raju and cycled
to her school. I made some enquiries and found out that the
stalker was named Venkataswamy but called himself Kuri
(Sheep). His father worked with a minister in the state
government and that gave Kuri an amount of clout in Revajitu,
the slum where he lived. As soon as they learnt I was looking
for him, three of Kuri's friends approached me and said he had
a long-running bet with them that he would 'get' Gowri by any
means possible.

'Don't do anything here, Sir. Let's take him to Konankunte
Lake and "repair" him,' they suggested.

At around four in the evening, Kuri came to the school. He
was about nineteen years old and was short and dark. I stood
at a distance with Raju while his friends walked up to him and
talked animatedly for a while. I then walked up to him.

'Are you Kuri?' I asked.

He looked around for support. I yanked him by his collar
and hoisted him onto the bar of my cycle. His friends then
walked up to us and he pleaded with them to help. 'Let's go,
Sir,' was all they said and Kuri knew he was done for.

All through our ride to the lake, I head-butted Kuri.

Back then, Konankunte Lake was a swamp: dank, murky
and deserted. We pushed him off the cycle and proceeded to

beat him senseless. We took off his clothes and kicked him with all the strength we had. Between yelps, he promised to never again look at another girl, but we wouldn't listen. He mustered up some hidden reserve of strength and broke free. He sprang for the lake and disappeared into the mist. His friends said he couldn't swim and called out for him. 'If I come back, you will kill me,' he screamed in the fading light and swam out further. We waited there till eight in the evening, an hour after the attack. By then, an ink-black night had settled on the swamp and we gave up Kuri for dead. His friends handed me his clothes and left. They hardly seemed to care that they had just contributed to the demise of their friend. I was far more worried. This was my first major offence. I returned home at around nine and tried unsuccessfully to sleep.

At around midnight there was a knock on my door. I opened it to find two police constables, who said they were from the Basavanagudi station. They asked me if I knew what had happened to Kuri. I told them everything I knew, thinking I would be charged with murder. But that wasn't the case. 'What have you gone and done? A case of attempt to murder is being registered against you,' one of them said.

It turned out that Kuri had survived after all. He had waded out to a cluster of reeds and hidden there till he thought it was safe to venture out. He eventually made it to a hut on the shore and told its occupant what had happened. The man gave him a lungi and took him to Jayanagar police station, where a complaint was filed.

That morning, I was taken to the police station. Though I had passed it before, this was the first time I actually saw the structure up close. It was old; probably dating back to the British Raj. A red tiled roof ran along its length and small green windows framed old iron rods.

I climbed up the long flight of steps leading to the station and at the top, I found a clutch of about nine boys gathered. They were from Kuri's slum and yelled at the police to let them have a go at me. 'Don't look at them. Just go straight in,' one of the constables told me.

Inside, the inspector asked me why I had done it and I told him the story about Gowri and how Kuri had stalked her. 'Why didn't you call the police?' the inspector asked me and called in Kuri.

I couldn't recognise the boy. His face was swollen and his left eye was bruised so badly, he could hardly open it. His right eye was partially shut.

I apologised to the police and Kuri immediately said he didn't want to press charges. His father, who was soon summoned, was in agreement. I was asked to leave.

That was that. I was free. I could go home.

A few weeks later, I would be back in the police station. This time, accused of murder.

Five

In retrospect, it isn't so much the first charge of murder levelled against me that is important. What is significant is that the alliances I had formed and the series of incidents that lead me to that day in the police station, when I stood before sub-inspector Wajid Khan as he accused me of murder, were completely arbitrary and more a function of chance than of design, or of the precise calculus of crime with which I would later become so intimately acquainted.

The fights in the hostel, the plans to attack Mune Gowda, my meeting K.M. Nagraj, the first encounter with Razor Vasu, the first conversation with the domineering Mohammaden Block Ali, and the assault on Kuri—these were all incidents that occurred, now that I think about them, by chance.

Even the murder that was to follow—the killing of a man named Bhasker—was an aspect to the events unfolding that I had no control over; indeed I was not even aware of the murder till the police came to my door to arrest me for it.

While such random incidents in a man's life may well appear commonplace within the larger context of the many daily lives that experience such unpredictable instances, tempered by hindsight, the story I have told thus far marks an important passage in my life. For one, however arbitrary the events may seem, they prepared me, albeit without my knowledge, for a life in crime. If it weren't for the people I met and befriended or the situations I would find myself in, I might never have worked up the courage to pick up a weapon or kill a man. I might never have become the man that forged some of the most dangerous coalitions in this city's underworld.

~

After the attack on Kuri and my fortuitous escape from imprisonment, I lay low for about a week. I wasn't scared about the boys who swore allegiance to the man who called himself Sheep—they wouldn't dare touch me because of my connections to Vasu and Ali.

But then, just when I thought I was out of trouble, I became embroiled in another murky and complicated conflict that involved Lankesh's family. His wife, Indiraji, ran a saree shop behind Basavanagudi National College. At first, she had entered into a partnership with a man named Dinakar, but later operated the establishment by herself after a falling out with him. Her estranged (and bitter) partner decided to take the fight to her and opened up a similar shop of his own right next door to Indiraji. Dinakar, though not in an obvious manner, used the services of his stepbrother, Bhasker, to intimidate his former associate.

Bhasker was a one-time precious stones dealer from Pavgada near Tumkur. He had affiliations with the notoriously violent Basavanagudi gang and was particularly close to Gandhi Bazaar Nagendra, a man of considerable clout and ill-repute. While threats were being directed at Indiraji almost daily, none was actually carried out because I knew the Basavanagudi gang just as well as Bhasker did. He, however, began to issue warnings and accusations at me, claiming that I had initiated plans to attack him.

One day, tired of this constant barrage of rumours and allegations, I confronted Bhasker and told him that it was about time he stopped. He wouldn't see reason and issued one final warning to me. 'I will finish you,' he said. I came away very angry.

The next day, Bhasker's body was found near a storm drain near Shankar Mutt Road, close to Basavanagudi. He had been murdered.

There was talk that it was an accident and that he had slipped and cracked open his skull on a stone. Another theory doing the rounds was that his stepbrother Dinakar had hired some men to do the job. The third and most obvious premise was that I had killed Bhasker.

Apart from being secure in the knowledge that I hadn't done it, I had two additional bits of information I was prepared to present to the police. One was that Krishna Masadi, a scriptwriter who was my roommate at the time, was playing chess with me in our room the night of the murder and would be ready with an alibi. The other, a tip that would serve more in aiding the investigation than proving my innocence, was that Bhasker, who never ventured out without footwear on, was found dead without his slippers on, suggesting that he had been murdered at home by Dinakar or members of his family, and his body later dumped near the storm drain.

So when I was summoned to the Central police station by sub-inspector Wajid Khan, and when he accused me of the murder—though it was clear to me that he didn't believe I was the killer—I told him as much.

'Who killed him then?' he asked, more intent on my physical reaction than my answer.

'Sir, the whole world knows who killed Bhasker. I know it and you know it. Why do you still insist on hearing the name from me?' I replied.

'Okay. Where's the evidence that he killed Bhasker?' he shot back.

'Don't mistake me, Sir, but it's not my job to find out, is it?' I replied.

'You are very clever, aren't you?' he mumbled.

Later, the rigmarole would be repeated with police inspector Kowri, and later still, with the then deputy commissioner of police, P. Kodandaramiah. The DCP, when he met me, looked as though he were convinced I was a killer. He said as much. I told him my version and said I was innocent. He listened, but his look didn't change. I was told to leave.

Sixteen years later, I would stand before Kodandaramiah again. This time, my name firmly established in the city's underworld, and his attached to the words 'police commissioner'. He wouldn't remember the Sreedhar of sixteen years ago, but his look would remain exactly the same as the one he fixed me with the last time we stood facing each other.

After my meeting with the DCP, I expected another call from the police, but I heard nothing for two months. Later, the case was transferred to the Corps of Detectives, not a usual occurrence, and I was asked to meet with officers from that department. I took along my roommate Krishna Masadi and presented my version of the story. They laughed and said, 'Be happy you haven't been "fixed" in this case. Forget about the murder, we will take care of it.' I knew that was that.

After that incident I stopped visiting Lankesh's house. Bhasker's murder was never solved. The CoD closed the case, attributing his death to 'unnatural causes'.

~

It was now 1979. I was twenty-four and had played small roles in about six movies. I was determined to produce a film and also firm that I would somehow create a life for myself in the cineworld.

One day I travelled to Mangalore, hoping to convince officials of Karnataka Bank to offer me a loan to make my movie. I had a day's worth of talks with them and, after a six-hour bus journey, returned to Bangalore.

At the time, my roommates were Masadi and Venkatappa, the boy who had introduced me to P.M. Ashok. We were no longer in Basavanagudi, but had shifted to Ashoknagar nearby.

That day, after I returned from Mangalore, I was on my way to the room, when a tailor, who lived in lodgings behind ours, stopped me and said, 'I am very sorry about what happened, Sir. It shouldn't have.'

'What happened?' I asked.

'Were you not in Bangalore, Sir? Then you don't know?'

'Tell me what happened,' I repeated.

'Yesterday, some people attacked your brother with swords and machetes. His legs are badly hurt. You must go to the hospital.'

For a moment, I couldn't think straight. My brother, Basant Kumar, lived in Kanakapura and had come to Bangalore to watch the Test match between India and Pakistan. He loved cricket, and would come to the city every time there was a match on. He didn't know too many people in Bangalore so he would always stay with me. Why would someone attack him?

The tailor had no answers and my room was empty. I got into a rickshaw and went to Victoria Hospital, where the tailor had told me he had been admitted.

My roommate Venkatappa and two friends, Raju and Mahadeva, were at the hospital. Venkatappa came up to me and held my hand. 'There is no need to worry. It is not serious,' he said. It seemed to me that they were more concerned about convincing me that all was well than showing me to my brother's room.

When I walked in, I was relieved. Basant's legs were bandaged to the knee, but he seemed quite collected.

He then told me what had happened.

Like me, Basant was obsessed with fitness. Whenever he was in Bangalore, he would exercise regularly at the Hanumanthanagar gym I frequented. The day I was in Mangalore, Basant and a friend, Nagaraju, were near the gym, discussing the day's cricket match, when a man in an auto-rickshaw charged at them, almost running the two over.

In a rage, Basant had shouted at the auto-rickshaw driver.

The man merely stared at him.

Suspecting the driver had had too much to drink, Basant told Nagaraju that this wouldn't be the best time to confront him and they decided to head back to my room.

In about five minutes the driver returned with a gang of men in two auto-rickshaws and on three motorcycles. The moment he got off, the driver pointed at my brother and said, 'That's him.'

One of the men screamed, 'I know him guru, he is Hariprasad's boy.'

Another man from the gang attacked my brother, slashing his leg with a machete.

'Who is Hariprasad?' Basant screamed, but the men ignored him. Somehow, despite his wounds, he managed to escape. He ran for the nearest house. Seeing that the door was open, he rushed in, blood now gushing from his wounds. Once inside, he forced the door shut. Inside, two women and a man rose in terror. The gang fell upon the door.

The man in the house peered out of the window and, recognising one of the attackers, shouted at him, 'You, Gowri, go away. This boy is badly injured.'

'The bastard is Hariprasad's boy,' the man yelled back, 'this isn't the end of the matter.' He then led the others away.

As soon as my friends heard about the incident, they took my brother to the hospital and informed Venkatappa, Mahadeva and a few others. The doctors immediately wheeled my brother into the operation theatre and performed what they said was a major procedure to save his legs.

When I spoke to one of the doctors later, he said, 'An inch more and he would have been a cripple for the rest of his life. But your brother is strong. He should recover completely in a couple of months.'

I decided then that I wouldn't spare the men who had attacked Basant.

But my brother wouldn't have any of it. He put up his hands and pleaded, 'Annaiah, those bastards beat me up for fun. Don't take this seriously. Go to the police, but stay away after that. Nothing has happened to me, you heard the doctors say so yourself. Please, just don't do anything.'

But I had to find out who had attacked my brother. The next day, I went to Basavanagudi police station. News had come in that the police had arrested eight members of the gang that had charged at my brother. It turned out they had carried out a similar attack on another man the same day. It seemed they had been on a marauding spree in the city, and without reason. No one at the police station had an inkling who these men were or to which gang they belonged. All anyone knew was that they seemed to have no apparent motive and that, before they launched an attack, they would ask their victims the same question: 'Are you with Hariprasad?'

Inside the police station, the officers didn't help much either. The sub-inspector, Madhav Rao, looked up at me and said, 'What can possibly happen? You will lodge a complaint and we will record it. That's it. Why don't you do something—since you are all here and so are the people who attacked your brother, why don't you chop them to pieces? Or tie them up to a pillar on the street and set them on fire? We will not interfere.'

I did manage to glean some information from the different conversations I had that day. Apparently the assailants were cohorts of a man called Dadi (Beard) Puttaswamy. In Hanumanthanagar, the gang's leader was a man named Ruby Krishna. The police wouldn't touch him because he knew Devaraj Urs, the chief minister.

I tried to collect as much information about this gang as possible, but made little headway. It appeared everyone was scared of these men, even the city's rowdies. All I learned was that, unlike any other gang in the city—including Jayaraj's—this bunch seemed to have no qualms about attacking blameless commoners.

Then I remembered that, when my brother was telling me what had happened, he had mentioned a name—Gowri. And that the man who had sheltered him knew this Gowri.

I decided to visit the man and his family.

They turned out to be simple milk sellers.

It was evening when I made my visit and I first thanked them for helping Basant. 'They are all bastards. They should attack Hariprasad if they have the guts. Gowrishankar, M.C. Prakash, Ruby Krishna . . . there were many in that gang. You are an educated man, don't speak to them. God will take care of them, either today or tomorrow,' said the man.

Things were getting clearer now. It turned out Krishna was the man driving the auto-rickshaw that almost ran over my brother. Prakash and Gowri (Gowrishankar was his full name) were the men who had assaulted him later with machetes. But Krishna, by all accounts, was too old to be a ringleader. I asked the man who their boss was.

'Why do you want to know? What will you do if you know?' he asked.

'Please, if you know, tell me. All I want is to find out who did this,' I said.

The man sat silent for about two minutes before replying, 'They call him Robbery King Kotwal Ramachandra.'

I had never heard this name before. No one, not Ali or Vasu or any of the several thugs I knew had ever uttered his name. Kotwal Ramachandra, as far as I was concerned, had emerged out of nowhere.

PART II

One

I decided to kill Kotwal. I had to kill him. But before I could even so much as formulate a plan, I had to amass as much information as possible about the man who had attacked my brother. I decided to ask Venkatesh, the rowdy whom Vasu had introduced me to. 'Kotwal doesn't drink more than a peg of alcohol and he's a notorious womaniser, this much I can tell you,' Venkatesh said, 'but he doesn't trust anyone so no one knows where he sleeps or his exact whereabouts.'

That didn't help much: I still didn't know how to find Kotwal; I didn't even know what he looked like.

It appeared his associate, the rowdy Ruby Krishna, was the man to begin with—after all, it was Krishna who first picked a fight with my brother, prompting Kotwal to attack him.

Krishna proved far easier to trace—he came from a wealthy, well-known family in Hanumanthanagar and, unlike Kotwal, maintained a very public profile.

While this plan—to attack Krishna—took shape in my head, I met a man named Chandru, from Gandhi Bazaar. He was very fair and short and was well known in the area for his agility and the fearsome temper he displayed during fights. He idolised B.K. Hariprasad, mentor to many of Bangalore's thugs, and after the recent skirmish in Hanumanthanagar, was just as eager to get Kotwal as I was. It also helped that Chandru had seen Kotwal and could pick him out in a crowd if necessary.

At first, he suggested that we approach Hariprasad for help, but I was reluctant—I wanted to get rid of Kotwal, not make a career in the underworld. However, Chandru did introduce me to a number of thugs in Gandhi Bazaar—Prakash, Viji, Benne Krishna, Huchha Raja, Chittur Ravi, among others—all of whom were united by a fervent hatred for Kotwal. They had heard about the trouble I'd found myself in after Bhasker's murder and were sympathetic. Besides, everyone in that gang knew I'd acted in a Kannada film, and that made me a little glamorous. Though initially reluctant to take on Ruby Krishna, a corpulent and dangerously violent man, the gang finally agreed to the project.

Four days after the attack on my brother, at nine in the night, we went to Hanumanthanagar and waited for Ruby Krishna to return home. We had just one vehicle, an auto-rickshaw, which we parked in a small lane near his house. Venkatappa and I sat in the auto-rickshaw while Raja, Chandru, Mahadeva and a few other boys paced the street. We had planned this operation well: I knew the exact spot where Krishna would be attacked. I had a switchblade while Chandru had a knife. We would charge in unison.

It was now eleven, and I was bored witless. Only when an auto-rickshaw approached would I tense—my limbs trembling and my eyes seeking out Krishna in the night. At one point, two constables approached us and asked what we were doing this late at night. We told them an acquaintance of ours had died and we were here to pick up a relative. 'There's a rowdy called Ruby Krishna who lives here. If he sees you, he might think you are from Hariprasad's gang and attack you. Park the auto at a distance,' they warned and walked away. We laughed.

At a quarter past twelve, an Ambassador and an auto-rickshaw drove up to the house. This had to be Krishna, returning from his nightly binge. We hadn't expected two vehicles, so we crouched in the darkness, thinking Kotwal was with him. A few minutes later, we heard a howl from within Krishna's house. We turned the auto-rickshaw around, ready to scamper home, thinking the two constables had picked up our quarry. But no, we had to find out what had happened.

Venkatappa said he would go look. By this time, a large crowd had gathered outside the rowdy's house.

Venkatappa returned ten minutes later, and as he approached he thrust his thumb down and said, 'The bastard is gone.'

Ruby Krishna was dead.

Venkatappa hadn't made enquiries of any sort so we didn't know how it had happened. We were back in my room at three in the morning.

At seven, Chandru came in saying Krishna had had too much to drink and had died of cardiac arrest.

Later, we stood atop a building and watched his funeral procession. Kotwal was not among the mourners.

Eight days later my brother was discharged from the hospital; the doctor had warned me that full recovery would take at least three months. Basant was up and about in one.

Fifteen days after Krishna's death, Venkatappa got married. My roommate Krishna Masadi and I took our belongings and moved to a room near Vidyapeetha. I all but abandoned plans of taking on Kotwal and instead began working on a film with a few friends.

~

Two months later, Kotwal and his gang chased an auto-rickshaw driver into a house in N.R. Colony, dragged him out into the street and hacked his hand off in front of a hundred people. They then set his rickshaw on fire. Chittur Ravi, the Gandhi Bazaar rowdy, happened to be in the vicinity and witnessed the attack. He was spotted by Kotwal and, terrified for his life, rushed to Gandhi Bazaar and told the gang what had just happened.

It appeared the auto-rickshaw driver was assaulted over a petty issue: one of Kotwal's associates, a man named M.C. Prakash, got into his auto-rickshaw and demanded that he drive as fast as he could. The driver refused, and as a consequence, Kotwal set his men on him.

The entire Gandhi Bazaar gang was up in arms—no one, not

Mohammaden Block Ali, or Mavalli Shetty, or Netkallappa Circle Johnny had ever struck an innocent man. This latest incident only proved that a virtual nobody from south Bangalore had a free run of what was essentially their turf. Hariprasad told the gang to finish Kotwal and his run of terror.

But the Gandhi Bazaar crowd couldn't trace Kotwal, no matter how hard they looked. So, they directed their ire at a member of his gang instead—M.C. Prakash.

Prakash, who was tall, dark and looked like he was from the West Indies, was, by all accounts, a sexual predator and pervert. Like Kotwal he would prowl in parks and isolated areas in search of young couples. His favourite spot was Bugle Rock, near B.M.S. Women's College in Basavanagudi. Usually Prakash and his men would accost the young lovers and, pretending to be members of the college staff, ask the boy to go to the college and submit a written statement about his amorous doings, and when he was gone, would rape the girl.

Days after the attack on the auto-rickshaw driver, Chandru, Viji and Benne Krishna trapped Prakash in Bugle Rock Park. Positioning him squarely in front of them, the three men spelled out what they would do to him: pour acid on his face, cut off his ears and pulverise his legs with large stones. Prakash was an incomparable actor—he whimpered and pleaded with them. 'I will lay down my life for the Gandhi Nagar boys,' he assured them. Viji and Chandru weren't convinced, but Prakash had managed to win over Benne Krishna. 'Why don't we give him another chance?' he asked. When the other two refused, Krishna threatened to cut off all ties if they didn't agree to spare Prakash. With that, the two had to yield. It would cost them, though.

Prakash rushed back to his boss Kotwal and told him exactly what had happened, and as was his wont, embellished with abandon. Kotwal asked his men to put together a small team to retaliate.

A few days after the incident, Kotwal and his men went to Gandhi Bazaar in search of Viji, Benne Krishna and Chandru.

They couldn't find them, but instead chanced upon Viji's brother, Prakash. 'Take him,' Kotwal directed.

Prakash, who was drunk, made the mistake of not yielding quietly. He was taken to Bugle Rock and the men slashed at his face and stomach and were about to leave when he screamed, 'You sons of bitches, why don't you take me on one by one?'

Kotwal was enraged. He came back and cut up Prakash so badly that when he was discovered the next morning by a milkman, he was soaked in blood.

Two days later, when I visited Prakash in hospital, I was told he had five hundred and ninety-four sutures on his body. The doctors were astonished that he'd managed to live. But it was not by chance that the wounds had merely caused intense bleeding and not death—this was Kotwal's way of sending out a message while keeping the law at bay; assault was a bailable offence, murder was not.

By now, the Gandhi Bazaar gang had grown in number, with over sixty boys joining in the campaign to eliminate Kotwal. Every day, there would be knots of people in the area, all discussing ways to kill the man.

Four days after the attack on Viji's brother, a meeting was called at Chandru's house in Gandhi Bazaar and just about every mobster from that part of Bangalore was in attendance. This would be one of several gatherings where plans to kill Kotwal would take shape—during one such meeting we even discussed the need for a weapon, and I actually borrowed a shotgun from a friend in Kanakapura. During these meetings, I also met my namesake, Sridhar, who had once charged at Kotwal with a nunchaku, and also a man named Sardar Sultan. I became close to both and they would play a significant role in my life during my days in the underworld.

Sardar was convinced that criminality was merely a prelude to a life in politics—he was hankering after a position in the Youth Congress. He was entrusted with carrying out the actual assault. He was aggressive, bold and fearless, and more importantly, he was one of the few rowdies in Bangalore that

Kotwal didn't know by sight. For us, considering Kotwal was a man obsessed with gathering as much information about his rivals as possible, this was a big advantage. With Sardar spearheading the campaign, we began what would be a series of—ultimately unsuccessful—raids to locate and eliminate Kotwal.

I was witness to Sardar's methods on one of the first of these campaigns: we received information that Kotwal would be at Olympia, a bar opposite Hotel Sarovar near Richmond Circle. We made our way there in a car and as soon as the vehicle stopped, Sardar jumped out, a machete tucked into his trousers, and headed for the bar with little fear. Though we didn't find Kotwal at Olympia that night, this would be an oft repeated scene: Sardar, machete tucked out of view, walking purposefully up to bars, dives, hotels.

After many such attempts we sat down to review our strategy. We figured that Sardar needed an associate, someone who was young but experienced. Sridhar came up with an idea: he wanted to bring in Bala—also known as Mysore Road Bala, or Vinayaka Bala—from Bombay. This man was a bit of a legend in the city's criminal class. Rumour had it that he had fled to Bombay after assaulting twenty-three rowdies and a few policemen in Bangalore. I don't remember where I met him first, but the image of a short, dark man with broad shoulders and eyes that betrayed no emotion whatsoever remains with me to this day.

Bala was introduced to us by Sridhar, and he almost immediately became a part of the raids we were carrying out. Unlike Sardar, his weapon of choice was a razor. I found out during several meetings with a gaggle of his admirers that Bala didn't particularly like gangs and preferred to operate alone or with just one other person. He had earned a terrible reputation for himself and, pursued relentlessly by the Bangalore police, had escaped to Bombay. There, he joined a fellow Tamilian in brewing illicit liquor. Bala would work at the tiny factory by day and spend time at cabaret clubs by night.

At one of these clubs, he met and took to a particular dancer. As was typical of him, Bala treasured the girl and would stave off all attempts by other men to even talk to her. I was told that, one night, a few boys who had been warned off earlier by Bala returned to the club to fight. After an intense encounter, with Bala and a friend battling eight men, he was injured so badly he couldn't move and had to be admitted to a nursing home. That night, convinced his life was in danger, Bala, still bleeding, escaped from the hospital and flagged down a truck on its way to Bangalore.

Bala and I became close friends, spending many hours in the rooms of his cronies at B.M.S. Engineering College Hostel. We drank, talked (these sessions frequently featuring him on the harmonica, which he would play when he was in a sentimental mood) and continued to chalk out plans for Kotwal's death.

At around the time Bala was getting reacquainted with Bangalore and had almost made up his mind that Mysore Road would once again resound with his name. Kotwal, who had remained underground for a while, carried out an attack very much like the one on the auto-rickshaw driver a few months earlier. This time, the victim was Vijaynagar Kanthi, a man who was known to idolise B.K. Hariprasad. Kotwal had had a run-in with Kanthi in 1965, well before he became the terror-monger of south Bangalore and, more recently, Kanthi had led an attack against a student leader Anjanappa, a protégé of Kotwal's.

It was nine-thirty or so at night, and Kanthi was in the midst of a conversation near the Shanishwara Temple on Magadi Road, when seven men, perched on two motorcycles—a Bullet and a Java—rode up to him. Later, Kanthi would identify five of those men: Daniel Kumar, M.C. Prakash, Pachchakari Shekhar, Mico Venkatesh, and Kotwal. The leader of the gang had no time for words; he merely pointed at Kanthi and told his men to 'beat him'. Six of them pulled out knives and razors, and just as they had with Viji's brother Prakash, slashed at him until he was a quivering bloodied mass. Kanthi managed to pull himself into a rickshaw and lodged a complaint with the police before being taken to a hospital.

For the first time, the police formed a special squad to tackle Kotwal. The team was headed by the city's finest: Sangram Singh, Ravindra Prasad, Nagarajiah, and the constable with an encyclopaedic knowledge of the underworld, Giriappa. The squad tapped all its contacts and fanned out across the city. This meant we could do little, and Bala, a man notorious for his fidgetiness during moments of idleness, had to be contained by any means possible—the ruffian had begun to create trouble near Vinayaka Theatre, his turf, and the police were determined to take him in. Chandru and I decided this had to stop and marched Bala to Sridhar's house, where he reluctantly agreed to take the next bus back to Bombay. Sardar was entrusted with the task of making sure Bala was indeed on that bus. The next day, a relieved Sardar waved goodbye to Bala.

Two days later, word came in that officers from Central police station had Bala in their custody. It turned out that the lure of Vinayaka Theatre and his old hunting grounds were too much for Bala to resist and he had returned after Sardar left. Once back home, he had strolled about, telling his minions that he had the personal blessings of the politician Gundu Rao, and that the police wouldn't dare touch him near Vinayaka Theatre. Those illusions were soon dispelled when two constables, faced with a very abusive and belligerent rowdy who claimed they had no business on his turf, took him into custody.

Sardar and I went to the station to try and catch sight of Bala as they brought him in. We stood at a distance and waited. Soon, we saw him being escorted into the station. He walked slowly and looked like he was in great pain. We knew instantly that the police had done the 'horseshoe' on him—tied him up by the ankles and pounded on the soles of his feet with sticks. They had worked on him for three days. Bala saw us and gestured for us to leave.

The next morning, word came in that Bala had died in police custody.

I have witnessed several funerals of rowdies in the last twenty years, but I have never seen one that was as tense or had so many mourners as I did the day Bala died. There were over twenty thousand people in the procession and every shop on its path was shut.

The death of this dark, violent man who played the harmonica and was oddly smitten by something as humdrum as a movie theatre didn't really sink in that day. But when it did, I was overcome with disgust and frustration. I decided I would sever ties with the underworld.

Two

During the meetings we'd had to chalk out plans for raids against Kotwal, I had begun to come to terms with the fact that I was being drawn inexorably into the city's criminal network. During my days as a student I had stood at the periphery of this world, occasionally stepping in; now, it appeared there was no option but to become a part of it.

After the search for Kotwal petered out, losing steam largely due to Bala's death, I continued to keep in touch with members of the Gandhi Bazaar gang, all of whom held day jobs: Chandru was in the Karnataka State Road Transport Corporation, Viji owned a shop, Benne Krishna ran a club. I began to hanker after money, and started to think of ways I could employ my connections in the underworld and my own growing stature in it to amass some wealth.

I began with small extortion jobs, merely taking away someone's money or something of worth, like a watch, and refusing to return it, threatening violence at even a hint of remonstrance. But that was hardly big money—I once took a Citizen watch off a boy from Hanumanthanagar, sold it for fifteen hundred rupees and threw a party for four at a nightclub on Brigade Road. One day, a bus conductor I knew, Krishnamurthy, spoke to me about the thriving counterfeit currency racket and said Coimbatore was where I should go if I wanted to get in on the trade.

Through people I knew, I got in touch with a man named Razak, who operated out of Coimbatore. He showed off freshly minted counterfeit notes and, to me, they looked exactly like the real thing. I gave Razak ten thousand rupees on the understanding that he would return in a week with one lakh rupees. I was thrilled. At this rate, I would make at least ten crore rupees.

But when Razak returned the next week, it was without the money. Another customer had needed the fake currency urgently he explained, adding that I would definitely receive my consignment the week after. Razak left after taking five thousand rupees from me. Seven days later, there was no sign of the man. Over many months this pattern continued, and in a year I had given Razak fifty thousand rupees with not a single rupee in fake currency to show for it.

Finally, just when it appeared my patience was wearing thin, Razak introduced me to a man named Thangaswamy, also from Coimbatore. This man seemed to me a miracle worker: I don't know how he did it, but when we met, Thangaswamy dipped rectangles of paper in a chemical and pulled out impressively real currency. 'If you need a lakh in fake currency, you need to bring me the same amount in real money,' he told me. 'And I don't do anything less than two lakh rupees.'

I looked up everyone I knew and somehow managed to cobble together the money. I even convinced a friend, Vijayendra, to allow me the use of his house to 'prepare' the fake money.

Thangaswamy and his assistant arrived the next day and began work at ten in the night. They worked late into the night, and at one point, awakened by the noise, I saw the two of them filling the chemical into syringes to coat the paper. I went back to sleep, happy.

The next day, the two left for the hotel in which they had booked rooms. Just before he got into the auto, Thangaswamy turned to me and asked, 'What would you say is the greatest act of charity?' I shrugged, waiting for him to answer. 'Patience; you need to take it slow,' was all he said.

I waited till late that evening for Thangaswamy to return but heard no word from him. I went to his hotel and was told that he had checked out at eleven that morning. I knew then that I had been cheated, but holding on to hope, I decided to wait for a day before unwrapping the bundles of fake currency he had given me, in case the chemical needed that amount of time to work to full effect.

The next day, when I opened up one of the parcels, I found a note bearing the message, 'You need to take it slow.'

Enraged, I took two boys and went to Coimbatore. I found Razak but couldn't trace Thangaswamy or his assistant despite scouring the city. I had lost two lakh rupees.

But I didn't give up on the counterfeiting business. Back in Bangalore and convinced that I could make money out of the trade, I tracked down a real estate broker, Shetty, who had once mentioned to me that he knew someone in the counterfeit business. Shetty introduced me to Gangadhar, who lived in Basaveshwar Nagar. A couple of days later, Gangadhar took me to Sandhya Lodge in Gandhi Nagar and introduced me to Altaf, a counterfeiter from Krishnagiri in Tamil Nadu. I was asked several detailed personal questions and Altaf finally agreed to sell me some currency—a few lakh rupees were coming in from Madras, and I thought I'd buy a lakh and forty thousand. He asked me for an advance of twenty thousand, but I refused, still chafing from my recent encounter with Thangaswamy. Altaf reluctantly agreed to wait for payment till the counterfeit money had come in, and asked me to return to the hotel the next day.

It was four in the evening when I reached Altaf's room and walked in to find him alone. 'The *maal* will arrive at five,' he said, and asked if I had brought money with me. I nodded. He asked me to hand it over, and I said it was with a friend who was waiting outside. 'But we never do these transactions without an advance. That's the rule of this business,' he said.

I knew then that Altaf was a cheat. I sprang up and held him by his neck, pressing him up against the wall. 'If you don't tell me exactly what you're up to now, I'll break your teeth and hand you over to the police,' I hissed. He begged me to spare him and said he was just a 'briefcase exchange expert' and not a counterfeiter. I didn't understand.

There were no counterfeit notes anywhere in Bangalore, he said. But there were several ways to cheat people using the currency racket as a front. I was already familiar with two. One was the method Razak used: sell the proposition so well that the victim would simply hand over real money and wait endlessly while Razak repaired to Coimbatore. The second was the method Thangaswamy used—concoct a story about a miraculous chemical that would turn sheets of blank paper into hard currency. The third ploy involved making a few fake notes and placing them atop a bundle of blank sheets, convincing the victim that the suitcase was indeed full of fake money and making a getaway before he could ascertain the veracity of that claim. The fourth was a little more dramatic and required the use of a few accomplices with decent acting abilities: pass off real notes as fake, and just when the suitcases exchanged hands, have your accomplices—dressed as policemen—barge in and pretend to carry out a raid. I asked him how many people were in on this racket in Bangalore. 'About two thousand,' he said. I decided to join their ranks.

My first mark was Gangadhar. Accompanied by two well-built friends, I went to meet him a few days after my run-in with Altaf.

'Did you get your money?' he asked, feigning innocence.

'How many other people have you cheated like this?' I shot back, beckoning my friends, who were in a parked auto.

'Do you know who they are?' I asked him.

He looked them over and shook his head.

'Have you heard of the name Daniel?' I asked, referring to the rowdy, Daniel Kumar.

He blanched. 'Isn't he Kotwal's right-hand man?'

I turned to my two accomplices as if about to order them to attack Gangadhar.

He pleaded with me to stop. 'Look, I do a few small jobs. Please. Don't ruin me,' he begged.

'Since we are all in this business, I think we should share the spoils. Don't you?' I asked.

He gave me fifteen hundred rupees and asked me to come back the next day, when an 'exchange' was scheduled to take place. He promised me a cut from that caper.

It was a simple enough racket, and though the earnings weren't large—the 'party' brought twenty thousand rupees and I made three—it was a beginning. Over the next few months, I was involved with a few similar jobs—we used the fake police method for one job and, in another instance, employed force. Over time I withdrew from active participation in these hits and instead settled for a cut from the jobs Gangadhar carried out.

So the counterfeiting business became a means of income for me, although none of my friends really knew I led this sort of a life. I had a few small roles in films and continued to associate with the writer (and my former roommate) Krishna Masadi, the cameraman Gowrishankar and a few others from the arts and cinema fields. One day, however, my role in the underworld became public. That was also the day I came into contact with Bangalore's world of homosexuals.

It was 1984, and I had a fairly strict fitness regimen in those days, often going to Krishna Rao Park in Basavanagudi to exercise. One day I finished working out on the parallel bars and was walking towards the gate when I noticed a man in his fifties following me. He had been there earlier, watching me exercise from a distance, and had even picked up my shirt when I finished. He didn't look at all dangerous—he wore simple clothes and spectacles; he might well have been an officer in a government department. That day, as I walked towards the gate—in a deserted corner of the park near the Basavanagudi police station—the man approached me and said, 'Haven't I seen you somewhere?'

'I think so too,' I replied, 'but I'm not sure where.'

By then we were out of the park. 'You know, some people look very familiar. You might never have met them, but you still feel you've always known them. It's some sort of a spiritual connection,' he said, and put his hand on my shoulder.

I've never been comfortable with physical contact; it takes years of getting to know someone before I can let him touch me in a familiar manner, so this stranger casually putting his hand on my shoulder irked me. I shrugged it off, and continued to walk. He didn't say anything to this, but asked if I'd like some coffee. We went to Sanman Hotel in Gandhi Bazaar nearby. He ordered sweets and snacks.

As we ate, he turned to me and asked, 'What do you think of two men liking each other?'

I knew then he was gay.

I have always been straight and, at that point, had only heard of gay men—there were a few writers I knew of who were homosexuals, but I had never met them. The man's question angered me. 'I have never felt it necessary to explore that idea,' I replied.

He seemed to relax, as though smug in the knowledge that all was going well.

We finished eating and returned to the park, stopping at a dark little clearing surrounded by trees. 'What's your chest measurement?' he asked, looking at me curiously and placing his hand on my chest.

In a flash, I grabbed his hand, twisted his arm around, and kicked him hard in the knees. He screamed.

I first groped around in his pocket, looking to see what he had.

'What are you doing?' he yelled in pain.

'Bastard. How many boys have you preyed on like this?' I shouted, removing his watch and wallet and reaching for his ring.

'Please, not the ring. It's a gift from someone,' he begged.

'You don't deserve gifts,' I said and took it off.

I kicked him a few more times and asked him to leave the park and never come back.

For the next four months, I was on a golden streak—picking

out gay men in the park and robbing them of everything they had. It was easy; unlike all the straight men I knew in the underworld, the gays had only one thing in mind. They wanted to have sex with as many boys as possible. So, accompanied by a young man who ran a hotel nearby, I baited and attacked these homosexuals. Things would have gone swimmingly well if I hadn't let greed overpower me.

Usually, the boy from the hotel and I would sit on a particular bench, either at Krishna Rao Park or Cubbon Park, and at sundown we would be approached, invariably, by a gay man. Once I had sized him up and decided he was wealthy enough, we would ask him back to a room my accomplice had in Hanumanthanagar. Once there, I would sit on a chair, make that night's victim kneel before me and begin the questioning. 'How many boys have you ruined?' 'How many years have you been at it?' 'Aren't you aware that what you're doing is a sin?'

They would tremble in fear and usually hand over all the money and valuables they had. This continued for many months, till I decided to do more than just rob gay men. I decided this could well move up to extortion and began ordering them to bring me more money, threatening to 'out' them to their families if they failed to follow my orders. Almost all of them obeyed—some begged, others argued and a few stood up to me, and when they did, all I had to do was show them my switchblade. Until one day, I met the wrong man.

Let's call him Amarnath. I snared him just like the others and used my usual threats. He agreed and said he would come back the next day with a thousand rupees. What he did was register a complaint with the Basavanagudi police. The next day, a few constables took me to the station. Once there, I was confronted by Mahalingayya, a stern, righteous sort of man. I explained to him that the men he was talking about were gay and that they were picking up boys right under his nose. 'If what you say is true, I'm willing to help you, but if you're lying to me, I will break your back,' he said.

So the two of us went around Krishna Rao Park, him in

plainclothes, and me, the guide. We met about twenty gay men that day and he stopped to lecture each one of them. He then turned to me and said, 'I should reward you for what you've done, but you've committed a crime and you'll have to go to jail.'

It was March 1984 and that was my first night of incarceration. As chance would have it, I didn't even get to think about what it felt like to be a prisoner. Other inmates in the police lock-up that night included six gay men. For hours they harangued me: 'What have we done to you? Why did you have to attack us? God will surely punish you.' The next day, I was marched into court. I was denied bail and sent to prison.

The first time a man spends time in a cell, he thinks about things and either decides he's had enough of the life he's leading or figures a life of crime is what he wants despite the possibility of going to prison. I hated jail. I never wanted to go back in there. Not ever. Besides, I felt bogged down, crushed. Not because I was disconsolate that I had taken to a life that had led me to prison, but because I had been foolish enough not to take precautions. That I had gone about terrorising Amarnath the wrong way.

Resolutions, of course, always sound good in theory. Six months after my first two days as a prisoner, I would find myself back where I didn't want to be.

Spending time under lock and key had obviously done a lot for my reputation. The moment I was released, two days after the incident with Amarnath, people I knew came up to me and said kind words. Then, perhaps because of the notoriety I had earned, and because my association with crime was finally public knowledge, all manner of jobs began coming my way: a lady called Begum, who had a falling out with the famous trial lawyer Devdas, sent word to me through a politician that she wanted the advocate murdered. I refused. I was prepared to kill Kotwal because I had a grudge against him, but this was completely different.

Soon I received another offer, which I took. A diamond

merchant in the city was being blackmailed by a woman, and he asked me to take care of his problem. This young lady was in the business of providing film extras to rich businessmen. All I had to do was scare her. It seemed an easy enough job to do, so I arranged for the diamond merchant to have her contact me through an acquaintance, and drove to the outskirts of Bangalore, on Kanakapura Road. There, I threatened her and told her that if she continued blackmailing the diamond merchant, she would see a lot of trouble.

A few days later, she decided to go to the police and I was arrested for the second time in my life. By now my links with gangsters and crime were far too firm for people to ignore. All my friends from the arts—writers, poets—distanced themselves from me. We were now nearing the end of 1984. Soon, I would be back in prison, and experience, for the first time in my life, the brutality that the police inflicts upon inmates. Soon, I would also meet Bachchan, the tall, gaunt man, completely devoid of fear, who would become my friend, accomplice and auxiliary in crime.

Three

This is how it happened.

My second stint in jail caused my stock to grow even more—the dailies had made much of the case—and a trader from Madhugiri got in touch with me through a mutual friend. A holy man had approached this trader and told him he had become a 'vessel for divinity' and that, in a state of rapture, he'd been told that if the trader were to put all his jewellery and gold into a large container and bury it, the next day, following several prayers to the goddess Devi, the trader's wealth would grow two-fold.

In his naïveté, the trader buried his gold, and, as he recounted it, much to my astonishment, even believed the holy man's words that the vessel, now heavier, should only be opened in the temple town of Dharmasthala. Upon reaching the holy city, the trader discovered that his recently buried wealth had turned into large, black stones.

The trader returned to Madhugiri and sure enough found that the holy man had decamped. It turned out, upon several enquiries being made, that many others in Madhugiri had been cheated in a similar manner. The trader was furious that not only had he been had, but that the holy man had been allowed to bless the womenfolk of the household. I was told I would receive half the jewellery if I found the cheat and recovered the stolen wealth. The trader gave me an advance of fifty thousand rupees and said he would deduct that amount from our final settlement. I was elated. Not only had I acquired a reputation, but this man was willing to bet half his wealth on it. I set about finding the cheat.

Since I'd gotten out of jail, I always had four men around me—I don't want to mention their names, because they all lead respectable lives now—and with them, I began the search. We soon ascertained that the holy man didn't operate alone, and that there was a significantly entrenched network at play. We learned that at the heart of this network lay a powerful, elderly man known as Ramanna, who had introduced the trader to the holy man. Hard to get to and of powerful build, Ramanna operated out of Tumkur. He was fifty, had two wives and six children.

We continued making our enquiries, and through a man named Kempaiah, an employee of Hindustan Machine Tools (he had introduced the trader to Ramanna), learned that the holy man was now married and had constructed a house for his family near Hebbagodi, on the Bangalore-Malur highway.

Hebbagodi, in those days, didn't have a police station, just an outpost. We went there and told the police that we were in search of the holy man. We were asked to register a complaint, but because we had instructions from the trader that under no circumstances was a complaint to be lodged, we asked the police if they would summon the man so we could arrive at a compromise. When he was brought in, the holy man was shocked to see Kempaiah. We decided to take him back home in a rented Ambassador to recover the money.

On our way, he pleaded with me to spare his life (Kempaiah had told him I was a police officer, an identity I would have to slip into several times over the next few years). It turned out he didn't have much money—fifty thousand in cash at home and a lakh in a fixed deposit. The rest, Ramanna and his gang had grabbed as their own. I felt pity for this sad, mewling man and his elderly wife, and decided I would only take twenty thousand from him. We didn't tell the trader we had found his man.

Later, back in Bangalore, we convinced Ramanna to travel to Bangalore—a friend of mine in the CoD, Yusuf, helped me out by threatening to expose him if Ramanna didn't come to the city to meet me. He was asked to arrange for fifty thousand rupees to hand over to us as recompense for our efforts and for cheating the trader. He arrived soon enough and we asked him to check in with us at Hotel Madhuvan while his son gathered the funds. We talked and drank through the night and Ramanna kept us entertained with accounts of his exploits. The next morning, at around eleven, the doorbell rang.

I opened the door and saw four well-built men. One punched me in the face. I was strong enough to take the blow and tried to hit him back. 'Stop it. We're from the City Crime Branch,' he shouted, fending me off. A little while later I found myself with those four men in a CCB office. I was made to sit on the ground and the interrogation began.

'Look, this Ramanna cheated a friend of mine,' I said, 'I only–'

'We know everything. Tell us where the money is,' one of them said, cutting me off.

'What money?'

'Don't do it. Don't pretend you're innocent. Where's the nine lakh rupees?'

I realised they didn't know what had actually happened, and the tone they took began to scare me.

'Sir, this Ramanna . . . and there was this holy man . . .'

I felt something pricking me in the back. I turned, but could see nothing. A second later, I felt it again. It happened two more times, and I begged them to let me go.

'Sir, please. What are you doing?'

'Are you a girl? What have I done?' one of them asked, smiling.

The one sitting on a stool in front of me looked at the others and in mock-seriousness, said, 'Why are you torturing him? Why don't you tell him how good he looks instead?'

The man behind me pulled out a small torch and pressed it to my neck. I was shaking.

'What is this, Sir?'

'This is the CCB. We don't bring the good guys here to chat. And those who do come here don't leave without talking. Tell us the truth and we'll spare you. If you don't, you'll die,' he replied, pressing the small device further into my neck.

'Sir, please believe me. I—'

One of them punched me. 'Look at his arrogance,' he said to the others, and then, turning towards me, 'You want to speak in English? Speak!' and slapped me hard across the face.

There were five of them and I was alone. I thought then that they would kill me, slowly and painfully. I began to sweat.

'Sir, please. You have to believe me. I haven't done anything wrong.'

'If you keep at the same story, you *will* die. You haven't done anything wrong? What about pretending to be a cop?' asked one.

'That is the only mistake I made,' I replied, now realising that I had to begin from the beginning and also let on that I was not without patronage.

'Look, Sir, I haven't committed a crime. All this while I have only worked for people like Lankesh and Rajkumar—'

'You think those names will scare us?' one of them shot back, and whacked me across the arm with his lathi. I thought he had broken a bone.

'Sir, I don't know what else to say. Please, listen to me,' I begged.

'Fine. Let's do some listening!' he barked, and dragged me to an adjoining room.

It was a small enclosure with no windows. A pulley was rigged to the ceiling and in one corner was a large stone.

One of the men pointed at the stone and said, 'Do you know what this is? It covers a small tunnel that leads to Ulsoor Lake. It isn't uncommon for people to die during questioning. What can we do with the bodies? We just dump them in the lake.'

Then he turned to one of the others and said I needed to understand what 'work' really meant. 'Has anyone ever "worked" on you?' he asked.

'No.'

'Then it's time you found out. Everyone should be "worked on" at least once in their lives, I think. That's the only way to salvation.'

'Tell me, what have you studied?' one of the others asked me.

'Law.'

'Oh, really. Look at him, a lawyer. Did they teach you what third degree was in college?'

'No.'

'Don't worry, we'll teach you.'

They asked me to strip to my underwear.

'He has a good body,' one said. 'How do you maintain it?'

'I go to a gym.'

One of them reached over and stroked my arm. 'Look Sreedhar, what a fine body you have. Tell us what you know and I'll ensure you get to keep this good body.'

I opened my mouth to say something, but he stilled me. 'Not now! Wait! Loosen your arms.'

Two of them then held each arm and turned each so hard that I was now kneeling.

'We don't want to harm you. Whatever happens here will only make you a better person,' they said as they tied my arms with rope. They then put one end of another rope through a pulley on the ceiling and tied the other to an iron rod, which went through the cord that bound my arms. Slowly, they began to tug at the truss till I was suspended, my legs barely off the floor. My shoulders now bore the entire weight of my body. My legs, too, were fastened.

One of them pulled at the loose end of the rope while the other tugged at my legs. I cannot describe the pain I was overcome with. I had never flinched at physical agony, but this was too much to take. I opened my mouth to scream, but one of them thrust a towel in it.

While the rope and my legs were being pulled, the two other officers went to work on my body with lathis and bare hands. One of them hit me repeatedly on the lower back and thighs, while the other pinched me with such force that there were little florets of clotted blood underneath my skin. They then directed their blows at those angry weals.

'Where is the nine lakh?' they asked repeatedly, punctuating the question with more blows.

'I don't know. I swear. The only money I have is the fifty thousand I took from the trader and the twenty the holy man gave me,' I screamed, when they finally removed the towel to allow me to talk.

'You can keep the seventy thousand. Just give us back the remaining money. The eight lakh thirty thousand.'

Sweat was pouring off me by now and the pain was beyond anything I knew. I relented. I told them I had the nine lakh.

They refused to let me go. 'Where have you hidden it?'

I told him it was buried in the compound of my house. At that, they let me down.

When my arms were untied, it was as though they had been hacked from my body. I felt I had nothing attached to my shoulders.

My throat was dry. My heart felt like it was ablaze. I asked for water.

'You shouldn't drink water now. Sit down and stretch your legs.'

'Please, just let me go!'

'Listen to what we say. Stretch your legs.'

I did as they demanded and two of the officers grabbed me by the thighs.

One of them began to hit me on the soles of my feet. This went on for about ten minutes. Though they had maintained a hailstorm of questions when they had tied me up, now, for these tortuous ten minutes, not one of them spoke. All I heard was the angry thwack of the lathi and the grunts that interspersed their exertions.

I was then dragged to a cell and locked in.

I could not stand. And because they had 'aeroplaned' me, I could not move my arms or my shoulders. I tried to slow down my heart by drinking water, but that didn't work.

That night, sleepless, I writhed in pain.

Four

The day after the beating, I was escorted out of my cell, my wounds still smarting. The CCB officers had arrested the holy man and brought him to the station. He didn't look at all like the whiny cheat I had met in Hebbagodi. The police had obviously worked on him: he was missing clumps of hair in his moustache and his face was blue from repeated blows.

'This is the real culprit,' one of the officers said, 'he did everything, and you were the one beaten up.' The taunting tone was unmistakable.

'Where is Ramanna?' I asked.

'You'd best look after your own interests. There's no need to worry about anything else,' the officer snapped back.

It occurred to me then that they were trying to shield Ramanna, and I was right. In the afternoon, Ramanna came to the station. He hadn't been charged. 'A simple fellow like you should not get into all these things,' he said to me. 'Don't worry. The police know you are innocent. They'll let you go this evening.'

And, sure enough, I was released a few hours later. I was put down as a witness to the crime and told to hand over the twenty thousand I had taken from the holy man. I gave them twelve thousand the next day. A case of cheating was registered against the holy man and Ramanna and I were named as witnesses.

Later, the merchant who had first asked me to take up the job called and said that, apart from the nine lakh he had been cheated out of and the fifty thousand he had paid me, his losses now included an additional lakh and a half, which he had paid the police. 'I would have been glad if the holy man and Ramanna had been murdered. They've just eaten up my money,' he said.

I had learned my lesson. No one was to be completely trusted and I had to remain on my guard during every single job I carried out. The next time I was involved in a counterfeit racket, I would ensure my back was covered.

That next time came soon enough. Kamaal Pasha, a counterfeiter living on Tannery Road, had cheated an acquaintance of mine of two lakh rupees and I was commissioned to recover the money.

My involvement in this racket was twofold: offloading currency in exchange for real money and recovering money for people who had been cheated by people like Pasha. This last method, I found, was far more profitable than actually cheating people: all I had to do was be tough and I would get a share of the recovered money.

But Pasha, unlike most others, was proving to be a bother. He always maintained cover and a small posse of about twelve men accompanied him at all times. Anyone who had any business with Pasha had to go to his house to complete the transaction; he never conducted meetings anywhere else.

I decided Sardar, the man I had met while on the hunt for Kotwal, would prove an ideal accomplice for the job. Sardar spent all his time in the Jayanagar Shopping Complex.

It was when I sought out Sardar that I realised that the city's underworld had gone through a significant churn. Peace had been brokered between Sardar and Kotwal. M.C. Prakash—Kotwal's lieutenant and the man who had been attacked in Bugle Rock—had been murdered by three nondescript boys (he had slapped one of them and the three retaliated by chopping him to bits). B.K. Hariprasad had not just severed his ties with Sardar, but had detached himself from the underworld. Sridhar, my namesake, who had once attacked Kotwal with a nanchaku, was now a practising lawyer. By way of various machinations, an uneasy calm was restored in Gandhi Bazaar as well, with that gang, once staunchly against Kotwal now maintaining cordial relations.

Sardar's and Kotwal's pact had been overseen by the Youth Congress leader Nissar. And as things came to pass, Sardar and Kotwal became such thick friends that the two appeared in all political posters, along with a third person, the politician and future chief minister of Karnataka, S. Bangarappa.

When I met Sardar in Jayanagar, he at first assumed that I was renewing my campaign to eliminate his newfound ally, and yet he was friendly towards me. I told him that this was about Kamaal Pasha. Sardar said the simplest way to approach this would be to kidnap the man.

We gathered seven men and went to Pasha's home on Tannery Road. A few of his gang members were milling about outside and Sardar asked one of them to summon Pasha. The man refused. Sardar, instead of pressing his demand, just left.

Later he told me that he'd recognised the man who had refused to summon Pasha. He was an associate of the much feared Shivajinagar gangster Koli Fayaz. Sardar said it would be both foolish and impossible to kidnap Pasha without Fayaz's explicit consent. This was too small a job to ask of Kotwal, who could easily have told Fayaz to agree to the kidnapping, so instead we decided to approach Fayaz directly.

There are three kinds of people that hold value in Shivajinagar: the politicians, the rowdies and the butchers. That last group, especially the ones who sell beef, are a large, well-knit clan and they don't normally associate with rowdies. Since this community was, in a sense, neutral, we took one of its members along with us: we picked Khalandar, who lived in Banashankari.

Khalandar was a former state boxing champion and was once ranked fourth in the country. Seeing no future in pugilism, he had opened up a butcher's shop in Yarabnagar, near Banashankari. He counted many of his relatives as members of the Shivajinagar butchers' group. When we spoke to Khalandar, he suggested that we also take someone called Lamboo to talk to Fayaz. Sardar immediately agreed.

'Who is Lamboo?' I asked.

'Lamboo is Bachchan,' Khalandar replied.

'A cousin of the actor?' I asked.

'He's called Lamboo because of his height,' Sardar replied, and added, 'You must meet this man. He simply doesn't know fear.'

Bachchan wasn't in his Banashankari home and we learned that he was watching a movie at Nanda Theatre in Jayanagar. We went there and asked the manager of the theatre to fetch him.

Bachchan emerged, tall, angular, powerful and smiling. He looked much like the actor.

The four of us discussed how we would approach Koli Fayaz and what we would say to him. The thing was, I had never met the man before, and he had a formidable reputation. I suggested that we take Nissar, the Youth Congress leader, with us. Fayaz would not refuse him. Though Nissar was a career politician— he was close to the then Congress leader S. Bangarappa—and not a gangster, he maintained close ties with rowdies. Kotwal and he were particularly close and Nissar was the man who always mediated between Kotwal and the police whenever there was trouble.

So, here I was, in the company of Sardar, now an associate of Kotwal's, on my way to becoming a friend of Nissar, another man close to the gangster whom I so badly wanted to kill. By way of a series of incidents, and without having to go through a traditional *raaji* or *kabooli* (compromise), I found myself with people who were in close proximity to Kotwal.

Bachchan, Khalandar and I got along famously. Khalandar would often speak of his fitness regimen. Bachchan was a man of few words, but always had a ready smile for everyone. Nissar, being the elderly statesman, remained the group's cynical adviser.

There were eighteen of us the day we decided to meet Koli

Fayaz. We travelled in a Matador, an Ambassador and two bikes. It was eight at night when we reached the chowk in Shivajinagar. Several people came up to Nissar to pay their respects. Several others approached Khalandar and invited him home for dinner. We merely asked about Fayaz and were told he would only be available after ten. We decided to eat dinner while we waited.

This was the first time I had a chance to observe Muslim gangsters. Unlike the Hindu boys, these men didn't drink, and paid more attention to their physical appearance. They were a band apart in matters concerning gastronomy as well: if Hindu members of a gang were at a restaurant, they would most likely order a few plates of food; the Muslim gangs would always call for a couple of dozen plates of food. When I thought of these two worlds, it seemed to me that the Muslim gangs were far more interesting and colourful. I liked their mannerisms and the way they talked.

After we were done with dinner, we went back to the chowk to wait for Fayaz. When he came, he had seven men around him. We stopped the car and he walked toward us slowly. As he got close, Bachchan, Khalandar, Sardar and a boy called Mehmood walked up to him and shook hands. Nissar and I remained in the car. Nissar called out to Fayaz and said, '*Kaisa hai Fayu*?'—How are you?—and held out his hand. '*Aao . . . Mubarak! Baitke baatein karenge*?' Fayaz said, inviting Nissar to sit and chat with him.

Nissar, rather mysteriously, said he wouldn't be able to get out of the car and that we should talk right there.

Fayaz got in.

As he sat, Nissar pointed at me and said, 'This is Inspector Sreedhar.'

Fayaz was taken aback, albeit for just an instant. As he proffered his hand in greeting, I noticed his left eye twitch a little.

Nissar told Fayaz that a close associate of mine had been cheated by Kamaal Pasha and that we needed his help to sort things out. Fayaz appeared delighted that a police officer had sought his help.

He asked Nissar to return the next day, at eleven, with Khalandar and Bachchan. He said I needn't come, and asked me which station I worked in.

I didn't know what to say, but Nissar chipped in, 'Special Branch.'

A few pleasantries later, we left.

I asked Nissar why he had introduced me as a cop, and he said, 'He wouldn't have taken this seriously if I'd said anything else.'

'But why Special Branch?'

'These Shivajinagar *pehelwans* don't understand or care which branch you belong to. They have a lot of respect for the police.'

The next day, Nissar returned to Shivajinagar with Bachchan and Khalandar. Fayaz was there to meet them. Kamaal Pasha, as it turned out, was too scared to come, so he had dispatched one of his boys instead. Pasha had spent a lot of the money he had taken, so he could only muster up a lakh. Fayaz handed this over to Nissar, who offered him twenty thousand as 'pocket money'. Fayaz refused, saying, 'I did this for Inspector sahib. His goodwill is more important to me than anything else.' Before they left, he asked Nissar to bring the Inspector sahib home for dinner sometime.

~

After the Kamaal Pasha deal, I made Jayanagar my *adda*, my main haunt. We would spend all our time in the shopping complex, working out of the second-floor office of a small-time black marketer called Subhan. I would walk into this office, above the vegetable market, at ten in the morning and leave at eight at night. Subhan ran his scams in the meanwhile—he mainly targeted people who had inserted 'for sale' ads in newspapers, buying their video recorders and television sets with fake cheques. He had interests in almost all the con rackets, from fake currency to fake overseas employment. His list of victims was as varied as it was amusing—everyone from gullible Marwadi businessmen to some of the most dangerous men in Bangalore (the Shivajinagar gangster Kareem Lala, for one) had been his targets. And this had a telling effect on Subhan; he was forever in trouble with people, often receiving bone-smashing blows from a recent victim (Kareem Lala being one). We were thoroughly taken with Subhan's exploits and I was often called to offer him protection—several times, I had to step in, physically, between an attacker and Subhan.

Because of this I gained quite a reputation in Jayanagar, and soon the boys there anointed me their leader. Sardar even told them I was now a bigger gangster than Kotwal.

As always, that man, my nemesis, remained in our conversations. Though Sardar was close to him, I still insisted on discussing ways to eliminate Kotwal. Sardar steadfastly refused, reasoning, 'If we get rid of him, who will support the gangsters of Bangalore? Hariprasad? He has given up all ties with the underworld. And besides, if we do manage to kill Kotwal, his men will not spare us.'

His arguments made sense. Kotwal's coterie included some of the most reviled killers the city has known: Kitty, Kariya, Satti, Muni, Hajaama Venkatesha and Daniel. One of Bangalore's most successful trial lawyers, C.H. Hanumatharaya, handled his cases. He had the blessings of politicians like R.L. Jalappa and Jeevraj Alva. Getting Kotwal was an impossibility.

And then, as luck would have it, a few months later, I found myself standing face-to-face with the man whose life I wanted to take.

At the time, *Lankesh Patrike*, P. Lankesh's popular Kannada tabloid, published a number of articles against Kotwal which had, obviously, made him very unhappy.

One day, I had to go to Channapatna and Sardar dropped me off at the bus stand. Once there, I found a bookstall that Lankesh owned. I befriended Siddappa, the man who ran the shop. It turned out that Siddappa was also the manager at *Lankesh Patrike*. Sardar suggested to me that, if I could manage a meeting between Kotwal and Lankesh, I might finally get to meet the gangster.

After I returned from Channapatna, Siddappa and I met up at Elite Bar after he had shut shop. As expected, Kotwal was the subject of discussion and I lied to him, saying I had met the man.

'You know, Lankesh doesn't have anything against Kotwal. And just the fact that Kotwal hasn't once reacted to everything that's been written against him must mean that he doesn't have anything against Lankesh,' Siddappa said.

I asked if it would be possible to arrange a meeting between the two. 'Lankesh is very temperamental. I don't know if he'll agree. Let's first see if Kotwal will meet me, then we can discuss Lankesh,' he said.

I reported back to Sardar, with the happy news that we had made some headway. He was delighted. 'Who cares if Kotwal gets to meet Lankesh or not? This is your chance to finally meet him,' he said. That afternoon, Sardar met with Kotwal to ask if I could see him.

At around five in the evening, the two of us went to Kotwal's office, on Double Road.

I would finally confront the man who had hurt my brother. I had rehearsed for this day a hundred times, going through what I would say and do. Sardar, who was far more pragmatic, warned me to betray no emotions and in no way reveal how much hate I harboured for Kotwal.

There were a few boys milling about and we were asked to wait inside for Kotwal. 'They are going to see the *pasar* (loosely, reconnoitre). If everything's clear, they'll let Kotwal know and he'll come.' As he said this, I heard the roar of a Yamaha 350-cc bike outside, I looked out of the window and saw a man I knew was Kotwal ride up.

We went out and waited. Sardar wished him. Kotwal kept the engine running and looked this way and that.

Sardar then introduced me to him.

Kotwal turned the engine off, took off his helmet and shook my hand.

He was over six feet tall, dark and well built. He had coarse, curly hair and was dressed in a blue shirt, pressed trousers and boots with heels. Around his neck dangled a gold chain. He wore a bracelet of the same metal on his right wrist, and on his left, a Rado. On his left cheek, I noticed a curious mark.

'Sardar has told me a lot about you. I believe you know Lankesh and can arrange for me to meet him? When are you going to make this happen?' he said, very loudly.

'As of now, it's the *Lankesh Patrike* manager, Siddappa, who will meet you,' I replied, in a low tone, fearful that he may refuse.

I was wrong. 'Right! I didn't think Lankesh would agree to meet me right away. It is better to meet the manager first. He will figure out how to bring Lankesh,' he said.

'Where should this meeting take place?' I asked.

Kotwal looked at Sardar and smiled. Sardar squeezed my hand, in disapproval. Kotwal noticed this and said to him, 'Perhaps he is not aware of our ways?' He then turned to me and said, 'You fix up the meeting and inform Sardar. Maybe we could do it at a star hotel.'

As he said this, a Fiat drove up; Kotwal walked up to the car to speak to the people in it.

I whispered to Sardar, 'Kotwal doesn't have anyone here. He doesn't look all that strong to me. What if we do something to him right here?'

'Don't even think about it,' he hissed.

Kotwal spoke to the men in the car for about five minutes and came back. He talked to Sardar about Bachchan for a while until four boys drove up on two motorcycles.

'We are going for a ride, Sardar. Will you join us?' Kotwal asked, directing the question at me as well.

'No,' Sardar replied, 'we need to be somewhere else.' I was disappointed. It would have been an ideal chance for me to observe Kotwal.

Kotwal nodded, said goodbye, and wheeled his bike after the boys.

Five

At nine that night I rang Siddappa, Lankesh's manager, to set up the meeting. A woman picked up the phone and wanted to know who was calling. When I told her, she said he wasn't at home.

The next day, the same thing happened.

I got the feeling Siddappa was avoiding my calls so I asked Sardar to ring him and say he was Bhimappa from Vidhana Soudha. Siddappa answered immediately. I took the phone from Sardar and asked Siddappa why he was avoiding me. He confessed that he'd become nervous about meeting Kotwal and had gone to his boss, Lankesh, for advice. Lankesh, furious, had told him to stay the hell away from rowdies and the underworld.

The meeting wasn't going to take place.

I knew this was a huge setback. Kotwal was notorious for abandoning people who had failed him. Even in the smallest way.

Sure enough, a few days later Kotwal expressed his disappointment to Sardar, who tried his best to placate him, but to no avail. We had to figure out how to get back in his favour.

At the time, we were in contact with a man named Moiuddin, who sold the spare parts of HMT watches in the black market. He had a countrywide network and frequently dealt with people from the underworld in the northern parts of India. Through him, I met a man from Bihar named Rafiq—a fair, ill-tempered thug.

Rafiq was a gun runner and was looking for potential customers in Bangalore. I immediately asked to look at his wares, and Rafiq, cool as daylight, pulled out two country-made pistols from his pocket. The only time I had actually seen a gun was when I had met my namesake, Sridhar, the man who had assaulted Kotwal with a nunchaku: he carried a small pistol with him.

But these guns were entirely different. Though they had been made locally, they looked and felt like something you'd buy on the international market—I couldn't make out a single defect.

Rafiq said each cost three thousand rupees and that if I bought more than five, I would get one free.

I turned to Moiuddin. 'Do you intend that I get into terrorism?' I asked.

'No, no. This is not for you . . . *woh admi joh hai . . . usko hona to* supply *karenge*,' he said, referring to Kotwal. This could be my chance to get back on track with the don, I thought. For his part, Rafiq was convinced that a man of Kotwal's stature and might would want at least fifteen of his guns.

Later, I laid out the plan to Sardar. Though he was a hard-boiled rowdy, Sardar wasn't a man to take risks easily. 'Where did you get this kind of dil?' he asked, using the prevalent term for bravado. 'If we get the guns, we'll be caught. We're doing just fine now. We don't need this.'

But I persisted and eventually persuaded him to meet Kotwal and make the pitch.

'I don't believe him. He said he'd set up this thing with Siddappa and nothing came of it,' Kotwal told Sardar, who again pleaded my case. Eventually, Kotwal agreed and asked us to get the guns.

Rafiq insisted that he be present when they were inspected so we took him to the general hostel, where politicians from the state stay. The whole time Sardar remained silent, refusing to even so much as look at Rafiq.

Kotwal soon joined us, and after inspecting the weapons, came outside the hostel with us.

It was eight at night.

Rafiq picked up one of the guns and pointed it at the Central College building near KR Circle.

'Do you have any sense? What if the *kuttas* (dogs) come running?' Kotwal screamed, referring to the policemen on their rounds.

Rafiq smiled. 'Don't worry, the *kuttas* won't hear a thing. Here, why don't you go stand there and watch,' he said, pointing to a spot ten-feet away. 'I'll fire from here.'

We were behind the hostel now and there was no one in the compound. Outside, the street droned with vehicles.

Rafiq fired at a tree. The .32 calibre pistol made a sound like a small firecracker going off. Though he had fired without warning, Kotwal was pleased. 'Fantastic! This is fantastic!' he exclaimed.

Rafiq was asked to return in a week, and though Kotwal insisted on meeting the gun runner alone, I knew we were in.

The next day Moiuddin told us Rafiq had left for Bihar, and later still we discovered he was avoiding us. But it didn't matter: we had delivered the man to Kotwal and now we were trustworthy. Now we had to begin working on a plan to kill Kotwal and also mull over what we would do once he was dead.

At around this time, we met another man who would eventually join us in the plot to finish Kotwal. His name was Varadaraj. This is how we met him.

Though there were many visitors to the office we had in Jayanagar, one of the most frequent, and most odd, was Muneer Ahmed Kureshi, or Rizwan as he liked to be called. He was very close to Sardar. Rizwan was an inveterate liar: you could never tell if what he was saying was the truth or fiction.

Once Rizwan came to us and said he'd been cheated by a man named Umesh Babu, a counterfeiter who lived in Madivala. We set up a meeting with Babu at Kamat Hotel near Minerva Circle under the pretence of wanting to work on a deal and as soon as he came there, kidnapped him and decided to work on him a little. Rizwan accompanied us and while we were about to launch into Babu—we would normally kick and punch people we wanted to threaten—we saw a side to our accomplice that was entirely new. Rizwan didn't stop at just kicks and punches, he made Babu take off all his clothes and beat him mercilessly, just like the police would. Later we learned that Rizwan had spent two days in a Pakistani jail and that there was even a case registered against him at a Delhi police station for the unlawful possession of a firearm.

Babu's father, who had encouraged him to pursue the currency racket, registered a case against us at the Madivala police station. We let Babu go. He promised us there would be no further trouble with the police. That same night, a few constables landed up at home. I was not named in the case and Rizwan applied for and obtained anticipatory bail.

Babu was admitted to hospital and was discharged in two days. He never returned Rizwan's money. Though we saw nothing of Babu after that, we did see a lot of Rizwan. He introduced us to Varadaraj—his childhood friend.

Before we met, I was told that Varada was impetuous and headstrong; he was only twenty and had dropped out of college. He was rich and privileged—his father owned a large and successful chemical plant. Much to his father's annoyance, he was seeing a girl who didn't belong to his caste. One day Rizwan was summoned to Varada's house by his father and asked to talk his friend out of these 'silly notions' of love. Rizwan, who didn't care much for the girl or his friend's dalliances with love, agreed and went straight to Kotwal, asking him to do something about it.

Kotwal decided to approach the matter indirectly and threatened the girl's brother. She was incensed and told Varada as much, shouting at him for letting his father run his life and use rowdies to threaten her family.

Varada went straight to Rizwan, seeking his help, not knowing that it was his friend who had asked Kotwal to get involved in the first place. Rizwan, trapped between friendship and his dislike for Varada's girlfriend, decided wisely to just hand the whole thing over to my friend Sardar.

It was decided that Varada would be taken to Kotwal and some sort of a compromise brokered. We picked Khadar, the younger brother of former Congress minister C.M. Ibrahim, as the intermediary. The meeting with Kotwal was to take place at Khadar's house (he lived on the floor above Ibrahim). The day the meeting took place, Sardar and Varada were accompanied by Nissar, the Youth Congress leader. Kotwal brought a large part of his coterie with him—Daniel, Kitty, Satti and Muni, among others. Nissar introduced Varada to Kotwal.

'Why have you gone and messed things up?' Kotwal asked. 'You're still so young, there's no need to get into all these things.'

Varada, arrogant as ever, and completely unmindful of the thugs around him, said, 'I haven't interfered in your affairs. I don't understand why you should interfere in mine.'

'It's not possible for you to interfere in my affairs even if you wanted to. I've been asked by some very important people to get involved. So you listen to me and—'

'How much money are they giving you?' Varada butted in. 'Whatever they gave you, I'll give you more. Just stay out of my life.'

'Listen! I don't care if you want to marry that girl. Just don't see her for a year,' Kotwal said.

Varada, as dramatic as ever, said he'd rather kill himself than stay away from her.

Kotwal began to bargain: he brought down the forced separation from a year to three months. But Varada remained adamant.

Frustrated, Kotwal turned to one of his men, Muni, and said, 'Convince this boy.'

At that, Muni, a large and well-built man, pulled out a sword and growled, 'Listen child, don't do this. Listen to what the boss says or else we'll have to kill both you and your lover.'

Varada remained steadfast.

Kotwal spoke up again, 'Don't meet her for a month at least. After that, I'll back you.'

Varada stood silent.

Later, he told Sardar that nothing would stop him from seeing the girl every day. Convinced that this would lead to trouble, Sardar met Kotwal the next day and advised him to deal with Varada with a little less harshness.

'I don't care if he wants to meet the girl, but his father has promised me a lakh if I take care of this. Once I get the money, the boy can do what he wants,' Kotwal told Sardar.

So Varada was encouraged to exercise a little caution while planning his trysts with the girl.

Two days later, Sardar introduced Varada to me.

I thought he was very handsome—he looked Kashmiri, with a sharp nose and chiselled features. We instantly became friends. That night Varada took us to a cabaret. He began to drink at eight and didn't stop till it was past midnight. As he drank, he became increasingly angry: at his father, who had hired Kotwal to threaten his own son, and at the gangster for his attempts at intimidation.

'Who the hell does he think he is?' Varada screamed in a drunken rage. 'Is this any way for a man to make money? Why can't he go rob banks or something?'

He had had too much to drink, so we decided to take him to a guesthouse that a friend of ours had built in Koramangala. But Varada didn't sleep. Continuing to drink, he looked at me and said, 'No matter how much it costs, we should finish this guy, Sreedhar. You look like a man who has the guts to do it. Why don't you think of a plan?'

I was a little wary of saying anything: Varada could, if he let such ideas slip while drunk, alert Kotwal to our motives by way of Rizwan. I told Varada that we should try and settle things by talking to his father. He refused. 'You don't worry about my father. If you have the guts, let's talk about Kotwal. If you don't, I think you should go become his *chela* (minion).'

Though I didn't say much, I felt good that night. If I try to finish Kotwal, this rich kid might actually come in handy, I thought.

The next day, Varada severed all ties with Rizwan and began visiting us at the Jayanagar office. He also said he'd cut off all links to his father who, knowing how stubborn Varada could get, had refused meet his son to discuss the matter further.

However, Varada did continue to go to his father's factory, if only to bring a vehicle to drive us around; each day a different one. We didn't have a problem with the police or the city's underworld then, and we didn't really need a different car every day, but what this did for us was boost our standing in Jayanagar.

Varada's entry into the group produced a few other changes, the most significant of which was Sardar's waning influence over what we did and how we went about conducting our affairs. The man who had been so loyal to us for such a long time didn't like the way Varada, Bachchan and I got along and, through a series of stratagems, made it known that he wasn't about to let things slide without a fight. The last of these little plots that he hatched proved to be his undoing. Sardar charged one of his boys, Zuber, the man everyone called 'Maam', with attacking my friend Subhan. Unfortunately for him, Bachchan and I were at Subhan's house the night Maam walked up the stairs with an accomplice and a knife. We intervened and sent out a message to Sardar that his ways had to change.

Wounded, Sardar came to me one day and said, 'What is this Sreedhar? I never imagined you would play such a game.'

Angered at his impertinence, I replied: 'I didn't plan anything more devious than what you did with Subhan.'

He sat silently for a few minutes, then he looked up and said, 'The boys don't trust me anymore, Sreedhar. They only like you. I will stop coming to Jayanagar from now. I will come only if you summon me.'

I felt a little sad for him. 'What will you do? Start another gang?' I asked.

'What are you saying Sreedhar? How can I build a gang and stand against you and Bachchan?' he replied, clearly hurt. 'I have been asked to work on a new business idea. I'm just going to do that.'

'What if Kotwal asks you to join him?'

'That will never happen. I swear on the Koran. I know you have taken a vow to finish him.'

The day after that, Sardar stopped coming to Jayanagar.

A while later, Bachchan and I, now fully in control of the Jayanagar gang, would get involved in a rather messy extortion job that would bring us head to head with almost every major rowdy in Bangalore. This is what happened: Khalandar, who we had included in the plan to kidnap and kill Sardar's man Maam after we got wind of his intent to go after Subhan, had a friend named Dhanvanth, who came to us and said he had been cheated of fifty thousand rupees by a man named Babu (this was not the Babu from Madivala). Babu, who operated out of Viveknagar, was a stunt man in movies and also supplied filmmakers with dogs and horses during shoots. We sent for him, but Babu refused to come. We decided to pay him a visit.

Babu lived in a three-storey building at the edge of the heavily Tamil-populated Sunnadgood slum near Viveknagar. I asked him to accompany us, but he refused. I struck him with a nunchaku and Bachchan and I carried him to the car. It took Babu just ten minutes to begin talking. Until recently, he told us, he had been running a brothel, with about thirty girls. The police had conducted repeated raids on his establishment and he had no recourse but to switch from prostitution to cheating people like Dhanvanth.

Upon completing our interrogation, we drove to Imperial Hotel on Residency Road for dinner. It was Babu's treat.

It was late in the evening when we headed back to Viveknagar. As soon as we arrived, people from the slum gathered round the car. They had been waiting for Babu. Clearly, he was a man of some importance in the area. He asked us upstairs and showed us into the house. The place had ten rooms. Babu pointed to what looked like a cupboard and opened it. It led to a hidden room.

Just before we left, we told him no one would interfere with his business, as long as he returned the fifty thousand rupees. He asked us to return in two days for the money. When we did, he said he had no cash but was willing to give us a television and a video recorder, claiming they were worth half of what he owed Dhanvanth. The other half, he said, would be ready a few days later.

I handed these over to Dhanvanth and in due course asked Bachchan and Subhan to fetch Babu so the rest of the money could be collected. I waited for two hours and when the two didn't return, hailed an auto and rushed to Viveknagar. The moment I reached Babu's house, a few men surrounded the auto and asked me to step out. They were from the crime branch.

I was taken to Viveknagar police station, where I saw Subhan, Bachchan and Babu. I wanted to know why we had been brought there. After much persuasion, one of the constables said Bachchan, Subhan and I were being charged with five murders. At around seven o'clock, a sub-inspector walked up to me and asked me about the murders. 'Sir?' I said, incredulous.

'Look, I can tell you are an educated man. I don't want to work on you,' he shot back.

'Sir, I'm not connected to any murder. This man Babu cheated us, so we're here to collect money,' I said.

'I know about the TV and the VCR. They don't belong to him. He'd rented them. We're charging him with cheating,' the sub-inspector explained. 'He's the one who told us about the murders.'

In a few minutes we managed to convince the policeman that we were innocent of homicide. A case of cheating was filed against us and we were taken to court the next day. Since there wasn't a lawyer to defend us, we were sent to judicial custody.

I was back in jail for the third time.

Six

This stint in jail was distinctly different from the first two. For one, I knew several people interred there and most of them knew me, if only by reputation. The moment Bachchan and I walked in, Mysore Road Kaalu, one of Koli Fayaz's lieutenants, met us and took us straight to his cell.

Later I met Daniel, one of Kotwal's most feared accomplices, in the upper block of the prison. Daniel, who knew Bachchan well, was angry with Kotwal—he had spent two months in prison but hadn't heard a word about Kotwal making arrangements for bail. He vented to Bachchan for a while, but eventually, as appeared to be the norm in prison at the time, talk turned to one of the most fabled rivalries in Bangalore's underworld: the unrelenting stand-off between Kotwal and Jayaraj.

Every night, from Kaalu to Daniel, people would speculate about how this impasse would end: would Kotwal kill Jayaraj and surrender to the police? Or would it be the other way around? Would peace be brokered? Would the police just pit the two against each other and watch, waiting for one of them, or both, to die?

Jayaraj had spent ten years in prison for various crimes and had recently been released. Everyone expected him to return to a life of crime very quietly, building support and re-establishing his hold over the city. But Jayaraj had other plans. Rather than slinking back, he made sure that his return home was marked by a triumphant procession through the city's streets. Indeed, even before he reached home, Jayaraj sent a message to Kotwal through a lawyer that he had now reclaimed Bangalore and that it would be in Kotwal's best interests if he moved back to petty crime in Shimoga, his native place.

Kotwal faced a further setback when the Kalasipalya boys decided to back Jayaraj, instead of remaining neutral. Though Kotwal had a deep-rooted dislike for the gangs of Kalasipalya, he couldn't ignore their dominion over the locality they were named for—a hub of cargo-trafficking, power-broking, and also where the city's old quarter, or pete, home to Tipu's Palace, is located. They were brutal: in 1977, when a rowdy named Mallaya attacked and killed a man named Kamalendra in front of Hotel Anand Vihar near Tipu's Palace, three men from the Kalasipalya gang, Nagaraju, Narayana and Mental Shiva, all friends of the murdered man, tracked down Mallaya and—in full view of a gathered crowd—hacked him to death.

In the four days that it took for Nissar to post bail for us, we had gathered information about the rivalry between Kotwal and Jayaraj and decided that we would play a significant part in it in some manner.

A few days after we were released, Sardar came up to me and said Kotwal was in J.P. Nagar and wanted to meet Bachchan and me. I was surprised. Why would he want to talk to us of all people? When we went to see him we were told it was to witness a petty scrap, but I later determined that it was because Kotwal was mustering his forces to battle Jayaraj. A week after our encounter in J.P. Nagar, Kotwal drove up to the Jayanagar office in an Ambassador and summoned Bachchan, Sardar and me. We didn't know where we were going, and Kotwal didn't offer an explanation. After we had crossed Sadashivnagar, I asked if we were headed for Chikkaballapur or Nandi Hills. Kotwal said we were going to Gauribidanur, about seventy-five kilometres from Bangalore. The home minister, Jalappa, had offered him a job, he said. Our mark would be at a bar in Gauribidanur and we had to carry out a '307'—attempt to murder. We wouldn't have to actually visit violence on anyone, he explained. 'I have two other men for that. You just have to offer them cover.'

Though, as it often happens with these things, we never managed to carry out the plan—we were thwarted by a few enthusiastic locals in Gauribidanur who recognised Kotwal and thought it fit to make a song-and-dance over his arrival at their little town—it occurred to me that I was being asked with increasing frequency to participate in Kotwal's underworld dealings. And in fact, the next time he would ask me to join him would be very soon, for a very big project. It still resonates: in my mind and in the minds of both former underworld dons and that of policemen who were handed the case at the time.

Because our clout in Jayanagar had assumed some significance, the police had begun to take an interest in us. We were harassed relentlessly and eventually decided to shift base to Triveni Lodge in Majestic. It was now 1986.

On the third of January, at around four in the afternoon, Kotwal summoned Bachchan, Khalandar, Sardar and Nissar to the general hostel. When the four got there, they saw a few hundred young men gathered around. Nissar sought out Kotwal amidst the mob and asked what was going on. 'Listen, we have to deal with an old man. He is from (chief minister) Ramakrishna Hegde's side. This is a very big job. Nothing should go wrong.'

But why these many boys to kill one old man? Kotwal wouldn't answer. He shook Nissar's shoulders in barely-concealed excitement and said: 'This is the biggest deal of my life. If I pull it off, nothing can stop me.'

At seven o'clock, Kotwal gathered all his men and picked out twenty boys, including Bachchan, Khalandar, Sardar and Nissar. Among others in this group were Bomb Krishnamurthy from Shimoga, who was dressed as a Sikh, Hajama Venkatesh, Arakere Naga and Seetharam Shetty, Kotwal's personal secretary.

'No one should attack before I give the word, and no one should reveal their identity: everyone should address each other as "Govinda". Each of you must come back in the same vehicle you used to get to where we're going. Don't worry, the police will not arrive till our work is done,' he said, before pulling a woollen monkey cap over his face. Shetty drove him to their destination.

When they reached Hotel Kanishka in Gandhinagar, Kotwal stood under a tree and signalled the others to form groups. Nissar said he had to go to the toilet. Kotwal asked Arakere Naga to accompany him and said, 'Check if the old man is in the toilet.'

When they got there, Nissar turned to Naga and asked who this old man was.

'Jayaraj,' Naga replied.

After having determined that Jayaraj hadn't yet arrived at the hotel, Kotwal split the group into three and asked one bunch to go into the building. Of the other two crews, one stayed with Kotwal near the hotel and the third stood guard outside. Nissar, who was a part of this last clutch, was worried for Bachchan's safety and decided to fetch me from Triveni Lodge, which was five minutes away.

When Nissar and I reached Hotel Kanishka, it was a quarter to eight. A few minutes later, we saw a heavyset fellow walk towards the hotel accompanied by another large man. Nissar went stiff. 'That is Jayaraj,' he said, indicating the first bulky figure. 'The one next to him is his lieutenant, Samson.'

Jayaraj went into the hotel while Samson stood outside and lit a cigarette.

A few seconds after he struck the match, Kotwal shouted, 'Charge!' and ran toward Samson. 'Jayaraj . . . today you die!' It was almost inhuman, that scream, and it felt like you could hear it in all the streets of Gandhi Nagar.

Bachchan and Narasimha raised their swords and swung at Samson, who fell to the ground yowling. Kotwal too joined in the attack, screeching: 'You bastards . . . you want me to leave this city?'

Bachchan, towering over Samson, didn't let up. Narasimha too was relentless with his blows. The man on the ground put his hands up in defence, but they wouldn't stop. Kotwal grabbed at them, and said, 'Okay. Enough. If you go on, he will die.' Then they went after Jayaraj.

'Inside, see inside!' Kotwal shouted. 'The bastard must be hiding there.' By now the shouting and the cries had reached such a pitch that people began to gather outside the hotel. Women and children spilled out of the hotel, screaming. But there was no sign of Jayaraj. He had escaped.

It took about five minutes for us to regroup and scamper away. Bachchan eventually emerged and entered the van I was in. Nissar continued to stand outside, in shock. 'Hey, Nissar, what are you doing? The bastard escaped . . . we'll meet again tomorrow,' Kotwal shouted at him, before jumping on a bike and disappearing. By now a police vehicle had arrived. We started up the van and sped in the direction that Kotwal had taken as the policemen rushed to Samson's aid.

~

The attack against Jayaraj was all Bangalore could talk about. Every single newspaper dedicated pages and pages to it and, in fact, such was the significance of what had occurred, that the ganglord Muthappa Rai, when he assembled his posse many years later, would first ask the men if they were a part of the Kanishka attack.

As a result of all the attention it received, continuing to work out of Bangalore became impossible for Kotwal and his gang. The police, sensing that this was an opportune moment to target a disadvantaged Kotwal, mounted severe pressure: making arrests, recruiting informants and subjecting several of his men to the third-degree. Jayaraj, seizing the opportunity, began to systematically whittle down the Kotwal gang. His men roamed the streets, seeking out people even remotely associated with Kotwal and beating them up. People like Kalasipalya Fort Nagraju, Narayana, Bekkinakannu (Cat-Eyed) Rajendra, Pushpa, Mahadeva, Balaram, the student leader Diwakar Hegde and Kurubara Pete Raja aligned themselves with him. It was a time when no one in Bangalore dared to even say he knew Kotwal. Things got so bad that many gangsters used the face-off as an excuse to settle old scores: pointing out people they had a problem with to Jayaraj's men as members of Kotwal's gang.

We decided to stay in Tumkur for a while, where a man named Muddappa had arranged rooms for us. We visited Bangalore every three days to gather information. We learned that the police had formed a squad, headed by the inspector at Central police station, Muddaiah, to track down Kotwal. This team included B.K. Hariprasad's brother B.K. Shivaram, Venkatachalapathi, Bagewadimutt, Ravindra and Kauri.

In Tumkur, we had little to do apart from play cards with local thugs, spend time with Varada, who visited us frequently, and, as was the case when we had time on our hands, plot Kotwal's murder. Now that we were in his inner circle, it seemed the right time to kill him. Though Bachchan was wary of any such plots, I pressed on and convinced him that we should arrange for a meeting with Jayaraj, so he could ensure us immunity in exchange for Kotwal's life. At the time, among the people who came to our rooms to play cards was a man named Ninge Gowda, who owned an eight-acre sugarcane farm in a village called Aralalusandra, in Koratagere. This farm, which we frequented, would hold special significance in the events that followed.

It had been fifteen days since the attack on Jayaraj and I was itching to meet him. Since no one in his gang knew me, we thought we should use Jayaraj's man Samson as an intermediary. As it turned out, this was easier than we thought. Varada, who had fallen out with Rizwan, had become close to Samson, and when he realised we had renewed our plans to get rid of Kotwal, he offered to set up the meeting. It was to take place at Victoria Hospital, where Samson had been admitted.

When I went there, Samson was swathed in bandages. As soon as he saw me, he asked all the boys in the room to leave. I got straight to the point: lend me support and I will end Kotwal's life.

Samson seemed sceptical; after all, Bachchan and I had been there the night of the attack. I convinced him that none of us knew, until minutes before the plan unfolded, that the target was Jayaraj. Finally he agreed to us meeting his boss. I said Kotwal's murder would take place in Jayanagar, but we had to wait. Bangalore was still too dangerous for us to lure Kotwal back. Besides, Bachchan's name cropped up every time the police discussed the attack at Kanishka.

While we waited for the tumult to die down, we thought we'd make some money. Muddappa, the man who had arranged our lodging in Tumkur, suggested smuggling sandalwood. He said he knew of a consignment that was coming to Shikaripura in Shimoga and there was easy money to be made.

One night, Bachchan and I were outside our room in Tumkur, two days before we were to leave for Shikaripura. Varada had come down to see us. As we leaned against the young man's vehicle, talking, we heard a bike approaching. It was travelling at great speed and squealed to a halt at our feet, its headlights blinding us. There were two men on the bike—the one riding was Seetharam Shetty, the man behind him was Kotwal Ramachandra. It turned out that, after they fled Bangalore, the two went into hiding. Four days earlier they'd moved into a farm owned by a man named Devanur Kumar. The farm was a few hundred metres from where we lived.

We went into our room and Shetty, whom I had never met before, looked around suspiciously. He didn't know either Varada or me. Kotwal asked us if we could find him a place to stay. We suggested Ninge Gowda's sugarcane farm. He agreed and went there at once.

Shetty was quickly dispatched to make preparations for the move and we then piled into Varada's jeep and headed out into the night, with Shetty following us on the bike. This was trademark Kotwal: he was always nervous about things going wrong or being trapped, and would insist on asking for a backup of some sort—in this case, Shetty on the bike—to make sure he had a getaway vehicle if something went wrong.

Ninge Gowda's farm was situated between Tumkur and Koratagere, and to reach it we had to turn right at a village called Urdigere and drive a distance of about ten kilometres on a muddy road.

It was February and because the heat was oppressive, people usually slept out in the open. On our way to the farm, we had to stop a couple of times and clear the path of sleeping villagers before we could move on. They were all surprised to see the two vehicles in the dead of the night; this made Kotwal even more jittery.

It was past midnight when we reached the farm. I woke up Ninge Gowda and explained the situation to him, telling him who our companions were. He smiled; Kotwal had gained immense notoriety not just in Bangalore but in several parts of Karnataka, and for someone like Gowda, it was an honour to host such a man.

The house was at the entrance of the sugarcane farm. To its right was a large hall sheltering rows of large circular bamboo trays for silk cocoons. Next to the hall were living quarters, behind which was the pump house. And beyond this was a well. Four acres of floppy sugarcane heads stretched into the distance behind the well. A few trees lined the perimeter. A small footpath beyond the fields led to a hillock.

We were told to sleep in the hall housing the silk cocoons. Gowda moved beds into this room and we settled down. It was two in the morning.

Kotwal slept by the side of the door. I was right next to him. The other three lay down at the far end of the hall.

It has been several decades, but I can never forget that night. It was ink-dark. None of the houses or streets displayed lights. I began to consider our situation: here he was, the man I loathed, snoring loudly next to me. And there, on the other side of the hall, slept the two other men intent on murdering Kotwal; a man so deeply suspicious and cautious, yet utterly unaware of his vulnerability. Clueless that he slept amidst his enemies.

To this day, people talk about Kotwal's murder as the most significant event in the history of Bangalore's underworld; that it changed the very nature of this city and that it shaped its future. And people still credit me for the efficiency with which the murder was carried out. But thinking back to the events of his last days in the farmhouse, I wonder if there was any cunning to it at all. Maybe it was just stupid luck: if Kotwal had succeeded in killing Jayaraj at Kanishka and, as he'd planned, surrendered to the police, he would have gathered a huge following in the underworld. He wouldn't have had to worry about a single thing for the rest of his life. For a man who prided himself on meticulous planning, Kotwal would be undone by the vagaries of fate.

But the murder wouldn't happen that night. Or, indeed, for many nights after those first few hours in that hall full of bamboo trays. Before the killing, I would lose all interest in murdering Kotwal.

Seven

Since the police were looking for Kotwal, and Bachchan was linked to the Kanishka attack, we spent most of our time inside the farmhouse, playing cards and drinking. Kotwal was a very secretive man; it was only once, when he was drunk, and I was the only one around, did he talk about his life.

'I am not as educated as you are,' he said to me one night, after Bachchan and Shetty had left for Tumkur to take care of some work. 'I have bizarre beliefs . . .' he trailed off, and after a while said, 'See, my two wives are suffering in Bangalore. My younger wife has no one but me. She left her family for me.'

I was a little embarrassed by this conversation, but out of politeness, asked: 'And your elder wife?'

Kotwal stared at his glass for a while and said: 'She is a good woman. Which other woman would tolerate her man having another wife?'

That Kotwal cared for and looked after his two wives was not the only thing I learnt about him. He was consumed by several things, including cleanliness and superstition. There were two aspects to him that peeved me. One was his hatred of beggars—he despised them with an intensity that was shocking; he would often throw stones at them and sometimes beat them senseless. The other was the casual way in which he cadged money off people, as though they owed him a debt of gratitude.

Surprisingly, Shetty, Kotwal's constant companion, shared my disgust. 'He is inhuman Sreedhar . . . mental,' he told Bachchan and me at a bar in Tumkur. 'Because of him I am in trouble. My brothers are in jail and he does not have the slightest sympathy.'

I was surprised at this outburst; I had assumed Shetty was loyal to Kotwal. I let him talk.

'I gave up my life for this, Sreedhar. But this, this *thing* only wants pimps and *chelas*. Not me,' he wept. And this would become a common scene over the next few days: Shetty would have a few drinks and spew his anger. One day, he said to me: 'Sreedhar, if you stand by me, I will kill him.'

I didn't know what to make of his rants—if he was indeed plotting to kill his boss or if it was just a combination of frustration and drink, so, going by Bachchan's advice, I decided to let it rest for a few days.

Meanwhile, in Bangalore, Jayaraj had begun to plan a final confrontation with Kotwal and, for some reason, he sought me out for information about his enemy. One day, Varada and I went to Bangalore to see how things were and heard that Cottonpet Pushpa was looking for us. And the enquiries he was making were on behalf of Jayaraj.

I was both surprised and alarmed. Pushpa, by all accounts, ran a gang that was not involved in the Kotwal–Jayaraj battle. Why then was he asking about me for Jayaraj? Did he know, somehow, that Kotwal was with us in the farmhouse? Had Pushpa, who had never before been associated with Jayaraj, finally decided to join forces with him?

Pushpa, who was raised by wrestlers in Cottonpet, had gained notoriety after a much-talked about murder in Vijaynagar. This was what transpired: Pushpa was in a gang peopled by ruffians like Market Raja, Layout Manja and Loki. Prabhakar, or Vijaynagar Prabha, was the leader of this gang. As it turned out, Prabha and Market Raja developed differences and Oil Kumar, the wily gangster from Mysore, seeing this as an opportunity to create a third force in Bangalore—one that would take advantage of the rivalry between Kotwal and Jayaraj—plotted to deepen the rift between them.

Backed by Kumar, a gang of twenty men, including Pushpa,

Raja and Loki, barged into Prabha's bar in Vijaynagar, pulled down the shutter, butchered him and burnt the shop to the ground. It was a brazen attack and seven of the twenty were booked for murder, Pushpa among them. Given the nature of the case and the impunity with which the campaign had been carried out, everyone was sure the trial would lead to a conviction. Oil Kumar picked the lawyer C.V. Nagesh to plead for the accused. All seven men were acquitted.

Though Kotwal was initially sceptical about us meeting Pushpa, he eventually said we should find out why he was looking for us. 'Don't tell him I'm with you,' he warned. 'If he's with Maharaja (that's what Kotwal called Jayaraj), the dogs will be upon us.'

It was decided that Varada, Bachchan and I would meet Pushpa, but when we reached Bangalore, Bachchan thought to go meet Sardar and Nissar first. Varada and I made our way through the narrow streets of Cottonpet, asking for Pushpa. Eventually, we were directed to a lane. It was lined with thugs and the moment we walked into it, we were surrounded. After I explained who we were, a boy ran up a flight of stairs and returned a couple of minutes later. We were led down an alley and told to sit on a raised platform outside a small house. Five minutes later Pushpa limped into view—he had recently been in a car accident in which he'd lost his mentor Patri Narayana. He came up to us and shook hands. He got straight to the point.

'Samson suggested that I speak to you. We figured the only way to get to Kottu (that's what all Kotwal's enemies called him) is through the Jayanagar gang. Since you head it, I think you should help us,' he said. I learnt that he knew about the attack against my brother.

'When I first mentioned attacking Kotwal to Samson, he didn't seem too interested,' I said. 'I'll need time to think about it.'

'Look, I meet Jayaraj daily. This is what's happening: that coward Kotwal is trying to arrive at a compromise with Jayaraj through the lawyer Hanumantharayappa,' Pushpa said. 'But Jayaraj is not interested in making peace. He is determined to kill Kottu.'

This was unexpected news. A compromise? Kotwal had mentioned no such thing to us. I feigned innocence and said, 'Even if we do manage to corner Kotwal, what can be done? Bachchan may support me, but what can just the two of us do?'

Pushpa thought for a while and said, 'Look, I'm a fighter, not a planner. We'll have to think of something, come back after two days.'

We returned to the farmhouse. That night, Kotwal asked us about the meeting with Pushpa and I only apprised him about talk of a compromise between the two gangs, with Hanumantharayappa playing the mediator. Kotwal was furious. 'I don't know what that Maharaja is thinking. I told him not tell anyone about this whole compromise thing. Now everyone will know.'

Then, given that we knew, Kotwal let us in on what was going on. Oil Kumar, who was gaining muscle in the underworld, had begun to bother Kotwal and Jayaraj. Kotwal was convinced that if he were allowed a free run, Kumar would 'spoil the market'. Since Jayaraj and Kotwal had ruled Bangalore for the longest time, it was his opinion that the two men should devise some sort of a pact, kill Kumar, and from then on share whatever bounty the city yielded. 'Since Maharaja is the senior of the two of us, I don't even mind if he gets a larger share of Bangalore,' Kotwal said. He decided to travel to the city the next day to assess the situation.

Usually Shetty would be the one to accompany Kotwal on his trips, but that day, I was asked to get ready. 'I don't want him, that wretched fellow,' Kotwal said and began to prepare for the journey. Though it was only a day-trip, Kotwal took an hour to get ready—he tried on different clothes, shaved twice and put on perfume; that was one of his quirks. He slid two machetes into a bag and handed it to me. At three in the afternoon, we left for Bangalore.

Kotwal, who drove slowly so we could reach the city after nightfall, slowed the bike to a halt near Dobbaspet and asked me to hop off. A white Ambassador, travelling toward Tumkur, had passed us and Kotwal, ever suspicious, followed it. He turned the bike around and went off, back in the direction from where we had come. Ten minutes later, he returned. 'All will be well,' he said. 'Do you know who was in that car? Jalappa.'

I wasn't sure if he was telling the truth. I knew Kotwal was close to the home minister, but to casually wheel your bike around on the highway and flag down an elected member of the state legislature seemed a bit of a stretch. 'But doesn't he use a government car?' I asked.

'Only when he has government work,' Kotwal answered.

'What did he say?'

'He said I should wait for a few days; he will talk to (Jeevraj) Alva and (Ramakrishna) Hegde and then I can surrender. Till then, we should be careful,' Kotwal replied.

Just before we reached Bangalore, Kotwal stopped at a phone booth in Peenya (the first one we encountered after Tumkur; the one-rupee phone booths were very new then). Kotwal pulled out several coins and made calls for about half an hour. He walked up to the bike smiling. 'Everything's going well,' he said and handed me a monkey cap. 'So no one will recognise us.'

When we reached Bangalore it was six and the light was ebbing. At Gangenahalli, Kotwal stopped the bike and asked me to wait. He walked briskly into a house. I stood waiting, the machetes in the bag on my shoulder. Twenty minutes later Kotwal returned, followed by a short man. 'Tell them I need more the next time,' Kotwal told him, before waving the man away. He turned to me and said, 'I know you're not that kind of a person, which is why I didn't invite you in.' He'd just visited a brothel.

We headed straight for Kotwal's house in Indiranagar. I wasn't sure this was such a good idea, considering how closely the police were keeping the place under surveillance. Kotwal told me not to worry, that we'd only watch from a distance. When we got there, a group of boys, excited to be in Kotwal's presence, surrounded the bike and asked what they could do for him. Kotwal wanted to know if anyone had come asking for him. Not for a while now, a few boys said. A couple of them claimed to have seen plainclothesmen snooping around.

'Who should we call if someone comes, boss?' one of them asked.

Kotwal gave him a number and said, 'Lawyer Varadhamanayya. Tell him.'

From there we headed for the petrol bunk near the entrance of Cubbon Park. Oil Kumar owned it. Kotwal wanted to send a message to Kumar through one of the employees there. He instructed me to act very tough.

As soon as we got there, a fair, bald man called Lakshman Rao came scurrying out and said, 'How are you, Sir?'

'We are fine . . . where is Kumar?' Kotwal demanded.

'He is all right . . . he was asking about you, Sir,' the man replied.

I butted in: 'We trust him and he is planning to attack us?' I yelled. 'Now that we have left the city, he is roaming the streets claiming to rule Bangalore?'

The man went quiet—usually Shetty accompanied Kotwal, but here was someone he'd never before encountered.

'Ask him to meet me soon,' Kotwal said, and we left.

On the bike Kotwal laughed and said, 'That man will go tell Kumar about what happened just now. And Kumar will go insane trying to figure out who this new guy with Kotwal is.'

We then went to a TV service shop near the race course, where I was told to look for a man named Syed. Kotwal and Syed talked for a few minutes and before we left, Kotwal pointed to me and told him, 'If there is something urgent, I'll send him.' On our way to Jayanagar, he told me Syed had spoken to a sub-inspector who admired Kotwal. The sub-inspector had asked him to reach word to us that B.K. Shivaram, one of the police officers in the squad formed to hunt down

Kotwal, was intent on killing him and that we should be wary of him at all times.

At Jayanagar, Kotwal stopped at a newsstand and bought a few magazines before heading toward Double Road. When we went past the cremation ground at the head of that broad street, Kotwal turned to me and said, 'Maharaja lives on this road. If we come across him, I'm more than willing to finish him and then surrender to the police.'

Minutes later, a white Ambassador, cruising slowly, passed us from the other direction. The driver's elbow jutted out of the window. He was balding and had a round face. As the two vehicles crossed, he stared at us. Kotwal screamed, 'It's him! It's Jayaraj!'

'Shall we go back?' he said, more as an instruction than a question. I was thrilled. I was set to meet the man the next day and here he was, witness to how close I was to Kotwal. Nothing could have worked better. I seized the machete in the bag and said, 'Let's go.'

We turned around at the gap in the median in front of the bus depot, thinking we would now be chasing him. Instead, we found Jayaraj had turned the car around and was pursuing us. Kotwal was shocked. 'What do we do now?' he shouted.

There was no one in the car with Jayaraj. We were two powerful men with weapons—we could take him on. But Kotwal didn't wait for my response. He turned left at the cremation ground and switched off the headlight. Jayaraj followed about five hundred metres behind us, but instead of slowing down to face him, Kotwal revved the engine, and in a few minutes, we were on Bannerghatta Road. Jayaraj wasn't anywhere to be seen.

'What arrogance,' Kotwal fumed. 'Maharaja chases us? If we had stopped, we could have killed him.'

I was very disappointed. 'Why didn't you slow down?' I asked.

'How do you know what he was carrying with him? He was alone . . . he could have had a gun. Or maybe someone was following him,' Kotwal replied.

I got the feeling that Kotwal was trying to convince himself. 'I don't think there was a car following him,' I said. 'Besides, he too didn't know what we were carrying in the bag.'

'You don't know Jayaraj, he always has someone following him,' Kotwal said, signalling that this discussion was at its end.

We were now travelling back in the direction of Double Road, and when we went past Richmond Circle and reached Kanteerava Stadium, Kotwal hesitated. He was paused, considering which road to take, eventually choosing the one that skirted the northern flank of the stadium (where Mallya Hospital now stands). Soon, we heard the sound of an Enfield Bullet to our left. Back in those days, there weren't too many vehicles on the road and you could clearly distinguish a bike's sound when you heard it. Kotwal instantly stiffened. He turned in the direction of the thumping engine: it was a bike approaching us from the Pallavi Theatre side of Kanteerava Stadium. 'Don't look . . . don't look,' Kotwal hissed. 'Shivaram . . . it's Shivaram.' The Bullet speeded up in pursuit.

When Jayaraj had chased us less than an hour ago, I wasn't scared. He was a rowdy and we could have taken him on. But this time, we were being chased by the police. My legs began to quiver. The Bullet was closing in. Kotwal switched off the lights and continued to yell: 'Don't look back . . . don't look back.'

But I couldn't help myself, I turned around. The bike was less than a hundred metres from us. There were two men on it. The policeman who rode pillion had pulled out his revolver. It was pointed at me.

I began to shake. My mouth went dry. I was terrified. In seconds, I could be dead. Kotwal hit me hard twice with his left hand, shouting at me not to look back. But I was transfixed. I would be subject to this kind of danger only twice in my life as a criminal: three years later, trapped in just as frightening a situation. But in that instance, I'd be presented with the opportunity to escape. Now, I could do nothing.

The Bullet was to our right and the policeman at the back

was having difficulty aiming his pistol at us from that direction. I shut my eyes. When I opened them again a few seconds later, the Bullet was to our left. It was an easy shot. I clenched my jaws and prepared for impact. But it didn't come. I waited for a few more seconds and then looked. We had put some distance between the police and us. By now we were at the traffic junction where Tiffany's once stood. An Ambassador approached from the other side, and seeing us travelling at such great speed, it slowed down. We missed it by a whisker and sped into Cubbon Park. It was completely dark. The sound of the Bullet receded. We raced toward Maharani's College, passed through Malleswaram and reached Yeshwantpur. We'd lost them.

Five months later, when Shivaram arrested me for murdering Kotwal, I would get a chance to ask him about the chase.

The man riding pillion was a sub-inspector called Chikkanna. Shivaram pointed to him and said, 'The two of us were on our way to dinner when we chanced upon you. In fact we were discussing Kotwal at the time. When we spotted you, I told Chikkanna that I would ride at whatever speed it required to catch up; all he had to do was shoot. But Chikkanna's hand trembled and he just couldn't do it.'

Chikkanna, a kind man with a large moustache, smiled and said, 'Yes, Shivaram kept telling to me shoot. I don't know why, but my hand began to tremble. I tried, but I couldn't squeeze the trigger.'

'Good thing you couldn't, Sir. I don't know about Kotwal, but I certainly would have been dead,' I said.

'That is why I did not shoot,' Chikkanna smiled.

We were now past Yeshwantpur and approaching Peenya. Though Kotwal seemed to have calmed down completely, I was still very rattled. Just as I was beginning to feel a little normal again, there was a loud crash and I was flung from the bike. Kotwal had lost control. I saw him picking himself up. I felt my arms and legs for broken bones, but I was only mildly bruised. I turned toward Kotwal, but he was gone. Soon, a boy came running up to me and said 'Boss' was calling me. I followed the boy to the back of a liquor store, where I found Kotwal on a chair.

'Are you hurt badly?' I asked.

'Just scratches,' he said. 'You?'

'Small scratches.'

By then a group of boys, who claimed to know Kotwal, had gathered around us. A few of them had propped up the bike. 'It's not too badly damaged, Sir,' one of them said. 'Just a broken taillight.'

Kotwal started the bike and we were back on the road.

He was silent for the rest of the trip, occasionally shaking his head in annoyance.

When we got to the outskirts of Peenya, it was around eleven. Kotwal stopped the bike when he saw a long line of vehicles in front of us. The police had set up a blockade. A sub-inspector began walking in our direction and Kotwal, cursing under his breath, turned into a small lane.

'Hey! You! Where are you going?' the policeman shouted.

'Nothing . . . urgent work . . . we have to go . . . thank you, thank you!' Kotwal yelled back, and headed off in the direction of Aralalusandra. We weren't sure if Shivaram had ordered the roadblock to stop us or if it was something the police had put in place because of the recent spate of dacoities in the area.

It was midnight when we reached Aralalusandra. Bachchan, Varada and Shetty were waiting for us, worried. We were late by over an hour.

Kotwal began recounting the events of the day. He embellished the story liberally, saying there were four men in the car with Jayaraj. Even while describing the chase, Kotwal lied, saying the two policemen got within ten feet of us and that it was because of his deft riding that we got away. That's when I asked him why he yelled at me not to look back. 'If you look back, it only spurs them on,' he replied. I knew there was more to it than that, and glanced at Shetty. He merely winked at me.

After Kotwal had gone to sleep, the three men pressed me for my version of that evening's events and I told them what had really happened in Bangalore. Shetty looked at me and said, 'He didn't ask you not to turn back because it would have spurred them on,' he said. 'It was because you would have ducked if they had fired, putting him in danger. That's the kind of man he is, always looking to save his skin.'

The next evening, accompanied by Varada, I went back to Bangalore to meet Jayaraj. It was six when Pushpa met us. I told him about our encounter with Jayaraj the previous day. Pushpa seemed to relax a bit, as though satisfied that it was indeed I who had been with Kotwal the previous day. He asked us to wait a while and returned with a man named Kurubara Pete Raja. We sat in an Ambassador and drove to the road where Kotwal and I had seen Jayaraj the previous day. The car turned into a large compound. In the middle was a small house with yellowing, deformed walls. A thin, bearded man looked us up and down. He smiled at Pushpa, asked us to wait at the door, went in and returned in a few minutes. '*Anna* is calling you,' he said.

~

Jayaraj—short, bald and fair—was sitting behind a desk when we entered. He had all the features of a Marwadi. He kept his eyes trained on me, never once looking away. He seemed like a very determined man. I put out my hand and announced, 'Sreedhar.' He gripped my hand firmly and motioned to a chair on the other side of the desk. There was a man with a scar running down the left of his face by Jayaraj's side.

'Yesterday, we saw Kotwal. Were you the man with him?' Jayaraj asked.

I told him our version of the story and how we'd given Shivaram the slip.

Jayaraj turned to the man with the scar and said, 'See Nagaraj, I told you. It was Kotwal I saw.' He then turned to me and said, 'All these fellows thought I had made a mistake. That I had chased the wrong man yesterday. But you look tough.

Why didn't you stand and fight? Why did you run away?' he asked.

'Look, I have no interest in fighting you. As soon as Kotwal saw you, all he wanted to do was run away,' I said. 'When he saw you were by yourself, I thought he would stop and fight, but he trembled.'

At this, Nagaraj mumbled, 'What sort of a gangster is he? I have never heard of such a cowardly rowdy.'

I turned to him and asked, 'And you are?'

'Kalasipalya Nagaraju.'

I have mentioned him earlier. He led the gangs that Kotwal wanted to have nothing to do with. The two murders he had committed clothed him with enough respect, ensuring that his supremacy over his cohorts went unquestioned.

It was clear from what Jayaraj and Nagaraju said that they knew of my intention to kill Kotwal and the reasons for it. Jayaraj said: 'Look, we know you are the man that can get to Kotwal. You know he is seeking a compromise. But that's not what we want. You have to do something very soon.'

I told him in no uncertain terms that I had no intention of making a name for myself in the underworld and that I only wanted to get rid of Kotwal for personal reasons. 'Also, if I kill him, I don't want to go to jail,' I said.

'What do you suggest we do?' he asked.

'Can you give us a gun?'

At this he burst out laughing. 'How many cases of crime have you been involved in?' he asked.

My three periods of incarceration were for petty offences so I remained silent.

Nagaraj chipped in. 'The easiest way, and this never fails, is to use a razor,' he said. 'When you are in a car, where does he sit?'

In the front, I said.

'Then all you have to do is run it across his throat. All the way,' he said.

I told him I had never held a razor in my life.

'No one is born clasping a weapon,' he retorted.

I suggested that I could lead them to Kotwal so they could finish the job.

'You saw how cowardly he is,' Jayaraj shot back. 'The moment he suspects something's amiss, he will run.'

That was that. It had to be me.

'Okay, if I finish Kotwal, you tell me how you will help me,' I asked.

'What do you want us to do?'

'Like I said, I don't want to go to prison. Also, I want Bachchan and Varada protected,' I told him.

'You leave that to us. Once we drink tea with someone and give that man our word, we never go back on it,' he said.

By then, we had had three cups of tea.

We finished at around nine and Pushpa insisted that we stay for dinner. He went out with Kurubara Pete Raja and brought back beer. We drank late into the night.

Pushpa woke us up the next morning and put us in an auto. We reached Tumkur by bus and from there we drove in a jeep to the farmhouse.

Everything seemed unchanged there. Kotwal was his usual boisterous self and Shetty continued to grumble about how he was being treated. We told Shetty about our meeting with Jayaraj. For the next four days there was no talk of killing Kotwal. Then, five days after my meeting with Jayaraj, something unexpected happened. Something that would see Kotwal dead in a matter of four hours.

Eight

Varada and Shetty had personalities that were polar opposites. Varada was born into money and his father spared no expense in surrounding him with every luxury imaginable. He'd attended the best boarding schools in Ooty and Kodaikanal. But Varada was a hot-headed rebel. He had fought consistently with his teachers and, once, walked out of school, trekking twenty kilometres to Salem. His teachers tracked him down and took him to his father, but despite all manner of cajoling, Varada refused to go back to school. He dropped out when he was in the ninth standard. But that turned out to be a godsend for his father's chemical factory. At seventeen, Varada began managing the business and did so with great efficiency.

But he remained arrogant and stubborn. He would insist on arguing a point, no matter how trivial—if a shopkeeper charged ten paise extra for a pack of cigarettes, he would quibble endlessly and even drive four kilometres to buy another pack at the correct price.

He had no reason to be here with us: he was privileged, rich and young. It was only because he'd fallen in love with a girl that Varada found himself in the company of criminals, living a fugitive's life on a sugarcane farm far from home.

Shetty had a very different past. He came from a poor family and had worked hard at several hotels in Bangalore as a young boy. He took on the task of raising his four sisters and three brothers. He placed two brothers in good jobs and set up a small shop for the third. He lived in Mariyappana Palya and was deeply involved in the regionalist organisation, Kannada Sangha. He was big and strong and fought hard. His battles with the rowdy Bekkinakannu Rajendra were storeyed. When the two became rivals, Kotwal stepped in and asked Shetty to join him.

Unlike Varada, Shetty always spoke of his family. He would look out for them and see to it that they were provided for.

The two had a problem with each other from the day they met, and now, with the annoyance of being away from home and in hiding, things came to a head.

Five days had passed since our meeting with Jayaraj in Bangalore. It was seven in the evening, and there were members of Ninge Gowda's family, Kotwal and the four of us at the farmhouse. A boy called Kitty, who held Kotwal in great respect, and who had joined us a few days earlier, stood guard at the gate. One of Kotwal's wives, unable to bear the constant harassment of the police, was with us as well.

Kotwal had now settled down to a life on the farm and would spend hours at a clump of rocks nearby. That day he had walked off at around five and, two hours later, was still missing. Before he left, he had asked Kitty to investigate a suspicious-looking van nearby. At the time I was in the house, reading a book. Bachchan, Varada and Shetty were playing cards.

Kitty, who had gone to the rocks to report to Kotwal about the van, returned saying he was nowhere to be found. At seven-thirty, we began to panic. Varada and Shetty went to the rocks, but couldn't find Kotwal. Shetty was very anxious: though he wanted Kotwal dead, he didn't want it to be at the hands of rivals or the police. He asked Varada to go a little further to look. Varada didn't like being told what to do, and shot back: 'Let him go to hell. I'm not going to look for him.' Shetty couldn't search for Kotwal in the dark by himself so the two men returned.

Shetty's anxiety turned to anger, and he began to scold Varada, who retaliated by calling Shetty 'cheap'. Incensed,

Shetty grabbed Varada's collar and began to shake him. The young man brushed him off and, screaming obscenities, grabbed a stone to hit him. I heard their loud voices and went to see what was happening. I stopped Varada just as he was about to hurl the stone. I shouted at them and while Shetty calmed down instantly, Varada continued to fume. 'Let Kotwal come back,' he told Shetty, 'I'm going to tell him what you think of him.'

'Do what you want. What has to happen will happen,' Shetty retorted.

At that moment Kotwal walked in through the gates.

I thought the two men would calm down when they saw Kotwal, but they continued to argue and curse each other.

'What is this?' Kotwal asked me.

Varada walked back into the farmhouse while Shetty stood there mumbling.

Kotwal and I went into a small hut and sat on a mat. 'Where have you been for such a long time?' I asked.

Kotwal laughed his fake laugh to mock me, indicating that if he didn't want to be found, no one would find him. 'If I go to the same place every day, anyone can find me. I have found several safe locations nearby,' he said.

It saddened me at that moment that this big tough man who had been raised in the underworld could find no peace anywhere and had to incessantly watch his back. I stayed quiet.

'What were those two fighting about?' he asked. 'That Shetty can't survive without picking fights.'

I told him they were bickering because he could not be located.

'Is it?' he laughed. 'But Shetty knows that if I make up my mind, there is no way anyone can find me.'

He left it at that and began to talk about his situation at the moment. He said he was considering sacrificing a sheep to a local deity in the hope that it would hasten Jayaraj's demise.

I looked sceptical.

'Why don't you believe in these things? Look at us, we have

been in the field for so long and faced such dangerous people, and escaped near death so many times. Do you think it's because of our intelligence and strength? It is the divine force that protects us and it will continue protecting us for the next twenty years,' he shouted.

Shetty walked in. Kotwal looked at him and said, 'What is this? Why are you fighting with Varada?'

'Keep quiet,' Shetty said. 'It's all because you went missing.'

I set out in search of Varada, who was smoking under a tree. Despite my entreaties he refused to calm down. I gave up and went away to talk to Bachchan. 'Let's get out of all this Sreedhar,' he said. 'Varada is too unpredictable and Shetty keeps erupting at the smallest things. We're planning something very dangerous, and with people like this, you never know what's going to happen.'

'Let them sleep it off,' I said. 'Tomorrow everything will be fine.'

But it wasn't to be. The night of 22 March 1986 would change everything for us forever. And it has been visited and revisited to this day. Every time the police have called me in for questioning, they've asked me the same things: Who all were there? Who decided to commit the murder? Did you do it for money? Was it for fame? How did you carry it out in such a precise manner?

I have no clear answers.

After a while, we decided to eat dinner. Varada, still smarting, didn't join us. Kotwal told me to do something about the boy, but I told him Varada was not one to be easily convinced.

We finished dinner and headed back for the hut. On the way, Kotwal noticed that the bamboo trays were lined on either side of the path. He carefully set them all to one side—walking through a corridor of bamboo is a sign of death, he said.

Shetty, meanwhile, had cheered up. In the hut, under a small bulb, he entertained Kotwal. He danced and pranced around, much to his master's delight. I fetched Varada who, growing very bitter, had begun to cry. It was ten in the night.

Though the men in the hut seemed to be having fun, I didn't join them. My head was feeling heavy so I went into the house. Varada, who had gone in by then, was on the bed, snoring. I lay down and stared at the fan for a while. I don't know when I fell asleep, but I soon awoke; Bachchan was shaking me by the shoulder, whispering urgently that I had to get up.

'What?' I said, sleepily.

'Kotwal is asleep in the hut,' Bachchan hissed, 'Shetty says now is the time.'

I tapped my forehead twice and told him to ask Shetty to go to sleep. 'We don't want to kill him anymore. We just want to escape,' I said.

By then Varada had also woken up. He goaded me: 'What's the matter Sreedhar? Don't turn off your meter. Come on, let's finish him.'

He said it with such certitude that it was impossible for me to disagree.

I walked towards the hut with Bachchan and Varada. On our way, a mongoose scampered across the path. Once, when the same thing had happened to him, Kotwal had said this was a good omen. 'Something good is going to come of this,' Bachchan whispered.

Shetty stood waiting outside the hut. We hadn't carried any weapons with us. I took him aside and whispered tersely: 'What are you doing? If we finish him now, what will we do next?'

Shetty had large eyes, and they would become larger still when he was excited. He looked at me with those saucer-shaped orbs and said, 'Sreedhar, this is the best chance we will ever get. No one is here. His wife is gone. Tundyala Shiva (one more of Kotwal's goons) isn't here either.'

'What about Kitty?'

'Why are you asking me this Sreedhar? You are his boss. He treats you with so much respect. He will be the first to attack Kotwal if you just say the word.'

I said nothing and went looking for Kitty. Though Shetty

had told us the boy was loyal to me, I had no doubt in my mind that he would refuse to be part of any plan that involved attacking Kotwal. I was sure he looked up to Kotwal more than he did to me.

I called him aside and asked him to go to the main road to check if all was well.

'But I just did. At eight,' he said.

'Look Kitty, I told Kotwal the same thing, but he wants to make sure. You know he's going away tomorrow, just go and check one last time.'

His face fell. 'But why is he going away?'

'How long will he stay at one place? Let him go.'

'No, no. Let him stay here,' Kitty pleaded. 'We will take good care of him.'

'Go.'

Kitty walked away in the direction of the main road.

I went back to the hut and told the others that I had sent Kitty away.

It was almost midnight. Shetty and Bachchan brought out the machetes that Kotwal always carried. I went into the house and returned with my nunchaku. Varada didn't carry anything. We went in and stood near Kotwal.

This was Seetharam Shetty's statement to the police three months after we were arrested for the murder: 'When the moon went behind the clouds, I looked at everyone. They all nodded. I hit Kotwal on the head with the machete. Bachchan landed blows to his neck and head. Sreedhar struck with his nunchaku. Kotwal died without offering resistance.'

It took less than a minute.

After the first blow was struck, Kotwal tried to sit up, but Bachchan proved too powerful for him. The dogs at the farm began to bark.

When it was done, we sat down. Blood was flowing freely from Kotwal's body. The wooden plank supporting the hut had given way. Varada lit a cigarette. Shetty and Bachchan too began to smoke. I never touch the stuff, but I lit one as well.

Nobody dared to smoke when they were in the same room as Kotwal. He didn't like it, and whenever someone lit up in his presence, his men would force them to stub the cigarette out.

That night, the four of us sat around Kotwal's corpse and smoked—not feeling elation, but strangely, sadness. We looked at each other. Shetty was crying. Bachchan's face had fallen. Only Varada sat stone-faced.

I stepped out of the hut and walked to a canal nearby. The moon had come out. My mind felt empty. I looked into the distance and stopped. I thought I saw two people standing there, staring at us. I called for Bachchan to take a look. It turned out we were staring at the silhouettes of a wall and a tree. We went back inside the hut.

I asked Shetty what we should do now.

'Come on. Let's clean the place,' he said, springing up.

Feverishly he mopped the hut with an old cloth. He cleaned the area around the body, but didn't touch Kotwal. He ordered us to get a bucket and brooms. Everyone, even Varada, followed his orders instantly.

Once we were done we found a spot near the canal where the earth was soft and dug a shallow pit next to a cactus plant. It was now past one.

Several people have asked me how I felt that day, when we killed Kotwal. My three accomplices will lend voice to my response: I was deeply pained. My hatred for him had disappeared and all I can say to the people who question me is that I did it because Kotwal attacked my brother.

In the underworld, people commit murder for one reason: it will bring you fame and that fame will translate to money. When we killed him, Kotwal was notorious, more than the smuggler Veerappan was in his prime. People used to say that the man who killed him would rule supreme in Bangalore. If we had brought his body back to the city the next day, hacked it to pieces and displayed our quarry in public, we would have been heroes. I doubt even the police would have had much to say about the killing—in fact several officers have chided me since then for not taking advantage of the murder.

The truth is, right until the instant a crime is committed, the criminal is unsure about what he is about to do, or what the outcome of his actions will be. There's always a niggling doubt that perhaps he can put off the act or altogether abandon the plan.

Till the first blow was struck that night, we did not believe Kotwal would be killed.

While we were digging the pit, Kitty came back. I went up to him before he could reach the hut.

'There is nobody on the main road. I don't know why Boss is so tense,' he said.

I put my hand on his shoulder and took him aside.

'Listen Kitty, we have a problem.'

'What is it, swamy?'

'Kotwal had become a nuisance. He is playing me against Shetty and Bachchan against the both of us. I don't know what to do.'

'What are you saying? He is here because of you. How can he do this? Let's do something about it.'

'That is why we've decided to kill him. If you agree, we can do it right now.'

He looked like I had struck him. 'No, no. People know we are with him. Let us take him to Tumkur and do it tomorrow night.'

I knew then that Kitty had no intention of doing anything to Kotwal. His outrage was just pretence. 'Kitty, if we let him go tomorrow, we will never find him.'

'I don't know all that, swamy, but I will not allow any killing here. There has never been a murder committed in this village and I am not about to start now.'

'What? What kind of a rule is that? This is Ninge Gowda's farm, what's it to you if we kill him here.'

By now, Kitty had dropped the 'swamy' he used to address me respectfully, and began to call me '*ree*'. 'Don't talk like that *ree*, this village belongs to my taluk. I will not allow such things here.' At that he began to run towards the hut. Shetty and Bachchan emerged from within it and stopped him.

'*Lo*, Kitty, what do you think that thing will do for you? I have been with it for so many years and have got nothing,' Shetty told him.

'Don't tell me all those things. I will not allow any killings to take place here.'

Bachchan lost his cool. '*Lo*, Kitty, he is already gone. What will you do now?'

Kitty rushed into the hut and began to wail. 'Murderers! What have you done?'

I told him that if he continued he would be next. He went quiet and asked me, 'What should we do now, swamy?'

We finished digging the pit and placed the body in it. We covered it with sand and planted a sapling so we'd recognise the spot later.

It was now four in the morning. Bachchan, Varada and I returned to the room we had rented in Tumkur. Shetty and Kitty told Kotwal's wife that her husband had fled along with us because the police were planning to raid the farmhouse. They put her on a bus to Shimoga and came to meet us at around ten.

We met Ninge Gowda and told him that Kotwal had left for Madras and that we would go back to the farm at night. He seemed relieved. That evening, Bachchan and I left for Bangalore to meet Jayaraj.

~

Jayaraj welcomed us with warmth. Without preamble, we told him that Kotwal was dead.

He sat silently for a few minutes and finally said, 'Is he really dead?' He was stupefied and trying hard not to show it. He stared at Bachchan and me and asked again, 'Did you really finish him?' We nodded, but he seemed not to believe us. He said, 'Please sit for a while,' and went out, leaving Pushpa with us. While he was gone, we were questioned incessantly.

Jayaraj returned with two thugs. One was of medium build and the other short and dark; he looked like a wrestler. 'What do you want to do now?' Jayaraj asked.

Since I didn't want my name to crop up during investigations, I suggested that Kotwal's body be shifted to another location and burnt. I told him that we could easily have done this ourselves, but wanted to show him evidence before we disposed of the corpse.

Jayaraj gave us an Ambassador, gunny sacks and rope. The two thugs, who I later learned were called Kalasipalya Narayan and Mysore Ganesh, came along to help. Pushpa, still recovering from the accident, was disappointed he couldn't join us.

We drove in silence, reaching Tumkur at one. We headed straight for the room and picked up Kitty, Varada and Shetty. We ate lunch in town and went to the farm in Aralalusandra. It was now evening. By the time we reached night had fallen and Gowda and his family thought nothing of the fact that there were two new men with us and that we would only be spending a night at the farm. They were happy to be rid of us.

We talked for a while and decided to dump the body in the car at four in the morning and leave. We went to bed at eleven.

I woke up at five in the morning. Everyone else was asleep. I tried rousing them, but they refused to budge. I gave up and practised karate in a corner for a while. They all woke up twenty minutes later, but still showed no signs of wanting to shift the body. I began to get angry when one of the thugs smiled at me and said the body had been moved at two in the morning.

We ate breakfast at Tumkur and reached Bangalore at ten. Near Double Road the two thugs parked the car in a small lane and walked away, leaving us with the body in the boot. After thirty minutes, they hadn't yet returned. We began to get anxious. What if Jayaraj had betrayed us to the police? But then, one of them came back and said, '*Anna* is calling you.'

When he met us, Jayaraj beamed. He seemed very relaxed and satisfied. 'Don't worry about anything. I'll take care of it. You relax,' he assured us.

Soon, Jayaraj's men started trickling in. Pushpa, Balaram, Anil, Malleswaram Venkatesh, Suresh and Ravi trooped into the house. Bekkinakannu Rajendra, Shetty's rival, also came in.

At around three we left for Hosur in six cars. We reached a place called Sampangere at around five. We stopped at a mango grove outside the village. A freshly dug pit, about twenty feet deep, was where the body would be burnt. A cartload of firewood and several cans of kerosene arrived. It was late at night when Kotwal was hoisted onto the wood and the pyre lit. Before he put the glowing torch to the wood, Jayaraj stared at the corpse and spat, '*Thoo ninamman*'—you motherfucker. He seemed to say this more in remorse than anger. Remorse that Kotwal had somehow brought this upon himself.

Seetharam Shetty wept endlessly.

It appeared Kotwal Ramachandra's murder had made nobody happy.

PART III

One

After the killing, we began to take every precaution to ensure the trail did not lead back to us. True to his word, Jayaraj went to great lengths to cover our tracks—he could have handed us over to the police, but he was a man of principle and wouldn't even imagine betraying us (this was a rare trait in the underworld and one that would hasten Jayaraj's downfall).

We were now sequestered in Malleswaram, in the house of a man called Club Narasimha. Jayaraj would visit us for a few hours every day and talk would invariably veer toward the murder of the one remaining obstacle in Jayaraj's ascendancy—Oil Kumar.

Unlike Kotwal, Kumar was secretive and wily. And while the man we had just killed prided himself on being mercurial, Kumar sat in the safety of his home in Vijayanagar and ran his fiefdom. There was a boy, Murthy—also called Huli—who accompanied him at all times. Huli, meaning tiger, had been trained by Jayaraj and had since shifted loyalties. He would sit by the window in Kumar's house and keep watch. At the slightest hint of trouble, Kumar received an alert, following which the police was summoned. And since it was established that Jayaraj was now gunning for Kumar, the law made haste in turning up each time an alarm was raised.

Besides this, it was common knowledge that Kumar carried guns with him. Apart from a .22 calibre pistol which he brazenly displayed, it was rumoured that there were four more firearms—far more powerful than the one he brandished—on his person. Above all, the fact that the police despised Jayaraj worked to Kumar's advantage.

Jayaraj didn't hesitate to show his contempt for the city's police force, launching attack after attack against them in *Garibi Hatao*, the disreputable tabloid that he ran. This too would prove to work against him.

For ten days after we moved into Club Narasimha's house, we collected information on Kumar. Finally, I decided that given the number of times the police had been summoned to Kumar's house, it would work best if we attacked in the guise of cops. Jayaraj was immensely pleased with the idea and promptly put me in charge of carrying out the killing.

First I had to select my men and train them to pass off as police officers. Then we began to discuss the actual details of the attack. I suggested that we stab Kumar inside his house, but Jayaraj maintained that it would have to be done outside. I yielded. We planned to print a fake warrant, arrest him, bring him to the van outside, and then stab him. Kumar's body would be cremated at the same place on Hosur Road where we had recently set fire to Kotwal's corpse.

Nine men were selected for the job. Tumkur Muddappa and Venkatesh would dress up as sub-inspectors, Balaram, Mahadev, Bachchan and Suresh would play plainclothesmen from the crime branch. Two men would wait in the van. Seetharam Shetty, Rajendra, Pushpa, Narayan, Nagaraj and a few others were left out of the plan because Kumar knew them by sight. Moreover, Shetty was very wary of the plan from the beginning. 'Just when we've gotten out of one mess, you want to get into another one?' he asked me.

I brushed aside his remark. We were too deeply mired in this plot to back off.

We went to Shivajinagar to buy uniforms. We even got Muddappa and Venkatesh fake medals. Everyone was asked to cut his hair short. I was to shave my beard the day before the attack.

On the day we were to go to Vijaynagar, we assembled at

Narasimha's house in the morning and rehearsed. At around four in the afternoon, I went in to shave. As I was walking into the bathroom, Pushpa walked up to me and said, 'Sreedhar, do we really have to do this?'

I was taken aback. I thought Pushpa was excited that we were going to eliminate Kumar. 'You have no idea how the police operate, Sreedhar. It's only a matter of time before people discover that Kotwal has been killed. If we go ahead with this, we'll have two murders hanging over our heads.'

'But what about Jayaraj?' I asked.

'He agreed to do this because you came up with the plan. You can easily dissuade him. No one—not even Rajendra or Narayana—wants to be a part of this.'

My enthusiasm evaporated.

I walked back into the room and said we would surely be discovered by Kumar and that the disguises would not work. I called off the attack. Everyone seemed relieved.

The next day, Seetharam Shetty announced that he wanted to leave town. Jayaraj gave him twenty thousand rupees and he left for his village near Kundapur.

Four days later, Jayaraj came to Malleswaram and warned me that rumours about Kotwal had begun to spread in Bangalore. He told me that this should be my last brush with crime and that I would be much better off with a regular job. 'It doesn't matter how much it pays, stick with working at an office. Being a criminal might earn you lakhs, but it's not worth it.'

'Right now, I can't think of a life other than the one I have now,' I replied.

'Sreedhar, it's only a matter of time before Kotwal's murder becomes public knowledge,' he replied. 'I will take responsibility for the murder and keep you out of this. Make sure you say nothing of your involvement.' He left it at that.

The next day, Bachchan and I moved out of Narasimha's house.

Varada, who was now married, wasn't in touch with us.

We were on our own.

An acquaintance of ours from the counterfeit racket days, Gangadhar, made arrangements for a room in Kamalanagar and we moved in.

It was now a month since we had killed Kotwal.

The papers were replete with reports about the crime, much of it speculation. The home minister, R.L. Jalappa, held a press conference and assured the public that Kotwal would be arrested soon. While people in the city spoke of Kotwal's appearances now and then, thugs in the underworld began to talk of his death.

Though Jayaraj had warned us to stay away from crime, with time on our hands and nowhere to go, we talked about the next big racket and began to look around for work. Soon, we got an offer from Tumkur. We had to get rid of a swami in Siddhaganga mutt.

Serious differences had cropped up between the senior seer and his underling; the fate of the entire mutt and its devotees, not to mention the members of the caste that prayed at the mutt, was at stake. One of the associates of the senior swami approached us and asked us to kill the junior seer. We would be paid ten lakh rupees for the job, he said, including one lakh in advance.

We hadn't the slightest intention of killing for money, but we were running low on cash. We told the emissary that we could threaten the junior swami instead, but he insisted he had to be killed. 'If you manage to escape and lie low, we'll take care of the rest. In fact, there are even some boys prepared to take the blame. We'll get them out on bail,' he said.

We told him we'd think about it and asked for an audience with the senior pontiff—we wanted to make sure this wasn't a harebrained scheme that we were getting caught up in. Also, since we were desperate for money, we thought it might be a good opportunity to simply take the one lakh and not do anything about the junior swami. What could they do if we disappeared with their money?

The man who approached us took us to the senior seer. 'Swamiji, these are the people I told you about.'

'I see. God bless you,' the swami said, and raised his hand sanctimoniously. The seer did not bring up the topic of murder. We were told by the emissary that the junior swami went for a walk early in the morning near the railway tracks and that this would be a good time to carry out the assassination.

Although we had no intention of hurting the man, we told the people at the mutt that he would be killed in four days. We were assured that we would receive the advance payment in two days.

That night, we were asked to stay at the mutt. We went out to watch a movie at one of those small halls where a few people gather to watch sleazy films played on a videocassette recorder. At around eight, Muddappa, the man who I had picked to impersonate a sub-inspector, traced us to the hall and walked in with bad news. Seetharam Shetty had been arrested. The well-known lawyer Vardhamanayya had heard about his whereabouts from one of Shetty's many mistresses and had told a lawyer friend of his. The lawyer promptly called the police.

We left for Bangalore. We had no idea what Shetty had told the police, but were pretty certain that after working on him, the police would eventually know we had killed Kotwal. We called Jayaraj.

'Don't you know Shetty has been arrested?' he asked.

'Yes,' I said.

'Then why are you still in Bangalore? Get out now.'

With very little money, Bachchan and I left for Tirupati. We got in touch with a man there who worked for the government and he made arrangements for us to stay at one of the rooms adjacent to the temple. We waited for news.

According to the Criminal Procedure Code, anyone arrested by the police is meant to be produced before a magistrate twenty-four hours after being captured, but this is almost never done. For four days we heard nothing about Shetty or the case.

On the fourth day, the news made it to the front pages of all the papers. Jayaraj had been arrested. Our names were in the reports. The police had begun the manhunt. It was now three months since the murder.

The newspapers were broadcasting that the police had unearthed Kotwal's bones. We didn't think this could be true—Jayaraj had thrown whatever was left of Kotwal into the Bay of Bengal. Later, we learned that Jayaraj actually buried the bones and it was these that had been found. We would find out why he did this in prison. They were, in fact, the bones of a dog! Jayaraj had decided that if the case was proved on the basis of witnesses, he would ask the court to examine the bones. Once the court realised that the bones presented as evidence were those of a dog and not a human being, it would dismiss the case, he had felt.

The papers also said that we had met Jayaraj at Victoria Hospital and planned the attack. The city police had fabricated this story so they would be in charge of the case instead of the Tumkur cops. Apart from a few such lies, the reports that appeared by-and-large hewed to events as they'd actually occurred.

A week later, Pushpa, Rajendra and Narayana were captured. Balaram, who had been in a brawl of some sort, was placed under arrest in a hospital. We stayed in Tirupati for a fortnight and then went back to Bangalore, heading straight for the room in Kamalanagar. Varada joined us there.

By then seven people, including Jayaraj, had been arrested and moved to the city's Central Jail awaiting trial. Jayaraj sent word through his emissaries that he would keep his word and say nothing about our involvement, but could do nothing about Shetty confessing to the police.

At around the same time, the police eased up on us: for them Jayaraj was the big catch, as was Shetty. The entire force was focused on amassing evidence against these two men. Kitty, the only other person present at the scene of the crime, had been detained twice and interrogated. Muddappa, Ninge Gowda and Nagaraju were all held overnight at the station and statements were beaten out of them. But to Jayaraj, it was vital that Bachchan, Varada and I remain hidden. He knew that our arrests would strengthen the case. He issued several reminders to us to lie low.

But since we weren't exactly luminaries in the underworld till Kotwal's murder, there were no pictures of ours published and we remained relatively safe, whiling away the time munching bread and bananas, and playing cards.

At around noon one day, we were immersed in one such game. I had been dealt a series of weak hands and was trying hard to get back when we heard shouts. Before we could react, we were being bound with lungis and being dragged into a jeep. Our attackers were from the crime branch. We were taken to Vijaynagar police station, but were allowed to sit outside on a bench. I was a little surprised. Surely, the men who murdered Kotwal would be trussed and thrown into a cell. At around three, one of the constables asked us if we wanted anything to eat. We told him to fetch coffee.

An hour later, the inspector came in. He looked at me and asked what I was doing at Gangadhar's house. 'We came to consult him on matters of astrology,' I replied.

The inspector burst out laughing and said, 'You look like a decent man. You don't know who this Gangadhar is—he's a cheat.' He turned to Gangadhar and said, 'So, you seem to be doing well for yourself. I hear you cheat people in the range of fifty thousand rupees now?'

'Swamy, all that was in the past,' Gangadhar replied. 'Now, I'm an astrologer. Nothing else.'

He asked us to leave.

It was settled. We would avoid Gangadhar as much as possible.

A few days later, the police arrested Muddappa and Ninge Gowda and detained them for two days, threatening them that if our whereabouts weren't revealed soon, they would be brought back and thrashed. We met Muddappa a few days later and though he promised us he wouldn't talk, we were too nervous to trust him. With barely a few hundred rupees to our name, we left for Madras. Gangadhar came with us. We booked a room at Udupi Hotel near the railway station and waited for news. Because of our financial worries, we cut down food to one meal in the evenings. We would sleep the whole day and, after supper, go to the beach.

On our third night in Madras, Gangadhar said he would go to Bangalore to survey the situation and call us when he had something of significance to report. He took the ten o'clock bus. We decided to stay for at least a week.

We waited the whole day for his call, but it never came. By the time we sat down for dinner, we were convinced that the police had picked up Gangadhar. We ate and left for the beach.

The sand was cool to the touch and the place was deserted. In the distance, the ships out at sea, their lamps bobbing, looked like little houses. We remained on the beach till about midnight. Bachchan said he would spend the night in one of the boats lining the shore. Varada, never one for too many words, merely lit a cigarette and stared at the water. I paced restlessly, often glancing at my watch.

At around three in the morning, I heard a van. It was the police. They walked towards us with torches raised and lathis poised. Varada didn't budge. Bachchan snored in his boat. I stood still. They asked me what we were doing this late on the beach. I told them we were from Bangalore and that I was a scriptwriter. They spoke to each other in Tamil: 'He's probably at the beach for inspiration.'

At half past five, we were back in the room. That night, we took the bus to Bangalore.

We went straight to Gangadhar's house. He lied unashamedly: 'I tried to call you at the hotel, but the line was always busy.' We said nothing.

It was Varada's opinion that, since the police didn't seem to care about our arrest, it was safe enough for him to move back in with his wife. We laughed and told him our arrest was both inevitable and imminent; we would be in Madras if he needed us. We went to Mysore instead.

We headed for Chamundi Hills and found a place to stay. For four days we watched movies to kill time. But Mysore was too small a town for us to hide in. I remembered I knew this man in Tirupati. That's where we went next. We were given rooms in the temple guesthouse. This would be a good opportunity for me to resume exercising, I thought. Idle for months, I had put on weight. For a week, I trekked up and down the hill twice every morning.

Then, news reached us that Diwakar Hegde had been murdered in Bangalore.

Hegde, a popular leader among student groups in Bangalore, quarrelled with people over the most trivial matters—he had recently picked a fight with Seetharam Shetty for the sole reason that Shetty was Kotwal's driver.

We had to determine if the troubling news about Hedge was indeed true, so we left for Bangalore.

Dairy Shivu was our informant. He told us that Tambu—a man who had entered the underworld early in his life, and who confined his dealings to running small rackets in the taluk office—had killed Hegde. Hegde, as was his wont, had fought with Tambu over some small matter and had slapped him. Enraged, Tambu retaliated two days later. We thought this was good for us—the police, now busy in pursuit of Tambu, would ease up on us. We decided to stay in Bangalore.

Bachchan had a relative who lived near Tannery Road. He was building a new home next to his old one, and it was all but complete: only the doors needed to be installed. We moved in. Apart from Bachchan's relative, the only man in Bangalore who knew where we were was an auto-rickshaw driver named Raja. He was our informant. Every evening, we would meet him and other such thugs at Coles Park and keep track of the progress that the police was making in tracking us down, and other goings-on in the city.

I would go to Ulsoor Lake for a walk each morning at five.

One day, unable to sleep, I got out of the house at around four and stood by the compound wall, staring up at the sky. A few minutes later, I went back to bed. Barely ten minutes had passed when I heard voices. 'Ey, the gate is locked, open it.' Someone jumped over the wall. It was too late to wake up Bachchan. I pulled the sheet over my head and pretended to sleep. Someone pulled it off me and shone a torch in my eyes. I saw a revolver a few inches from my face. 'Don't move,' the man barked. It was Shivaram, the cop who had chased Kotwal and me into Cubbon Park.

I was relieved. It was finally over. I asked Shivaram to lower his gun. It turned out that Raja, the auto-rickshaw driver, had been arrested and had broken down during interrogation. Shivaram was astonished that we'd had the audacity to hole up a short sprint from KG Halli police station. That's where we were taken. When we were bundled into the van, Varada was sitting there, looking at us. 'They didn't even abuse me,' he whispered. 'They just kept me in Madhuvan Lodge for a week.'

We were held at the police station for a few hours and at ten o'clock, were moved to Shankarpuram. There, we met Muddiah, the inspector in charge of the Kotwal murder case. He was one of the finest officers in the force—patient, intelligent and well regarded. The other three men with him, Shivaram, Appacchu and Chikkana, were just as good. They treated us well. It was Jayaraj who had drawn their ire. Since he had been arrested in the Kotwal case, Jayaraj had spared no time in attacking the police, printing articles against them in his tabloid, telling the court that he had been forced to confess (he had not) and giving all manner of statements against the police to the papers. 'You killed Kotwal to avenge the attack on your brother, but this fellow ... he behaves as though he has conquered the world,' the police would often say to me.

We were taken to Central police station, but it was hardly incarceration. Prison to us was more like a hotel. Dairy Shivu brought us food every day and we regularly received visitors. I got the chance to exercise regularly and spent time with several people we knew in the underworld. For a week this continued: we weren't taken to court. Finally, we were taken to a magistrate's house and permission was sought to hold us in custody for seven more days. Later, Samson, Jayaraj's man, told us that we were to proclaim in court that the police had detained us illegally for a week. We refused.

Jayaraj was clearly upset that we weren't adding our voices to his tirade.

I was worried. If Jayaraj was produced in court the same day as us and we refused to speak against the police, he might turn against us in prison. I waited nervously for my date in court, hoping it wouldn't be the same day Jayaraj was there. This was not to be. When I was marched up to the magistrate, Narayana, Pushpa, Rajendra, Shetty and Jayaraj were there waiting for me. Jayaraj walked up to me, glowered at Shivaram, put his hand on my shoulder and said, 'Tell the court everything Sreedhar. Don't hold anything back. Tell them how you were treated.'

Fortunately, one of Jayaraj's aides, Chindi, was also going to be produced before the judge with us. I had told him about my fears when we were in lock-up and he assured me that no matter what we said in court, and no matter how angry Jayaraj was, he would calm the don down. When the magistrate asked us if we had been mistreated by the police, we all said no. Chindi's voice was the loudest. The magistrate ordered that we be taken to jail. When we came out, Jayaraj had left. We knew he was angry.

In prison, although heroes to just about everyone interred there, we were still worried about encountering Jayaraj. We had disobeyed an order and jeopardised his case. What would he do?

Two

Seetharam Shetty received us at the gate of the prison and led us in after we signed the register. We followed him to our new lodgings, the 'koranti', a corruption of the word 'quarantine', used at the time the British operated the prison. When it was built, the koranti was reserved for men who had committed the most heinous sort of crimes. Now, it was more of a halfway home, set aside for new prisoners who would be interred there for a few days before being sent to finish their sentences with the rest of the men in the barracks. Shetty had secured the use of one of the four rooms in the koranti for us.

Before the Central Jail moved to its present location at Parappana Agrahara, off Hosur Road, it was in a neighbourhood central to the city's geography, near the race course. It was set in a forty-acre plot, and in addition to the barracks, housed offices, workshops and a library. When I was there, the barracks held about forty to sixty prisoners each. Prisoners sentenced to life terms were charged with guarding each barrack.

However, not all prisoners there were convicted: there was a significant population of under-trials as well. These men were provided with just the basic necessities—food, water and the like. Unlike the convicts, they didn't have to wear white uniforms and weren't trained in carpentry, tailoring, printing and other such skills in the prison's workshops, which convicts then put to use inside the penitentiary to earn money.

The koranti, unlike the barracks, was like a block. When we

were brought there, it was unoccupied. A man serving a life sentence was assigned to watch us. The prison 'opened' at six-thirty in the morning and 'closed' at five-thirty in the evening.

On our first morning in prison, at around eight-thirty, the four of us went to meet Jayaraj. We were worried that our statements in court would have angered him.

Jayaraj was in the twelve-bed prison hospital, used primarily by rich and well-known criminals. Prisoners who were genuinely sick were taken to the prison ward at the Victoria Hospital nearby. Jayaraj was strolling with Kote Narayana when we met him.

'Why did you say that in court?' he asked, not sounding irked in the least.

Unable to contain himself, Narayana interjected angrily, 'You should have done as you were told. Why did you go and say those things?'

'Ey, they are scared of the police,' Jayaraj told him. 'Not everyone is like you.'

I was relieved that Jayaraj said what he did. He appeared to divine that we were in need of money, and much to my embarrassment, thrust five hundred rupees in my palm. I politely refused. He told me to come to him if ever I was in need.

I was to be presented in court every fortnight. Jayaraj had already applied for bail and had promised us that he would get us out as soon as he was released. He had retained the services of Devdas, a popular lawyer known for his command over English and thunderous voice. Devdas was consumed by studying the minutiae of a case and used the loopholes he discovered to impressive effect. A lawyer named Sambamurthy would argue for the rest of the gang. We didn't have legal representation so Jayaraj asked us to pick someone. We chose a little-known fellow called Yusuf, who, given the nature of the case, said he would appear in court for free. He even asked us if we needed some money to tide us through.

I was A2, or accused 2, in the case. Shetty was A1; Bachchan and Varada were A3 and A4 respectively. Jayaraj was A5. The list went up to A14.

Prison is a strange place. Nowhere else do clashes, plotting and gossip take on the proportions that they do here. The fearsome stone walls, the barracks, the faces and names that count the hours behind the iron bars—all these things kill a convict's sensitivity. A man who spends six months in jail will come away a hardened criminal even if he was innocent when he entered.

The days in jail began to seem long and empty. As I said, we had to attend court once a fortnight, but the rest of the time we had to spend in jail. As per rules, each inmate was allowed one 'entry' or visitor every week, but Jayaraj and his group, including me, had twenty to twenty-five entries every day. Again, as was the norm, inmates would be behind bars and their visitors on the other side. But for us, some visitors were allowed inside. In prison, anything can happen with some negotiating. We got our meals from Jayaraj's house and two litres of milk a day from the hospital, courtesy Seetharam Shetty.

People serving long sentences in jail usually align themselves into groups. Gang fights and petty skirmishes are not uncommon. It's a well-known fact that no one who goes into prison ever comes out without having been embroiled in a fight. We were fourteen notorious gangsters serving time for a much-publicised murder case, and it should come as no surprise that we had more than our share of brawls.

Among us, there was one person who stood out both for his appearance and his reputation: Rajendra. He had several nicknames. His light eyes earned him the tag Bekkinakannu or 'Cat-Eyed' Rajendra and the curious redness of his skin caused people to call him Kencha. Rajendra always read Tamil books, and his knowledge of everything, including rowdyism, was extensive. He had entered the underworld at a very young age and he knew just about every gangster in Bangalore.

In my experience with the underworld, I cannot think of anyone else who was discussed as much as Rajendra. Perhaps this was because no one had as many enemies as he did. He seemed to believe that it was important to keep one's friends close and one's enemies closer. Just like he did not trust even the people closest to him, there were things about his enemies that Rajendra respected and even liked. As a testament to Rajendra's paradoxical nature, even those who were against him usually started liking him after the first meeting. He was straightforward and humble and this gave him the kind of charm and allure that other men in our line of work lacked.

I was introduced to Rajendra when I first visited Jayaraj's house. Rajendra had pretended to be a resident of Mysore and had tried to dig out information from me when he saw that I was drunk. I had always admired his cunning, and in prison we became close.

Seetharam Shetty and Rajendra did not get along at all. Shetty, a popular member of the Kannada Sangha, disliked Rajendra for his Tamil leanings. To counter this perceived threat, Rajendra formed a group of his own, ironically made up entirely of Kannadigas. Once, at three in the morning, Shetty's gang attacked Rajendra in his house and beat him senseless before discarding him in a ditch. Within the next three hours, Rajendra's group had retaliated and thrashed up every member of Shetty's group. Fights like this occurred often between the two gangs, although Shetty and Rajendra never encountered each other directly. Instead, many guiltless people were caught in the crossfire.

Rajendra preferred to stay away from Jayaraj. I was surprised to find that Jayaraj often made fun of Rajendra. This began to irritate me, and I spoke to Pushpa about it. Pushpa explained that Jayaraj's antagonism towards Rajendra took shape when he tried to advise him on how to go about his business in the underworld. Jayaraj was a man who commanded fear and respect and did not appreciate counsel from a youngster.

Rivalries, differences of opinion and fights of this sort kept us occupied most of the time, in a place otherwise devoid of life.

These days, jails are equipped with television sets. Back in the 1980s, there was nothing. Even pocket radios, if acquired, were to be hidden from the guards. Each morning at six, the *Suprabhata* from the clock tower would wake us up, but other than that there was very little music to mark our days. However, I will never forget a certain Tamil song that I heard in prison, which came to mean a hundred things to those counting the hours there:

Ponaal poguttum poda;
Inda ulagattil nilayey valdavaryarada.

Let it go, forget about it
Who in this world can claim to live forever?

Although I yearned for physical strength and fitness in jail, I smoked a joint every day. Opium was easy to procure in prison, and there was an illicit compact between the jailors and prisoners in these matters. There has been much said against this practice, but the critics don't understand a simple truth. The availability of opium in prison—like the rampant gambling—was not an issue that went ignored due to laziness or corruption on the part of the police. It was more a tactical decision that helped control the inmates. No one apart from jailors and the prisoners themselves understand the state of mind of people who serve out long sentences. There is no future for these people. There are only failed projects, worries about family, agonising loneliness and remorse. These things can drive a man insane if he doesn't have something to take his mind off it, or at least distract him temporarily from the overwhelming emptiness of prison life.

In a way, even jailors are imprisoned. Their houses are close to the jail, and even when an inmate is free, the jailors are not; their work continues. Their sole responsibility is to cope with notorious criminals and thugs. But when you meet these people every day, they cease to be fearsome offenders; they become nothing more than weathered men caged like animals behind bars. A curious relationship develops between jailors and criminals. It is in light of this fact that the significance of opium is better understood. Without opium it is impossible to regulate the behaviour of inmates. Trivial differences can lead to big fights; an aggressive man becomes a monster.

Our only other distraction in prison was to observe and size up the new arrivals. Fresh batches of prisoners were first housed in the koranti and then, later in the morning, shifted to the barracks. Every day, barring court holidays and Sundays, brought a different set of faces. The new arrivals were lodged in the room next to ours, so we got to see them daily. Usually they were marched in when it was evening and time for locking up, so we would summon them for our own internal 'questioning' on the following morning.

In the first week of our being in jail, a rape accused was brought in. When we summoned him and asked him for the details of his case, he was boastful and told his story with pride, thinking we would hold him in respect. We beat him up with a lathi borrowed from a jailor. All prisoners accused of rape received such treatment.

Once a week, Jayaraj would go out of the jail to Victoria Hospital on the pretext of getting a health check-up. Since he was in fact in good health, the check-up would be over in a few minutes. Jayaraj would then go and spend a couple of hours with some girls that had been arranged for, in secured places. The jail police who escorted him would look the other way for a few thousand bucks. I felt anxious about these visits of his. Samson too was worried and asked me to speak to Jayaraj. When I did, he said, 'One should not be that scared. If you want, you too can go. I will cover up for you saying you have gone for a check-up.' After that I did not mention it again.

Jayaraj didn't take opium but he would drink alcohol. Sometimes, when he drank, he would get emotional and talk to me about the past. He once told me that no one could be trusted, not even family. 'They come to you now, because you have done something big whether right or wrong. They come to you because you will make money in the future and take care of them. Tomorrow if you are sentenced, no one will come near you.'

Jayaraj had fallen in love at a young age. He had eloped with the girl, but when he was jailed in Mysore, she could not cope and filed for divorce. He had a son and a daughter, and he loved his family dearly, but seldom spoke about them. He once told me that he mentioned them because I was not like everyone else; I was not a rowdy. 'You are not capable of cutting anyone with a knife like we are,' he said. 'Somehow you managed to kill Kotwal, but you have to choose some other line of work. We can face anyone, but this will be difficult for you. You are not like us.'

Although Jayaraj was the centre of attention throughout his stay in prison, there was something about him that went against his status as an underworld don. He was a kind-hearted man, and a lot of people received favours from him whilst he was in jail. Several convicts who were sentenced to life, who couldn't even afford to appeal to the Supreme Court, would come to Jayaraj, requesting money to pay lawyers' fees. He would always help them to the best of his ability. Jayaraj was always getting people to submit petitions that allowed prisoners over seventy years of age to be freed.

It was interesting that only the lower and upper class criminals were not ashamed or upset about being in jail. Middle-class morality is truly a universal affliction; it was only the middle class offenders who were mortified about their imprisonment. They would wail and mourn for days because they were the only ones from their families who had ever been jailed, and it was difficult to console them. They would refuse to eat for days and flounder in their grief. But in prison, the older convicts would take the new ones under their wing, and teach them how to come to terms with the grey life of a prisoner.

Three

After a few months in jail, Jayaraj was shifted to Victoria Hospital on health grounds. Anything was possible in Central Jail for underworld dons! Two months later, he managed to get me shifted to the jail ward of the same hospital as well. He wanted me beside him to discuss and plan our defence for the trial.

Ninge Gowda, Muddappa and Nagaraju were witnesses in our case, and they came often from Tumkur to meet me. I had complete faith in them, but Jayaraj didn't; he asked me to keep them in fear of him and his gang.

Among Jayaraj's frequent visitors were two burly men, Cottonpet Gopal and Meese (Moustache) Bala. Both had huge moustaches and bodies to match, and presented an intimidating front. Following Jayaraj's orders, I would use them to threaten the Tumkur witnesses. 'I don't know what they have been sent for,' I'd say, my demeanour suggesting anxiety. 'Surely some heads will roll. Who knows whose turn it could be?' These tactics were successful enough, as Ninge Gowda, Muddappa and Nagaraju were in constant fear of the two men.

Within a month of being with Jayaraj, I met several rowdies from the oil business. Because I had played a major role in Kotwal's murder, I enjoyed much fame, and people like Ramalingam, Deena and Mohan were eager to talk to me. Oil Kumar—who had settled his differences with Jayaraj—visited often, but when he met me in Jayaraj's company he pretended not to notice me, and would merely smile politely. I knew it was a façade, because underneath his nonchalance was a very shrewd man.

When I was a suspect in the Bhasker murder case and was questioned by the CoD, I was not known in the underworld at all. It was nine years before Kotwal's murder and my imprisonment. Yet, somehow, Oil Kumar managed to ferret out this morsel of information. Jayaraj learned about it through Kumar, and he teased me about being a seasoned criminal. He even reached the conclusion that it was Lankesh, my friend from old times, who had instigated the murder. Jayaraj laughed and teased me about my association with the Kannada writer, but thankfully this stopped soon enough, when he realised I was uncomfortable with his prodding.

A few days later, Jayaraj got temporary bail and was discharged from the hospital.

A year had passed since I had been imprisoned. In spite of this, I was still learning things and familiarising myself with life in jail. Every now and then something would happen that would remind me to be more careful, like the incident involving Khalandar.

Khalandar was an old friend of mine. One day, I saw a group of constables walking him into the jail, his hands bound. Immediately I exclaimed, 'What is this, Khalandar?'

He turned away as if he did not know me, and Jayaraj looked at me and said simply, 'You should not have spoken.'

I realised I was in trouble. The next minute, three sub-inspectors and many members from the crime branch were upon me, asking me questions about Khalandar and his men, and trying to rough me up. Thankfully, Shivaram, who I knew, was one of the sub-inspectors present, and he calmed the flaring tempers. Because of this incident, although I wanted to stay in the hospital after Jayaraj's discharge, I got discharged as well and went back to jail.

Inside the confines of the prison, the clannishness and gang fights continued unfettered. There were now two groups, one loyal to Pushpa and Rajendra, and the other aligned with Kote

Narayana, Vijayanagar Ravi and Anil. In spite of being neutral, we had to side with Narayana's faction because of Jayaraj's loyalties—Vijayanagar Ravi was a relative of his. We were friendly with both Rajendra and Pushpa, but were part of the group they were plotting against, and it felt strange. Everyone was talking about 'finishing off' someone from a rival group, so I wasn't worried when I first heard similar talk about Rajendra.

One night, while we were drinking, an altercation broke out between Pushpa and Vijayanagar Ravi—Ravi pushed Pushpa, who'd had a little too much to drink, and he keeled over. They created a huge scene that night, with Pushpa insisting on having the gates opened so he could go to Rajendra's ward. The next morning, just as we were questioning Narayana and Ravi about the fight, Rajendra walked in and attacked Ravi, punching him in the face. I was taken aback, but held on to Rajendra and dragged him out of the ward, while he swore at Jayaraj. In the exchange of curses that ensued, Narayana pulled out a razor. A huge crowd gathered to watch the fracas, and the tower bell was sounded, which is done to warn the police of a crisis.

That fight could have been a serious one had the jail authorities not intervened immediately. Eventually, the skirmish had serious consequences for our relationships. It was then that I saw a side to Rajendra that I didn't know existed.

Because Rajendra and Pushpa had clashed with Ravi, it was clear that the two could never gain Jayaraj's favour again. It was also clear that none of us could be friends with them.

So far, though there had been clear factions, I could get away with talking to Rajendra or Pushpa because nothing concrete had happened. The fight established firm grounds for enmity, which, although we did not want it, had to exist if only in the form of outward silence between the groups. I asked Rajendra what should happen henceforth if we had to save ourselves, and I received the most intelligent, sensible and selfless answer from a man who was attributed with great selfishness.

Rajendra told me that, although we were both a part of the underworld, we were different people. I was new in this business, and if I were to join hands with them, Jayaraj would ensure that I never got out of jail. Although we were all in prison for the same reason, the risk I was running was greater since I was charged with murder, not with conspiracy or abetting the act. Jayaraj and the others would get away with a seven-year sentence, which they could later appeal and get bail for, but Seetharam Shetty, Bachchan, Varada and I could get life sentences, or even the death penalty. If Jayaraj ever felt betrayed by any of us, he could immediately hang the blame on us and get himself and the others acquitted.

Rajendra told me that there was no way we could be on the same side under the circumstances. The most I could do for them was to warn them if I learned of an attack planned. No one else could ever find out about this compact between us as it was too dangerous for me.

That night, Seetharam Shetty, Bachchan, Varada and I talked about this at length and concluded that we would remain committed to Jayaraj.

Jayaraj, however, was more street-smart and cunning than any of us could hope to be. He told me not to cut off contact with Rajendra and Pushpa. I was to feed them specific information, made up by Jayaraj, so they would always be in the dark about what was really brewing. Jayaraj told me there were no plans to kill either of them. He said the person he wanted out of the picture was Kurubara Pete Raja, the short, slim, smooth-talking thug who had links with the oil and club barons of Bangalore. But I knew that Jayaraj would not stop anyone from killing Rajendra. To this end, the city's criminal networks were in agreement. Kote Nagaraja maintained an army of goons; Gedda was a strong force; Koli Fayaz was an ardent Jayaraj follower; and then there was Balaram. The Tamil boys who did not like Rajendra were with Balaram. The intensity of his arrogance and courage were rare even in the underworld, and he commanded the respect and fear of many.

One morning, when Jayaraj and I were on our way to the court along with Balaram, Jayaraj said to me in confidence, 'If someone wants to finish Chappar (Rajendra), don't stand in his way.' I couldn't believe what I was hearing. I had only affection for Rajendra and the thought of someone killing him was unnerving. More than anything else, the idea of being a part of another murder case when I was already in jail for killing someone was untenable. I tried to reason with Jayaraj, but all he told me was that he did not expect me to kill Rajendra; but if someone else seized the opportunity, I should not stand in the way. I knew that he had mentioned this to me only after having discussed it with Narayana, Nagaraju and Samson, and from that day on, I feared for Rajendra's life.

People who are not a part of a life of crime believe that killing is a routine occurrence in the underworld, and the smallest reasons are enough to warrant murder. This is far from true. The number of such premeditated slayings in the underworld is far less than outside it, and there is a reason for this. In the outside world, the issue ends with the death; in the underworld, murder is just the beginning. Yes, killings are planned daily, but they are seldom carried out. Once a man is established as being a part of this system, he encounters the police at every turn, keeping a close watch even when nothing is going on. This isn't all: everything in the underworld happens in groups, so leaks in the system are common. Even the most tightly-held secrets fall free from tongues loosened by alcohol. And the moment one of these shady schemes comes to light, the people who are being plotted against spring to shifty wariness. This is what happened in Rajendra's case.

Because the plotting against Rajendra had become public, Jayaraj was very particular that the killing should not be done with a sharp instrument or by bludgeoning, since this would incriminate him. Everyone was in a fix: how could Rajendra be finished off without anyone suspecting Jayaraj and his men? At this point, an unexpected development offered a solution. Cyanide entered the jail through the machinations of Gedda.

Although Gedda claimed that he'd had fifty grams of the poison flown in from Bombay, we discovered that he'd acquired it from a compounder in Victoria Hospital. I had read a little about cyanide, but did not fully appreciate how dangerous it was. I came by this information in a book on medical jurisprudence. When I'd first heard about the plan to kill Rajendra with cyanide, I'd laughed it off. But it was no joke. Cyanide administered in any form takes just four seconds to kill a person, and the quantity required is a mere 1.5 mg/kg of body weight. With the fifty grams that had entered the jail, we could end the lives of thousands of people.

We hid the packet with us in the koranti and tried it on a cat four days later. We fed the animal a piece of mutton laced with about half a gram of cyanide. Within half a minute it began to act strange and collapsed after throwing up the food. Just as we were beginning to think the beast had died, it slowly revived and walked away haltingly. We wondered if cats required a higher dose of cyanide, or if the powder we got was adulterated. Its effects had shocked us though, and it was decided that the poison would be used on Rajendra.

We were all terrified of getting caught administering cyanide. If the police got wind of this, we would find ourselves in deep trouble. I took the problem to Jayaraj who said, 'You don't worry about all that. You only think about how you will hand over the cyanide to me.' He added that the jail staff would cooperate with us.

The plan was to invite Rajendra and Pushpa for drinks. When the two had had enough alcohol and had loosened up, we were to mix the cyanide in Rajendra's drink. Jayaraj, along with some of the others from the gang, wanted me to do it. I didn't think I'd be able to bring myself to do it. How would I bear to look at Pushpa after that? Also, Bachchan and I were worried that people would know it was us, since we were the only ones Rajendra and Pushpa talked to. There was too much risk involved. Days turned into weeks, and we found excuses to put it off, until finally, Jayaraj and his gang took the task upon themselves.

Every morning, we ate ragi ambali—ragi balls left over from the previous night's dinner mixed with onion and curds. We ate in our rooms, but Ravi, Narayana and Rajendra dined in the hospital upstairs. One morning we received news that Rajendra had been poisoned and was very ill. We rushed up to find him sitting at a table labouring for breath. He told me between gasps that he had been poisoned. However, after a few minutes, he forced himself to throw up and was fine. Rajendra did not die of cyanide poisoning that day.

As I wrote these words, I thought I'd talk to Rajendra to refresh my memory. Strangely, till I mentioned it to him, he had no idea that he had been poisoned with cyanide.

In spite of the foiled plan to kill Rajendra, Jayaraj didn't give up. Even when he was out on bail, he continued to plot Rajendra's murder, and even decided that I should play an important role in it. This time, it was to be death by strangling. Before this plan took serious shape, Jayaraj's bail was cancelled, and he was brought back to jail. He had to abandon the plan, since if the murder was committed in his presence, he would be mired in serious trouble.

Four

As the months passed, our names gradually become strongly linked with Jayaraj. Bail was out of the question.

Out of the fourteen arrested for Kotwal's murder, eight of us remained in jail: Seetharam Shetty, Bachchan, Varada, Jayaraj, Pushpa, Rajendra, Narayana and I. We had our differences within the group, and someone was always plotting against someone else. Seetharam Shetty was petty. He would lose his cool over the smallest things. He wasn't even interested in making it big in the underworld; in fact, he was trying to get out of it. He fought with Bachchan and Varada often and even had arguments with me, although I never let them turn into fights. But it was very hard to remain calm. Prison changes people; boredom is all-consuming, and they become suspicious of everyone they encounter. To keep my wits about me, I distracted myself by reading, exercising and running.

Meanwhile, Jayaraj toiled on in his efforts to dominate the underworld. He planned killing after killing.

The murders of a boy called Sheeru and Kurubara Pete Raja took place in quick succession.

Sheeru, who was Pushpa's disciple, had earned quite a reputation. Jayaraj had never taken him seriously, but people started complaining to him that Sheer had become problematic. Jayaraj advised them to take matters to the police and leave it at that, but there was someone else who would not be content with this.

Tambu, short and slim, was a student leader and the main

accused in the Diwakar Hegde murder. He had been bailed out of jail a month earlier. He was from a traditional family. But he had a formidable reputation in the Bangalore underworld at the time (and a strange glimmer in his eyes that made people shudder). He came to jail one day and revealed that he and four of his boys had decided to murder Sheer, and that they needed Jayaraj's help.

When I mentioned this to Jayaraj, he said, 'Let them finish him off first. Don't commit to them now, but tell them that once the job is done, you will convince me to extend support.' Jayaraj knew that if the news of his approval spread, he would be in trouble. I passed on Jayaraj's message to Tambu, and within two days, Sheer was killed. The same day, Tambu was richer by thirty thousand rupees and received the promise that a lawyer would be appointed to bail him out.

But Jayaraj's real target was Kurubara Pete Raja. In fact, he probably hated him more than he hated Rajendra; the latter kept to himself, but the former spoke disparagingly of Jayaraj. What threatened Jayaraj in the first place was that Kurubara Pete Raja had tried to meet Oil Kumar. A liaison between Oil Kumar and Kurubara Pete Raja meant that the former would get stronger, which was a threat to Jayaraj's life. Raja mocked Jayaraj openly, referring to him as Muduka or 'old man', and didn't think too highly of the don. This was enough reason for Jayaraj to plot his murder.

The rest of us had always liked Kurubara Pete Raja. He was warm and friendly, and always took the time to address us when we met in court. As far as we knew, he didn't disrespect Jayaraj or speak against him; in fact, on one occasion when Pushpa had said something against Jayaraj, Raja had snapped at him. Although it was the perception at the time that Raja had a criminal bent of mind, to me he always seemed innocent. He had two children and, when his wife became pregnant with the third, I advised him to consider vasectomy. He said, 'How can you, an educated man, say this? Children are God's blessings. On no account should we stop them from being born. Who knows what greatness awaits which child?'

I made it clear that I was against Kurubara Pete Raja's murder, but left it at that. It was not my place to plead with Jayaraj beyond a point; he would become suspicious of me.

In the past, Jayaraj had tried but failed to track Kurubara Pete Raja's movements. He had to monitor him secretly, since raising any suspicions would foil his plan. If Kurubara Pete Raja lodged a complaint against him, that would be the end of it. This time, however, things worked in Jayaraj's favour.

A man called Cubbonpet Gopala or Meese (moustache) Gopala brought us breakfast every morning. He was on amicable terms with Pushpa, and was Kurubara Pete Raja's friend. It is possible that Gopala was unaware of Jayaraj's hatred for Kurubara Pete Raja, because one morning, he mentioned that he would not be able to bring breakfast for us the following Thursday. We weren't certain why he was forewarning us a week in advance, but Jayaraj asked him why he would be unable to come that day. Kurubara Pete Raja had purchased a site in a new layout that Gopala had in Hosur, we were told. Raja had called him there next Thursday so he could have the site registered.

Gopala remained ignorant of what he had set in motion. He held Raja in great affection, and never imagined that he would play such a pivotal part in the murder of his friend. That night the plan to kill Kurubara Pete Raja was drawn up. Jayaraj had initially decided to get it done by Mysore Ganesh, but realising that he may not be able to take the lead, he decided to hand over the reins to Tambu. He had not forgotten Tambu's swift handling of Sheer's murder.

Jayaraj asked me to tell Tambu to finish Kurubara Pete Raja. I did not have the courage to talk about Raja's killing with Tambu. I was worried that if the information did leak out some day, then Rajendra, Pushpa and their gang would feel that I had abetted Raja's murder. Since Tambu had no personal enmity with Raja, I would have had to take on the responsibility for ordering his death. I was also worried that, in case Jayaraj fell out with Tambu and refused to foot the expenses, then naturally Tambu would hold me responsible as the middleman.

All these thoughts crossed my mind, and I told Jayaraj that it would be better if he spoke to Tambu himself. He agreed. When asked to be the front man in Kurubara Pete Raja's murder, Tambu agreed readily. He was willing to do anything for Jayaraj.

A year later, exactly what I had feared occurred, and I was very glad I had not agreed to be the middleman. In mid-1989, Jayaraj was arrested and sent to Mysore jail. Samson, Kote Narayana and Nagaraju were also arrested. Jayaraj had developed a strange anger and hatred towards those outside the jail. He stopped giving money to Tambu for court expenses.

Around this time, Bachchan and I were on a motorbike in front of Vani Vilas Hospital when we met Tambu at the traffic signal. We had not seen him for a long time and we asked him to Kamat restaurant for a chat. It was his *adda*. A group of seven or eight boys surrounded us. We were surprised because we had no enmity with Tambu.

Tambu came to the point right away.

'Sir, we carried out Kurubara Pete Raja's murder because we are friends. Now you must take care of the court expenses.'

That made me angry, and I said, 'Was I giving you the money all along? Didn't Jayaraj give you the money? Now he has gone to jail, wait till he comes out.'

'I don't know, Sreedhar . . . I did it for you . . .'

As soon as he called me Sreedhar instead of Sir, our defences were up. Bachchan's hand slipped into the bag he carried, containing a pair of machetes.

But I did not want a fight. I looked at Tambu and said, 'What do you mean? I did not ask you to kill him. Is Mysore Ganesh my boy? How can you blame me now? We are sitting here because we're friends.'

Tambu relaxed. He sighed and said, 'That is right, Sir, what can you do if that bastard does not behave properly? I had to talk like this because of my problems . . .' and continued to make light of the issue.

If I had not insisted that Jayaraj speak to Tambu directly, I would not have been in a position to defend myself that day.

The Monday after Jayaraj spoke to Tambu about killing Kurubara Pete Raja, Gopala—still in the dark about his friend's impending death—confirmed that he would be in Hosur on Thursday with Raja. By then careful preparations had begun. In the underworld, it is a rare occurrence for two notorious dons to unexpectedly encounter and kill each other; everything takes place with precise planning.

The first big issue to settle was the boys who would be part of the team. Jayaraj left it up to Tambu to work with whomever he was comfortable. Besides specifically mentioning that he wanted Kote Shiva and Ganesh, Tambu didn't name the rest of his boys, and no one asked him to.

Then, there were the courts to contend with: since Jayaraj was in jail, he was sure that he would not be accused in the case, but he was anxious that Samson and Kote Nagaraju not be accused either. He asked them to get admitted into a hospital before the date of the murder, and emerge only after Raja was dead. (He didn't tell them why they had to do this. They assumed that Oil Kumar was the target.)

On Wednesday, a day before the planned murder, Jayaraj invited Meese Gopala to have a drink with us. Usually it was only Jayaraj and I, but the special invitation was extended to Gopala in order to find out the details of the bus they were boarding to reach Hosur. After some carefully planned 'casual' questioning, we found out that registration started at eleven in the morning and Gopala and Kurubara Pete Raja intended to wrap things up by noon. Gopala was sent away within five minutes of delivering this news, so that the final details of the plan could be put together. Tambu and Ganesh joined us, and it was decided that they would go to the Kalasipalya bus stand to check that Gopala and Raja were on the bus, before going to Hosur and waiting at the main bus stand there.

Jayaraj said the attack had to take place as soon as Raja got off the bus, failing which they should finish the job on the way to the sub-registrar's office. He also asked that they confirm Raja's death before leaving the spot. Finally he cautioned them against getting caught and insisted that they take off from the scene immediately after.

In spite of all the instructions and warnings, Jayaraj was very nervous and restless after Tambu and Ganesh left that Wednesday night.

On Thursday morning, the substitute appointed by Gopala brought us breakfast. It was eight o'clock. Tambu and his assassins wouldn't call us immediately after the attack, but by my calculations, the news was likely to reach us by two in the afternoon. We went about our business as normally as possible, but we didn't hear from them at all that day. We began to worry about the possible reasons: maybe our boys had met with an accident or maybe Raja had not been killed at all.

The next morning, we were stunned to read about Raja's murder in *Prajavani*. While the article did not mention the details of his death, it went into great detail about how the murderers had been caught and arrested. The killers had been escaping the scene of the crime in an Ambassador, when the Hosur police got on the wireless and instructed the police at Attibele to stop them. While they failed to catch the speeding vehicle, the Attibele police noted the car number and flashed it on the wireless. Finally, they were stopped in Hebbagodi police limits. Seven men were arrested.

Jayaraj was worried when he read the news. If seven people had been arrested immediately after the murder, it was hard to be certain that none of them had talked. Later that morning, the lawyer from Tigalarapet, Vasu, arrived and berated Jayaraj for what he had done. By afternoon, the news of Jayaraj's involvement had spread. Except for a few of Jayaraj's supporters, everyone was upset about Raja's murder. They all found it shameful that the normally straight-shooting don had resorted to such cowardly methods.

Five

By the time Kurubara Pete Raja was killed, lawyers had begun arguing the Kotwal case. Charges had been filed, and witnesses summoned. We were required to present ourselves in court.

It so happened that we had an appearance to make the day after Raja's death. No one questioned Jayaraj about the murder at the time. Tambu and the others had tried to convince the Hosur police that the Bangalore police had 'worked' on them. In truth, since they were taken into custody after bringing it to the notice of the court, the police had not employed forceful interrogation techniques on them at all. More important, although I had no clue about this at the time, the minute Jayaraj formulated the plan to kill Raja, he had reached out to the Hosur MLA. By the time the Bangalore police went to Hosur, the MLA had softened up their colleagues in Hosur.

When we went to court after Raja's murder, Pushpa's face was mangled with grief. He had grown up with Kurubara Pete Raja and been very close to him. As soon as he saw me, he began to weep like a child.

'Could you not give me an idea, Sreedhar? He has two small children . . . How can I bear this?'

It was difficult for me to console him. I said I did not know about the murder plan, but he did not believe me. I did not try hard to convince him.

Rajendra, too, was upset, but did not show his anger like Pushpa did.

In the evening, Jayaraj asked me to recount our conversation in detail. Then he suggested that the next time I met them, I should advise them to surrender to him. He thought they would have collapsed after Kurubara Pete Raja's murder. However, they were hurt, but had not lost courage.

Over the next few days, we put aside thoughts of Raja and turned to our case, which rested almost entirely on Kitty's testimony. Our future depended on what he would say to the judge. When the court sends summons to a witness, the police have to sign and receive it. Now our main concern was how to bring Kitty from Oil Kumar's hide-out and place him in Koratagere. Kumar had hidden Kitty in a guesthouse owned by Annachi, a petrol bootlegger from Madras because Jayaraj was worried the police would take Kitty into custody before he got on the witness stand and force him to make a statement against us. The police had taken Kotwal's murder case very seriously since Jayaraj was involved in the case. Matters were darkened further because Jayaraj had annoyed the police by alleging in his paper, *Garibi Hatao*, that the police had framed him. Jayaraj knew that no matter how notorious a rowdy was, he quailed when confronted by a policeman. He reminded the lawyers several times over that they were to prevent this.

The Central station inspector Shivanna had become close to Jayaraj through our lawyer Yusuf. Jayaraj spoke to him and they came to an understanding. Shivanna agreed to call the main witnesses—Kitty, Muddappa, Ninge Gowda and others—to the station and issue summons to them in his presence. Inspector Muddaiah had been transferred, which was good for us.

No one testifying against us could create as many problems for us as Kitty. He was the participant witness and his statement could get us sentenced. To test what the police would do, we called Muddappa and Ninge Gowda and told them to receive their summons. The police did not threaten them or take them to the station, so Jayaraj was emboldened enough to send for Kitty. There were now only ten days left for the enquiry.

Jayaraj called Oil Kumar and asked him to bring Kitty. This

is when we found out that Kitty had escaped. We immediately called Muddappa, Nagaraju and Ninge Gowda and told them to bring in Kitty if he came to their place.

Jayaraj suspected that Kumar may have either handed him over to the police or instigated Kitty to escape by telling him that Jayaraj would give him a large amount of money. If he was in the custody of the law, we were in deep trouble. The police could file a case against us, along with Kumar, for having illegally confined Kitty for more than a year. Kumar would surely support the police and get them to file a case against Jayaraj. This would have serious consequences against us in the Kotwal murder case. If the police held Kitty in their custody and made him stand before the judge, we had no doubt that Kitty would issue a statement against us.

If Kitty had indeed escaped, then it was impossible for us to get our hands on him. If the court found out that summons were issued against him, it would issue a warrant to arrest him and the police would find him and keep him in custody before producing him to the court. However we looked at it, we were in trouble.

In twenty-four hours, we received news that Kitty had reached Koratagere. However, he refused to come to us, no matter what our men tried. We sent the police with Samson and Nagaraju and made them issue summons to Kitty. Everyone advised him not to implicate us. He only said, 'I will not allow them to get into trouble for any reason.'

With six days remaining for the enquiry, Muddappa brought a local rowdy called Johnny to us. He would lure Kitty out, we were told.

Johnny, who had come at seven in the evening, was drunk. Muddappa introduced Jayaraj to him. Jayaraj asked him what Kitty had said.

'Ayyo, why do you ask about him? It is not so easy to make him agree. Why did you keep him away for one year? Now police summons . . . you know . . .'

Jayaraj listened with his jaws clenched. It was evident Johnny understood that Kitty was important to us, and was trying to extract as much money out of the situation as possible. It angered me that he showed us no respect.

'Do you realise to whom you are talking?' I said and head-butted him in his face. Jayaraj did nothing to contain me. He looked approving. I picked Johnny up by his hair and asked, 'Now you tell us, how much money do you want to bring Kitty?'

'Nothing *anna*, he is my disciple. Don't kill me. I will get him tonight . . .' he pleaded.

We sent Johnny with Mysore Ganesh and two other boys to a hotel. We then talked to Muddappa and Ninge Gowda. They were stunned at the beating Johnny had been given.

After everyone left, Jayaraj called Ganesh back and asked him to work on Johnny. He said that others would not create trouble after they saw Johnny being thrashed in their presence. He was right. The next day Muddappa and his gang convinced Kitty to come with them. They brought him to the hospital.

Jayaraj asked him, 'Did Kumar trouble you?'

Kitty did not provide a clear answer. He only said, 'Don't trust that bastard.'

It seemed like Kumar had had nothing to do with his escape. But judging by his behaviour, we were worried that if the police caught him, Kitty would testify against us in court. So instead of turning him back home, we sent him to a relative in Channapatna. We told Muddappa and Nagaraja to accompany him.

The day of the inquiry arrived.

The previous night, we had been very anxious. We were scared the police would snare Kitty before he entered the court. If that happened and they forced him to give a statement against us, we could not tell the court that we knew Kitty supported us. That would have meant we had illegally confined him, which would amount to trying to influence witnesses and complicate the case more. The lawyer Devdas advised us to send Kitty to court under the protection of a lawyer.

We were called to the stand at half past eleven. Nothing could be said until Kitty's evidence was recorded. When he stood before the magistrate, the court fell silent. He placed his hand on the *Bhagavad Gita* and swore that he would tell the truth. After asking his name and other details, the public prosecutor pointed to us and asked Kitty, 'Have you seen them before?'

Without a minute's hesitation, he said, 'No,' and even shook his head.

The Kotwal murder inquiry was practically closed. The rest was a matter of routine.

Some judges close the case as soon as an eyewitness refuses to testify against the accused, but in our case, although the evidence of none of the witnesses in Ninge Gowda's farm went against us, everyone's testimony was recorded. Only Kotwal's wife testified against us, and since her statement amounted to hearsay, it was of little concern to us.

The forensic evidence took the most time. The prosecution had called several technical experts and one doctor to testify. Our lawyer Devdas had determined that the most robust defence would be to attack the evidence of the experts who had examined the bones and blood stains. In his booming voice he asked each expert, 'Are you competent to talk about murder?' The expert, confused, would blurt out, 'No, certainly not', and leave.

Except for one. He was a doctor who had been brought in from Madras. He countered all of Devdas' jabs. When Devdas asked him in his usual baritone, 'Are you qualified enough to dissect the murder?' he answered, 'Very much'. Questioning the doctor took four days. There was nothing in his evidence that could help us, but Devdas's pride would not let him leave the expert alone.

The strangest thing about the entire case was that the prosecution had shown that the blood found on the bones was B negative. We had records to prove that Kotwal's blood group was O positive, but despite this (and the fact that the bones were that of a dog) Devdas did not produce this information in court or bring it to the notice of the court.

When the inquest drew to a close, we each had to make a statement. Devdas told us what the judge would ask and what we had to say in response. He told us that we would have to say, 'All lies, Banavat Mahaswamy.'

When he asked me what I would say, I said, 'I will say, all lies, Your Honour, it is all fabricated.'

He got so angry, he started screaming. 'It is because of people like you that people get convicted. Absolute featherbrain! Just say what you are being told to say!'

I had never addressed anyone as 'mahaswamy', but this time I had to. After our statements were committed to the records, the date of judgment was set at a month thence.

That night, one peg down, Jayaraj said, 'We will get out in this case. And then we can get rid of one more headache.'

'Which one, Sir?' I asked.

He looked at me and said coldly, 'Somehow we must get rid of Oil Kumar.'

Six

Kumar was no ordinary man: he held a special place in the telling of Bangalore's criminal history. He did not posses one quarter of the guts that Jayaraj did. He had none of Kotwal's cruelty or ability to escape danger. Though he had participated in a few small fights, he did not have their physical capabilities or courage. Yet, he was revered as a don.

Much later, another great gangster—Muthappa Rai—would be counted among these men. But Rai had the support of a few police officers and strongmen. The threats he issued on the phone were laced with menace.

Kumar could do none of that. All his supporters, except for Kunta (Lame) Kumar, were forever planning schemes against him. Though he bribed the police liberally, except for one or two constables, no one on the force liked him.

However, he was so full of guile and cunning that he could manipulate the thugs in his employ by his wiles alone. He had a flashy lifestyle, and even in the times of two super dons, he was able to maintain his place in the underworld owing to his tact.

Once, at a wedding that Kumar attended, a man approached him and said the gangster Kotwal Ramachandra's threats against him had become so incessant and inexorable that he'd been driven to the verge of suicide. Kumar asked him coldly, 'Have you seen Kotwal?' The man said he hadn't. Kumar asked him to stay put for a while, called Kotwal and asked him to come there. Then he took Kotwal to the man who had complained and said, 'See this is the Kotwal you keep hearing about.'

This was a time when people were rattled at the mention of Kotwal. Even those close to him did not address Kotwal by name. Kumar's behaviour gave the impression that he was bigger than Kotwal.

After he had failed in his attempt to kill Jayaraj, Kotwal began to worry more about Kumar than Jayaraj. Kotwal was confident he would finish Jayaraj someday, but he did not know how to defeat Kumar. 'After a few months, if we rush in, everyone except Maharaja will run. Only he will stand tall, then we can blow him up. But this Kumar ... we have to handle him carefully,' Kotwal used to say.

Jayaraj also had the same problem after Kotwal's murder. He had been certain that someone would finish Kotwal, if we did not. But Kumar had sent emissaries even while Kotwal was alive. After his murder, Kumar went to Jayaraj along with his wife and brokered a successful compromise. Yet Jayaraj knew that Kumar was making use of an opportune moment. Kumar felt safe with that one act. Though his status was a little dented, his ability to stay alive amidst the clash of the titans was seen as a great achievement.

Jayaraj began to feel that he could be happy and trouble-free when he got out of jail, if he finished Kumar. He knew that Rajendra and Pushpa were angry with him for getting Kurubara Pete Raja murdered, but he was aware that they would not challenge him openly. However, he was also aware of the possibility that Kumar could someday use them both as his pawns. Hence, he decided to settle the matter once and for all.

Once his ideas start taking definite shape, Kumar's end started haunting me. Every night we would walk after dinner and discuss how to finish him. But all plans reached a dead-end. It was not possible to barge into his house and attack him because he always had two or three men guarding him. Also, the entire underworld knew that he had a foreign pistol. To attack and finish him on the road would be suicidal because the Bangalore police, who clenched their teeth at the mention of Jayaraj's name, would not just arrest him but possibly finish him in an encounter. To lure his associates with money was impossible because Kunta Kumar and Huli Murthi were loyal to Kumar.

Finally Jayaraj came to a decision. I have seen dons taking risks in the underworld before, but the risk that Jayaraj was ready to take to get rid of Oil Kumar was beyond anybody's imagination.

Jayaraj was an old-time rowdy. He became a rowdy to show off his physical strength. He was a regular at the gymnasium and was rumoured to do four to six thousand sit-ups at a time, even doing twelve thousand once! He had grown up watching constables and small-time rowdies trouble his father, who had an arrack shop, which had made him hate the police. Although he was just over five feet tall, he was extraordinarily strong. As a teenager, he got involved in local fights. Then he confronted Dhobhi Lakka and Munegowda and was thus noticed by M.D. Nataraj, the son-in-law of the then chief minister Devaraj Urs.

Jayaraj was the very first proper underworld don in Bangalore. To exact revenge on Tigalarapet Gopi for gathering a force of thugs to mount an assault on him when he had no one to rely on for support, Jayaraj charged at his attacker in full view of a court, for which he had to serve a seven-year jail term. He was, however, deeply compassionate towards the downtrodden, and had an aura of a godfather about him.

Kotwal, on the other hand, was a very different man. He had changed the very nature of Bangalore's underworld. Scheming had replaced straightforward fights. It is likely that, had Kotwal had easy access to Kumar like Jayaraj did, Kotwal would have finished him a long time ago. However, Jayaraj felt that if he killed Kumar when the latter came to visit him at the hospital, his image of a straight fighter would suffer.

Once, Jayaraj, Samson and I were standing at the hospital talking when Tigalarapet Gopi slowly walked past our ward. Samson's jaws clenched, and he said, 'This one must be removed somehow.'

'If you say yes, we can do it in one week,' Samson said.

'Be quiet, Samson. I must strike myself, or I must keep quiet. What respect will I have if I let someone else attack?' Jayaraj had responded.

After Samson left, I asked Jayaraj, 'Didn't you allow someone else to kill Sheer and Kurubara Pete Raja? Why the discrimination?'

'*Dadagiri* is like wrestling . . . the pairing must be correct,' he answered.

This is why he was determined to eliminate Kotwal.

Since Kumar was a don to match, he could not delegate the job to anyone else. But the problem was that Kumar was not challenging him: a compromise had been reached. It was a strange situation, which he could neither ignore nor accept.

Finally, he decided to call Kumar to the hospital and finish him. He asked me several times whether what he was doing was morally right.

I only replied saying if I had posed such ethical questions while participating in Kotwal's murder, I could not have finished him.

He laughed. 'The one who had to think was not you but Seetharam Shetty,' he said, defending my actions. 'You did not kill him to become a don.'

Finally I convinced him that, since it was a war, everything was fair. The next thing to decide was what to do with the body after Kumar was killed. Jayaraj was sure that, if Kumar's body were found in front of our ward, the police would hang him. I shared his anxiety. We finally decided that, after killing Kumar, we would hand the body over to Samson and Nagaraj and get them to dispose of it.

We were left with the problem of how to tackle Lakshman Rao, who would come there with Kumar. We argued for a while when I suggested we kill him as well. I was very upset when Jayaraj accused me of being a cold-blooded murderer.

Jayaraj was certain that Rao would do as he was told once Kumar was dead. His plan was to make Rao call Kumar's wife and tell her that they were going to Madras to attend to a pressing matter. Later they would circulate the rumour that Kumar had gone with a girl and was missing. He was sure that when the body was found in a car near Mahabalipuram beach, along with flowers, drinks and perfume, the police would decide that Kumar had been killed because of a woman. And by the time the case was transferred to Bangalore, it would be cold.

Jayaraj worked out every detail without overlooking a single aspect, even preparing to prove which hotel Kumar stayed in on the day of the murder.

Kumar usually parked his car right in front of our ward. If there were no serious issues to discuss, he would come in. On such occasions he would give me a tepid smile and ask, 'How are you, Sir?' which embarrassed me. It was like a chief minister addressing a corporator as 'Sir'.

If there were serious matters to discuss, Jayaraj would sit in his car and talk. We decided that, when Kumar came, I would sit at the back and ask him for his help to set up an oil business in Mandya. Jayaraj and he would be in the front seat. I would then strangle him from behind with my arm; Jayaraj would hold his hands tight so he would not be able to escape.

Jayaraj asked him to come at seven in the evening. I kept a button knife as a stand-by in case it was not possible to strangle him.

Although we did not tell them anything, we called Samson, Nagaraju, his younger brother Vasu and their supporters, so they could threaten Rao and keep him quiet.

No one would be able to see inside the car, but Jayaraj arranged for three lakh rupees to bribe the policemen guarding us in case they got suspicious.

That evening, my heart beat wildly, but Jayaraj remained cool. When Kumar came, Jayaraj got into the front seat.

The police, as usual, sat in a corner and were immersed in conversation. Samson, Nagaraju and the others stood under a tree on the road. Rao was loitering around. Jayaraj called me into the car. I went in and sat. I could not hear what they were saying. Jayaraj signalled to me with his finger. I leaned forward, but my arm didn't go all the way around his neck. Just then, an old Impala car drove up and parked next to our vehicle. I hastily withdrew my arm, scared. Kumar had not even noticed it.

In the Impala was Chetan Kumar, Jeevaraj Alva's brother-in-law. Jayaraj, who had been talking about setting up an oil business for me in Mandya, got down immediately to greet him. When Jayaraj was in jail, Chetan Kumar would use his influence to get him out whenever he wanted on parole. Jayaraj had immense respect for him.

Kumar thought I would continue the discussion and stayed in the car. I did not know what to do, so I got out as well. Kumar too got down then, greeted Chetan Kumar and, calling out to Rao, got into his car, told Jayaraj that he would meet him the next day, and drove away. After he was gone, Chetan Kumar asked Jayaraj, 'Why do you still allow him near you? He will always be a danger to you. Can you not do something about him?'

Jayaraj just smiled.

After they left, Jayaraj exclaimed, 'See how lucky he is?'

We decided to kill Kumar when he next visited us, but the time never came. Two days later, Kumar went to Madras and did not return for some time. When he did show himself, it was just five days before we were due to be released, and we did not want to take any risks. Instead, Jayaraj turned his attentions on no less than police sub-inspector Kauri, and this time, instead of murder, he wanted to plan an acid attack.

At the time, Kauri was a sub-inspector at the Kalasipalya police station. Before Jayaraj was arrested in the Kotwal murder case, Kauri had arrested and kept him in lock-up for a day in connection with a false complaint. Since Kote Narayana, who was involved in the case, was an associate of Jayaraj, the complainant had included the don's name as well. There was no way the police could have known it was a false complaint.

Jayaraj had created a ruckus in the station saying he was not involved, but daredevil officer Kauri had not given in and had instead insulted Jayaraj. This had always bothered Jayaraj, and he wanted to take revenge before leaving jail.

But I shuddered when I heard the name, and said there was no one I could use for such a serious act. Jayaraj said, 'The educated think too much about the law and get scared.' I did not deny it, and he did not talk about it again. He was also aware that if he mentioned it to someone else, it could be dangerous for him.

Seven

May 14, 1988. After one year and eight months in jail, we were due to be released.

We did not sleep the previous night.

Our lawyer Vasu had come to see us and told us that the judge had not yet dictated the order to release us. This was usually done three days in advance. Also, the judge had called the inspector and advised him to ensure that we had protection, adding to our confusion, since such instructions are usually given in the case of notorious criminals who are sentenced.

Though no witness had testified against us, Vasu had said that the judge might give a moral conviction since Jayaraj was a known underworld gangster and don and we were not. Although I did not know of any such provision, I was terrified. Jayaraj said philosophically, 'We only know how to get into jail; getting out is not in our hands.'

At eleven-fifteen we were called into the court hall, and a minute later the judge pronounced the judgment, 'I have released you all, you can go.'

When those words were spoken, even Jayaraj's eyes filled with tears.

We returned to the hospital ward and waited. Since there were cases pending against us in other courts, we had to obtain several clearances before we found release, but this was a routine procedure. A team of lawyers who were working would attend to this.

Anxious, we finished our lunch and waited for the legal

team. Just then a police van and two jeeps arrived. By the manner in which they came, we anticipated trouble. Shivanna, the Central station inspector, was in one jeep. Jayaraj asked me to find out what the matter was. Shivanna took me aside and, putting his hand on my shoulders sighed, 'We also thought you would be released today, but you won't.'

'What's wrong, Sir?'

'Another case has been booked,' he said quietly.

An important incident that amended the course of Jayaraj's life must be mentioned here.

Two months before the day we were to be released, the Rasheed murder case was reported. A Malayali named Sadashivan had arrived in Bangalore. He was shrewd. The then home minister Jalappa had previously applied for permission to start a 'Devaraj Urs Medical College'. Sadashivan too had submitted an application to start a 'Sanjay Gandhi Medical College'. He bribed Jalappa's personal assistant and, instead of Jalappa's application, his own was placed in front of chief minister Ramakrishna Hegde. Hegde thought it was Jalappa's application and approved it.

Jalappa discovered the trickery the next day. He met Hegde, had the application cancelled and obtained permission for his college to be set up. Sadashivan didn't take kindly to this. He employed a lawyer called Rasheed and obtained a stay on the permission granted for Jalappa's college. Rasheed was a lawyer practising in Kerala. He was happy to find a client in Bangalore and constantly created trouble for Jalappa by serving several legal notices. One day, while he was travelling from Cochin to Bangalore, he disappeared. His family filed a complaint with the police, alleging he was murdered.

The day the case was registered the lawyer Vardhamanayya came rushing to Jayaraj. That day, which spelt the fall of Jayaraj, is still fresh in my mind; I can remember every detail. The interrogation of witnesses in the Kotwal murder case was in progress at the court. Important witnesses had already deposed in front of the judge and we were sitting and chatting in the police van after having eaten some biryani. Vardhamanayya came up to us and showed Jayaraj a typed letter. Jayaraj asked me to read it (he was illiterate). It was the petition filed in court by Rasheed's wife. In it, allegations were made that the Bangalore police, in particular DCP Narayan, had murdered Rasheed. The home minister Jalappa was also one of the accused.

Jayaraj was always looking for ways to put the police in a tight spot. Now that Rasheed's wife had accused a deputy commissioner of police of being involved in a crime of such a serious nature, he saw another opportunity to target the police. DCP Narayan had even sent for Samson to deliver a message of caution to Jayaraj. He had threatened to put a stop to all the black market activities in which he believed Jayaraj had a share. But Jayaraj was not worried. When Vardhamanayya showed the petition to Jayaraj, he immediately said, 'Tell us what you want us to do, Sir, we will get it done.'

After Vardhamanayya left, I told Jayaraj, 'Sir, this is not a simple case. DCP Narayan commands great respect in the police department. We should not get into this.'

Jayaraj looked at me as though I was the biggest coward in the world.

Two days later, Rasheed's body was found on a beach in Tamil Nadu.

Bangalore lawyers boycotted court. Ramakrishna Hegde handed the case over to the Criminal Bureau of Investigation. To this day, many politicians feel that Hegde should not have handed over a case against a Cabinet colleague to the CBI. Hegde's critics say he did it to curb Jalappa, who had turned into a powerful leader of the backward classes.

Jayaraj became so deeply involved in the case that, thrice a week, CBI inspectors visited our ward. They wanted Jayaraj's support, as the local police were hindering their investigations.

The CBI had concluded that Rasheed was murdered in Hotel Satyaprakash in Seshadripuram in Bangalore, and then transported to Tamil Nadu. They were keen to arrest Kulla

(Shorty) Shantha, who was accused of transporting Rasheed's body. In those days, Kulla Shantha was notorious in the Gandhi Nagar film world. He was rumoured to be in Mandya, and the CBI wanted Jayaraj to find him. Twice, the chief of the investigating team had come to the ward in a hired vehicle to talk to Jayaraj. I had several discussions with him as well.

But who had killed Rasheed? We heard many rumours from people who had migrated from Doddaballapur to Bangalore, which we then passed on to the CBI. They all turned out to be false.

One morning, DCP Narayan was arrested, along with four constables and one sub-inspector. Jalappa, who had been absconding, resurfaced, beaming, having been given anticipatory bail. Jayaraj was jubilant, and the Bangalore police was furious.

It was at that time that the judgment in the Kotwal murder case was announced and we were acquitted.

But Bekkinakannu Rajendra had submitted a petition that he faced a threat from the Jayaraj gang. Usually an officer of the rank of inspector disposes of such petitions. If there is some evidence of truth, the accused is given a warning and let off. But the police were seething at Jayaraj's stand on DCP Narayan and, making the petition an excuse, did not let us go for two days.

We stayed in the hospital for two days and then sought permission from the court. We were released, but all of us, including Rajendra, were summoned by the police and interred in Upparpet station. After two nights, we were finally released.

When we were in jail, we imagined a hundred different ways of how the outside world would view us once we were released. We talked for hours about what we should do and how we would behave once we were released. Strangely, in less than twenty-four hours, everything felt normal. It was like you were meeting someone who had been away on work for two years and had just returned. In ten minutes the excitement had subsided. It was as if we'd never been away. But our time in jail had earned us a fearsome reputation. Even those who had known us for a long time looked at us with fear mixed with curiosity.

Seetharam Shetty, Bachchan and I rented a small house in Ilyasnagar near Banashankari. Our days of *dadagiri* started. We dreamt of becoming the richest people in Bangalore in the span of a year. Jayaraj always used to say it was not easy to earn money, however much people put you on a pedestal. But several big crooks would come to the jail and insist that we stay with them after we were released. Regardless of what Jayaraj had said, we had high hopes. But the bubble soon exploded.

The week after our release was spent in visiting temples along with Jayaraj. Then we began to contact, on a war footing, those whom we thought would support us. Nothing has changed in the underworld. It is the same story. Young boys who take to weapons dream big, they dream of one big attack or murder that will establish them in the field. But they slip into the abyss very quickly.

The land mafia was then just reaching its peak in Bangalore. We knew that Kotwal had been given two sites and fifty thousand rupees by Krishna Bhat, who had formed a new layout called Girinagar. Even in jail we were strongly attracted by real estate—prices were spiking.

A man called Muniraju from Kattariguppe had promised us that all that we had to do upon being released was to solve a few land disputes and our lives would be made. He showed us an acre of land that had been causing trouble for him and said that if we sorted things out, we would be paid one lakh rupees. But when we found out who the claimant was, we refused to even consider it. It was a senior civil lawyer.

A scrap dealer called Chotu had promised us a car. When we contacted him, all he furnished us with was a good lunch at Taj hotel in City Market, and six thousand rupees. He then got rid of us. Kaleem, another friend, fed us lunch at home and slipped us five thousand rupees. Ismail, who had promised us fifty thousand rupees, gave us the slip. Mandi Raghu, who always said with pride that we were 'his', gave us a thousand rupees.

Within twenty days of being free, we realised it was not easy to make money. Jayaraj would occasionally slip us a couple of thousand rupees with a casual, 'Keep this', but had not fixed up anything for us. With me, he was very affable.

All around us there was talk that Jayaraj made lakhs every week in the club and oil business. One evening, I casually mentioned that it would be easier for us if he fixed something for us on a weekly basis. He laughed aloud and exclaimed, 'What! You have got such a big reputation and you don't know how to convert that into money!' Then he asked me to meet Jagadeesh of Sampangiramnagar. Jagadeesh had been instructed to collect *mamool* from a few brothels and give half of the money to Seetharam Shetty, Bachchan and me.

We felt miserable. We knew that even Kotwal collected a share from such businesses, but we thought it an insult to take money from brothels. When I told Jayaraj this, he called us immature. 'You don't know anything. All illegal trades should be in our control, whether it is prostitution or currency cheating. Otherwise someone else will take control and oust us.'

Jayaraj made sure we were paid around three thousand rupees a week. In those days, it was big money.

At the time, massage parlours were doing a roaring trade. Every lane had such an establishment. Jagadeesh took us to one on Residency Road. Our method was simple. The three of us would visit the parlour and put up a 'show', which meant that we could create fear without actually committing any violence. We would make it very evident though that, if required, there would be an attack. Jagadeesh would later settle the deal.

Rowdies are like Dobermans. If you go to a friend's house and see the dog, despite all assurances that it will not bite, you still feel scared of it. It's the same with rowdies. No matter how much they assure you that they will not trouble you, you still fear them, because you know that they have the capacity to hurt you. Middlemen convert this fear into money.

Just as we were calculating that we would get a good income from the Residency Road parlour, Jedarahalli Krishnappa got in our way. I don't remember talking to Krishnappa in jail; perhaps I did not notice him because we were in the hospital most of the time. By the time we were released, he had become very close to Balaram. We used to meet Balaram near Jayaraj's house, but we had never met Krishnappa.

Two days after we finished a 'show' at the Residency Road parlour, we went to one in Shantinagar which had just been inaugurated. We met Krishnappa there. He had a peculiar irritated look on his face. At that time, he was always preoccupied with wanting to finish Srirampura Kitty (not the same Kitty who was a witness in the Kotwal case). When he met us at the parlour, he said that since we had hundreds of other ways to make money, we should shun extorting from parlours and instead leave this business to him. I said we would talk to Balaram about it.

Balaram knew we had got into the parlour business only with Jayaraj's knowledge. By the time we reached Jayaraj's house that evening, he had already spoken to Jayaraj and made him agree to hand over all parlours to Krishnappa.

In front of Balaram and Krishnappa, Jayaraj told us we had to step aside as Krishnappa was looking for Kitty, and Kitty was frequenting parlours to collect money. Also, Krishnappa had already murdered Sidda in this connection and was therefore the appropriate person to take charge of the parlour business.

There existed no enmity between Jayaraj and Kitty; nor was he at odds with Balaram. But Krishnappa, who had been viewed as Kitty's shadow in jail, had become his enemy after his release. Since Balaram was with Krishnappa, Kitty had become Balaram's enemy too. Jayaraj was Balaram's boss, and so naturally Kitty considered Jayaraj as his enemy. And since we supported Jayaraj, Kitty was our enemy.

Eight

I have always enjoyed street fights. Even before I became a rowdy, I used to brawl on the roads, in hotels, at film shootings. Now, newly released from jail, I was embroiled in at least one such scuffle every week. Earlier I was a nobody, but after being involved in Kotwal's murder, I had become a big name.

In the beginning, although the fights were over petty issues, they helped build our image. Seetharam Shetty, Bachchan and I were always together, Seetharam on one motorbike, and Bachchan on the other. I would ride pillion on Bachchan's bike. I always carried a bag on my shoulder: it held two books and two machetes. This was at a time when there was no one in Bangalore who could challenge Jayaraj, so we were not scared that we would be attacked. But Jayaraj always insisted that, after making a name in the underworld, it was not right to travel through the city unprepared. He reminded us that we could be attacked by anyone, at any time. He recounted several incidents where common folk had chased and beaten up notorious rowdies. So we never ventured out without machetes.

Once, near what used to be Tiffany's restaurant, a group of boys in a car went past us and almost grazed our bike. I abused the boy driving the car. He stopped and made an obscene gesture. Bachchan protested, but I made him stop the bike and went up to the car. The boys also got down and started making a show of wanting to fight. I went up to them and delivered two strong kicks to two of them and caught hold of the collar of the third. The rest ran away. A large crowd gathered and tried to stop me, but we did not relent until they had apologised.

In another incident, I was with Bachchan and another friend of ours in a car near Russell Market in Shivajinagar. Two Muslim boys, arrogant in their stance, blocked our way. We rarely got into fights in Muslim areas, since a large crowd can gather in no time. But we'd had beer in the afternoon and were charged up. Bachchan abused one of the boys and they opened the door of the car. I used my karate skills to kick the boys away and told my friend who was driving the car to leave immediately, before a crowd gathered. He pointed towards the back in fear. Bachchan was fighting with the boy I had kicked first and they had pushed and shoved each other into Russell Market.

Bachchan, though courageous, is not trained in martial arts like me, so I ran to his aid. Though we were strong and had almost bested them, our attempts to flee the scene surprised the gathered crowd. They determined that we were Hindus (in fact, Bachchan is a Muslim) and began to advance, screaming.

We managed to get into the car, and though some boys ran behind us, we sped out of the area.

After several such incidents, an encounter almost out of a film made me resolve never to get into a fight again.

Around eight months after we had been released from jail, we shifted from Ilyasnagar and rented a big room in Shantinagar. One day, Bachchan and I were on a motorbike just behind Johnson Market when we almost scraped against another motorbike. We continued on, but the boys on the other motorbike chased us. We had to stop near the football stadium since the two boys, who were Muslims, were eager to fight. I ignored the thin boy and kicked the big boy. Within seconds, Muslims in the entire area had gathered and we began to fear for our lives. Just then one of the boys recognised Bachchan and he told the others to calm down. Bachchan sent me home in an auto-rickshaw. When I reached, I sent Seetharam Shetty to help Bachchan. He also knew people in that locality. Between the two, he and Bachchan managed to pacify them.

In the evening we found out that the boy I had kicked had

broken his right shoulder. He was a motor mechanic, and the doctor had advised him to wear a cast for two months. Although he had cried in front of Seetharam Shetty, I did not feel guilty since he had started the fight.

Two months later, I was riding the motorbike—I had just learnt to ride—when I hit a car. My left ankle was fractured and my leg was bleeding. Bachchan, who was on a scooter behind me, tried to hail an auto to take me to a hospital. Just then the mechanic whose shoulder I had broken drove past. As soon as he saw Bachchan he stopped the car, took me to a hospital and gave me blood. He visited me over the next ten days that I was in hospital.

His concern troubled me more than my broken ankle.

One day I apologised to him and said I had been punished for breaking his bone, and I would never get into fights again. From that day, I haven't been involved in a street fight. Except once. That was the night when Balaram, Krishnappa and I created terror in the city. Three cases were booked against us in that one night.

This is what happened.

None of Kotwal's followers had challenged Jayaraj after his murder. Patti went into politics, Muni became a contractor, Hajama Venkatesh joined Jayaraj, and Daniel became a drunk. Except for Srirampura Kitty. Krishnoji Rao, or Kitty as he was known, was a Maharashtrian like Kotwal and very dear to him. Kitty was a kabaddi player. He was an expert in running and fighting—strong and efficient. While we were in prison, awaiting trial in the Kotwal case, he was incarcerated for the Chotu and Sidda murder. He had almost joined Jayaraj once, but Seetharam Shetty had convinced Jayaraj that he was more dangerous than useful.

Kitty and Krishnappa were together in jail and, as it often happens, were staunch enemies by the time they got out. There is a belief in the underworld that when a group gets into jail together they come out as fragments. It was so in our case, too. We were fourteen when we went in. By the time we got out, Pushpa and Rajendra had left the group.

Krishnappa came to see Jayaraj occasionally, when he began to spend time with Balaram. They both complained to Jayaraj that Kitty had become unbearable. At first Jayaraj did not take them seriously, but later decided that he should put a stop to Kitty.

One morning he called us and said we had to go with Balaram and Krishnappa to all of Kitty's regular haunts and put up a 'show'.

That evening, a group of us set out on four motorcycles and in two cars. Samson, Bachchan, Kote Nagaraju, Seetharam Shetty and I were in one car; Kote Narayana, Balaram, Jedarahalli Krishnappa, Dadiya Ravi and two of Balaram's boys were in the other. Anila, Chandru and eight other boys were on bikes. We left Jayaraj's house in Wilson Garden at around seven and went to Jayanagar. Balaram and Krishnappa had decided the spots where we had to 'show'. We had never heard about Kitty being in Jayanagar, and we had many contacts there, so we did not want to go to that neighbourhood. But they did not agree. They said they had accurate information about Kitty's *addas*.

First we went to Venkatesh Reddy's office in Yediyur. Before we stopped our car, Balaram, Krishnappa and the others had barged into the office, flashing their 'longs', the colloquial word we use for swords. Bachchan, who was sitting next to me, went in with them and so did Shetty and Kote Narayana. Samson and I did not get out of the car. Seeing them rush in, the people there scattered, terrified. The neighbouring shops began to pull down their shutters. Venkatesh Reddy was not in the office. We threatened them saying if they let Kitty in we would set fire to the office.

We then went to a wholesale kerosene shop run by Putta on KR Road. Balaram wanted to do a '307'—attempt to murder—on Putta, but he was not at the shop.

From there we went through Mysore Bank Colony to Kattariguppe and raided a wine store owned by Palani. Palani's younger brother Venkatesh was a notorious rowdy who had been jailed in connection with M.C. Prakash's murder. He wasn't to be found, but Palani was at the shop. Because he had a large gang, Palani was not intimidated by us. He calmly asked Seetharam Shetty, 'Why, guru? Don't you know who I am? Why should I allow Kitty or for that matter any other rowdy here?'

Yet Balaram and Krishnappa flashed their longs.

Venkatesh's boys had looked after me the first time I went to jail. I had not known that the wine store belonged to Venkatesh. After I found out, I felt bad and shouted at Balaram for coming there. He did not care.

From there our group went to Common Club in Jayanagar 4th Block. It was situated on the first floor of a building. I had sat in the car during the previous two attacks, this time I wanted some action and barged in with others. The players there were engrossed in their cards, but as soon as they saw the longs, they scattered. One of the young men swore that Kitty had never stepped into their club.

Wherever we went we had just one question: 'Where is Kitty?'

We drove to Sarakki, searching for Putta's house. If he was not at the KR Road shop, we knew he would be at home. We searched but could not locate his house. We headed in the opposite direction from there and, passing through Vijayanagar, rushed into Kamakshipalya. We raided a bar where, Krishnappa said we would definitely find someone from Kitty's gang. This time I too held a sword. Balaram laughed when he saw this: he thought I was not fit to hold a long. We climbed a narrow staircase and went up. We all rushed in, except for Samson, and all the seventy people there started screaming.

I lifted the sword with both hands as if to assault a big man standing there, over six feet tall.

He pleaded with me to let him go, holding my hand in a tight grip.

I did not hate either Kitty or anyone else there, and I began to feel that my holding a sword over the head of big man, and him pleading with me not to hit him, was quite farcical. But I knew I couldn't let him go as soon as he pleaded, so I shouted at him, 'Why do you want a rowdy's friendship? What is your connection with Kitty?'

'Guru . . . I swear on my wife and kids . . . I don't know any rowdy . . . I have not even seen Kitty,' he said, shivering. He asked a thin man next to him to please remove his watch.

It was a thick Rado watch.

Till he brought it up, it hadn't occurred to me that I looked like a notorious rowdy to him. When he tried to give me his watch, I felt disgusted. I just looked at him and said, 'Okay, fine, I will not do anything to you.'

I climbed down the stairs and sat next to Samson. Balaram and Krishnappa emerged next. The rest followed and sat in the cars or on bikes. All except Krishnappa. He was still at it, charging at anyone he could find, pummelling people with the blunt edge of his sword. Even the waiters weren't spared. He hated Kitty to such an extent that he was attacking anyone who might have exchanged brief words with the gangster.

In the heat of battle, what we hadn't noticed was that less than three hundred feet from where we had parked was a police station. The police had not noticed us when we had gone up, but when Krishnappa started flashing his sword on the road, a sentry on duty outside the station saw him.

'Ey . . . who is it?' he shouted, and aimed his rifle at us. We started the car in a hurry. Krishnappa ran and got in. We didn't think the sentry would take a shot, but within seconds the thundering sound of a .303 rifle shook everyone in the car. Luckily the bullet did not hit the automobile but swished past it. The sentry screamed, 'Catch those bastards,' and took one more shot. It missed our car as we sped away.

We were shocked by this unexpected turn of events. We thought the police would send out a wireless message and we would be stopped any minute. Balaram and Krishnappa got down and went to Malleswaram. We sped through small by-lanes and finally reached Jayaraj's house.

The next day Jayaraj was very upset. He said we had not understood what a 'show' was. He said we just had to give the impression that we were ready to strike; we were not meant to have brandished weapons. That was the secret of a 'show'. He said Samson, who was experienced, should have guided us. What Jayaraj did not know was that neither Balaram nor Krishnappa had been inclined to listen to Samson.

The night we had the 'show', three cases were registered against us: in Kamakshipalya, Jayanagar and Banashankari stations. But in all the complaints, the accused were recorded as 'unknown'.

The *Prajavani* reported the next day that rowdies were shot at in Kamakshipalya. We thought that if we lay low we could get away with it, but in twenty-four hours it was the talk of the town that we were responsible. Venkatesh and his brothers came to Jayaraj and complained against Balaram and us. Kote Narayana shouted at them but Jayaraj calmed him.

Though the police did not search for us, Samson and Seetharam Shetty obtained anticipatory bail. Bachchan and I pretended not to know anything, but sub-inspector B.K. Shivaram called to threaten Jayaraj that sub-inspector Kauri was looking for us and demanded that we surrender. We said we would go to the station the day he asked us to, but he did not agree. He said we were to follow his plan: Kauri would find us drinking beer in a bar; we should then try to escape but eventually surrender. If that happened Kauri would gain repute (and so would we), he said. Since we had decided not to stand up to the police as far as possible, we agreed to everything he said. But it turned out that Kauri wasn't interested in becoming popular (nor did he show any interest in catching us).

However, the result of our 'show' was that Venkatesh and others thought Sunkenahalli Gauri was responsible for the attack on the wine store and Gauri was forced to leave Bangalore and settle down in Ramanagara. Also, Jayaraj decided to keep Balaram and Krishnappa at a distance. He felt that these two would someday prove to be trouble for him.

Nine

After this dramatic incident, things turned relatively calm, the mob was passive for the most part. Jayaraj was invited to a number of programmes in Bangalore, Mysore and Kunigal. He sat on the dais alongside the likes of Gundu Rao, Jeevaraj Alva and Aziz Sait, and was felicitated as well. Jayaraj also held parties regularly for all kinds of people, from inspectors to lawyers to MLAs. Liquor was plentiful. Jayaraj drank no more than two pegs.

Meanwhile, Samson took care of the oil business. The 'income' from clubs went straight to Jayaraj. He preferred that all dealings were finalised without threats and violence. He said that since we were capable of both, there was no need to prove it.

We were approached for two deals. A man called Purushottam asked if we could help him alter property papers: so a site registered in the name of a man called Mallayya would be transferred to him. Mallayya was a well-known man, and he had contacts with police officials. Purushottam said we had to get the job done; even if it meant kidnapping Mallayya. We needed money, whether we did the job or not, so we took one lakh rupees from him and asked him to wait at the MTR restaurant while we went to Seshadripuram to bring Mallayya.

We went straight to Jayaraj and told him about the deal. Jayaraj was furious. 'It is such bastards who keep us rowdies ... *avanamman*, motherfucker ... why should we kidnap anyone to get the site registered in his name? Tell him that you pushed Mallayya into the car and the police came after you and you escaped. Also tell him that the police are searching for you and take one more lakh from him.'

We made Purushottam wait till afternoon and then sent word through a boy that we had encountered a police problem. We never heard from him again.

Another deal we got was from Hassan Raghu, who worked as a stunt master for Kannada films. He was in Bombay then, in connection with a television serial. He had contacts with the don Haji Mastan. A man named Shetty had cheated Raghu's friend of ten lakh rupees and was refusing to return it, no matter how he was threatened. Hassan Raghu brought this friend to us.

When we went to Shetty's house, he came out in a chaddi and banian, looking ferocious. He was huge. Seetharam Shetty whispered in my ear that if he was cut into pieces, a hundred people could have a hearty meal. We began the conversation by saying we were involved in the Kotwal murder.

'I have wrestled with Jayaraj, I will talk to him,' he said, and even as we were watching, went in, returned fully dressed, got on his scooter, and rode away. We called Jayaraj and gave him the news.

When we reached Jayaraj's house we heard him telling Shetty, 'These people are the new generation . . . we cannot get them to agree by mentioning old connections. Why don't you set it right by giving what is due?'

The next day Shetty returned the ten lakh rupees.

For our efforts, we got one lakh rupees and an invitation to go to Bombay to meet Haji Mastan. We were thrilled and decided to leave as soon as we could.

By now, we thought it best not to use intimidation and thuggery to earn money. We wanted to keep our business propositions legitimate. One member of our group, Devaraj, had connections with Marwadi businessmen. He promised to get us a friend's shop in Chikpet without rent if we could start a textile business with one lakh rupees. He also impressed upon us the large profit margin possible in the textile business. We planned to use the one lakh rupees to buy textiles from Bombay on a three-month loan and sell it in Bangalore at a profit. We spent twenty thousand rupees on furniture and gave the remaining eighty to Devaraj.

Devaraj and the Marwadi businessman said they'd go to Bombay, and I thought I'd join them since I wanted to meet Haji Mastan. On the appointed day we went to the railway station but a shock awaited us. Devaraj came empty-handed—he had lost all our money on a race. It is difficult for me to explain the helplessness and anger I felt.

We took Devaraj to our house and thrashed him mercilessly. The next morning he pawned some jewellery and gave us twenty-five thousand rupees. We eventually collected forty thousand rupees more from him.

We went to Bombay and Devaraj and the Marwadi purchased textiles worth four lakh rupees by paying an advance of a lakh. Hassan Raghu took us to meet Haji Mastan, who was quite old by then. He looked after us well, and put us up in a hotel run by Ahmed Chua, a smuggler friend of his. We were also introduced to three men in Dawood's company. One was Nadeem, who lived in Musafar Khana. It was an area populated predominantly by middle-class Muslims and Tamilians. Nadeem's house was an old building, but like a fortress. Arshad and Shareef also stayed nearby. All of them knew Hassan Raghu.

Although they were respectful towards Haji Mastan, they called Dawood 'Bhai'. They were in their thirties then, and had one dream: to rule Bombay. Unlike the Bangalore rowdies, they were not simple and straightforward. They moved fast, and constantly. There was no night in their Bombay: they returned home at five in the morning, slept till two in the afternoon, got up and went to work in the evening. They would order everything in dozens. Guns were everywhere.

When I was in Bombay, a Shiv Sainik had shot a Tamilian. Though badly injured, he did not die. That night, Shiv Sainiks were ready to attack the Tamilian's gang, but the police wouldn't let them. The underworld always had the police on their side. Before they committed a murder, they would inform the police and would discuss at length who should be framed. Compared to the Bombay police, I felt, Bangalore police, though corrupt, had retained their integrity.

We did not sleep for the six days that we were in Bombay. We were taken to Caesar's Palace, a hotel then run by the Dholakia brothers. It was the flashiest disco in Bombay. Over the next four to five years, Dawood would get rid of the brothers and their children, and take control of the hotel.

I became tired of Bombay, and though they kept insisting that I should stay, I left and returned to Bangalore.

Back home, Bachchan, Seetharam Shetty and I convinced Devaraj that if he had more money, especially with Haji Mastan mediating, he could purchase textiles worth a large amount and make money. We sold our stock for three lakh rupees, collected our investment along with an additional fifty thousand, and quit the textile business.

By then the investigation into Rasheed's murder was nearing completion. DCP Narayan and the other accused were in Coimbatore jail. Jayaraj continued to take a great deal of interest in the case. When the CBI police tried to take the eyewitness, Subbaraju of Satyaprakash Hotel, to Coimbatore to give a statement, the local police protested. The lawyers of Bangalore, however, supported the CBI. Jayaraj sent a large group of advocates along with Subbaraju to Coimbatore. I could see very clearly that he was unnecessarily taking on the police and I warned him against it, but he ignored my words.

The *Garibi Hatao* office—which funnily enough was in a building belonging to the Central Jail—was always full of small-time editors from all over Karnataka. It was sickening to see newspaper editors, reporters and owners trying to ingratiate themselves with Jayaraj, who could neither write nor read. I was the only one in that entire group who opposed and analysed whatever Jayaraj said, hence they were all very suspicious of me. When Jayaraj was with them, he behaved as if he felt more secure with them than when he was with rowdies.

~

Just when we thought everything was proceeding swimmingly, Srirampura Kitty attacked Balaram near Highlands Hotel.

Kitty had not retaliated after our raids on all his *addas*. We calmed down, but Balaram and Krishnappa were dogged in their pursuit of Kitty. They had even barged into his house. Kitty, who had only been waiting for an opportunity, went with Anil and his other boys and attacked Balaram, who had to be driven to the medical college in Vellore for treatment.

We did not take much interest in the incident. When Jayaraj heard the news, he was more disgusted with Balaram than angry with Kitty. 'One must not enrage the enemy and make him pounce,' he said.

It was around this time that Seetharam Shetty suggested that we go to Rose Guesthouse. It was a ten thousand square foot place in one of the small bylanes off Brigade Road. There was an old bungalow on the grounds, and the place was owned by a British woman called Rose. The property was entangled in a legal tussle for a long time. When Kotwal was alive, a man called Nagesh had given him two rooms in the bungalow as payment for threatening his opponents. Of the two rooms, Seetharam Shetty claimed, one now belonged to him. He said he would get his share once all the disputes were settled and builders bought the property.

At first we didn't care all that much about this wrangling, but one day, with nothing else to do, we went to see the place.

We sped through the gates, pushing them open with our legs, and parked very close to the bungalow. We sat on the chairs in the veranda and put our legs up on a teapoy as if the house belonged to us. A boy dressed like a waiter in an Udupi hotel came out of the house and asked who we were. Bachchan and I didn't say anything, we just stared at him.

Then Seetharam Shetty asked, 'Who are you?'

That boy looked at Shetty, scared.

Shetty switched to Tulu and the boy relaxed. They chatted for a while. Shetty told us that Nagesh was killed in an accident a few months earlier. Then he told us the name of the man who had taken charge of the bungalow.

Muthappa Rai.

'Who is Muthappa Rai?' we asked Shetty, who in turn questioned the boy. We were told that he was from Puttur and was known to Samson. We gave another 'show' around the house and left, teasing Shetty about another Mangalorean coming to Bangalore. Shetty said he would get him to vacate the place in no time.

We met Samson in Jayaraj's house and asked him about Rai, who we were told was a partner at a cabaret on Brigade Road, called Omar Khayyam. Patti and Hajama Venkatesh, who were Kotwal's associates, were also with him. He was employed at a bank and had resigned from his job to start a hotel. He also ran a cards club. He was close to Samson and, according to him, 'a good man'.

In those days, we used to go to former chief minister Gundu Rao's house every evening. His personal assistant Adugodi Sreedhar was friendly with us. At that time, not a soul passed near Gundu Rao's house. Gundu Rao, who had once led a luxurious life and was courted by many, was now lonely. When he saw us he would smile, probably glad to see someone coming to his home. His son and Congress MLA Dinesh Gundu Rao was then a teenager. He frowned whenever he saw us. He probably realised we were up to no good.

Adugodi Sreedhar knew Muthappa Rai. One day he casually mentioned Rose Guesthouse and said it was filled with criminals who had come from Mangalore and Bombay. He said the cars they drove looked like they were stolen, and it also seemed like they carried guns. He warned us that they would take over the city's crime network. We laughed.

Underworld dons believe they are practically invincible, that nobody can displace them. Occasionally a stranger may rise up in the underworld, but it is very rare for one group to completely take over the underworld. We told Adugodi Sreedhar, 'Their gang may rise from stealing cars to stealing aeroplanes, but they won't take over the underworld.'

We never imagined that his prediction would one day come true.

Ten

We were introduced to Purushottam, a theatre owner in Mandya and DCP Narayan's brother-in-law, through a mutual friend. He was troubled by Jayaraj's view on DCP Narayan in the Rasheed murder case, and spoke to me about it. I assured him that I would arrange for him to meet Jayaraj.

I spoke to Jayaraj about the situation, arguing that, at a time when officers belonging to the backward class were rare, troubling Narayan, who belonged to a backward class, was wrong.

Jayaraj was upset. 'You have lost your mind, spending time with the likes of Lankesh. I don't know of any social justice. According to me there are only two castes: one is us and the other is the police. We have to confront them.'

I finally managed to convince him to meet Purushottam. After talking to him for half an hour, Jayaraj relented, and soon after he left, decided to work on getting bail for the DCP.

The next morning, however, there was a big write-up in the *Indian Express* about Jayaraj. It alleged that Jayaraj had divided Bangalore into thirty-six divisions and distributed them amongst his followers. It also said that lakhs of rupees flowed from shops, hotels and other activities in each division.

Crime reporters are anti-social elements. I say this without malice. They don't attempt to learn the truth, or if they know the truth, they are more interested in glamorising the crime world for young impressionable readers. That article was one such report. Neither Jayaraj nor his followers had divided

Bangalore. Although they were collecting money from illegal trades, they still feared the police.

Just one week prior to the publication of the article, S.N.S. Murthy had taken charge as the commissioner of Bangalore. Although honest and committed, like many IPS officers, he too was unaware of the situation as it existed. He believed the report completely, and arrested Jayaraj.

That morning, we went to Jayaraj's house as we usually did, and found a large battalion of policemen. More than ten jeeps were parked outside. We remained at a distance. At around noon, Jayaraj was taken to Wilson Garden police station. We were told by constables that he would be produced in court the same afternoon. Since the lawyers Devdas, Samba Murthy and Partha were doing the running around, we returned to our room in Shantinagar. But Seetharam Shetty was not one to keep quiet. He pleaded with us to go to court. I opposed this plan. Finally he asked me to stay in the room and left, taking Bachchan with him.

When they had not returned by four in the evening I began to get worried. I made a phone call and found out that Jayaraj had not been produced in court yet. I also learnt that, while in the court, Seetharam Shetty and Bachchan had been taken into custody at gunpoint. It was B.B. Ashok Kumar—famous for having arrested the chain-snatchers who had terrorised Bangalore—who had arrested Shetty and Bachchan.

I was scared the police would 'work' on them. I started looking all over Bangalore for someone who knew Ashok Kumar. Finally, I found Khan in Shivajinagar, who knew the policeman through an acquaintance, Muthanna, an inspector from Coorg in the CoD. At around eight in the evening, I went to Khan and requested him to get Shetty and Bachchan released, since Ashok Kumar had arrested them without a complaint being registered against them.

Usually the police start to work on people after midnight; I had to find out what Ashok Kumar was planning before that. Though there were no complaints against Shetty and Bachchan, it was enough that they were associated with Jayaraj. There was a coconut tree in the Vaiyalikaval station, where Ashok Kumar was sub-inspector, and it had become big news in the underworld when he had tied Srirampura Kitty and others to the tree and worked on their backs.

At ten that night Khan brought news. He had been assured that no one would hurt Bachchan and Shetty as Ashok Kumar felt they were harmless, and also because he had to produce them in court the next day. Still, I felt uneasy.

All three were produced before the court and Section 110 was imposed on them. Section 110 of the Indian Penal Code deals with the regulation of rowdies. Under this clause, arrests can be made even if there have not been any complaints. The tragedy was that not one of them was involved in any activity over which Section 110 could be applied, but police officers use it on several occasions based on newspaper reports.

When Jayaraj was released, he returned with a grim face. The constant smile had vanished. Although former chief minister Gundu Rao and the very powerful Jeevaraj Alva often visited his house, the police had arrested him without any reason. He was not about to listen to reason. He wanted revenge. He sent for me to come immediately as a petition had to be drafted. I was an expert in drafting petitions.

That night Bachchan praised Ashok Kumar and said he had promised the sub-inspector that I would meet him. The next day, with a lot of hesitation, I went to see the cop. He met me at a hotel about a hundred metres from his station.

I was immediately taken by his cultured mannerisms. He said that, since Jayaraj was trying to create a rift in the police force, especially with regard to DCP Narayan whom all of them respected, it was inevitable that he would be arrested. He told me to warn Jayaraj and expressed his displeasure against some police officers who were using Jayaraj. He also said I could contact him any time of the day in case of an emergency.

I went straight to Jayaraj's house after that and advised him to stop attacking the police. He was adamant though, and started shouting at me. 'Has any officer made any money in a just manner? Don't they take money from brothels? We are not as bad as them. If I listen to you I will have to hang myself. If we back out now they will finish us.'

He wanted to call a press meet the next day, at which he planned to attack Ashok Kumar and police commissioner S.N.S. Murthy for having insulted him. I tried my best to dissuade him, but in vain. He held the briefing at Hotel Cauvery Continental the next day and released a press statement that he had me compose.

In the press release, he called S.N.S. Murthy a 'Hundred and Ten Commissioner' because Murthy's own staff had ridiculed him in front of Jayaraj, saying Murthy was fond of Section 110 and would apply it all the time, even in matters concerning insignificant rowdies. He accused the Bangalore police of being more corrupt than the underworld.

All the dailies gave prominence to the news. Jayaraj bought a half-page advertisement in *Kannada Prabha*, and had the press release published. Everyone spoke highly of Jayaraj's daring, and his confidence soared. He was always surrounded by editors and owners of small newspapers and every time he saw me, he would chide, 'At least now stop getting scared of the police.'

There was no reaction from the police to his statement or press conference, but their silence did not seem to me to be helplessness; I felt as if they were preparing for something big. When I told Jayaraj this, he laughed it off. He boasted that no policeman would touch him. But his laughter and daring did not last long. He was arrested again five days after the press meet, and that too in a case in which he was innocent. Srirampura Kitty had lodged a complaint that someone had shot at him on Goodshed Road. Krishnappa was guilty of the crime; he'd shot at Kitty with a country pistol, but the bullet had scraped him without causing any damage.

I have always wondered what would have happened if I had been arrested with Jayaraj. My life would have taken a different turn. The police had barged into Jayaraj's house in Lakkasandra within ten minutes of us leaving.

We had no word of the arrest till the next day. When we were on our way to Jayaraj's house as usual at eleven the next morning, a boy who met us at Akkithimmanahalli gave us the news. Jayaraj, who believed that he would not be arrested because he had journalists on his side, had argued with the police, who had in turn bellowed at him, finally persuading him to go with them.

Everybody—including the police—knew that Jayaraj had nothing to do with the shooting. The police also knew that if Jayaraj had committed the crime, he would not have been sitting at home waiting to be arrested. But Jayaraj's war against the police commissioner, his allegations in several small instances against the police, had driven them to implicate him.

The police had also arrested Samson, Nagaraj, Narayana and his relatives. More than fifteen people were taken in. The only people in the gang who were not arrested were Bachchan, Seetharam Shetty and me. We first thought it was because they did not know where we lived. But later we found out that they had intentionally let us off. One reason was that they knew that we had met Jayaraj only after the Kotwal murder and were not hardened criminals, and secondly, there were no instances of us being cruel to the general public.

A handcuffed and barefoot Jayaraj was paraded on the streets of Bangalore the next day, starting from his *Garibi Hatao* office in Gandhinagar, through Majestic, to Kengeri Gate police station. We were deeply hurt as we stood at Mysore Bank Circle and watched him. Jayaraj's face was a mixture of pain and dignity. He walked with heavy steps.

It was the first time in the history of Bangalore that an underworld don of his stature was treated like this. Usually, only small-time rowdies were paraded through the city. Anyone could tell that the police were determined to crush Jayaraj.

The way the police system works is strange. Yet, if the system did not exist for even one day, it is unimaginable what would happen. There is a saying about the police: you shouldn't be friends with them, nor should you be enemies with them. I don't think it's possible to describe the police system better than this. I, who have been troubled by the police without any reason, know very clearly that they not only trouble me, but also my enemy. I feel angry when they torment me, but when they go after my enemies, I feel happy. While dealing with this system, one has to be extremely cautious. This applies to both those in the underworld and commoners.

Jayaraj had not understood this. When he first lent support to the lawyers in their battle against DCP Narayan, a few police officials had encouraged him. But the same officials did not utter a word when Jayaraj was arrested in a case he had nothing to do with. That is where the contradiction lies. However much police officers support a rowdy, when a crack officer stands against him, no one will protest.

That day, when he was being taken in a procession, I felt it foretold Jayaraj's last journey.

The members of his family kept me updated on what was happening. Jayaraj had gone on strike at the station, refusing to eat. Finally, several officials convinced him that, while they knew the commissioner was wrong, they could do nothing about it, and they forced him to eat. Though the papers had carried the news of his arrest, he was not produced in court, but was instead taken to a magistrate's house and then into police custody. The next day when he was produced in court, lawyer Devdas' bail application was rejected. Jayaraj went to jail. The police began to harass his family members and his associates.

Except for the three of us.

Not only did they not trouble us, they did not even search for us. Rumours began to make the rounds in the underworld. Even our friends started asking, 'Why are the police not arresting you?'

We began to think: if Jayaraj gets to hear of this, how will he react?

It was the lawyer Devdas who picked up the rumour, dressed it up, added feathers to it, blew life into it and let it fly high.

I knew that Jayaraj's weakness was his strange fear of the court, mainly because he was illiterate. Lawyers used this to keep him quiet. The top lawyers ran their cases however they wanted. If the case was complicated, there was money to be made. Devdas was no exception. The fact that the prosecution had noted the wrong blood group for Kotwal could have gotten the case dismissed very soon, but he never brought it to the notice of the court.

This time, although Jayaraj was innocent in the case, he did not get bail although a month had passed. Since there was no one apart from Jayaraj's elder brother Jayadev to do the running around, we offered our services. We could also get the latest updates on the case this way.

We went to Devadas' office opposite Mount Carmel College in Vasanth Nagar. It was impressive. He sat in a large room, from where he could watch over the eight juniors working for him. We waited for half an hour before we were asked to go in. Devdas was usually nice to me, but that day he seemed aloof.

'What?' he asked, looking up at us.

'What happened to the bail, Sir?'

'What bail?'

'Sir, Jayaraj's bail . . .'

'Oh that! Why do you want to know?'

'What are you saying, Sir? What's wrong in asking when my boss will get bail?' I said with a mixture of anger and surprise.

He looked at me for some time without speaking. Then, 'I think you are asking this to give information to someone,' he said, glancing at all the juniors.

I was stunned. 'Inform whom?'

'Who else? Police!'

I could not control my anger. The allegation Devdas was making was so ridiculous, my lips began to tremble.

'What information shall I give, Sir? Don't they know that Jayaraj's house is in Wilson Garden? Don't they know that you are his lawyer? Should I tell them that he runs a newspaper? Are the newspapers not reporting on his other businesses every day? So do I need to tell them when his bail hearing is . . .?'

As I continued, all his juniors started laughing. They realised the truth in what I was saying.

Devdas also laughed aloud and, after glancing at his juniors again, said, 'What you say is true, what is there that is not known about Jayaraj? It is not me who is questioning you . . . Nobody knows why the police are not touching you . . .' Then he said the bail would be granted in two weeks.

That night we could not sleep. We thought someone had accused us of being informants. We cursed the police for arresting the entire group and not even looking for us. The next day we met Jayaraj's elder brother Jayadev. We told him about what had happened in Devdas' office and expressed our anguish. He told us not to worry about it. But in two days, rumours began to course through the city. Someone said that Devdas had sent us out of his office after condemning us as informants. We decided to stay quiet till Jayaraj's release was secured and then speak up.

Jayaraj was denied bail. The police filed case after case against him. They would go to the judge's chamber and beg him not to give Jayaraj bail. They made the judges believe that if Jayaraj were released he would be dangerous to the public.

Then a group of people who ran the small newspapers planned something new. They asked Harbhajan Singh, president of the 'Association of Small Papers of India' to organise a function in New Delhi and invite Jayaraj, who was the president of the Karnataka unit, as a special guest. Before going to jail, Jayaraj had invited Harbhajan Singh and others for dinner and given them money and lavish gifts. Now it was their turn to repay him. A convention was scheduled and Rajiv Gandhi was invited as the chief guest. Jayaraj was given special bail for three days to attend the ceremony. He was to go to Delhi the day of his release, attend the convention and return to the court the next day, from where he would be taken back to jail.

Jayaraj planned to meet a few ministers from Karnataka to persuade them to secure his release. He also felt that once he'd got temporary bail, it would not be difficult to get permanent bail.

By then it had been two months since Jayaraj had gone to jail. We asked the lawyer Vardhamanayya—who met Jayaraj every day—to convince him to meet a few police officials after his return from Delhi. He did not agree to our suggestion. If Jayaraj was angry with the police, Vardhamanayya was livid with the entire world. Not only did he not pass on our suggestion to Jayaraj, he threatened that if we passed it on, the rumour that Devdas had spread alleging that we were police informants would be proved true. We kept quiet.

Jayaraj was released and he went to Delhi. We planned to meet him upon his return. That night we heard that Gandhi Bazaar Chandru was looking for us. We went to his house after midnight. He recounted what he'd heard that afternoon: there was going to be an attack on Jayaraj the following night. Not an ordinary attack, but a '302', murder. Srirampura Kitty had said this to a mechanic, who in turned relayed it to Chandru.

Chandru gave us one more piece of information. He said that when he had not found us, he had gone to Jayaraj's house at eleven in the night to tell the others about the attack. Jayaraj's younger brother, Ramesh, had heard what Chandru had to say, and then said, 'Don't tell this to Sreedhar on any account.' When a surprised Chandru asked him why, he had said, 'Don't you know? He is now a police informant. That means he must be in the good books of the enemy gang also.'

Chandru knew we were genuinely concerned about Jayaraj and he said, 'Don't listen to those fellows. Let us first get him back safely and then we will make him take these guys to task.'

We ignored Ramesh's remarks and the next evening went to the airport with a gang of boys. Ramesh had also brought a large group. I borrowed a cigarette from Bachchan and went to Ramesh and asked him, casually lighting my cigarette, 'Have you asked all the boys to keep watch?'

He had thought that, after what he'd said to Chandru, I wouldn't dare come to the airport. He was shocked. He just nodded and bowed his head. Bachchan, Seetharam Shetty, Chandru and I stood at one end of the waiting area. Jayadev, Ramesh and the others stood at the other. Two men stood at a distance and watched us curiously. We were expecting Kitty, Pushpa, Rajendra and the others. Along with them, we expected some new boys, and hence I was very suspicious of the two strangers. I did not want to make the others anxious, so I stayed silent.

It was a year-and-a-half before I became acquainted with those two strangers: Muthappa Rai and Satish Shetty. I found out later that they thought only Jayaraj's family would come to pick him up. When they saw all of us, they called off the operation they'd been planning.

Jayaraj landed at around nine in the night. He was happy to see us. He called me and made me sit next to him in his car. 'Why have so many come?' he asked curiously. I told him about the rumour. His eyes flashed. 'You think they would dare?' he asked.

'Shouldn't we be careful, Sir?'

'Raghu and Rao visited jail twice ... Kumar will not be behind this ... no?' he said, talking to himself.

On our way home, there were cars in the front and at the back, as well as seven to eight motorbikes. The men wanting to kill Jayaraj could not take the risk, and nothing happened on the road.

When we reached Jayaraj's home, he began talking about bail. His entire family gathered around him. I whispered in his ear that I wanted to speak with him confidentially. He sent everyone out.

I told him about our conversation with Devdas, and what Ramesh had said to Chandru.

'I have never addressed you as *"anna"*, but you really are like my elder brother. When I was with you at the hospital, I developed that strong feeling. Now what can I say about such cheap allegations? Perhaps some people might suspect that I am meeting Shivaram. I am telling you the truth: I have neither met Shivaram nor any other police officer.'

When I finished I had tears in my eyes.

Though Jayaraj grew up in a tough atmosphere, he was still very sensitive. He did not have that cold-blooded cruelty that Kotwal did. He put his hand on mine and said, 'Sreedhar, this is very common in this field. I also heard these rumours. Everybody is wondering why you have not been arrested ... But maybe Shivaram has a good impression about you ... what can we do about it? Don't I know that even before you came to us, you were on good terms with them? Don't worry about all this. Whatever they say, I know what you really are. All will be well after I come out.'

Then as I was sitting there, he left the room. After five minutes Sampangiramanagar Jagadish came to me and said, '*Anna* scolded Ramesh. He said, "Do you realise what would have happened if they had not finished Kotwal". He warned him strictly not to talk like that again.'

We were at Jayaraj's house till eleven-thirty, and when we left, he told me again not to worry about the rumours. Relieved that he believed us, we told him we would send a few boys to the court and left.

The next day, we asked Chandru to go into the court hall and stood at a distance. At eleven o'clock Jayaraj arrived and was sent to judicial custody. At eleven-thirty, Jayaraj left court in his white Ambassador to go to jail. Chandru and another boy followed on their motorbike and Jayaraj signalled them to stop. He was suspicious that the police might nab anyone following him.

Chandru came back to me and said that, even in court, Jayaraj had said several times, 'Tell Sreedhar not to feel bad.'

'Whatever anyone says, at least he trusts you,' Chandru said, and went to work.

We went to see an English film and, in the evening, walked around MG Road and Brigade Road. It was around eight when we met Sampangiramnagar Jagadish who brought disturbing news.

Jayaraj had been attacked in front of the jail.

He said that when Jayaraj had stepped out of the car and was about to enter the jail Rajendra, Kitty, Mahadeva, Sakkare, Manibharathi and others had arrived in another car and attacked him. They shot at him and also hurled bombs.

Nobody knew what Jayaraj's condition was, he said; he'd been admitted into Victoria Hospital. Since we'd spent so much time there, I knew many of the staff members. I went to the hospital. Hundreds of boys had gathered there. Jayaraj's brother Ramesh and his gang heckled us. I ignored them and, having sought the help of a doctor, went in straight to the emergency ward. Jayaraj's head and hand were bandaged. He was sedated, but opened his eyes slightly. I went and stood near him. He stared at me.

'Who attacked you, Sir?' I bent down and whispered in his ear.

With great difficulty he whispered, 'Bastards . . . not now . . . would all have run out of town . . . come after two days.'

My heart felt heavy and I did not want to leave, but it was not possible to stay on.

A year-and-a-half later, Rajendra described that attack to me. A man named Loka, who had been convicted in connection with the Vijayanagar Prabha murder case, was in jail at the same time as Pushpa, Kurubara Pete Raja and the others. He knew Muthappa Rai and, after Jayaraj was jailed, Loka introduced Muthappa Rai to Pushpa and Rajendra.

Muthappa Rai had connections with the Bombay underworld. Though he had no personal enmity against Jayaraj, he decided to support Pushpa and Rajendra so he would gain notoriety in Bangalore. He also helped them financially. They had initially planned to attack Jayaraj at the airport, but seeing such a large crowd of his followers, they had decided against it.

The next morning they met in front of Maharani's College—opposite the jail—where Kitty, Rajendra, Pushpa, Mahadeva,

Manibharathi, Sakkare and Isha had assembled. Each one of them was an expert assassin.

Just ten minutes before Jayaraj reached the jail, Oil Kumar's men Raghu and Rao had come up to the group and said that their boss had sent word not to touch Jayaraj in front of the jail. It was only then that Rajendra and Pushpa realised that Kumar was involved in the scheme as well. They ignored Kumar's words and remained seated in their Ambassador, waiting for Jayaraj. They had begun to argue about whether the attack should proceed as planned when Jayaraj's car rumbled into the jail premises and stopped. Their car followed.

Pushpa had gone into the college to meet someone, thinking there was time for Jayaraj to arrive. However, Rajendra was there, and he knew Jayaraj's habits: when Jayaraj got down from the car, he would stand, comb his hair, pull up his pant, glance all around and then walk ahead. He was such a fool; though we had cautioned him about the plan to attack him the previous day, he got out of the car and stopped to comb his hair . . .

Rajendra and the gang got out of the car and charged at Jayaraj, screaming. Though Jayaraj was stocky, he was very quick. As soon as he saw the gang, he ran towards the small gate which opened into the jail. But his loose pants were a hindrance and he tripped. By then Rajendra had come up to him. He hit him with force on his head and his back. Jayaraj got up in a flash and caught hold of Rajendra's machete. He gripped the weapon with such force that it bent. According to Rajendra, if Isha had not come up and stabbed Jayaraj in the back, Jayaraj would have snatched away the machete and struck Rajendra.

Kitty was standing at a distance, issuing instructions: 'Hit him on the head . . . hit him on the head.' Manibharathi and Sakkare had him covered.

Jayaraj's brother Jayadev screamed at the police, 'Shoot . . . shoot!' One sentry raised his rifle but did not fire.

Jayaraj, though injured, was still able to fight back.

Manibharathi set off a hand bomb. Yet, Jayaraj did not fall. Rajendra dropped his machete and fired a shot. Since he had no experience with guns, the impact of the shot caused the weapon to fall from his hand.

Jayaraj became rattled when he heard the gunshot. He managed to escape the men and slipped inside the jail. The gang escaped in the car they had come in. The police arrived half an hour later and admitted Jayaraj to Victoria Hospital. They claimed that the gun, which had slipped from Rajendra's hand, belonged to Jayaraj and filed a case against him. All those who had attacked Jayaraj were free to move about the city—not a single man was arrested. The police were taking revenge against Jayaraj for his role in sending DCP Narayan to jail.

Two days after the attack, I visited Jayaraj in hospital again. Though the bandages were still on, he was able to move about. He was able to talk normally as well. He asked me to find out if Kumar had had a hand in the attack, and also to track Kitty, Rajendra and Pushpa's movements. We became dispirited by the way the police supported our enemies. With the state of affairs being what it was, far from being able to keep track of our enemies, it was tortuous just trying not to get caught.

After ten days, Jayaraj went back to jail. There seemed to be indications that he would get bail. Four days later, Oil Kumar got all Jayaraj's enemies together and raided the don's oil *addas*. We were shocked: we'd never imagined that Kumar would ever declare open war against Jayaraj. Also, while we knew that Jayaraj had several oil sheds under his control, we had little knowledge about where they were located.

Jayaraj called us to jail and told us to do the 'rounds' against Kumar. He said Sampangiramanagar Jagadish would bear all the expenses. Seetharam Shetty did not like it, but agreed. Bachchan wanted to barge into all of Kumar's *addas*. He gathered twenty boys for this purpose. Jagadish, however, said he could not afford to spend that much money. We did not know any other way of getting the funds and decided to meet

Jayaraj again to convince him to arrange the money. By then, though, the police transferred him to the Mysore jail. We were crestfallen.

But there was one more group committed to Jayaraj: Anil, Kisan, Kalapathar and others led by Station Shekhar, the son of Acharappa, who had once ruled Majestic. We ran into Shekhar and Kalapathar at Taj Hotel in Shivajinagar. We saw that all of them had longs and bombs. The group was in the mood for a fight.

Station Shekhar was tall, dark and strong. His father Acharappa ran a travel agency near City Railway Station, hence the name Station Shekhar. The travel business was highly competitive at the time. There are several auto-rickshaws that stand at railway stations and bus stands to pick up tourists who come to Bangalore. They compete with each other to get passengers. The travel agency that Station Shekhar ran used to do very well.

Manibharathi and Sakkare often fought with Shekhar, but Kalapathar always followed him around like a shadow. When a rival gangster Rajendra began to trouble him, Shekhar killed him—in the middle of the day, in front of the railway station in the presence of thousands of people. After that he joined the list of dreaded dons.

That afternoon we had lunch with him and his boys. They knew all the *addas* that Kitty visited in Srirampura. Shekhar insisted that we had to take revenge for the attack on Jayaraj and asked us to support them. We tried to excuse ourselves saying the police were keeping an eye on us and that we had to be very careful. They insisted that they would not give out our names and that there was no need to even be seen. We said we would meet them after a couple of days and left.

The next day there was a fierce fight between Kitty's and Shekhar's gangs.

It was like how gang wars are depicted in films. The two groups faced each other less than fifty feet apart and began to hurl soda bottles at each other. They flashed their swords and stepped forward ten feet and then withdrew twenty feet. It was highly dramatic. Finally, Kitty threw two bombs at Shekhar's gang. Just then a BTS bus passed by. The bomb exploded and the windows of the bus shattered. People screamed and ran.

Up until then, the Bangalore police had only one aim: to finish Jayaraj's gang. But now, they focused on Station Shekhar and his gang.

Usually, rowdies who hide from the police lose their wits. They start to think that, because they are in hiding, they may as well do a few more deals. Station Shekhar was no different. He started rushing in everywhere. He and his boys started threatening his enemies. They raided clubs, bars, cabarets, oil *addas* and brothels. One of the cabaret joints they pillaged was on MG Road. There was a rumour that the owner was related to the then assistant commissioner of police Iqbal, and we heard that Shekhar assaulted the cabaret dancers in front of the owner.

That cabaret was within the Cubbon Park police station limits and B.B. Ashok Kumar was the sub-inspector there. Usually rowdies were scared even to walk in the areas that came under Ashok Kumar's jurisdiction, and we felt Shekhar should have refrained from doing anything there. He did not keep quiet even after that. He moved all over Bangalore, terrorising the city.

Then one day the news was in all the papers: Station Shekhar had died in a 'police encounter'. Ashok Kumar had shot him. The papers reported that Shekhar had tried to assault the policemen who had gone to arrest him, and so the cops had opened fire. But the truth was that the police had held Shekhar's man Kalapathar the previous night. Only he knew where Shekhar lived, and he had no choice but to show them. They took Kalapathar there and made him call Shekhar. When Shekhar opened the door, the policemen made Kalapathar stand outside and three sub-inspectors walked in.

Ten minutes later, Kalapathar heard a gunshot.

The next day a mammoth crowd gathered in front of

Shekhar's house. It looked like the situation might get out of hand, and the police was sure to be attacked. This had happened ten years before, when Vinayaka Bala had died in lock-up. At that time, the police was attacked with razors and soda bottles, and it looked like something similar was about to happen.

Somehow the Kengeri station sub-inspector K.V.K. Reddy, under whose jurisdiction Shekhar's house was located, managed to bring the situation under control.

Jayaraj later made Shekhar's wife file a case against the police. She submitted an application to the court asking them to hand over the case to the CBI as she had no faith in the state police.

Since the CBI had arrested DCP Narayan, the Bangalore police were nervous of their intervention. The CBI, on their part, was angry with the way the Bangalore police had behaved in the DCP Narayan case, and hence hoped that Shekhar's case would come to them. The lawyer Vardhamanayya was working day and night to make it happen. However, we were worried that, in the Jayaraj–police face-off, which had now intensified, we would get into trouble. We decided to convince Jayaraj not to go against the police. Whatever hatred Jayaraj had against the police, I knew he craved a luxurious life. He wanted his two pegs of Scotch every day and lots of non-vegetarian food; he wanted women. Though he claimed that he was only thirty-eight, everybody knew that he was closer to forty-five. I wanted to convince him not to think only of the short-term, but to think calmly about how he would live in the future. To this end, Seetharam Shetty, Bachchan and I went to Mysore to meet him.

At ten in the morning, we headed to the jail ward of Krishnarajendra Hospital, which is where Jayaraj had been interred. When we reached, there was a big crowd outside. Filled with anxiety, we parked our motorbikes. We saw that there were four or five police jeeps parked there as well. Our hearts started beating wildly. Just then we saw Jayaraj's elder brother Jayadev. We went up to him. His expression serious, he looked at us but didn't say a word.

We asked him what had happened. Sarcastically, he said, 'You still don't know? Jayaraj was attacked at seven in the morning.'

I held his hand and asked with fear, 'Who did it? What happened?'

He shook off my hand and said, 'What ... someone from their gang ... I can't talk now.'

It was evident he did not want to talk to us. Yet, I asked, 'Where is *Anna* now?'

'Where else, in jail,' he said.

'Can we go and see him?' I asked, my voice almost failing me.

'Whatever you wish,' he said and walked away.

As we were leaving, we saw Appayya, who had been bringing food to Jayaraj from the time I'd been jailed with him. Appayya was a lifer when Jayaraj was in jail, and after his release, he had stayed on at Jayaraj's house as a worker. Jayaraj had got him married and both he and his wife worked for him.

As soon as we saw him we felt relieved that there was someone who could give us news. We took him to a hotel and got all the information from him. At around three in the morning, he said, there was gunfire through the doors and windows of Jayaraj's ward. The police on guard had hid in the corner, scared. Luckily Jayaraj had been sleeping under the cot, and not on it. Five or six bullets fired through the window had struck the cot.

After the attack in front of the Bangalore Central Jail, Jayaraj always hid bombs with him. He threw two at the door and window. They were powerful, and the door was completely blown to bits. The attackers had run away, screaming.

Jayaraj had chased them with bombs in both his hands, swearing, '*Thoo ... gaandu sule makkalaa*. You want to attack me when I am inside ... if you are born of fathers come and face me when I come out ...'

By the time the police had come, he had gotten rid of the bombs. The police had scratched their heads and moaned, 'We are in trouble because of you,' and shifted him to the jail.

'It's all that Kumar's doing, Sir,' Appayya said.

We went to the jail. As soon as we wrote down our details in the register, Samson came up to us. It had been only half an hour since Jayaraj had come there, and Samson did not know all the details. 'Isn't all this common? Such things have been happening for the last fifteen years and we have managed,' he said casually, and then asked me, 'Sreedhar, you are brave and more intelligent than him. Can you not show a way to get rid of Kumar?'

'If the fight with the police is scaled down, we can finish Kumar in twenty-four hours,' I said.

'You speak to Jayaraj, I will call him,' he said and went in.

After five minutes he returned looking upset. 'Jayaraj says he cannot come now. Maybe his mood is not all right. Come back later.'

Immediately we realised that Jayaraj suspected we were connected with the attack. It was not difficult for us to guess that Jayaraj thought we'd been sent to find out the effect of the attack. That is why he had not come out to meet us. Already people around Jayaraj had suspicions about us. Now, the fact that we had visited the spot on the day of the attack would strengthen those suspicions. We knew nobody would believe it was a coincidence.

For a week we worried about it. We could not join Pushpa and Rajendra, who had got support from Kumar. And, on the other hand, Jayaraj suspected that we had joined hands with the enemy. On top of all this, we were scared of the police: for them we would always be part of Jayaraj's gang.

Because Jayaraj had started suspecting us, we stopped going to his house and his elder brother's house. Sampangiramanagar Jagadish had faith in us, but the Jayaraj gang core group did not take him seriously.

Around this time, I met with the accident that I mentioned earlier. I was never interested in riding, but Bachchan insisted that it would be good for me to start. I had just learnt to ride a motorbike and was speeding across a road when a car hit me. It drove away without stopping. I could not tell the number on its plates. I was admitted to a nursing home for an operation. After two days, a large man visited me and said it was his car that had hit me. After learning who he had hit, he had searched for me in all the nursing homes and finally just found me. He said he would pay the charges for the operation. We had spent about six thousand rupees, but we said it was fifteen thousand. He gave us the money without saying a word. Being a rowdy had its benefits.

The accident left me limping for some time.

One day I met Somanna of Maddur, who was a childhood friend of Jayaraj. I told him about the stand Jayaraj had taken against us. He said he would meet me in a week's time. When he did, he said he'd visited Jayaraj and argued on our behalf. Jayaraj had said he was unhappy about what had happened with us and had called us to meet him.

I knew Jayaraj never revealed what was going on in his mind. Though Somanna said Jayaraj believed in us because the plan he'd made with me to finish Kumar had not become public even after one year, I did not fully believe him. I had not forgotten Kurubara Pete Raja's murder. I knew that nothing stopped him. Even though the police were after him, Jayaraj refused to sit quiet in jail. He sent Anil to bomb the Padma Recreation Club, which was always crowded. When Anil threw the bomb there, at around eight in the night, it fell on one side and then exploded, so luckily no one died. If the bomb had fallen at a slightly different place, at least ten people would have died.

He also orchestrated the death of one of Jedarahalli Krishnappa's boys. Iliyas and Motte (Egg) Kanna had gone out for lunch. After eating, Iliyas kick-started his bike, which immediately exploded, blowing Iliyas to pieces.

Bachchan felt we should meet Jayaraj and explain everything to him and set right things. I did not agree, so we sent Chandru and Viji as emissaries. They met Jayaraj and came back satisfied. 'Forget what his family says, he is very affectionate towards you,' said Chandru. Only after this did we go to Mysore. This time Seetharam Shetty did not come with us. I felt he was distancing himself from the Jayaraj camp.

After we entered the jail, Samson came and spoke to us. The bars separating jail inmates and visitors were fitted with a thin mesh, which had not been there earlier. Jayaraj then came and spoke to us. Though he was smiling, I felt the old affection was missing.

He asked about Muthappa Rai and we said we knew nothing about him. Jayaraj said it was he who had introduced the Bombay boys to Oil Kumar. He should be finished before he gains fame, he said.

Instead of worrying about a non-entity like Muthappa Rai, it would be better to focus on stopping this enmity with the police and things would then set themselves right on their own, was my opinion.

He stared at me and asked, 'So what shall we do now?' He was curious about my response.

I said that since things had gotten so out of hand with the police, any attempt his gang made on anyone would lead to serious consequences. The best thing for him to do at this point, I suggested, was to try and get bail as early as possible and to set right his relationship with the police through Jeevaraj Alva and others.

He nodded and asked us to come again in the evening.

I thought that, though he had not shown us the usual affection, since I had explained our thoughts clearly, he would change his mind. When we returned to the jail in the evening, he agreed that I was right. He asked me to discuss the hurdles to getting bail, which I did.

Before leaving, I touched his fingers, which were resting on the bars, and said, 'Please do not put us in a difficult position by testing our loyalty. Please understand that we are not doing anything, even a small thing, against you.'

'No, Sreedhar,' he answered. 'Don't worry. All will be well after I come out ... go see Jayadev.' He always used the respectful plural to address me and for the first time he now used the familiar singular. I felt relieved, thinking his old affection had returned.

But three days later, when I went to see Jayadev, something occurred which made us never want to see Jayaraj again.

Eleven

I will never forget that day.

Fame in the underworld means making friends with death. It is always ready to pounce on you, and even a second's carelessness will allow it to do its duty. That does not mean we are not ever relaxed, but it does mean we are always aware of the possibility of danger. However, no matter how careful one is, since your enemy is putting as much care into a scheme, sometimes your calculations can go wrong. Years later, Muthappa Rai's men would shoot at the car I in which I was travelling; at other times, I missed being attacked because I happened to be elsewhere; but never have I been so close to death as I was that day.

When we went to meet Jayadev at four in the evening, he was not home. We were told he would return by seven o'clock. We went to the NIMHANS hospital compound near his house, sat under a tree and spent time eating groundnuts. We were in a philosophical mood and very happy; for three hours we did not utter a word about crime or the underworld.

Although Bachchan has studied only till the seventh standard, his intellectual capacity is very high, and I enjoyed discussing everything with him, from technical problems to the latest scientific invention, from problems of the mentally ill, to the atrocities committed the world over.

By the time we went back, Jayadev was waiting for us. As soon as we knocked on the door he opened it, came out, started the scooter he had parked in the front and said, 'Come, let's go to our bar.'

Jayaraj's younger brother Ramesh had a bar in Wilson Garden. We had often passed it, but had never gone in. There was a cinema hall diagonally opposite it, and the small lane was always crowded. When we reached, four boys were sitting on a compound wall next to the bar. Two of them greeted us as soon as we parked the bike, but one of them turned away. One boy stared at us, which irritated me. Then I realised they might be suspicious since they were all Ramesh's boys, and he was the first person to openly accuse us of scheming against Jayaraj.

The small bar, which had about eight tables, was filled with cigarette smoke and music was playing loudly. We sat down in a corner.

We had spoken to our lawyer Vardhamanayya two days ago about arranging a compromise between Jayaraj and the police. Vardhamanayya's entire existence depended upon making Jayaraj file case after case against the police, so though he agreed that Jayaraj should come out on bail at the earliest, he was not agreeable to a compromise with the police. We'd had a heated argument about it. Finally Vardhamanayya had said, 'I have no objection; you talk to Jayaraj.' We were sure he would go to Mysore the next day and wrongly advise Jayaraj. We shared this anxiety with Jayadev.

By then drinks were served. Usually I don't drink more than a peg, but this time, while we were talking, I was drinking whisky like water. Bachchan was very careful. At one stage he even said, 'You cannot handle it, why are you drinking so much?'

Jayadev said, 'Let him drink, Bachchan. With whom else can he drink but us?'

Even then Bachchan kept signalling me to stop, but I had already crossed the limit of reading those signs. Jayadev was not saying much; he just listened, slowly sipping his drink. I said there were three things in which Jayaraj had to take a step back. One, he must stop interfering in the DCP Narayan case. Second, he should take back the application he had submitted demanding a CBI inquiry against Ashok Kumar and others in connection with Station Shekhar's encounter death. And third, he must take back the application he had got the family of a thief to file against his death in lock-up in Kengeri.

I insisted repeatedly that we were very fond of Jayaraj and that I had made a mistake in introducing Vardhamanayya to him. Jayaraj was now unnecessarily taking on the police.

Jayadev stared at me for some time and then finally asked, biting his lips, 'Did you meet Shivaram?'

The coldness with which he asked the question made me shudder. 'You still believe that I am his informant? I swear on my wife and kids, I was never an informant . . .'

'No Sir, I am not saying you are an informant, I just casually asked if you met them . . . since you are close to Shivaram and Ashok Kumar.'

'Who said Ashok Kumar is close to me? I have seen his face only once.'

'Whatever anyone says, can they take anything from Jayaraj? He did not care for Devaraj Urs, how can these Shivarams and Ashok Kumars matter?'

The manner in which he was talking made me uneasy. Although he suspected that I had regular contact with Shivaram and Ashok Kumar, he abused and insulted them. The fact that he was speaking so frankly worried me: did he think I would not tell them—or did he feel that I would never see them again? I put away this thought because I thought it was impossible that Jayaraj's family would harm me.

Jayadev said he would be back soon and went out.

I told Bachchan I was worried.

'Then why are you drinking so much? And don't advise them—he is also drunk and talking rubbish. Let us just have a good conversation and leave,' Bachchan said.

But it was not that easy to leave.

Jayadev did not come back for a long time. Ten minutes after he left, a retired military man whom we had seen outside came to talk to us. He ordered drinks and talked to us for more than half an hour. There was no way we could leave.

When Jayadev finally returned we tried to leave, but he stopped us, asking, 'Why should you go; is this not your home?'

When we tried to say that the police were catching people if they were out late, he began to taunt us and abuse the police using vulgar language.

We continued our meaningless conversation with the military man, because we were hesitant to get up and say outright that we wanted to leave. The talk turned to Jayaraj.

'Have you seen Jayaraj's hand?' Jayadev asked.

I thought he was talking about his strength and said, 'What is there to talk about! He is invincible.'

'Not that, Sir. Have you seen the lines on his palm?'

'No, I am not interested in palmistry.'

'Whoever sees his palm tells him not to show his hand to anyone. Do you know why? Because from his birth, they have said he is in danger. But nobody can do anything to him. He is a great devotee.'

'Yes Sir, nothing is greater than devotion. It saves you from all dangers.'

'I know, Sir, I know you don't believe in God. That is why you are scared of the police. But look at Jayaraj—he does not worry about anyone. Even in jail he lives like a king. It is his devotion that protects him. People have attacked him many times, has anything happened? No. Even now, we know they are planning. But what will happen to them? Like Kotwal, their bodies will disappear.'

By then it was eleven o'clock and we'd had five or six pegs. Although deep down I was feeling nervous and helpless, I was also tipsy. Jayadev, who'd had a lot to drink before going out, started downing drinks even faster. He also began to ramble.

Bachchan got up to leave. 'Get up, enough is enough. Let's go,' he said.

Jayadev tried forcing him to stay, but Bachchan insisted. 'I usually sleep at ten,' he said, and pulled me up by my hand.

I stood up slowly, because I was high.

Jayadev followed us saying we should meet again and talk.

We came out of the bar and Bachchan took the bike off the stand. Near the compound wall there was now a large group of boys standing next to a matador van and four or five motorbikes.

I stared at the group for a few seconds. Ramesh was also amidst them, but he did not look at me.

Jayadev stood at the bar entrance and held my hand. 'Go carefully, Sir—you are drunk. If someone drunk like you were to hit you at a crossing, it will be a problem. I remember all that you have said,' he continued. 'I will talk to Vardhamanayya, and I will meet Devdas. I will tell Jayaraj to take back all the cases he has filed against the police. If he does not agree, you are there . . . he will not go against your advice.'

Bachchan looked down at the bike and said, 'Tyre is punctured.'

Jayadev called a young boy Shivu who said he knew where it could be fixed, and that he would go with us.

We bid goodbye to Jayadev saying we would meet him the next day, and went with Shivu. We took a small lane to the left of the bar and then turned right. The main road was about three hundred feet away.

Since I had not yet completely recovered from my accident, I was limping. Suddenly the street lights went off and it became dark. Bachchan said, 'It is difficult to push this bike, let me start it and then push.' He tried to kick-start it four or five times, but the engine would not fire. Bachchan bent down and checked the bike. 'Sreedhar, danger,' he said. 'Someone has removed the plug wire.'

Bachchan's words still ring in my ears. It was like a voice from a vacuum. Time stood still. Somewhere, a car started.

It was not possible to run.

Our death was certain. Nobody could prevent it.

It is now many years since that night, and most of my nightmares are of what happened! It is impossible for me to express in words what I felt from the second we found out our motorbike had been tampered with, till we escaped.

When Bachchan said, 'Sreedhar, danger. Someone has removed the plug wire', I immediately lost my high. I became fully alert.

Shivu's presence didn't register with Bachchan at that point. When he stood up and looked at me, he seemed more anxious than afraid.

We were both physically strong, but my accident meant I was unable to even walk properly. There was no way I could run. Also, we did not have the two machetes we usually carried with us in our bag. Before we'd left home, I'd picked up the bag, but Bachchan had said, 'We are going to our boss' brother's house. Why the bag?'

It was now midnight. I said, 'Bachchan, you run to the police station.'

The police station was two furlongs from where we stood. I knew Bachchan could run fast, especially under the circumstances. But Bachchan said, 'Let us go to the bar again.' Since we had not been attacked on the small lane, we were confident the gang would not attack us on the main road, which also had lights.

We talked as Bachchan pushed the bike and I limped next to him. Shivu walked beside us as if he could not hear us. When we reached the main road, we saw that the lights were still on in the bar. A few cars and motorbikes were parked outside.

I whispered, 'Bachchan, I will stay in the bar. If they attack, I will fight with whatever I can lay my hands on. You run to the station. Both of us should not get caught.'

Sub-inspector B.K. Shivaram was in that station, and I thought that if the gang knew Bachchan had gone there, they would not attack me either.

But Bachchan said, 'Just be quiet, don't talk nonsense, I am not going without you.'

I've never heard of someone responding like this in my entire fifteen-year life in the underworld. Usually, when one knows there is going to be an attack and that it is not possible to retaliate, the body acts on its own and runs. Just two months before, when the Kitty gang attacked Balaram, his boys had scattered. When Seetharam Shetty attacked Rajendra, and when Rajendra attacked Shetty, when Kote attacked Nagaraja, when Muthappa Rai's gang attacked Mysore Ganesh, in all these instances, the associates had run away. I've known instances when a man who is with as many as four of his associates has been attacked and they've all run away to save their lives.

But that day, with death staring in our face, my companion did not run away. And, although I was facing an assault, I wanted him to escape.

We went back to the bar. Jayadev was still standing at the door, smoking with his military friend. We passed Ramesh and his gang and went up to Jayadev. As soon as they saw us the entire group was shocked. Everybody started looking at us in surprise. I went and held both of Jayadev's hands very tight. His expression did not change. With the pretence of innocence, he asked, 'What Sir, what happened? Didn't you get the puncture guy?'

I did not speak but stared at him. There were two police constables standing outside the theatre and that gave me courage. As I stared at Jayadev's expressionless face, the fear and anxiety in me was replaced with anger.

The way he'd encouraged me to drink more, the way he'd abused the police officers although suspecting that I was in touch with them, the way he'd made us sit in the bar while he went out and planned the attack—all this flashed through my mind. 'Remember one thing Jayadev. I have not committed any wrong against *Anna*. I swear on my family. I didn't think you would resort to this . . .'

'Why, what happened? Why are you talking like this?' he said, trying his best to free his hands. I had decided that, although he was not likely to attack me there, in case he did dare to do so, I would give him a kick in his groin and kill him. Hence I held his hands in an iron grip.

By then Bachchan, who was bent over the bike, managed to fix the adaptor and kick-started it in one go. He called out to me, 'Come and sit, Sreedhar.'

I knew it was not possible to ride a bike with a punctured tyre, so I said, 'No, let these people drop us.'

'Just come and sit,' Bachchan said and put it in first gear. I sat on the bike.

Now it was Jayadev's turn to hold my hand. He came behind me saying, 'Sir, don't panic . . .'

I put my hand on his chest and pushed him away, saying, 'We are going, Sir. Good night.'

As we took off on the bike, we heard Ramesh and his gang start the van. We rode faster than a bike with new tyres and reached the police station. When we stopped outside the station, the van turned on to another road. We knew that Ramesh and his gang would think we would go inside and lodge a complaint. We stayed outside the police station for a while, and then returned to our room.

Before going any further with my story, I should tell you what had happened in Jayadev's camp that night. We learned the details six months after the incident.

That day, after our first visit to Jayadev's house, when his family had told him we'd come, Jayadev had immediately called Ramesh. First they discussed what would be the consequences of killing us. They came to the conclusion that since people outside the gang did not know that we had fallen out with Jayaraj's gang, the police would decide that it was the handiwork of Oil Kumar and accuse him of the murder. Then they discussed how to kill us.

They decided to get us to the bar, make us drink till the bar closed, and when we were completely inebriated, they would kill us. In case we did not stay till the bar closed, they would kill us on the bylane next to the Wilson Garden grounds. They decided to remove the plug and puncture the tyre of our bike so we would not be able to get away.

Their failing lay in the fact that there was not a single expert rowdy in their group. If there had been one, I would not be writing this.

Jayaraj's family told us all these details in the presence of

Balaram after Jayaraj was killed. By then they had realised that I had not betrayed Jayaraj.

We could not sleep till four in the morning. Seetharam Shetty had not come and we guessed he had gone to his place. Since Sampangiramanagar Jagadish knew where we lived, we locked the door downstairs and kept swords next to us. We were not scared anymore, just sad. We felt our strength had been drained out of us. Bars, boys and dark streets flashed before my eyes. Suppose Bachchan had not checked the plug wire?

I had participated in the Kotwal murder for personal revenge, not to get into the underworld. But over the past two years, my name had been firmly etched in the world of underworld camps. After being released from jail, although I had not assaulted any one, I had still got the title of a notorious rowdy. When I had gone with Jedarahalli Krishnappa and Balaram to give a 'show', I had been laughing inside.

That day, the failed effort to kill me made me realise that on no account could I go back now. Whether I liked it or not, I was part of the underworld. No one is given a chance to plead his innocence here: I could get killed any minute, without any reason, without anyone having either hatred or anger against me. Though we had not uttered a single word against Jayaraj, the mere suspicion that we had, had led to an attempt to kill us.

We lay in bed till the afternoon of the next day. I hadn't missed an exercise session even when my leg was hurt, but that day I felt my very life was a bonus. We didn't even want to eat breakfast.

Two boys from Banashankari came by to see us. Just by looking at our faces they realised something was wrong. They started pestering us to tell them what had happened. Bachchan and I sent them out and discussed whether we wanted to tell other people about the previous night's incident. We felt there was a chance of encountering more danger if we did not reveal anything. Most importantly, since we were still hanging out with Jayaraj's gang, they could try to kill us again. So we decided to tell everyone.

But by doing so, we knew another problem would arise. At that point of time the war between Jayaraj and Oil Kumar was at its peak. Muthappa Rai's name had taken centre stage in the underworld. If we confronted Jayaraj, what stand would Kumar take? He might invite us into his camp, or he could assault us and blame it on Jayaraj. We decided that we needed to keep a distance from him too.

The Banashankari boys flared up when they heard the news. There were several groups of boys in Gandhi Bazaar, Jayanagar and Shivajinagar who liked us and would stand by us if we retaliated against Jayaraj. But we were not strong enough financially to fight Jayaraj. If we got into that, we would have to go for 'roll call' (*hafta*) and extortion, and we were not ready for that. Also, since Jayaraj had been assaulted twice, we could not rule out the chances that there might be one more attack. We decided that we would talk to B.K. Shivaram after Shetty returned and then take a decision.

We finally left our room at around four o'clock. The first thing we did was to meet Sampangiramanagar Jagadish and tell him about the previous night's incident. Jagadish, who worked at the KEB, was Jayaraj's childhood friend. He was one of the few who addressed Jayaraj in the singular. He was also fond of us and to him the previous night's incident seemed like Jayaraj's end and a tragedy. Before we could abuse Jayaraj, he swore, '*Kantri sule makkalu* . . . they should not have done this. You were the only people who were loyal to Jayaraj. It was a mistake to give advice to them.'

For the first time since I met him, I referred to Jayaraj as *avanamman*, motherfucker, but Jagadish told us not to curse him. 'Jayaraj is not mean-minded. It is impossible to believe the attack happened with his knowledge. And if he did plan the attack, you would not be alive today.' It was six months before we found out from Balaram that Jagadish was indeed right. Jayaraj found out about the attack two days after it had taken place and he was furious. '*Thoo . . . sule makkalu!* With whose permission did you attempt such a thing? What mistake did they commit for you to kill them? Didn't Sreedhar always say from the very beginning not to make enemies out of the police? Just for that you attempted to finish them?' he had shouted.

But at that time, we were not in a state of mind to find out whether Jayaraj was aware of the scheme to finish us or not.

We met Seetharam Shetty that night. Rather than being shocked at the news, he was happy, because he had met Muthappa Rai through a police officer. After hearing from us the story of the failed attempt, he said, 'You never believed me when I told you, Sreedhar. Those fellows are dangerous. I knew it from the beginning. You may be shocked to know, but I have already met Muthappa Rai and spoken to him . . .'

We were as shocked at this as we were at the previous night's attack. Bachchan and I looked at each other.

Shetty explained the meeting. After the attack on Jayaraj in Mysore, Shetty had realised that it was dangerous to remain in his gang. He knew, though, that we would not agree with him, so he had decided to meet Muthappa Rai alone. He believed that since both of them belonged to coastal Karnataka and both were Bunts by caste, Rai would treat him well. But how and where would he meet him? Finally he had asked B.K. Shivaram to mediate. The sub-inspector had called Rai to the Ashok Nagar football stadium at night and introduced the two.

Even as Shetty was explaining all this, Bachchan flared up. 'How did you talk to him without telling us?'

I consoled him, saying there was no point thinking about that now. I asked Shetty what Shivaram and Muthappa Rai intended to do.

'They will finish Jayaraj someday,' Shetty said.

We went to Shivaram's house the next day and told him all that had happened. He told us not to lose courage, and said we could contact him whenever we wanted. I asked him the one question that had been bothering me for a long time. 'When the police arrested the entire Jayaraj gang, why weren't the three of us arrested?'

He laughed and said, 'To us you looked like the outsiders in Jayaraj's gang. We did not think you were rowdies who had to be arrested.'

When we were leaving, he touched my shoulder and said, 'Sreedhar, if you are in any financial trouble, come to me.' I remember it to this day. When a person identified with one leader or gang disengages himself from it, he encounters several kinds of problems. Shivaram, who knew the underworld well, understood our troubles.

That same afternoon, we met B.B. Ashok Kumar. He was on duty at Cubbon Park police station. We stood under a tree and talked. He was badly shaken up by Jayaraj's petition to the court to hand over the shooting of Station Shekhar to the CBI. We did not say anything about possible attacks on us as he did not have in-depth knowledge of gang fights. We assured him that we would get him as much information as we could to help him in the case.

To this day, I am surprised that Jayaraj's family suspected that we were police informants and tried to kill us. And the tragedy was that, by doing so, they were responsible for pushing us over to the police camp. Till the day of the attack, I had not met any police officer. After the attempt, however, we did not go to any other rowdy gang, but depended on the two officers who had the strength to control the underworld.

Amidst all this confusion, our differences with Seetharam Shetty grew. Shetty had been trained under Kotwal and our thoughts did not match. He did not trust anyone or feel loyalty to anyone. He strongly believed that everyone in the underworld was selfish, and that every rowdy should engage in some scheme for his survival. He suspected everyone, even Bomb Krishnamurthy of Shimoga. The minute Shetty introduced us to him, we had liked Krishnamurthy. We liked the fact that, though he was very strong, Krishnamurthy had the appearance of an innocent boy. It upset us when Shetty schemed against Krishnamurthy using Krishnamurthy's boys. Often, Bachchan and Shetty would get into heated arguments. Although such arguments are usually harmless, in the underworld they can lead to unimaginably dangerous situations. Both had their own gangs and boys; both were experts in fighting. In those days, to identify the differences between them, strike a balance and to pacify them was my main job.

Compared to Seetharam Shetty, Bachchan was straightforward. He stuck to his beliefs, and did not bother with scheming and plotting. But he wanted to make it big in the underworld. He was not interested in the fame and money that it would bring, but he wanted to be known as Bangalore's most daring fighter. Shetty had no such desire. He came from a big family and he wanted to make each one of his family members economically independent. Sometimes I used to worry that some day they might plot to kill each other, but fortunately they did not hate each other to that extent.

The one common factor between them was that both felt affection for me. Whatever arguments they were involved in, when I raised my voice they would both keep quiet. However intense the fight, when I intervened they would compromise immediately.

When we found out that Shetty had met Muthappa Rai without telling us, our faith in him was shaken. We wondered if that piece of news had been embellished and passed on to Jayaraj's gang. Perhaps that was the reason they had attempted to attack us. From the very beginning we were aware that if any one of the three of us got involved in a plot, the responsibility would lie with all three.

We also knew that I, being the most intelligent of the three, would have to bear a little more responsibility.

We decided to distance ourselves from Seetharam Shetty.

As if paying for his unjust act, Ramesh, Jayaraj's brother, was arrested by the police two days after he attempted to kill us, as were Jayaraj's nephews. At the time, the police did not need any reason to arrest anyone connected with Jayaraj. Our friends said, 'God has taught them a lesson for cheating you.' Actually, it was a strategy the police had adopted to break

Jayaraj's mental strength. Their intention was also that there should be no one in the gang to follow up with lawyers and jails.

Within twelve days after the attempt on us, we distanced ourselves from Seetharam Shetty. We vacated the Shantinagar room and rented a house in Ilyasnagar, which we felt was safe for us. When we vacated the Shantinagar room, the three of us had tears rolling down our faces.

People think men from the underworld are devoid of emotions. In reality, because they are always under the shadow of violence, they are more sensitive than many in the normal world. At one stage, Shetty started crying aloud saying, 'What wrong have I done? Am I a police *halkatti*, a lackey? Why are you going away from me?'

Both of us had to struggle to calm him down. We left with a promise to each other that we would never, under any circumstance, become enemies.

By then the differences between Jayaraj and us had become known to all the boys. Strangely, no one showed any sympathy towards Jayaraj.

The financial constraints we faced those days were known only to us. By the way we conducted ourselves, and the way we refrained from extortion gave the impression that we were very well off. Also, Varada, who had been with us in the Kotwal murder case, had started working in his father's business full-time and helped us to a large extent. He assured us, 'Don't be scared about anything, I am with you. Declare war against Jayaraj, I will take care of you.'

One month after we separated from Jayaraj, Kalasipalya Nagaraj and Jedarahalli Krishnappa were released from jail. We heard that, one week after his release, Nagaraj was doing the rounds of the city. We were very careful in our movements. Since we did not yet know what Jayaraj's reaction was to his gang's attempt to kill us, we decided to carefully watch their moves. We also heard that Jedarahalli Krishnappa was moving about in a car full of bombs. We knew from experience that exaggeration was very common in the underworld, yet whenever someone spoke about Jayaraj's gang, we felt uncomfortable.

Two weeks later, the police resumed their hunt for Nagaraj and his movements stopped. The police said that Krishnappa, who had assured Jayaraj he would make mincemeat of his enemies, was busy learning to drive a car.

By then Balaram, who was under treatment in Vellore following the attack on him by Srirampura Kitty, was discharged from the hospital and could walk about.

Balaram was a strange figure in the Bangalore underworld. He was like a zombie out of an English horror film—even when you cut their heads or hands or legs, they still have life left in them. Balaram was like that. No matter how many times he was assaulted, he bounced back, crueller and more courageous than ever.

When he was back on the streets, we were really anxious. Whenever he met anyone known to us, he would intentionally ask, 'Where are those two?' just to intimidate us.

We didn't show our anxiety, though. 'His hands and legs are already hurt; we will finish him in half a minute if we meet him,' we would say.

Balaram had been very fond of me when I was with Jayaraj in the hospital. Once when Samson and I had a heated argument, Balaram was angry enough to say he would 'deal with Samson'. Although we had no differences with him, Jayaraj had once mildly objected to our keeping company with Balaram. We had drifted apart without providing Balaram any explanations. Moreover, when he was in the Vellore hospital for a year after the assault, we had neither gone to visit him nor sent money. Initially, Jayaraj too had not sent any money, but after he was assaulted repeatedly, he did.

So had we met Balaram, a fight would have been inevitable. Balaram was always ready and itching for a scrap. Also, we knew that, unlike other rowdies, he did not worry about the fact that the police had declared a full-fledged war against the gang. Nothing would prevent him from attacking us, so we were careful not to cross his path.

In the underworld, it is very rare that two rival gangs come face-to-face. We were with Koli Fayaz and his two associates in a lodge at Shivajinagar when we heard that Balaram, Anil, Kisan, Korangu, Malayali Sridhar and others had come to the very same lodge and were two rooms away from us. They had arrived in two cars. We knew that they always carried weapons, and all we had on us were two machetes.

Balaram had never seen the two boys who were with us, but he would easily recognise rowdies. Our boys kept an eye on the gang standing outside, and came in every ten minutes with a report.

When there were no signs of Balaram going away, we began to feel anxious. We could not risk staying there too long. Finally I called Shivaram and Ashok Kumar from the telephone in the room. Both were unavailable. Those days there were no pagers or cell phones. Then I dialled 100, the police control room, and gave the name of the hotel and Balaram's room number and said there was commotion in the room. The control room must have transferred the information to the Shivajinagar police station for a police jeep arrived in twenty minutes. Just as the jeep was spotted at the street corner, one by one Balaram's gang disappeared. The police came up, checked the room and went back, talking amongst themselves that it must have been a prank call. We left half an hour after Balaram did.

The next day, when Balaram and Malayali Sridhar went to see Jayaraj in Mysore jail, they were arrested. The rest of the boys with them escaped. With the arrest of Balaram, Jayaraj's gang lost its strength. Jedarahalli Krishnappa and the Kalasipalya gangs were not seen at all because they were scared of the police.

With the downfall of Jayaraj's gang, rival groups gained strength. Muthappa Rai's name began to be heard everywhere. Among our associates, Gundu Rao's personal assistant, Sridhar Reddy, knew Muthappa Rai. He often described Rai as very smart-looking, well-dressed, and always surrounded by seven or eight boys. He looked as if he was always thinking deeply, Sridhar said.

Pushpa and Rajendra's names were also in circulation. They had done a '307' (attempt to murder) on Mysore Ganesh at a massage parlour and kidnapped him. The news spread, but no case was booked in any police station.

Hemanth was the owner of Ishwarya Bar and Restaurant in Majestic. Varada, who had business dealings with him, introduced him to us. In a matter of a few meetings we discovered that he was in touch and had business dealings with Muthappa Rai. Hemanth had entered into an agreement with the owners of Rose Guesthouse at the end of Brigade Road and had used Muthappa Rai to take possession of the place. We had not been to the guesthouse after Jayaraj was arrested.

We had once gone to Bombay with Hemanth, and he'd introduced us to a boy called Arish. Arish was from Bombay, a tough boy with contacts with everyone from Haji Mastan to Arun Gawli. Despite this, he had not been lured into the underworld. When he had gone to Germany, he had made contacts with the LTTE cadre. Rajiv Gandhi had not yet been assassinated, and the LTTE still held some weight in India.

When we were in Bombay, the police had just arrested Winsy, who was trafficking boys to Canada. Arish was trying to get him released. We also moved about with him, meeting lawyers, and so on. Winsy and Arish, who were tired of all the complications in Bombay, came with us to Bangalore on Hemanth's invitation.

Winsy had participated in several acts of the LTTE. As night fell he would get excited and drink a lot. When he asked us to take him to brothels, as it was his first visit to Bangalore, we shouted at him. He begged us to take him to a cabaret place at least, and we couldn't say no. We took him to a place at the end of Brigade Road. Arish and Winsy, who had behaved decently till then, went overboard as the girls started dancing. By the time the show ended, they had started acting inappropriately with the dancers. They tried forcing the girls to come with us.

The dancers did not agree, but Arish and Winsy would not take no for an answer. At around two in the morning, the dancers started leaving. We also left the cabaret. The girls got into an auto-rickshaw and left. Arish and Winsy sat in Hemanth's car and started following the auto. We had a motorbike and we followed them because we were afraid they would get into trouble.

The auto stopped outside the Rose Guesthouse, where, we knew, the cabaret dancers rented a place. The car stopped as well. We parked the bike at a distance and went up to Arish and Winsy to tell them it was better to leave. But they got down from the car and caught hold of the girls. The watchman tried to help the girls, but Arish and Winsy slapped him. The girls kept pushing the two away, but they began taking out bundles of money from their pocket and showed it to the girls.

By then a group of ten or twelve boys came to the gate and began to shout in Hindi, 'Who is that? Leave them!'

Arish and Winsy, who were very drunk, got into an argument with the boys. Both knew no fear. 'Cool . . . cool. We haven't come to fight, we've come for the girls,' Arish replied in Hindi, his arms stretched out and shrugging his shoulders.

One boy asked, 'You're from Bombay?'

'Haan, bhai,' Arish said, pushed the boy aside and went in.

One boy pointed his gun to the sky and pulled the trigger. Everyone was still for a minute. We in the car were stunned. No one in Bangalore had opened fire for a silly issue like this before. But Arish and Winsy did not calm down even after the gun shot. Arish said coolly, 'What bhai? You have to lift your gun for such a small issue?'

One man went up to the boy who had fired the gun and shouted at him. By then a couple of boys had begun pushing Arish. He said, 'Okay bhai, leave me. We'll go.' He returned to the car and sat inside, along with Winsy.

A big guy came to the car and said, 'Don't come here again.'

Arish started the car and said, 'We'll come back with guns and do a show.' He drove away quickly, the gang following and shouting, 'Catch them, catch them.'

I shouted at Arish, but he said, 'Cabaret girls do not have so many pimps on guard even in Bombay. How can it be possible here?'

I said they were not pimps, but were sitting there for a deal and that the place belonged to Hemanth. Immediately, they both became enthusiastic. 'Then if we take Hemanth, will we get the girls?' We asked them to go back to the room and got down where we had parked the bike.

We told Hemanth about what had happened the next day. He got alarmed, and that evening he managed to send Arish and Winsy back to Bombay.

Much later, after we developed contacts with Muthappa Rai, we mentioned this incident to him. Rai had not been present that day, but his boys William and Satish were there. He said that nobody had followed the cabaret girls so boldly till then. When the watchman had told them, they had come running thinking it must be Jayaraj's gang. When they realised Arish was from Bombay, they had calmed down. When I told them we had been there, they were surprised.

After the incident at the guesthouse, we shifted to Woodlands Hotel near Kanteerava Stadium. Ramanna, who produced the film, *Garuda Rekhe*, had a permanent room there. We would sit with him, chatting from morning till evening.

Later we found out that Oil Kumar also had a room in the same hotel, and that Muthappa Rai's gang stayed there all the time. We learned that they had watched our movements carefully: for the first two days they suspected that we were planning something. Then they guessed from our behaviour that we did not even know of their presence, so they kept quiet.

Then, elections were declared in Karnataka.

Elections are a colourful time for those of us in the underworld. We can move around openly with the candidates; there is no fear of being arrested; and there is loads of money coming our way.

Before we could decide whom we should support, we received news that Jayaraj had been released—he had obtained temporary bail from the court. Even more surprising was the news that Jayaraj was contesting the elections.

We were confident he would not attempt an attack on us: Jayaraj's speciality was that he never tried to finish anyone when he was out of jail; the plans were carried out only when he was in the jail. There was, however, some fear that there was a possibility of assault during elections, so we decided not to get involved and began watching Jayaraj's movements carefully.

Jayaraj was contesting from Jayanagar. The Congress candidate was Ramalinga Reddy, Janata Dal had fielded Chandrashekhar and Jayaraj was an independent candidate with the symbol of a tiger.

Underworld dons tend to have obsessions—Jayaraj's was the tiger. In his house there were several posters of tigers in various poses. There was even a statue of a tiger next to the chair on which he sat. When he spoke to people, he would caress the tiger's head. It was why he had chosen a tiger as his symbol in the elections.

Hundreds gathered outside his house every day. His name was all over the slums in his constituency. The crowd that went with him for canvassing was so loud and exuberant that everybody thought he would win. The papers started projecting him as the winning candidate. Jagadish and others said Jayaraj was too involved in the elections to think about us, but we were still very careful. We knew he would be accused in case of any violence, so he was not likely to attack, but we could not be overconfident because small-time boys would do anything to gain his appreciation.

We were always talking about finishing Jayaraj off, because he was dangerous to us. We knew that he had been released on bail on one condition: he had to sign attendance at the Siddapura police station between eight-thirty and nine every morning. The easiest way to attack him, we thought, would be when he returned from signing in at the police station. But we did not want to be seen anywhere near the spot. The minute he saw us he would know our intention, so we had to get somebody else to do it. We decided on Tambu, accompanied by two Muslim boys and two Hindu boys. We wanted them to be ready in two days. Before this though, we decided that it would be better to discuss our plans with at least one police officer, so one morning we went to see Shivaram in his house.

The first time we went they said he was asleep. The second time we went they said he was shaving. The third time we went they said he was bathing. The last time we went they said he had gone to the station! He must have definitely guessed that we had gone to his house to discuss Jayaraj. We realised that he was avoiding us and decided to implement our plan anyway.

The day after the decision was made, a friend of ours from Wilson Garden, Chand Pasha, came to see us at around nine in the morning. We realised he must have something important to tell us for him to come to see us that early. He hurriedly parked his car and came in. 'Don't you know yet? Jayaraj is gone,' he said.

We were not shocked, just curious. 'Who killed him? When?'

'Not murder—accident. His car hit the wall next to Lalbagh. He died on the spot.'

Now we were shocked. Such accidents were rare in Bangalore. Also, Jayaraj was an excellent driver. He manoeuvred cars like toys.

We went to see what had happened. Strangely, although we'd been planning to finish him ourselves, when we heard that he was no more, we felt a strange sadness. We reached the spot at around ten. There were policemen all the way from Siddapura Circle and the road to Wilson Garden was blocked. We reached the accident spot through a back lane. There was a lone policeman standing there. Nobody was allowed near the car. We asked innocently, 'What happened?'

'Murder,' he responded casually.

'Who did it?'

He shook his head to indicate he didn't know and then made shooting motions with his hand. So someone had shot Jayaraj. We left the place immediately.

By afternoon, the news spread all over Bangalore. The lawyer Vardhamanayya had been with Jayaraj, and he was injured. Jayaraj had died on the spot. We found out that they were bringing Jayaraj's body to the Victoria Hospital for post-mortem at eleven o'clock, and sent Afsar Khan of Shivajinagar there.

The police officers who had come to see the body were heard telling journalists, 'He deserved it.'

We met Varada in the afternoon. He was also upset. He did not go to the factory, and advised us not to go home. He put us up in a room in Victoria Hotel. We, who never drank during the day, started drinking at noon. We recalled all the times Jayaraj had treated us with affection. The image of him handing me fruit at the hospital, saying, 'Here', is etched in my mind.

We'd had no reason to hate Jayaraj. We had planned to kill him because we were worried he would pay heed to rumours and finish us. We had no personal enmity with him.

We did not bother to discuss who killed Jayaraj. Since guns had been used, it was obvious that Muthappa Rai had done the job. Pushpa and Rajendra would never have used guns, no matter who instigated them.

The next day, the papers were full of details on the murder. Strangely, there was no mention of Muthappa Rai; Pushpa and Rajendra seemed to be the suspects. Even Tambu collected information about who was with Rajendra and Pushpa, which car they had used, who was driving, etc. Only Seetharam Shetty, whom we met that night at Kattariguppe, said ecstatically that it was Muthappa Rai's people who had committed the murder. After killing Jayaraj, the boys had gone to see a film in Majestic, and since they were still on a high, they had a picked up a fight with someone and had shown their guns to scare them, he said.

Shetty's intention was simple: since Muthappa Rai was from the Bunt caste, belonged to Mangalore, and since he had spoken to him a couple of times, Shetty wanted to show us that he was close to the killers. I jokingly said, 'Looks like we can see even your hand in the murder,' and he said, 'Just keep watching Sreedhar, let's not talk about it now!'

Over the next few days, we found out the details of the plot behind the killing. The people who had killed Jayaraj were not from the underworld—it was an act engineered mainly by the police. The tragedy is, though they had unlimited resources to carry it out themselves, they made use of a group from the underworld, which later amassed great power.

The police supported Rai to such an extent that they had blocked the road from Siddapura Circle to Lalbagh Circle till Jayaraj went to the police station at eight-thirty, signed and started heading back home. Jayaraj had taken his brother Umesh, lawyer Vardhamanayya and three other boys in an Ambassador.

Muthappa Rai and his gang had waited for Jayaraj to emerge and had followed his car from Siddapura Circle. When the car was near Lalbagh gate, they shot at him with a rifle. If Jayaraj had been at the wheel, he would have noticed the van following them and tried to drive into it, but his brother Umesh was driving. Though the bullet did not hit him, a scared Umesh drove into the Lalbagh wall. Then, four men holding sten guns and pistols had leisurely got down from their van and walked up to the car.

Jayaraj grasped what was happening and pulled a slim Vardhamanayya onto his lap to shield himself. The killers came near him and pumped bullets at Vardhamanayya as well. Jayaraj, who was usually cautious, was caught unaware: he thought he would not be attacked near a police station, and that the killers would not shoot at the lawyer. Jayaraj died on the spot and Vardhamanayya died at the hospital.

Muthappa Rai had been heard of before Jayaraj's assassination, but with Jayaraj's killing, his name became firmly entrenched in the Bangalore underworld. That day the police used Muthappa Rai. The same Muthappa Rai is now posing a challenge to the entire police system. He organises killings and declares he has done so. Who is responsible for it?

Jayaraj was killed six days before the election. Though the newspapers were full of the details, the killers were arrested only ten days later; Muthappa Rai was not one of them. On the day Jayaraj was killed, two men who were in jail at the time of the murder were arrested as the main accused!

It is an incident that makes a mockery of our police system. November 19, 1989. Sunday. At around six in the evening, a police squad rushes into a lodge in Mudigere in Chikmagalur district. Two tough boys staying in a room are taken, along with their luggage, to the station. They are stripped and put in lock-up in their briefs. A case is registered as crime number 317/89. Nobody asks any questions. A sub-inspector, four crime branch officers and several police constables in uniform are present. After half an hour, the ACP arrives. He is surprised to see the two tough guys in the lock-up—usually such criminals are not seen at such stations. He asks the sub-inspector about it. The sub-inspector says the boys were creating a nuisance in a bar and the owner had lodged a complaint.

The ACP gets them both out of lock-up, delivers a few beatings, and inquires why they are in Mudigere. They say they are from Bangalore, had gone to Dharmasthala temple, and on their way back to Bangalore had gone to a bar for a drink. Everybody knows that casual fights are common in bars. The ACP cannot understand why the sub-inspector took such a small matter so seriously. But since the two do not look innocent, he decides to keep silent.

The next day the two tough boys are produced before Chikmagalur court which is forty kilometres away from Mudigere. The magistrate is on leave, and because the arrested men cannot be kept in police custody for more than twenty-four hours, and because the magistrate has gone somewhere only fifty kilometres from Chikmagalur, the police take them there. They make the accused wait outside and go in and get an order from the magistrate to take them into judicial custody. Usually magistrates do not force the police to produce the accused when the allegation is not serious.

The two are brought back to the Chikmagalur jail and put in a cell. It is eight at night now.

The next day, November 21, the jailor arrives and asks them about the allegations. The two explain what happened and request the jailor to inform their families as they do not know anybody in Chikmagalur. They give postcards to the jailor to be posted to their families, which he does that afternoon.

That same morning, at around eight-thirty, notorious don Jayaraj is killed near Lalbagh gate in Siddapura. A case is registered at Siddapura station as crime number 410/89.

On Wednesday evening, November 22, the two are released from the jail on bail. They pay an amount of five hundred rupees as guarantee in court. After they are released, the two boys do not come to Bangalore. They travel to Puttur and other places for a week and then go to Madras. They take a room in an ordinary hotel. They stay there for two days, never venturing out. Tiffin, coffee and food are sent to the room.

The two tough boys are Rajendra, i.e. Srirampura Bekkinakannu Rajendra, and Pushpa, Cottonpet Pushpa.

They had not been arrested without their prior knowledge and approval. The two had been involved in the previous two attacks on Jayaraj. For this, the third attack, when it seemed that the plan would definitely work, they had decided to get themselves arrested to be safe. They had been kept in the lodge from where they were arrested by Muthappa Rai's right-hand men Jayanth Rai, Pomma and Satish. The bar and the bar owner are not known to this day. It was part of the plan that a rumour be spread that Pushpa and Rajendra killed Jayaraj. And later, documents from Chikmagalur jail would be shown to prove that they were in jail on the day Jayaraj was killed, so they would be acquitted.

There was no enmity between Jayaraj and Muthappa Rai. Jayaraj's right-hand man Samson was so close to Muthappa Rai that, one-and-a-half years after Jayaraj's murder, when I convinced Samson to meet Rai and took him myself, Samson sat casually, with his legs stretched towards Rai's face, and spoke to him like a childhood friend. By then Rai was a big don.

So Muthappa Rai had no reason to kill Jayaraj. It was a case of contract killing: Oil Kumar and the police gave the contract to him jointly. But the contract to kill Jayaraj was not given by the entire police department, but by the one man who stood as a link between the underworld and the police: B.K. Shivaram.

Jayaraj's murder is the most complicated one in the history of Bangalore's underworld, and it was a turning point. For the first time, guns were used to kill in the city. And B.K. Shivaram did not stop at being the instigator of that murder; he started ruling the underworld from behind the khaki uniform.

More than anything else, money began flowing like water.

PART IV

PART I

One

Of the three main underworld dons of Bangalore during the '70s and '80s, Oil Kumar was the wiliest. As I mentioned earlier, he didn't have Kotwal's physique or Jayaraj's strength. He lived more opulently than the other two. Neither of them had any sort of affection for, or trust in, Kumar. Even before attempting the assault on Jayaraj at Kanishka, Kotwal had planned to finish Kumar within a couple of months if he was successful in finishing Jayaraj. Jayaraj always gritted his teeth at the mention of Kumar. 'While he is alive he is like a noose around our necks,' he would say.

Kumar introduced the oil business to the Bangalore underworld. He always had one or two police constables with him and acted as if the entire Bangalore police force was at his command. He also opened a film distribution office in Gandhi Nagar and identified himself with the film industry too. The only time he was briefly inactive was after Jayaraj escaped the Kanishka attack. However, within four months he had reached a compromise with Jayaraj.

The attack on Jayaraj in front of Central Jail was Kumar's declaration of dissent. He made friends with Muthappa Rai and even assured him financial backing for carrying out Jayaraj's murder. After this attack, Rajendra and Pushpa hid in a farm in Puttur, where Muthappa Rai went to meet them. When Muthappa Rai said he had just met Kumar, both of them were angry and upset. Rajendra had even declared that, when Jayaraj was killed, he would accept Muthappa Rai as his boss, but never Kumar. Until then it was never discussed who would be the don after Jayaraj. Rai was very happy that a notorious underworld man was openly accepting him as a don, but he convinced Rajendra and the others that at that point of time Kumar was invincible.

One day Rai took Rajendra, Pushpa and Mahadeva to Woodlands Hotel, where Kumar usually stayed. Before going there, Rai had warned everyone not to smoke in front of Kumar and also not insult him in any other way. Rajendra had seen Kumar several times before; he not only asked Kumar for a cigarette but also borrowed his lighter and lit it. That day, while they were conversing, Kumar casually showed his .32 pistol and Rai was stunned. It was the kind of American-made pistol that he had seen with Sharad Shetty and Ashok Shetty, men who had gone to Bombay from Mangalore and made it big in the underworld.

From that day onwards, Bangalore became a hub for killers from Bombay. Every week Rai would show a photograph of Bombay rowdies to Kumar, convince him that he could get Jayaraj killed by them, and collect a large amount of money. He would then get the killers to Bangalore, make a 'show', take them to Mysore where Jayaraj was kept, do a round of the jail and send them back.

The Bombay boys looked gigantic and acted like they had killed hundreds of men. Kumar was ecstatic just looking at them. During that time, Sharad Shetty, who was as famous as Dawood Ibrahim, had come to Bangalore. He was introduced to Kumar, who behaved like his life was finally worth living.

Even on that occasion, it was only Rajendra who did not stand up to show respect when Sharad Shetty walked in, and Muthappa Rai was annoyed with him for that.

During this period, all the notorious underworld men from Bombay came to Bangalore, enjoyed Kumar's hospitality, had a good time and went back. Subhash Thakur, who is in jail in Mumbai now and sentenced to hanging, sharpshooter Sautiya, who was killed in Dubai, Francis Cutinho of Mangalore, all came to Bangalore often.

~

Though most of the Bangalore boys frequenting Muthappa Rai were close to us, we had no intention of meeting him or joining his gang. But one deal led him to make contact with us. Our opponent in an important land litigation case tried to scare us by dropping the name of Oil Kumar. We chased those boys in front of Ramaiah Medical College and this became big news in Bangalore. The next morning, Gundu Rao's PA Sridhar met us and informed us that Rai wanted to meet. He hinted that the differences between Rai and Oil Kumar were brewing and Rai was happy we'd challenged his boys in the open.

Despite the fact that Jayaraj had been fond of me, I had always maintained a distance with him. Because of his huge size and fearless attitude, he had seemed larger than life to me and it was difficult for me to be casual with him. But with Rai, there were no such hurdles. Our conversations were more relaxed. Also, Rai was flexible. He was always open to new ideas. Whenever I expressed my displeasure, disregard and fear of guns, he agreed with me. He would say we should not kill anyone with guns anymore. But he could not give up collecting or carrying guns. 'I am not used to fighting with a sword like you,' he used to say simply.

He found guns unavoidable because of his connection with the Bombay underworld. The 'encounter' era had started in Bombay. It was just four or five months since Rama Naik had been killed in an encounter, allegedly at the behest of Dawood. Rama Naik's disciple, Arun Gawli, called Dawood 'Chuha' (rat). Dawood was in Dubai but he would often make brief appearances in Bombay. Sharad Shetty was a strong supporter of Dawood.

Ashok Shetty, whose name we had not heard much, would also come to Bangalore often to meet Muthappa Rai. I remember distinctly the first time Muthappanna introduced me to Ashok

Shetty. Muthappanna was wearing a pale red silk shirt with a floral print tucked into black pants. The tall, fair Ashok Shetty was wearing a grey Safari suit. Kini stood next to him.

They were inside when Bachchan and I came in from somewhere. The atmosphere was charged. Four tough boys were standing in one corner. There were a few chairs in the veranda and we occupied them as usual. Sardar came out from the hall and whispered in my ears, 'Ashokanna has come.'

When the door was opened Muthappanna saw me. He told Ashok Shetty something in Tulu and called me in. It was evident from the way he looked and talked that he had said something good about me. Even while introducing me to Ashokanna, he said good things about me. Kini did not talk, but his look indicated that he liked me. This is when Ashok Shetty brought up the Dholakia job, and I was happy that he told me about it directly. I decided that I must do it no matter what it took. Bachchan, who liked Rai as much as or more than I did, was very excited.

That was the truth of that day. We were very enthusiastic to identify ourselves with the Bombay underworld. We often talked about Bombay being the centre of India's underworld, and we did not want Bangalore to be excluded from it. We were also greatly drawn by Muthappa Rai's conduct.

What followed was a series of incidents that made it inevitable that we oppose him.

Dholakia had a house in Sadashivnagar opposite former chief minister Bangarappa's house. Our plan was to enter into the house disguised as income tax officials or some other officers, threaten him and make him call his father in Dubai to tell him that he was being kidnapped. We would leave after Ashok Shetty collected twenty-five lakh from him.

Kidnappings were not yet common in Bangalore those days. Rai called the Dholakia job a 'deal'. He also said, 'We have not done any favours for Ashokanna so far, so this time let him take the entire booty.' We felt a little disappointed about not getting a share of the twenty-five lakh, but we agreed to it.

Those days, Dholakia used to run the Bangalore International Hotel, which was very successful. It had rooms, live music, and was a popular pick-up joint. Dholakia had taken on lease a hotel running under loss and converted it into a successful business.

I told Rai it was not safe to threaten Dholakia and continue to let him sit in his house, and he agreed immediately. So, instead, we decided to kidnap him from his hotel. Bachchan and I went to Janardhan Hotel to study his movements. We saw that he always got into and out of his car from the hotel portico. Also he always had four to five boys with him. They looked like Mangaloreans.

We informed Rai about this. Rai knew about the Mangalore boys with him: we were told that they lived in Bombay and Rai had contacts with them as well. He considered involving them in the plot, but realised that, if it failed, Dholakia would find out about the plan and it would be impossible to get him after that. So he gave up the idea.

Rai was now getting worried about Kumar. He had control of all black market businesses in Bangalore, but was never cordial with his associates. Once, Rai had asked Kumar to make a phone call to someone in connection with a repayment deal. Kumar had said with arrogance, 'Just mention my name; tell them we are also with you and your job will be done.' Rai and Jayanth, his right-hand man, were furious that day.

Another issue Rai had was Kumar's relations with Amar Alva, the boss of another gang that had played a part in Jayaraj's murder. When Rai was a nonentity, Amar Alva had already made a name for himself as a student leader. It was he who had introduced Rai to contacts in Bombay. He also had the support of the notorious Sharad Shetty. Rai was now trying to prevent Alva from getting involved in Bangalore deals, but Kumar was always encouraging him. Rai received information that Amar Alva, along with Francis Cutinho and Ramesh Pujari, often came to Bangalore as guests of Kumar. Rai and his gang could not take it. Bachchan, Bomb Krishnamurthy and I were not scared of Kumar since he was not at all fit physically, but Rai was quite disturbed by him. Yet, for all his anger, Rai never spoke of finishing Kumar.

One evening, though, he called Bachchan and me and said, 'After much thought, I have decided to complete Kumar's work.'

We didn't know what to say. In the Bombay underworld, 'completing one's work' meant killing that person. Though I did not like Kumar one bit, I didn't think there was a need to kill him. I tried to say as much to Rai, but he did not agree. He was actually more scared of Amar Alva's gang than Kumar. He felt that if Kumar were removed, then Alva could not do anything in Bangalore. Also, he felt that if he did not finish Kumar, Kumar would finish him. He would tell me at least twenty times a day, 'Look Sreedhar, we have finished Jayaraj's work and helped Pushpa, Rajendra, Shivaram ... you must help me complete Kumar's work.' I told him I would threaten Kumar and see that he did not trouble Rai again, but Rai did not agree to this.

'We are doing it tomorrow. Let us plan for every eventuality so no fingers are pointed to us,' he said. Whenever Rai planned such plots, his face would lose colour and he would get a headache.

That evening, Jayanth told us another reason why Rai and Kumar's relationship was going bad. A man called Shankar, who ran a cards club in Majestic, had got into a quarrel with 'Blues' Kittynna. Oil Kumar was supporting Shankar's partner, while Kittynna had gone to Muthappa Rai. All the parties had sat down for a meeting. Rajarajeshwarinagar Jayanna, whom all the clubs in Bangalore contacted when they got into any sort of trouble, Oil Kumar, Muthappa Rai, Williams and others were present at the meeting.

Nothing Muthappa Rai could say would make Kumar change his stand against Kittynna. Finally Rai had lost his cool and yelled, 'Okay Kumar, I did not know that you would repay our help to you in this way. I can do anything to you right this minute, but I don't want to get a bad name, that I called you for a discussion and finished you. You can go out now . . . wait to see what will happen in one month's time.'

For the first time, Rai had addressed Kumar in singular.

Oil Kumar did not take Rai's threat seriously; he did not believe that a net was being woven for his death. He accepted the challenge, saying, 'You do what you can. You can even call someone with an AK-47 to shoot me.'

He was insulted that Rai had spoken like that in front of Jayanna.

'Call someone to kill you? Just see what happens,' Rai said sarcastically.

But after Kumar left, Rai felt he had been very hasty. Kumar was not small-fry. He had even made Kotwal and Jayaraj wait for him like small children. Also, he had been successful in getting Amar Alva, Francis and others on his side so Rai could not get to him. Rai felt he should not have thrown a challenge like that at him. But what had happened had happened.

After Rai mentioned finishing Kumar, several plans were hatched with zeal. Rai insisted that on no account should he be the accused in the case. As in Jayaraj's case, this time too he wanted to be in the clear. There was really no need for him to be so scared of the police: he knew most of the Bangalore police, not just as acquaintances but as friends. Despite his involvement in the murder of a big don like Jayaraj, the police had not troubled Rai at all. In all the time that we were in Rose Guesthouse, a police jeep came by only once, and that too in pursuit of a small matter.

Eventually, Oil Kumar was killed without any fuss; it was much easier than we had imagined.

We had one scheme and B.K. Shivaram suggested another to us. We planned to rent a big house, fill its sump with water from a tank, get Kumar to the house on some pretext and drown him in the sump. Then we would take him in his car to the same tank and dump the car in the tank. It would be registered as an accident. When we told Shivaram our plan, he said 'Brilliant', but gave us a simpler plan. He said an overdose of insulin could kill a person, and nobody would be able to detect it either.

However, it was impossible to get Kumar alone so we could implement either of these plans. Finally we asked Ashok Shetty to call him from Singapore to say that he was in Bangalore and that Kumar should come to meet him at an apartment in Sadashivnagar, with the two boys he was sending. Kumar believed him and came like a sheep. The two boys who went to bring him were Rai's special boys. Though the two boys had been told how to finish Kumar when he was sitting in the car, they didn't do anything, even after Kumar stopped the car.

Bachchan, Krishnamurthy and Mysore Ganesh, who were watching from a distance, rushed in and finished Kumar. Jayanth, Williams and I were watching from a distance in another van. As soon as Kumar was dead, Jayanth and Willy cheered and shouted, 'Now we are Bangalore's kings.' I, who can never enjoy a murder, felt disgusted with them.

The night Oil Kumar was killed—September 1990—Rai was not in India, but in Dubai.

Since there were no witnesses, the police, based on Kumar's wife's statement, filed an FIR alleging Muthappa Rai was the prime accused. After three days, the police arrested Mysore Ganesh and two other boys from Ulsoor who gave a statement to the police confessing that they killed Kumar, and also that they were Rai's boys. The police determined that Muthappa Rai was the prime suspect in the Kumar murder case.

Till a chargesheet was filed, nearly three months later, Rai did not return to India.

There was a rumour that I had a hand in Kumar's murder but I was not arrested by the police and I convinced everyone—from my friends to legal experts—that I was innocent.

Usually, secrecy plays an important role when a plot is being hatched to finish a don. In Kumar's case, however, Rai had told everyone around him that he would kill Kumar. Many people who ran clubs knew about it; in fact, several of them had left town the night before Kumar was killed. Even a few police officers knew exactly how Kumar would be killed. Strangely, Kumar, who had the reputation of being well informed, had no clue about the plot. Perhaps this had more to do with his 'don't care' attitude rather than Rai's intelligence.

Rai returned to India after the police filed the chargesheet, but he did not come to Bangalore—he stayed in Mangalore and Sullia. He invited us there once and we stayed at his relative's house in Sullia. Rai had changed in just three months. He had gone to Dubai for the first time and he already looked like a don. The entire morning he spoke about Dawood and Sharad Shetty. He described his two-day stay in Dawood's guesthouse with much enthusiasm. He also described Dawood and Sharad Shetty's relationship.

Those days, Dawood—who ruled the entire underworld in India—depended solely on Sharad Shetty. He had Rama Naik killed in a police encounter, and just when he thought he had no one to oppose him, Arun Gawli had sprung up on the scene and become a nuisance. He was known as the Hindu don. Dawood depended heavily on Sharad Shetty to control Gawli. Chota Rajan was not yet notorious then, and Chota Shakeel and Abu Salem had not yet arrived on the scene. Dawood and Shetty did not argue, not even as a joke. When they played cricket once a week in Dubai, they played on the same side. They never took a decision without consulting each other. While attending mujras, they would pull money from each other's pockets and throw it at the dancers.

In the underworld, especially at the level of Dawood and Shetty, there are hundreds of pressures, mentally and emotionally. To kill and to get someone killed is as easy as pulling a trigger. So Dawood and Sharad Shetty had decided to always live like 'two bodies and one soul'. Rai had been impressed by this.

We then began to talk about how to manage the Bangalore underworld. Rai was a very good listener, and had the ability to completely grasp what the person in front of him was saying. That night we had our drinks and started talking at around twelve. When we finished, it was past four in the morning. In that entire time he spoke maybe ten sentences, and just listened carefully to what I was saying.

We decided that we had to manage the Bangalore underworld cautiously and not give violence a chance to erupt. But it was easier said than done—the complexities were beyond words.

The man who had taken us from Madikeri to Sullia was called Gopal. He was short and his eyes held a strange attraction. That night, before going to bed, I asked Rai about him. He said his real name was Raghu. He was involved in several crimes in Mangalore and had gone to Bombay to lie low. He was Sharad Shetty's blue-eyed boy. If given a deal, he would follow the person day and night. He had no bad habits. He would just eat idli and vada for months together while searching for his victim. He did not talk much. He had a rivalry with the then notorious Yadu gang in Mangalore. The only issue he discussed with us was the friendship between Yadu and Balaram. At that time Balaram was in the Mangalore jail. He requested us to separate Balaram and Yadu.

I did not believe that Balaram would come to us, since we had become friendly with someone who had finished Jayaraj, but I did not tell him that. Instead I said that it was simple and I would do it. Raghu said, 'If you have any job in Bangalore, give it to me, I will do it for you.'

I laughed. 'In the entire Bangalore underworld, we have no rivalry with anyone to finish . . . tell me if you have a job for us in Bombay.' I said, acting like a professional killer.

The otherwise serious Raghu smiled. 'Sreedhar, a job does not mean revenge . . . You are behind the times. Money . . . money—one must work for money,' he said as if taunting me.

For a second I was embarrassed that he had exposed my ignorance, but I managed to recover and said there was no such work. After that I did not talk much with him. Sometime later he was killed brutally in Poona.

The next day, several incidents occurred that gave us an

insight into Rai's eccentricities. It was past nine when we woke up. There were several fighter cocks in the house and Rai organised a cock fight for us. Rai, who rarely showed excitement, was intensely involved in the skirmish. He explained in great detail the fighting spirit in cocks and he seemed to want to identify himself with this grit.

Later we went to a river about five kilometres away from the house to swim and to fish. Jayanth, who was the fittest in Rai's gang, and I competed against each other to see who could stay under water for longer. The others kept time. We started with thirty seconds and went up to seventy seconds. Finally Jayanth stayed under three seconds longer than me. I hate accepting defeat and was about to go down again but Bachchan and Krishnamurthy winked at me. I relented.

Rai said, 'Sreedhar's stamina is great—Jayanth is ten years younger than him!'

I said, 'Jayanth smokes two cigarette packs every day . . . I didn't expect him to have such lung capacity.'

Rai himself never tried to claim any physical abilities that he did not possess. Kotwal and Jayaraj had tremendous pride in their physique. They would often brag about how fast they could cut limbs once they raised their swords. Even the weakest rowdy in the underworld will brag about his abilities. But Rai never boasted about his capabilities, even with guns. He always remained straight and simple.

We left for Bangalore in the afternoon, after lunch. Though we were happy with his hospitality, we felt he would continue to give more importance to Bombay and Bunt boys, rather than Bangaloreans. Even though he could see that the role of the Bangalore boys was more important than that of his own men, he would still have the same attitude, and we were not happy about it.

I was happy with our discussion, however. I told the others about it on the way back. We took the fact that he had listened to me patiently as a sign of his approval. However, I was aware that there was now no one to challenge Muthappa Rai. Usually when there are no challengers, dons do not show much cordiality to their associates. We decided not to come to any conclusions till Rai came to Bangalore for talks.

Muthappa Rai was granted anticipatory bail. He was taken in for questioning for just two hours. He gave a statement regarding Kumar's murder and was then allowed to go. He is probably the only person who got out of a serious murder case so easily.

Then his exercises in image-building started. Rai stayed in a room in Akshaya Hotel in Sampangiramnagar for some time and then started his own office in one of the roads off Brigade Road.

It was a small office but it was convenient because it had several cabins which could accommodate many visitors. It was air-conditioned and tastefully decorated. The wall behind Rai's table had wood-panelling on which strips of leather were affixed. Holding a strap at one end and pulling it up would reveal a small box-like structure. Whenever police raided the place, the straps were used to hide the guns, and nobody could tell.

It took three months to get the office ready. During this time, Rai and I both became very fond of each other. I liked him more than I liked Jayaraj. I called him 'Muthappanna' with all sincerity. Rai never hid any information from me. Prominent people were received and deals discussed in my presence. He was quite open about the weaknesses of Willy, Kini, and others with me.

He had money pouring in from all the clubs then. In the beginning he had decided not to make any money in the oil business, but later he changed his mind, because he was worried that if he did not step in and take charge, small-timers would take advantage.

All the men who had already made a name for themselves began approaching Rai after Oil Kumar's murder. Kote Narayana and Nagaraj, and also Kunta Kumar, who was with Oil Kumar till the end, came to him. Pushpa, Rajendra, Balaram

Kotwal Ramachandra

Jayaraj (second from right) with three henchmen and
Kalasipalya Nagaraj (sitting) with a photo of the
maharaja of Mysore

ayaraj with an associate, a studio photo

Jayaraj at a public function before going to jail in 1974

'Dadi' Puttaswamy (first from right), one of Jayaraj's associates, with current Karnataka chief minister Siddaramaiah and the then chief minister Ramakrishna Hegde (1982)

Jayaraj in Central Jail, 1975

Jayaraj and Nagaraj (from the Kalasipalya gang known for their brutality) after th former was released from jail in 198

Jayaraj being greeted after his
release from jail in 1984

Jayaraj with M.D. Nataraj,
son-in-law of Chief
Minister Devaraj Urs

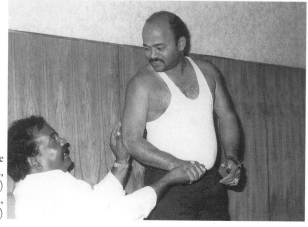

Kotwal's secretary and one
of the men who killed him,
Seetharam Shetty (standing)
and Kalasipalya Narayana,
in jail (1987)

R.V. Devaraj (currently an MLA, centre) with Kalasipalya Narayana (second from left) and friends

Gundu Rao, then chief minister, and Jayaraj at a function in 1988

Janata Dal minister Jeevaraj Alva being garlanded by one of Jayaraj's henchman

Jayaraj with his right-hand man Samson (wearing glasses) and Kalasipalya Nagaraj (in a checked shirt)

Advocate Varadhamanayya (first from right) who was gunned down along with Jayaraj

Kalander, through whom I approached Koli Fayaz

Balaram, one of the fiercest rowdies I've known

Nissar, a Youth Congress leader and an associate of Kotwal Ramachandra

Nissar (standing, second from left), Sardar (third from left) and Gun Muneer (fourth from left) with Daniel (sitting in centre) at the journalist's birthday celebrations

One of Balaram's close friends Jedarahalli Krishnappa (sitting, centre) with associates

Varadaraj Naik, one of the men who killed Kotwal Ramachandra

'Dadi' Puttaswamy (second from right), an associate of Jayaraj's, along with politicians

Bekkinakannu Rajendra, whose cunning I admired, had great knowledge about everything, including rowdyism

Sardar, who was part of my gang in the early days, and Nissar (centre) with henchmen

'Bachchan' Amanulla Khan, who has always stood by my side (second from right in the photo alongside, and second from left in the photo below)

I (third from left), with my new friends from the literary and media world just after I launched my tabloid, *Agni*

Muthappa Rai (handcuffed) being brought to jail after his return from Dubai

With Bachchan

and Jedarahalli Krishnappa were in jail. Rai was confident that all of them, except Balaram, would join him after their release. He wanted to keep an eye on what Pushpa and Rajendra would do after their release though. None of us trusted Rajendra and we suspected that he might plan something.

Rai was worried about Balaram because he was getting close to Yadu, Raghu's enemy.

Balaram and Malayali Sridhar had become so notorious in the Mangalore jail that an incident there made big news in Bangalore as well. Balaram was very rough. If he was not in a good mood, he would slap anyone who irritated him even slightly. Once, in the Mangalore jail, he slapped someone and all the inmates protested. That evening they all came together to attack him.

Just then Balaram and Sridhar walked in holding two hand bombs. All the inmates ran away screaming, and someone brought the jailor. He talked to them and made them hand over the bombs. When they did, the jailor realised that they were just balls made of paper and tied with thread! Despite this, the inmates stopped troubling Balaram after that.

We went to Rai's office every afternoon. One day, I received a phone call. I was taken aback when I heard the voice on the other side.

'It's me Sir, Balaram . . .'

I put my hand on the mouthpiece, and told Rai, 'Balaram.' He signalled for me to continue.

'What Balaram, when did you come?'

'Yesterday, Sir.'

'And . . .?'

'I want to see you.'

'When?'

'Sir, if you are free today evening, come to Airlines Hotel,' he said.

I agreed.

I told Rai what he had said. 'Go talk to him Sreedhar; find out what he's thinking.'

'I'll take Jayanth with me,' I said.

'Why?' he looked at me questioningly.

'See Muthappanna, you are important to me. Balaram has a huge following. When we were meeting him in Kanishka, Jayaraj had warned me about it. Any boy who looks stronger than the don he is under creates tension in a don. I don't want to have any misunderstanding with you later. If I go alone he may talk badly about you. If Jayanth is also with me it may send him a message that I do not do anything without telling you . . . isn't that right?'

Rai looked at my face for a few seconds and then nodded.

Balaram always had a big gang of boys with him and that day as well, when we went to Airlines, around fifteen to twenty boys were there, standing in groups. I had taken Bachchan and Jayanth with me. As soon as we got down from the car, I introduced Jayanth to Balaram.

When Kitty and his gang had attacked Balaram, they had severely damaged his hands and legs. So whenever someone was introduced to him, he would shake hands with a lot of hesitation. When Jayanth put out his hand, Balaram took it with a long face. He was not happy that I had brought Jayanth.

I took him aside. 'What shall we do now, Sir?' he asked.

I slowly explained to him that we had accepted Muthappa Rai's leadership. I said good things about his personality and told him that if he wanted to have a relationship with us, he had to accept Rai. He did not say anything, just stared at the faces of people who walked by. When he had not spoken for a long time, I said, 'Then shall I go?' I felt he would not go along with us.

'Sir, meet me here tomorrow afternoon, I will bring Kalapathar also,' he said, and then, indicating Jayanth with a glance, he added, 'Don't bring him.'

'But I don't want to meet without telling Rai, Balaram,' I said firmly.

'I am not saying don't tell him; I said don't bring him,' he said.

I agreed and we went back to the office.

Before I could explain what had happened, Jayanth briefed Rai in Tulu. When he was finished, I told Rai that Balaram had asked me to meet him the next day, but he did not want anyone from Rai's side to be present. Rai said, 'Sreedhar, maybe he feels strange that one of my boys is there. You go alone and talk, let's see what he says.'

Rai was still anxious about Jayaraj's brothers and associates, even after Kumar's murder. I had told him they were in no position to take revenge, but he was not completely convinced. Now that Balaram was out, his anxiety had doubled, and since Balaram had asked me not to bring his boys, Rai was all the more nervous.

When we went to Airlines the next day, Balaram was not there. Instead a boy greeted us and said Balaram was elsewhere. He asked me to follow him and led us by bike. It was clear Balaram did not trust us completely.

Balaram and Kalapathar were in Cauvery Continental. We chatted for about two hours. We discussed how Jayaraj's brothers had tried to finish us. It was then that Balaram told us that when Jayaraj found out about it, he had yelled, 'Who told you to do such a dirty thing? You ruined everything.'

Balaram was not angry with Rai for killing Jayaraj. He too had realised that it was not possible to live after taking on the police in the manner that Jayaraj had.

'See Sir, we liked you from the beginning. In the middle we separated. Now we will listen to what you have to say,' he said, stating that I was their leader.

I explained about Muthappa Rai to him. I clearly said we liked him and that we would not go against him.

He replied that it was not Muthappa Rai who was a problem for him. It was Rajendra. Balaram was extremely angry with Rajendra. Balaram had been a decent boy with no exposure to rowdyism. He had come from Hassan and worked as a paper agent in Bangalore till Rajendra had not only turned him into a notorious rowdy, but had even instigated a deceitful attack on him. He could never forget that.

I told him that Rai would never show Rajendra the same trust and affection that he showed us. Rai had already discussed Rajendra with me several times. When Balaram heard this, he relaxed. Kalapathar, who was seconding all Balaram's opinions, was also happy.

It was decided that a meeting with Rai would be arranged after three days.

When I went and reported the meeting to Rai, he also relaxed. After three days, I took Balaram and Kalapathar to Rai's office. Rai welcomed then affectionately. After some time, he mentioned Rajendra casually. 'Balaram, for us Sreedhar is like a family member, but we don't feel the same about Rajendra. All said and done, family is family and outsiders are outsiders ... don't you think?' Balaram's face broke into a wide smile—Rai had suggested that he was also family now.

After this meeting, Balaram and Kalapathar started coming to Rai's office whenever they wanted to see me. They would bring about twenty boys with them when they did. All the boys in their gang—Anila, Balakrishna (Kalakar), Huchche Gowda, Basava, sometimes Konagu—were seasoned rowdies.

Rai's office was on the first floor. Whenever Balaram came, we would go down to meet him. Balaram's boys would watch Rai's gang with curiosity. A few times Rai would come down as well, on his way out somewhere, and the boys watched him without blinking an eyelid till he got into his car and drove away.

We were bothered by that look. I mentioned it to Balaram once. 'Balaram, why do your boys watch Rai's comings and goings with such interest?'

'Nothing Sir, these boys, they come from nowhere and see how they preen,' he shook his head and laughed.

Balaram did not have the same trust in Rai as he had in me, but he never spoke disparagingly about him.

After Balaram and Kalapathar also accepted his supremacy, Rai started rising unhindered in the underworld. He would go to the court sometimes to talk to Pushpa and Rajendra. Money from clubs and the oil business was flowing in without any problems. He now turned to betting on races.

Rai loved betting. He would attend to office work till afternoon and then go to Brindavan Hotel on MG Road where he kept a permanent room to play cards. He would gamble till late at night and then go home. He never missed playing cards even for a day. One could meet him in the afternoon only on absolutely important work. His friends were addicted to cards as well. Only on race days would a cards game take a back seat.

Rai always goaded me to take an interest in cards and racing. 'Sreedhar, all these dealings, underworld are all nothing in front of racing. With your intelligence if you get involved in racing it will be good.' But I could never take an interest in them.

Rai was also involved in fixing races. There was great risk in this. Horses are, after all, animals and can be controlled only to certain extent. Sometimes, even when the other horses were held back, the designated horse would not run fast enough to win.

Rai would bet huge amounts. If his horse won, he would collect the money from the bookies immediately. If he lost, he would not pay but ask them to put it on credit. But since he had to pay some day, he felt very upset when he lost.

Rai was very involved with the racing scene in Mysore. His cousin ran a bar in that city and Mysore's rowdies and black marketers would assemble there. During racing season, Rai stayed in Mysore twice a week. Since not very many major races were held in Mysore, it was easier for him to fix races there. A couple of times, he bet ten thousand rupees on horses in Mysore and asked Jayanna to give me the profit, hoping that would get me interested in racing. Unfortunately, in both instances, he could not fix the winner.

Rai's gang had any number of Maruti cars, vans and guns, but we still moved about on motorbikes. When we came out of Rai's office, he would get into a car and we would get on a bike. He would be disturbed by this. 'Buy a Maruti car, Sreedhar, I will give you the initial amount. Buy a car on loan, if you can't pay the instalments, I will pay,' he said several times.

I did not agree. I used to say, 'For that I must first get a job that gets me regular monthly income.'

At that point, I believed that, as far as we were concerned, possibilities in the underworld had reached a saturation point. The underworld is alive only when you have enemies and intense disturbances. These had died down now, and I did not wish them to be rekindled.

Two

Bachchan and I began to search for a new path. We decided we would leave Bangalore, buy ten acres of land near Kanva, Channapatna, and set up a farm to raise cows and sheep. This was not a casual thought, but something we felt we should do to prove ourselves to the world.

We met a highly placed official in the Animal Husbandry department and went to Hesarghatta to study Australian sheep. When we found out that they would not survive in our climate, we were disappointed. We really wanted to extricate ourselves from the world of violence and live peaceably, close to nature. We studied cows and sheep in greater detail than we ever had humans, and we even looked at land near Kanva. We thought that if we had about ten lakh rupees at hand, we could get into the business.

One day I mentioned this to Rai. I said if Bachchan and I could get ten lakh rupees in a deal, we would go to the village and settle down.

'Then will you give up the underworld?' he asked.

'I have had enough,' I said.

He laughed aloud. 'If you are planning on leaving the underworld, then I will prevent any money coming your way.'

I immediately said, 'Look, this does not mean our friendship will end. We will come even at midnight when you call. But we don't want to depend on this for our livelihood.'

It was not easy for us to work on our project while we were still part of the underworld. Every day something would occur that made us change our way of thinking.

Because of Rai, the Bombay underworld began making inroads into Bangalore. Every week, four or five boys came from the western port city to visit.

I did not have a good feeling about these killers from Bombay. Some of them came to hide in Bangalore after committing a crime. Some came to carry out some 'work' in Karnataka. Usually they stayed at Hotel Gautam. They did not look rough, like the Bangalore rowdies, but like cold machines. I felt repulsed by these killers: they would murder for money, even where there was no disagreement or motive of revenge.

Rai did not favour them much either, but when Sharadanna or Ashokanna asked him, he could not refuse.

Meanwhile, he continued to be anxious about Amar Alva of Mangalore. Rai had believed that getting rid of Kumar would silence Alva, but this hadn't happened. While he did lose what little hold he had in Bangalore after Kumar's murder, he was still very strong in Mangalore.

In fact, a few months after Kumar's death, Kini and a few others had too much to drink and fired shots at the hotel in which Alva stayed. Alva did not buckle; instead, he continued to move around with a strong group. Francis Cutinho and Ramesh Pujari supported him and the former was quite used to Bombay boys.

Alva, who looked like Kamal Hasan, had a huge fan following in Mangalore as a student leader. He followed what other smart youth bosses did and established contact with Bombay dons who were from Mangalore. Once he reached the stage where he could call Sharad Shetty directly on his personal number, there was no holding him back. Alva came from an affluent family but got involved in havala and smuggling gold biscuits from the Gulf to Mangalore.

Alva had Sharad Shetty's support. Rai had Ashok Shetty's support. That was where the problem lay. Ashok Shetty and Sharad Shetty seemed to be on good terms on the outside, but they were in fact competing to take charge of the Mangalore boys in the underworld. Alva and Rai were pawns in this fight between Sharad and Ashok.

Just when the conflict was growing, Rajendra and Pushpa were released in Jayaraj's murder case. Rai went to Pushpa's house and spoke to them. Rai met Narayana, Pahilwan Naga, Mysore Road Naga and other boys there.

Rai talked to me about it the next day. 'They have good boys, Sreedhar. Pushpa says he has seven batches of boys. He said he could send boys even at midnight if I needed them.'

I knew he wanted me to report this to Balaram.

Rai was unnecessarily tense, now that Pushpa and Rajendra were out of jail. Rajendra is among the most intelligent and well-informed men in the underworld. He had not displayed anger or unpleasantness when we joined Rai. More surprisingly, he had not made any objections to Balaram. Rai said Rajendra had told him, 'Listen Sir, in Bangalore there are several groups. Whatever differences we have amongst ourselves, you be good to everyone. In case we have any problem with each other, you can then solve it.'

I was not confident about the two and Balaram and I always spoke badly about Rajendra to Rai. All that changed after their release.

What else do we have to do in the underworld other than to watch our enemies' movements? Balaram kept a close watch on Rajendra's every word and step. At no time did Rajendra give room for any suspicion.

Since Rai was getting close to Rajendra, I advised him to sort out the issues between Rajendra and Balaram. Rai became irritated. 'How do I get Rajendra and Balaram to come together, Sreedhar? Will Balaram accept someone who mounted an attack on him?' he asked. His tone suggested that it would be better if they didn't. He was also strongly influenced by the Dubai bhais, who advised him. 'Look Sreedhar, they say that I should not attempt to unite two fighting parties . . . I should only take care that they don't fight me. Aren't they right?'

We did not like his stand. We knew that it is a dangerous mind that takes care to be safe personally but tolerates others fighting. I often told him patiently, 'Muthappanna, Bangalore is not Bombay. It is not an extension of Bombay. Here we have no smuggling. In an hour's time we can go from one end of the city to the other. If you make up your mind, you can make both groups sit together and sort out their differences.'

'Why worry about it now? Let's see when the need arises,' he brushed it off.

One day the unexpected happened.

Usually Pushpa and Rajendra would come to meet Rai after calling ahead and fixing a time. Balaram would also take an appointment through me. Bachchan and I had the freedom of going any time we wanted and we usually went around noon, since Rai came into office at eleven o'clock.

One day, Bachchan and I went to Rai's office and one of his boys told us that Rajendra and Pushpa were inside. It had been three years, and I was not prepared to meet them without prior mental preparation. We sat in one of the cabins. We did not tell the boy to inform Rai of our arrival, but he did so anyway. Rajendra asked Rai, 'Sir, please call them in, I want to see them.' Rai had no option but to call us in. We went in, though we were reluctant.

In just one second Rajendra drove away all my misgivings.

Rajendra has been one of the very few associates who have been close enough to address me in the singular. I had no personal differences with him; we'd had to separate after we backed Jayaraj. We spoke for about half an hour in front of Rai. Jayaraj, Oil Kumar, Balaram, Jedarahalli Krishnappa—all of them figured in our conversation. It was like meeting an old dear friend; within minutes we regained that old familiarity.

I looked at Rai's face several times to check if this annoyed him, but I saw no such feelings. When Pushpa and Rajendra got up to leave, I went to see them off.

When we approached the steps, Kalapathar stood before us.

Kalapathar was Rajendra's staunch enemy and Balaram's friend. For a minute I was stunned. I recovered and said, 'See Rajendra, you were asking about Balaram and Kalapathar— here he is.'

I had told the truth. When Rajendra was in jail, Kalapathar was also there and he was quite friendly with Rajendra. After he came out, Kalapathar had joined hands with Balaram.

Rajendra spoke freely with Kalapathar. There was no malice or sarcasm in his voice. He wanted to forget the past.

Kalapathar always felt shy to talk in my presence. He had the look of Tamil film star MGR and an attractive smile. He gave Rajendra the same smile. Both of them shook hands.

Rai's boys, including Willy, looked at them in surprise. One boy went in and told Rai what had happened.

After Rajendra left I took Kalapathar in. Rai's face had lost its cool. He was upset that Rajendra had spoken to me and had met Kalapathar as well.

'What Kalapathar, what did Rajendra say?' he asked.

'Oh nothing much, Sir. Just met and said a few words,' said Kalapathar.

Kalapathar stayed for some time and then left. After he went Rai said with annoyance, 'Couldn't you have made Kalapathar sit here and reach a compromise with Rajendra, Sreedhar?'

His question irritated me.

~

Bangalore has seen some of the toughest and most efficient police officers, but in the early '90s it was Kempaiah who spread fear in the hearts and minds of those of us in the underworld. There is no one like him.

Kempaiah was already a legend in Bijapur and Shimoga by the time he came to Bangalore, but when Rai told me about Kempaiah the first time, I did not pay much attention.

When Kempaiah stepped into Bangalore, it was not an easy place. Though Jayaraj and Oil Kumar were dead, everybody was talking about Rai's guns. It was also common knowledge that he had the support of a section of the Bangalore police.

In those days, Bangalore was more plagued by massage parlours than rowdies. From commercial areas, they had spread their tentacles to middle-class localities too. They were run under the name of 'recreation clubs'. A few dumbbells, bars, plates and a carom board were set up, but what was really going on was the massage business. The parlours were filled with girls who were eighteen to twenty years old. It was a parallel trade to the flesh market.

The massage parlour owners first collected all the information they could about Kempaiah—from his brand of drink to his clothes and friends. Then they offered him, through a friend of his, a bribe of twenty-five lakh rupees to start with, and two lakh rupees a month.

How Kempaiah reacted to the offer was widely publicised. He looked down at his shoes and said, 'In my opinion, the offer you have made has no more value than the dust on my shoes.'

After hearing this, it was an unwritten rule for us not to operate in his jurisdiction.

At that time there were two DCPs in Bangalore: Kempaiah in the south and K. Ramamurthy in the north. Ramamurthy was also an efficient officer but he did his work according to law and did not yell like Kempaiah. On the odd occasion that Ramamurthy went on leave, all of Bangalore would come under Kempaiah, and at such times Rai did not even open the doors to his office.

The underworld was most scared of Kempaiah's 'work'. Usually it is crime constables who torture the accused. Notorious criminals are 'worked' on by sub-inspectors and inspectors; very rarely will an officer of the rank of ACP be present. We had never heard of a DCP being present when 'work' was going on. And Kempaiah would not just be present, but would take the rod and thrash the man himself. It would take months for the man to heal.

His style of 'working' was special. He would come to the station after midnight (there were rumours that he arrived on horseback). He would hold a rod—he never touched a lathi— and start the beating, asking, 'Have you seen Ambareesh's film?'

If an ordinary grade officer 'worked' on us, we could appeal or even complain to higher officials. But what could we do when a DCP 'worked' on us? Not that Kempaiah 'worked' on small-time rowdies. He would not touch them. He only tortured notorious dons.

There was a rumour that he did not sleep. Apparently after he left the station at four in the morning, he would go swimming.

Luckily none of us were subjected to his torture. Only Kalapathar and Tanveer were unlucky enough to be beaten by him. He had 'worked' on Kalapathar so much that anyone else in his place would have given up the crime world. But he was as strong as his nickname suggested, like stone, and took it.

Krishnamurthy from our gang was once 'worked' on by Kempaiah in Shimoga. After that he never went back to Shimoga as long as Kempaiah was there. Yet, Krishnamurthy said good things about him. He said anyone wanting to give up the underworld would get his support. Also, if a lower rank officer troubled an accused and if he approached Kempaiah, he would help.

Once, while drinking, we asked Krishnamurthy about Kempaiah's 'work'. He did not speak for some time. He looked down, trying to figure out how to explain it. After a few minutes, he lifted his head and said, 'When Kempaiah gets very angry, he does not "work" *Anna* . . . he kills.'

The underworld was abuzz with news that Kempaiah was collecting information about Rai. Several police officers who liked Rai kept telling him to be cautious. I suggested that Rai should go and meet Kempaiah.

The common people think the police should not have any connections with the underworld. They consider it a big crime. But if the police have no connections with criminals, how can they catch them? All over the world, the police-criminal nexus is a reality. The men in the underworld only resort to extortion; they do not engage in dacoity or rape, and the police need their help to find these other criminals.

So I thought it would be good for Rai to meet Kempaiah, but the question was, through whom. We did not know how

Kempaiah would react if Rai went on his own. We asked Krishnamurthy, and he said that Kempaiah would listen to Manjunath Bhandari of the Congress. Rai knew Bhandari. He immediately went to meet Bhandari, who organised the meeting.

The next day, I asked him what happened. He said, 'I should not have gone,' and explained.

Rai did not know how to go to meet an officer. He had on a treasury worth of jewellery and left the top two buttons of his shirt unfastened. Kempaiah was furious. 'Button up!' he had screamed.

A few days after Rai met Kempaiah, he was offered a house in Richmond Town. It was an old bungalow, a highly-priced one at a prominent location. We knew that Kempaiah's attention was directed towards Rai's office; it was not in his jurisdiction, but that did not mean he could not raid it, so we began to spend time at the Richmond Town house. We would go to the office in the morning for a brief time and then leave for the bungalow; we called it 'Society'. A smart boy called Lakshman cooked for us all. We had a TV, VCR, English films and also blue films. Kini, Rajan, Satish, Narasimha, Naveen, Pamma and others stayed there all the time and played cards. We spent our afternoons there.

One afternoon, Rai and Jayanth came over. Rai looked worried. He took me aside and said, 'Bad news Sreedhar, the one we trusted has cheated us.'

I looked at him in surprise.

'Balaram,' he said, and looked at me sadly.

I said that Balaram had never betrayed anyone and asked him what had happened.

This is what he told me. Kalasipalya Nagaraju and Samson together had a big site behind Jayaraj's house in Wilson Garden. They had each constructed small shacks on that site, where three or four people could live comfortably.

Three boys from Mangalore had been staying in Samson's shack for the past three days. They had got drunk the previous night and started talking disparagingly about Rai. The boy who took care of Nagaraju heard what they said. One of the three had even predicted that Rai would soon be murdered. The caretaker had reported the conversation to Nagaraju, who told Jayanna, who told Rai.

It was Balaram who had kept those boys there. We were not surprised about that, because ever since Balaram had spent more than a year in the Mangalore jail, he knew boys from the underworld in that city. Also, Balaram had good relations with Samson, so he must have let them stay in Samson's shack.

But what surprised us was that he had contacts with Rai's enemies. A long time before, when I had mentioned Raghu's request to finish Yadu, Balaram had refused point-blank. 'Let us try to get them to compromise, but do not even mention finishing Yadu,' he had said.

We always knew that Balaram would do anything for his friends.

I told Rai that it was unlikely that Balaram had backed his enemies; yet, I said, we could raid the shack that night. If the boys did have Balaram's support, then we should not let him go. Rai looked relieved.

We decided not to leave the place till the boys were picked up. In the underworld, suspicions spread very fast, and once chariness takes root, it is difficult to be rid of. We were very committed to Rai and his gang, and we wanted to sort out the issue.

Rai informed the police as well. In case the boys really had plotted to kill him, the police could make them talk and then we could take action. Everybody agreed with the plan.

At around midnight, we covered the shack. After ten minutes, the Wilson Garden police came and picked up the three boys. We watched from a distance. One boy did not have an arm. By midnight we'd found out the details. They were from Rai's enemy's gang from Mangalore. Jayanth had cut one boy's arm in a fight, and hence they had been talking angrily about Rai amongst themselves. They had never spoken against Rai to Balaram.

I met Balaram the next day and shouted at him. He was also very upset about the incident. He said if he had been alerted instead of involving the police, he would have thrashed the boys and sent them back.

Finally Muthappa Rai himself had to talk to the police and get the boys released and sent back to Mangalore.

That evening Rai spoke to Balaram and asked him to keep the Mangalore boys at a distance. The outcome of this incident was that Rai started trusting Balaram as much as he trusted us.

Because of his fear of Kempaiah, Rai began establishing contacts with politicians. It's a strange network. The politicians pamper the underworld because they are of use during elections. The police play up to politicians because they can be used during transfers. The underworld controls the police through politicians and the politicians control the underworld through the police!

We knew several politicians even before Rai came on the scene. Rai too had a cordial relationship with Vinaykumar Sorake, Jeevaraj Alva, Suntikoppa Ibrahim, Devaraj and others and he had indirect contact with Hariprasad and Janardhana Pujari. Rai had introduced me to Sorake in his office. Devaraj Urs' youngest daughter would also visit Rai's office.

One day, Hosakote's Chikke Gowda came to the office. He was a powerful minister at the time. One Sonnappa from Kodihalli had insulted him, and he wanted to finish the man, for which he had come to Rai for support. A man called Acharya had come with him. I was present when Chikke Gowda told Rai about Sonnappa.

After he left, Rai asked me what he should do. I said although it would be good to take up the assignment and get the support of an influential minister like Chikke Gowda, it would be dangerous to rush into a village and execute such an act. Rai wanted Bachchan, Krishnamurthy and me to take the lead, use his boys and get the work done. But when we did not show any interest, he left it at that.

When we later made enquiries in Hosakote, we found out

that anyone stepping into the village to kill Sonnappa would be killed even before he could attempt something.

One afternoon when we went to the office, we saw a large man with a beard. He was Sakaleshpur Sudheer Prabhu. He had a big coffee estate in Sakaleshpur which he'd sold to a Gowda, who had given him an advance of about fifty lakh rupees. The balance one crore thirty lakh rupees was due to him. The coffee was ready for harvesting and an income of about eighty lakh was guaranteed. He had come to request Rai to intervene and get the balance paid to him.

We did not know anything about estates.

Rai seemed intimidated by the person who was backing Gowda—a man called Vikram. He said the deal had to be handled carefully. I told him we could bribe the police and execute the plan. Rai agreed.

After a few days, Rai went to Puttur, intending to go to Sakaleshpur from there to put up a 'show' at Sudheer Prabhu's estate. We had some work of our own in Bangalore and couldn't go with him, but sent five boys, including Chandru, with him. Rai and his gang took eight cars for the journey: it was the first time Rai was visiting his native place after Kumar's murder, and he wanted to make an impression, hence the large number of boys.

But they didn't make it to Sakaleshpur. The news that Rai and Sudheer Prabhu were in Puttur reached that place and the Gowda's boys were ready to retaliate in the event of an attack. Rai found out about this and abandoned his plan. After the group returned to Bangalore, Sudheer Prabhu became a permanent member of the gang.

We noticed how quick Sudheer Prabhu was at playing cards, when we went over to Brindavan Hotel. We used to comment amongst ourselves that he would lose not only the money from the sale of the estate but also his entire family wealth.

It was not long before our words came true.

~

Meanwhile, Amar Alva was gaining a formidable reputation in Mangalore. He had plans to finish Rai. Since Alva used Francis Cutinho and Ramesh Pujari for his attacks, whenever they were out of Mangalore, Rai would be alerted.

Several times we heard that Amar Alva and Kumar's wife were planning to kill Rai. We did not take it seriously, and neither did Rai. One day, however, a boy from Bombay Kishore's gang came to Bangalore and told us that plans were on to kill Rai.

Rai immediately took notice. In the Bombay underworld, everything is systematically planned. People do not fight for personal revenge like they do in Bangalore. Killing is a business there. The Bombay underworld runs on the calculation of how much money can be made by killing whom. The boy who had given us the information was a 'planner'. Planners have the responsibility of deciding how their group will benefit by killing someone, when it has to be done, by whom, as well as how. They are very important in Bombay.

The planner in this case was Kishore—the same one who had played a major role in Jayaraj's murder. Parekh, who had hosted the Bombay killers at that time, gave shelter to Kishore.

After being released from jail following the Kotwal case, Balaram's gang had picked Parekh up. They suspected he was involved in shady business of some sort and they had tortured him in a garage. The next morning I had reprimanded them and forced them to release him. I could never have imagined that he would be spending time with the people who had killed Jayaraj. When Rai first mentioned his name, I thought it was someone else. But after he described him, I realised it was the same Parekh. Rai was worried about him so we decided to pick him up and get information about the Bombay killers who had landed in Bangalore.

Although we were eager to execute the plan, Rai wanted Pushpa and Rajendra to do it. He wanted to test their commitment. They assured him that they would bring Parekh to him in twenty-four hours, but even after one week they had not done so, giving one excuse after another. Finally, Rai asked us to do it.

We called Balaram to ask him to pick up Parekh. He agreed, but even after four days, we could not get Parekh. On the fifth day, Balaram and his gang did not join us; they said they wanted to relax. We had booked a room in Bowring Club for the last four days so we could wait near Parekh's house for him. However, he never spent the night there; instead he would come for a while during the day and leave immediately. We had a boy stand on watch. He called that day at seven o'clock and said Parekh had come home.

I immediately called Rai. Only Bachchan and Krishnamurthy were with me, so I said I wanted some more boys. We couldn't track Balaram down, and Rai tried to contact other boys but only Willy was available. Rai was angry that even when Bombay gangsters had come to Bangalore to kill, we were not able to find boys.

'What will you do?' he asked me.

We had been waiting for so long to catch Parekh, and since we knew that Francis Cutinho and the others were not with him but staying at a hotel in Seshadripuram, I said we could not afford to delay any further. If Willy were sent, I said, I would bring Parekh at any cost.

Willy came at eight. We went by Parekh's house in an Ambassador. Our boy was still there and said Parekh was still at home. At nine-thirty Parekh left on a scooter. From his house in Rajajinagar II Block he took a right on the West of Chord Road. We followed him in our car. The road was crowded with vehicles. Parekh turned into a road that leads to Mahalakshmi Layout. We sped up so our car lightly touched his scooter. He fell down. Krishnamurthy acted swiftly: without even giving us a chance to get down, he picked up Parekh and bundled him into the car. Immediately a crowd gathered and started asking what was happening. We said 'police' and 'smuggler'. You have no idea how scared people are of the police. They immediately said, 'Take him, take him', and the crowd dispersed. Come to think of it, there is absolutely no difference in the way the police and the underworld pick up a man!

Bachchan picked up the scooter and followed us.

Parekh first thought it really was the police who had picked him up. We took him to Society, Rai's new place in Richmond Town, and made him remove all his clothes, except his briefs. He had fifty thousand rupees with him, which we took.

I was furious with Parekh. What did he think of the Bangalore underworld, that he would first support Rai when finished Jayaraj, and then support Amar Alva to finish Rai? I began torturing him from ten o'clock. Seeing how angry and violent I was getting, the boys tried to calm me down. Willy, who usually tends to get rough in these cases, also kept quiet.

At around one o'clock Rai came with his boys, including Kini, Jayanth, Rajan and Satish. His eyes were burning with anger. He came rushing at great speed towards Parekh. '*Kya* Parekh . . . *mera* fielding *karega?*' he caught hold of Parekh, pushed him down and lifted his hand to beat him.

But his hand, which had gone up at such great speed, lost its spirit by the time it came down. I thought his humaneness must have stopped him, and my anger increased all the more. The fact was, I really liked Rai.

'*Kantri bolimagane*,' I cursed. 'You think of Bangalore as a brothel? You think you can finish anyone and make anyone the boss? We like Muthappanna and we have accepted him as our leader. Anyone who harms him—we will smash them and their family totally . . .' I shouted and kicked Parekh hard.

He staggered. I was about to kick him again but Rai stopped me.

Satish asked Bachchan, 'Why is he beating him so badly? Ask him to stop.'

I stopped hitting him and asked, 'Parekh, tell me, do you think Muthappanna has become a boss for nothing? Did he not finish Jayaraj by risking everything? Tell me . . .'

My punches did not perturb him. He just stared at me and did not answer.

'Tell me, who killed Jayaraj?' I prodded him. I was trying to get him to say that Rai was the undisputed don of the underworld.

But he said coldly, 'Subhash Thakur.'

I had not heard until then that Subhash Thakur, a notorious don from Bombay, had also been involved in the Jayaraj killing. I hid my surprise and said, 'Okay, he was also there . . . and who else?'

Rai watched it all silently.

'Sauthia.'

He was talking about Sunil Sauthia, who was known as the number one shooter in Dawood Ibrahim's gang in Bombay.

Now, instead of just forcing him to admit that Rai was the don, I was more interested in finding out who had really killed Jayaraj.

'Who else was with them?'

'Francis, Ramesh Pujari . . .'

'Okay, was Muthappanna not there?' I looked at Rai's face and asked.

'He . . . he too was there. He was the one who first shot at the car. Then Subhash Thakur and Francis got out of the car and finished him . . .'

Kini and Willy had told me several times that they had killed Jayaraj. That day I found out the truth. It is common in the underworld to claim someone else's job as yours. But in Jayaraj's case, nobody knew—not the police, not the underworld, not even we—who had really killed Jayaraj.

The paradox was that, although it was Rai who had fired the first shot, he had never claimed that it was he who killed Jayaraj.

Rai said, 'Sreedhar, let me speak to Parekh alone.'

We said we would return at night and left, cursing ourselves for all the wrong things we had imagined about Jayaraj's murder.

We returned later that evening, thinking Rai would have decided to kill Parekh, but Rai had sent him away.

I was unhappy that he had let someone who had been trying to kill him go. Rai said he had persuaded Parekh to come to his side. I argued that anyone else in his place would have kept him for at least two days and tortured him so he never attempted something like that again.

'You just watch, Sreedhar, I will bring down Alva's gang through him,' he said.

Not only had Rai let him go, he had also given Parekh back his fifty thousand rupees!

I have to record here something I found out after we separated from Rai.

The day we picked up Parekh, Bombay's 'master planner' Kishore was staying at his place! If Rai had acted as tough as I did, we could have seized him. If we had finished him, all the killers from the Bombay underworld would have been stunned. Also, we could have got Francis Cutinho, Ramesh Pujari and the other Bombay killer with them in the hotel. We need not have even done anything—if we had just informed the police, they would have done the rest. But as soon as Parekh told them what had happened, all of them vanished.

Did it mean picking up Parekh was of no use?

Of course it had its uses. Parekh gave us vital information. The day after we picked him up, Rai had to attend court. That day, all preparations were made to kill him. Since it was suspected that Rai would wear a bullet-proof vest, they had decided to shoot at his head. Rai did not attend court that day.

After the Parekh incident, Rai was even more cordial with us. He began to believe that he could depend on us for anything. Meanwhile, another incident occurred that once again put our trust in him to the test.

Three

That morning, Jayanna invited us to MTR for breakfast.

I had never been fond of the restaurant, but I learned that Venkataswamy Reddy, a close friend of the then minister S. Ramesh wanted to see me there, so I had to go. When we reached, we saw that the legislator Devaraj was also there.

While we were eating breakfast, Jayanna received a phone call. Since all his friends knew that Jayanna would be in MTR between ten and twelve, they often called the restaurant for him.

After speaking on the phone, Jayanna called me aside and said, '*Aa yappa* (that man—Jayanna called Rai *Aa yappa* affectionately) called and he asked me where you were. I said you are with me here. He asked me to send you urgently.'

I was surprised. It was around ten days since the Parekh incident had occurred. There was no chance of any attacks, and Kempaiah had no plans to raid Rai's office. Ashok Kumar had searched his office only a few days ago but did not find anything there. Since then we had been meeting in Brindavan Hotel and in Society. Rai too had stopped going to the office.

When I went back to join the others, Devaraj and Venkataswamy Reddy asked me what the matter was. I told them. Immediately they said they would leave with me because if Rai had called, there had to be some urgency.

We went straight to Brindavan Hotel.

Kini, Satish, Mahabala, Sudheer Prabhu, Pomma and a few others were standing outside. Rajendra and Pushpa were inside with Rai. As soon as they saw me, Rajendra and Pushpa bid goodbye to Rai, gave me a smile and left. But by looking at their faces, I knew something was wrong.

Rai's face had lost colour. He was courteous to Devaraj and Venkataswamy Reddy, but was not able to talk to them. Noticing this, Jayanna led them away. Rai took me to a small room in the front and we sat facing each other. Rai was looking at my face but I could not bear to look at him.

'What happened, Muthappanna? Why are you like this?'

He sighed. 'We have to murder a man . . . I wonder what you will say.'

'What's there to ask? If you say it, then it has to be done,' I said.

'No Sreedhar, I feel you may not agree.'

I was very confused by the way he was talking. 'Even if I don't agree, Balaram will execute the commission . . . you know how they all love you now.'

'I can't use any of them, only you can do it.'

I felt relieved. 'Tell me what the problem is. Let's see if I really don't like it . . .'

'Sreedhar, tell me the truth. How much do you trust me?'

I laughed despite the tense situation. 'Why? Do you suspect me?'

'No Sreedhar, tell me,' he insisted.

I was certain either Jayanth or Kini must have annoyed him. Naturally he could not confide in anyone else.

'I have a hundred per cent trust in you. Tell me.'

'Someone amongst us has challenged my leadership. In fact, he has even questioned my capabilities . . . tell me what should we do?'

Now I was very certain, but I did not want to rush. 'If someone has behaved like that and if it is serious we should find a way. First let us find out the reason.'

'My decision to finish him cannot be changed Sreedhar. He has challenged me in front of many boys. News has already reached Sharadanna's ears too . . .'

I realised the seriousness of the situation.

'Then there is nothing to ask. Tell me who it is and let's finish the job.'

Rai said slowly, 'Balaram.'

But those days Balaram was so fond of Rai that I could not imagine him speaking against him on any account. I thought Pushpa and Rajendra must have caused some mischief.

'What happened? To whom has he spoken? If he really has spoken like that, we must not let him go; but you cannot just listen to hearsay.'

Rai did not answer; instead, he called out to Kini, who rushed in as if he had been waiting for the call. Kini's face, which was usually calm when he was not drunk, was on fire now.

'Sreedhar, I don't have as much experience as you in the underworld. I respect you, but yesterday night the way Balaram came here and behaved was unimaginable.'

'Balaram came here? To this room?'

'Yes, he came here, at half past ten at night, with Malayali Sridhar and two other boys. I was getting ready to go out for dinner, Malayali put a cigarette in his mouth, picked up a matchbox from the table and, lighting the cigarette, asked me, "Is Rai available now?"'

Apparently, before they came to the hotel, Balaram, Malayali Sridhar, Kisan, Anil and Swamy had been sitting in a pub on Dickenson Road, drinking beer. The pub belonged to a dealer of foreign cars; his son looked after the pub in the evening. Balaram went there thrice a week and sometimes we went there with him.

That night, while Balaram's gang was at the pub, Sudheer Prabhu, Mahabala and a friend from Bombay had come in. They had earlier met Balaram through me. When they walked in, Balaram invited them to join him at his table. They greeted him, but refused and sat at their own table. Malayali Sridhar got up, went to them and invited them again to their table. Again, they refused.

In the underworld, pride is extremely important. A man can be killed just for glaring at someone. Once, Manibharathi, Kalapathar, Kantha and some other boys were going to a live concert. In the lift, a stranger stared at them. When they asked him why he was staring, he did not reply properly. Manibharathi stabbed him to death with his button knife. They went to jail for a year-and-a-half for this!

Balaram and his group felt insulted. Also, they got the impression that the pub owner's son was ignoring them after Sudheer Prabhu had arrived. The result of all this was that, after the other group left, Balaram's gang had assaulted the pub owner's son and destroyed tables and glasses in the pub. The pub's owner was in Dubai. He was a close friend of Sharad Shetty, whom Rai respected.

It was after this that the gang had gone to Brindavan, and that was when Malayali Sridhar asked, 'Where is Rai?' with a cigarette in his mouth.

Kini was stunned—nobody addressed the boss like that. In the underworld, it is unpardonable.

'Why? Why do you want him?' Kini had asked.

'Nothing much . . . we have beaten up someone dear to him because his behaviour was not right. We want to tell him,' said Sridhar.

The attitude with which he said this was as if he were saying, 'We have thrashed his man—what will you do?'

Kini told them that Rai was not available at that time even on the phone and sent them away. After they left, Sudheer Prabhu, Satish, Mahabala and the others came there. Kini told them what had happened. When they called the pub, the owner's son was crying, so they went over.

Meanwhile, Balaram and his gang were waiting near Ulsoor Circle. They had sent a boy to find out if the pub owner had lodged a complaint against them in the Ulsoor station (no complaint was lodged). When this boy went to the pub, Kini, Sudheer and the others beat him up, asking where Balaram was. He went back crying to Balaram and narrated what had happened to him.

By then Balaram had collected many boys from the area. They all headed back to the pub to attack Sudheer Prabhu and the others. When they reached, a police jeep from Commercial Street station was there, so they did not go in but watched from a distance.

Kini called Rai, who told him to finish Balaram. They searched for Balaram the entire night but couldn't find him. They did not know where I lived, and hence had been waiting for me to come to the hotel to inform me of the events.

Kini, who rarely lost his cool, explained the entire episode to me in a rage. I did not know how to react. I sat there stunned. I had not expected Balaram to challenge Rai like that. Just the previous afternoon Balaram had told me, 'Ask him Sir, where we can find Francis, Kishore . . . we will go to Bombay and finish them.'

'Sreedhar, tell me . . . what shall I do?' Rai said. 'He is close to you. The last time when I was doubtful about him you were not this close to him . . . now it is difficult for you to lift your hand against him. Just say yes and our boys will finish him. Just tell us where we can find him.'

The tragedy was that Rai also liked Balaram. He knew he had played an important role in getting Parekh. In fact, he had trusted him so much that he had asked me a couple of times, 'Shall we keep four or five guns with Balaram?'

That time I had said that on no account should he make that mistake. We did not know when Balaram would go over to whom, and we could not take the risk of giving weapons to him. Balaram had also been after me to get one or two guns from Rai. I told him Rai was ready to give him guns but I was stopping him. He had not argued about it again.

Rai said, 'I understand your anxiety Sreedhar—I am not shocked at Balaram assaulting that boy. Maybe after our men came away he might have done something, we can accept that. But what happened after that—in the hotel room, and him going back to the pub. What does it show? He did not like me; he was with us for your sake.'

That day Rai was in a dilemma like me. In the underworld, since friendship can change to enmity quickly, it is not easy to resort to violence.

Rai said, 'Pushpa and Rajendra are telling me to allow them to finish Balaram . . .'

'Why did you not have trust in me?' I asked.

'You know Sreedhar, I never trusted them as much as I trusted Balaram. But Balaram betrayed me without any reason. I cannot let him go. Whatever you say, it will be difficult for you to kill him . . . I need someone local, hence I called them,' he said.

'You should not have called them,' I said. 'Look, I don't know why Balaram did this. Definitely we cannot excuse his behaviour. Yet, please give me a chance to talk to him . . . if you trust me.'

Suddenly Rai's face relaxed. 'Please talk to him, Sreedhar, but whatever you say we cannot spare him,' he said, but his tone implied that the issue could perhaps be sorted out.

After this, Rai took us to the house of the boy who had been assaulted. He had bandages on his forehead and hand. His mother and sisters started crying when they saw us. Perhaps the father knew that Balaram was close to me: he kept asking me, 'If this had been your boy, what would you do?' trying to impress me.

The boy told us that after Sudheer Prabhu and the others had left, Balaram called him and slapped him, saying, 'Just because they were all there you want to put up your pride?' and then Malayali Sridhar and the others had trashed the pub. Then they forced him to sit down and asked him, 'Who is Bangalore's boss?' The boy had innocently said, 'Muthappanna'. They had beaten him with a bottle and asked him again. This time he had said, 'Balaram . . . Balaramanna.'

They had threatened him and left.

When the boy was narrating the incident, Satish, who had once tried to become a hero in films, was screaming, 'Woh Balaram . . . woh gaandu . . . we will show the Bangalore rowdies who we are . . .'

Rai gestured to him to not scream like that. He himself was sitting quietly without losing his calm. After we went back to the hotel he asked me, 'You heard him, Sreedhar. What does the question, "Who is the boss?" tell you? Now let us decide finally . . .'

I said I would still like to talk to Balaram one final time and decide.

'But don't make us seem weak in front of Balaram, Sreedhar. Later, if others follow him, it will be difficult,' Rai said.

The problem was that we did not know where Balaram lived. It had been nearly a year since he was released from jail, but no one had his address. He had not shown his house to even the boys who were ready to die for him.

I had found out just two months ago that he had gotten married to a girl he had been in love with for over a year. His wife did not know he was a rowdy. He had passed off Kisan, who looked older, as his uncle, and each of his boys as some relative, and had completed the wedding ceremony.

I had started using his marriage as a lever to advise him to behave properly. I always stressed that, now that he was married, he should not attempt any work that would send him to jail again—that even if a single case were filed against him his wife would find out about his past and it would shatter her dreams. I even told him that women were very sensitive and she might even commit suicide because of the shock. Balaram, who had nodded his head meekly in front of me, had then attacked the pub owner's son just because he had shown more respect to someone else. I was very angry. Also the fact that Rai trusted us and had never treated us badly made me wish to keep a distance from even Balaram. Yet in my heart I did not want to finish him.

We went to Cauvery Continental Hotel where we usually met him. Two of his boys had been waiting there for us from ten in the morning! They just said, 'Follow us.' We followed them through many lanes and bylanes and we finally reached the Kodavara Sangha building, which was actually very close to the hotel. We were stunned to see about seventy boys with Balaram. I became even angrier when I saw that group.

Balaram, Malayali Sridhar, Bachchan and I sat at one table. The minute we sat down, I started yelling at him. I said he would never improve; that he would never learn how to behave with people; that if Kotwal or Jayaraj were in Rai's place, things would have been totally different.

Finally, he said coolly, 'Sir, let us do one thing—you step aside, let them do whatever they want to, we are ready.'

'Balaram, what has Rai done to you?'

'I am not talking about him. We are as affectionate towards him as you are. But those *gojja nan makklu* ... his associates ... what arrogance! We invited them so many times, why couldn't they have just had a drink with us?' He did not allow me to talk further but poured out his anger.

Malayali Sridhar started explaining slowly as if to convince me. 'Sir, none of this would have happened if they had just come for a minute and then gone to their table. How can they rule Bangalore without local support? That chotu ... that soolemaga small boy ... he was not even standing in front of us! When they were sitting there, you know how he behaved? "They are all our Sharadanna's boys ... our daddy calls Sharadanna often. He has made Muthappanna Bangalore's don," he said! So you want us to listen to it and keep quiet? Sharadanna has made Muthappanna boss, it seems! Then why should all of us be there?' he asked furiously.

Balaram answered him vulgarly, 'To shave their balls.'

'Okay, in the pub the boy irritated you and you thrashed him. Why did you go to Brindavan Hotel?'

Malayali said, 'We did not want them to say we were sitting quiet when they were present and then showed our strength after they left, isn't it? So we went to challenge them directly. We thought those *gojja nan makklu* would be there, but apart from Kinianna no one was there. We left a message that we are ready for anything.'

Now, I started consoling them. 'Look, Balaram, just because

someone drinks and misbehaves, why are you angry with MR? (We often called Rai MR.) Why do we all go there? Is it not for MR?'

'Look Sir, whatever you say, however good MR is, we cannot do salaam to the dogs around him. And please understand one thing: we are ready to accept you as our boss, but not MR. Just because we like him that does not mean we are ready to accept him as our boss.'

When Balaram said that, I was shocked.

'Balaram, I don't know if all of you agree or not, but I have accepted MR as the boss. If you talk like this sitting in front of me, and if he gets to hear of it, will it not create a misunderstanding?'

'Then you tell MR that he should not involve those Mangalore gojjas. We will take care very good care of him.'

It took me three hours to convince Balaram. He said he would not beat anyone up even if his pride were insulted. He also assured me that when I called him, he would talk to the boy he had assaulted in front of Rai.

I have specific reasons for documenting this incident in such detail: it resulted in several developments.

To this day, neither the police officers who have sufficient insight into the Bangalore underworld, nor rowdies, nor Muthappa Rai himself know why I broke from Rai. The only reason was that he had decided to finish Balaram. I became aware of it six months after this incident. Even after Balaram spoke to him and totally accepted him, Rai did not completely give up his plan for revenge. It might seem irrelevant to record a few incidents that happened six months before, but I have to unveil completely the consequences of those incidents. Unexpected events result in strange twists, not just in the underworld but in life in general.

That was one such incident.

After talking to Balaram I met Rai and spoke to him. I didn't want to tell him about Balaram's challenge, because I did not want the group to break. I only stressed on things that would heal the rift.

Ten days after the incident, Rai called Balaram to Brindavan. Although Balaram had assured him that only he and Kalapathar would be present, there were about twenty boys with him. Some of them stood at a distance from the hotel and only seven boys, including Kalapathar, Kisan and Malayali Sridhar, entered. Balaram made them stand outside, but in a place visible to us from the room, and came in with Kalapathar.

Rai had called the owner of the pub, the boy's father, and he had come with two of his friends. I thought he would make a move on seeing Balaram, but he did no such thing. He behaved with respect and fear with Balaram. Rai told Balaram that if anything bad had happened he should have informed him before taking any action. The meeting was cordial, except when Mahabala came in and told Balaram, 'If we had met you there that day, we would have fired at you and you would be dead by now.'

Balaram gave him a fierce look and gestured carelessly, taunting him.

'Forget the others, Balaram, now the situation is such that if we give guns to you, even he would say it would be a mistake,' Rai said, pointing at me.

His intention was to tell Balaram that he trusted him more than I did.

The boy's father stayed for some time and then left. Rai got everyone juice. Just when Rai was telling Balaram not to attempt anything that would lead to a misunderstanding, Balaram's boy entered to say that the crime branch police had arrived and were asking for Rai.

Just look at the sequence of events: Rai's boys never watched the surroundings like Balaram's boys did, so if they had not been there, Rai would have definitely been caught along with enough number of guns to make it difficult for him to escape from Kempaiah's clutches.

In fact, even when Balaram's boy came and informed him that the police were outside, Rai did not take it seriously. However, I insisted that it was not safe to stay there. We sent

Balaram away, asking him to come some other day, and we left in a hurry.

Bachchan, Jayanth, Rai and I went in one car. Kini, Willy and Sudheer Prabhu were still at the hotel. We went for a drive to Indiranagar, and other places. Rai seemed relaxed after speaking to Balaram. He said anyone else in Balaram's place would have done the same thing. 'We all think from our own point of view, Sreedhar, but from Balaram's point of view, how else could he act when he was insulted in front of his own boys? He too has a status. And when it is damaged he can't act otherwise, isn't it?'

I felt very proud of him at that point. I really appreciated his leadership qualities.

After one hour we returned to Brindavan. We saw two police jeeps parked outside. Rai was not too concerned because he had not committed any crime. He drove the car straight into the hotel, but I stopped him. I knew that the police violate all rules while arresting underworld men. I said we should not go in unless we knew why the police had come. Rai reversed, though he did not want to, and we went away. It was night by the time we got the news: Kempaiah had raided Brindavan Hotel and arrested all Rai's men.

Kempaiah had had his eye on Rai from the time he'd arrived in Bangalore. He could not fathom why the Bangalore police had not arrested Rai though he had played a major role in Jayaraj's murder. However, all Rai's activities were conducted outside his jurisdiction, and so he could not take any action.

The same evening that we saw Balaram, we were to meet with the Sakaleshpur estate party (which I have mentioned earlier) regarding Sudheer Prabhu's land deal. They had contacted Rai through someone and wanted to come over to work out a settlement. Rai had agreed to meet them.

Rai had wanted to return to the hotel from our drive so he could meet with the estate party. Fortunately, we left. The next morning, we found out that the previous afternoon the Sakaleshpur party had casually mentioned to Tagore, the traffic

DCP in Shimoga, that they were going to meet Rai and asked if he knew anyone who was close to Rai since they needed a mediator. Tagore had informed Kempaiah. Naturally Kempaiah thought Rai would collect all his boys and try to threaten and bring pressure on the party, and so he had raided the hotel at that time.

In fact, Rai had planned no such thing. If he had, he would have asked Balaram to stay back. But he had told only Sudheer Prabhu and me to be with him. He had to go into hiding for no fault of his.

The day after we left Brindavan Hotel, Rai called me at seven in the morning.

I had always kept my place of residence a secret. In 1991, my younger brother Basanth completed his training in the police department and was posted in a police station in Bangalore as a sub-inspector. I could no longer hide where I lived. I tried forcing him to move out, but he did not agree. Still, we never invited anyone home. After Oil Kumar's murder, Rai had forced me to get a telephone connection. 'To look for you in emergency is very difficult. If not for you, at least for my sake you must have a telephone,' he insisted. In those days getting a phone connection was not as easy as it is now. Finally, we purchased a phone which cost twenty-five thousand rupees. The phone connection was most useful when Kempaiah conducted raids.

'The raid was by Kempaiah, Sreedhar,' Rai told me. 'He came to my house at midnight. Just half an hour ago, the inspector from the station where Kini was kept called me and said Kini had given my address . . . I escaped immediately.'

He asked me to meet him at the Magadi Road petrol bunk at eleven o'clock. I reached there on time and Rai came within five minutes. Jayanth and Pomma were with him. Rai was fuming. 'Why should they chase us? What have we done? Somebody has done it intentionally, Sreedhar. There is no complaint against us and we are not even in Kempaiah's limit . . . they are pushing us.'

I felt bad for him; I pacified him and said on no account should he be arrested. But even without my saying it, he would have been careful, because he was scared that Kempaiah would kill him in an encounter!

In those days, the Bombay police was hunting rowdies like flies. The entire Bombay police was divided in two. One was against Dawood and the other against Arun Gawli. Looking at it from another angle, one group was loyal to Dawood and the other to Arun Gawli. To this day the situation is the same in that city, except instead of Gawli, it is Chota Rajan.

In Bangalore, though, such a situation never arose. The police system was never divided based on dons. Yet Rai was scared that Kempaiah would be influenced by what was going on in Bombay and finish him. He had mentioned it several times to me. I tried to instil courage in him by arguing that the underworld never bothered about anyone other than the people in the number two businesses—oil, cards—and those who brought their problems to them. The police would not take such an extreme step.

But Rai was nervous that even if he did not kill him in an encounter, Kempaiah would torture him. He would touch his back and say, 'Sreedhar, nobody has worked on me till today. If he works on me like that, I cannot take it. If he does it to me I will not keep quiet, I will finish him.'

Bachchan, Krishnamurthy and I laughed at this. We told him that, after one or two thrashings, the body heat rises and the beatings that follow are not so painful. This was from our own experience. He would laugh at our explanation.

In the beginning, Rai would jokingly say that he would finish Kempaiah, but gradually the tone became more serious. We got anxious that Rai was making the same mistake that Jayaraj did with regard to the police. In any field, as a man climbs the ladder, he becomes blind to reality, to his surroundings. He starts believing that what he decides is the only truth. It is from here that the downfall begins. Rai was aware that the police system would crush him completely if he killed a police officer.

He also knew that, even in Bombay where the biggest of the dons were active, no one had attempted such a thing. Yet, he was considering finishing Kempaiah.

He was so tormented by the idea of Kempaiah that he had given one lakh rupees to the politician Suntikoppa Ibrahim to have Kempaiah transferred! Ibrahim had promised that he would get it done in one month, but it was not done. We had heard that Kempaiah would not give in to influence: not only in the underworld but also in the political world. Everybody said he was the then chief minister Bangarappa's protégé, so it was not possible for anyone to use influence on him.

Because of all these frustrations, Rai discussed with small-time boys how it would be if he finished Kempaiah. He was not aware that if talk like that floated, it would gather momentum— which is what happened in this case as well. Kempaiah used to go swimming at four in the morning. Rai asked a boy called Narasimha to check on this and confirm it. Since that boy was close to us from the times of Kotwal, he told us about it. I cautioned Rai not to talk like that about police officers with the boys. In case Kempaiah found out about it, Rai would not be spared and nobody would help him.

'I know that, Sreedhar, but what should I do?' Rai had pleaded.

I convinced him that unless someone complained, Kempaiah would not come after him. And if we were careful enough not to allow that to happen, then things would clear up on their own. Eventually, Rai put aside thoughts of killing Kempaiah. However, his Dubai 'controls' gave him another idea—to keep drugs in Kempaiah's house and get it raided by Bombay Narcotics! He discussed this idea for a few days and gave up on that too.

During those anxious days, Rai was contemplating another course of action. Once he asked me what I thought of his leaving Bangalore to stay in Dubai. I said it was a good idea. But when he revealed the name of the person whom he was thinking of appointing in his place, I was shocked. It was me.

'I will settle down in Dubai, Sreedhar. You be in charge here. If you have to finish someone, use my name. I will admit to having done it. Nobody will even have the guts to protest against you. In the police case too, my name will appear and you will have no problem whatsoever . . . what do you say?'

When he said this the first time, I laughed at his stupidity. 'Don't underestimate the police,' I said.

Also, since I was seriously thinking of giving up the underworld, the idea seemed meaningless.

Another day, in front of Kini, Rai said, 'Sreedhar . . . I cannot think of another person but you to take over. All my boys will accept you.'

I refused his suggestion point blank. 'If you are thinking of going away, appoint Jayanth or Kinianna in your place.'

'No, Sreedhar, if I leave this place, Jayanth will not stay here anymore. He will go to his place. Kini is here because of me. As soon as I leave he will take up something else.'

The problem with Muthappa Rai was that he buckled under pressure. Due to this weakness he complicated simple things that could be sorted out easily. Even his plan of running the Bangalore underworld from Dubai was a result of his fear of the police. In fact, except for Kempaiah, no other police officer had thought of crushing him. Many of the officers were friendly with him. But Kempaiah tormented him to such an extent that he wanted to leave Bangalore.

Before we could come to any serious decision, Kempaiah conducted a raid.

That afternoon, when Rai met me at Magadi Road, he first raved and ranted about Kempaiah but later turned his anger towards some of the politicians who might have instigated Kempaiah against him. He was suspicious of Chamarajpet MLA Devaraj. He had also figured out that, though he treated Pushpa and Rajendra cordially, they were not very fond of him. Their travel agency at Majestic was doing good business and he believed Devaraj was backing it.

He told me that he would not be available for a few days. He also said that Kini had been 'worked' on by the police, and was being taken to Sanjay Gandhi Hospital for treatment. He asked me to find out about his condition. In case of an emergency, I was to leave a message at his home. He also said he would call me often.

That evening we went to Sanjay Gandhi Hospital in a car and watched from a distance. Kini was limping badly. I felt terrible that the police had 'worked' so much on someone who had been happily chatting with me just the previous day. That night Rai called. He said he would get a doctor's certificate for Kini and file a case against the police. Even in the depressed mood I was in, I felt like laughing. Jayaraj had behaved like that and gotten into serious trouble. Yet I did not get into an argument with Rai about it but simply said it would be best if he got anticipatory bail at the earliest. He said he had spoken to the lawyer Sambamurthy.

After two days, Rai left Bangalore.

Four

One characteristic of Kempaiah was that the moment he began to chase somebody in the underworld he became relentless. I had met him and even spoken to him six months before he set his eyes on Rai.

Once the crime branch police were after Varada and me— we found out that one of Varada's relatives had reached an agreement with the police regarding their business and hence the police were after us.

I had taken Varada to the toughest cop in the city.

Kempaiah was writing something when we walked in. We introduced ourselves. 'Tell me what you want?' he asked, lifting his head for a second and then continuing to write.

'Sir, we need to talk,' I said.

'Talk,' he said.

'Sir, you must have heard our names.'

'No.'

'Sir, we were involved in the Kotwal murder case,' I said hesitantly.

He lifted his head, his eyes afire. He stared at my face. But just for a second. Then he calmed down. He must not have seen a killer in either of our faces.

Before I could say anything he said, 'No, I have not got any complaints against you; not even once.' He thought we were approaching him to ask for mercy.

'No Sir, we have not come because of any trouble. We have no case against us, yet the crime branch police are chasing us. Please inquire about it, Sir. For no reason they are—'

Before I could finish he said, 'The crime branch does not come under me. Tagore is there. Go to him.'

'Sir, it would be better if you tell him—'

'Just like you have come to me, go to him also. Nothing will happen if you are innocent,' he said.

We thanked him and left. What happened after that is irrelevant here, but I understood two things about Kempaiah from that meeting. One: he does not like to trouble innocent people. Two: he prefers to tackle matters head on.

In the Sakaleshpur estate affair, Rai was innocent. The one who had complained against him was the one who was in the wrong. The tragedy was that the police system supported him. If Rai had stayed back in Bangalore and proved his innocence, Kempaiah would have definitely pardoned him. But Rai was too terrified to even imagine standing before Kempaiah!

Then started Kempaiah's merciless attack on the Rai group. He chased everyone known to Rai. He had a squad of young officers with him like Surendra Naik, Kumaraswamy, D'Souza and Muniswamy, who were eager to implement anything he ordered them to. Though Rai was not in Bangalore, we tried to bring pressure on Kempaiah from political sources. There was no politician we did not meet in those days. Though in principle I did not like the BJP, I had come in contact with one or two leaders from the party. The BJP's Ramachandre Gowda was close to Varada's father. He had not even heard of Rai and had no clue about his activities. We briefed him and sent him to Kempaiah while we waited at Shamprakash Hotel, which was next to the commissioner's office.

When he did not return even after forty-five minutes, we relaxed, thinking that Ramachandre Gowda, who was not at all corrupt, must have convinced Kempaiah. We started feeling good. Just then Ramachandre Gowda came up. His face had lost its colour. He looked very disturbed.

'What did he say, Sir?' I asked curiously.

He gave me a sad look and said, 'I did not know your Rai is of *that* level. I cannot do it, it is beyond me . . . I should not have gone at all.'

Gowda had gone to tell Kemapaiah that Rai was good, but Kempaiah had convinced him that Rai was not good!

After Ramachandre Gowda's influence failed, we decided to get Gundu Rao to bring pressure on Kemapaiah. Pattanagere Jayanna of Rajarajeshwarinagar and I went to meet him. Gundu Rao's PA Sridhar arranged a meeting. But there were too many people surrounding him and we left saying we would return some other time.

When we were leaving the house, we ran into legislator Devaraj. He spoke to us cordially. He guessed the purpose of our visit, but we behaved as if we didn't know what he was talking about.

The next morning Sridhar Reddy was arrested. We were shocked. Forget helping us, Gundu Rao had to struggle to get his own assistant released! Those were the days when Gundu Rao and Bangarappa were staunch rivals. Gundu Rao's private secretary Shastri was extremely anxious about what information Sridhar would reveal to the police. He had sent word with some inspectors who were his friends that Sridhar should not be allowed to talk under any condition.

After this, we gave up the idea of using anyone's influence.

The day after Sridhar was arrested, the police came and took Jayanna from his house at Rajarajeshwarinagar at midnight. Nagaratnamma—Devaraj Urs' daughter—called Dharam Singh, who was the home minister then, and screamed and shouted and finally got him released at eight o'clock. I think that was probably the only instance when Kempaiah gave in to influence.

As soon as the men who were picked up by Kempaiah were released, we would immediately go and meet them and find out who else Kempaiah was looking for. We found out that he had mentioned me to Sridhar Reddy once or twice, but not seriously.

We all felt very bad that, while one by one his men were being picked up by Kempaiah and being thrashed mercilessly, Rai had left Bangalore. A feeling spread that he was not a dependable leader. The only one who did not think this was Balaram. This was because even he used to go into hiding if the police were looking for him. 'What use is it if he is also caught? It is better if he is outside,' he argued.

None of us knew where Muthappa Rai was. He would call sometimes and say he was trying to get politicians Janardhana Pujari and Oscar Fernandes to talk to Kempaiah. But we knew that they were all lying to him because no one dared talk to Kempaiah about Rai. Except for Dadi Puttaswamy.

Puttaswamy had been very famous during former chief minister Devaraj Urs' time, but retreated to the sidelines later. He belonged to the Kuruba community, like Nataraj, Devaraj Urs' son-in-law. I met him and he assured me that he would try to convince some officers of his community to talk to Kempaiah. I mentioned him to Rai. By then Rai was desperate and was clutching at straws. It was already two months since he had started going from place to place, and just before I'd called him, something had happened to make him even more desperate.

Rai had been staying at a hotel in Delhi. He had friends there, and he spent time with them and at the races. One day he was informed that he had been given anticipatory bail. An elated Rai immediately called home and informed his family about it. He was aware that his phone was tapped, but thinking he was safe now that he had anticipatory bail, he gave them the name of his hotel and room number.

The next morning, the Delhi police arrested him.

Kempaiah and his group had informed the Delhi police that a notorious rowdy was staying at that hotel and had weapons with him. Luckily Rai did not have even a single pistol with him at the time. As soon as he was produced before the magistrate he was released on the basis of his passport.

It was at this point that I mentioned Dadi Puttaswamy to him. I don't know through whom he approached Kempaiah, but Puttaswamy told me that Kempaiah had said, 'Now that he has bail, let him come to the police, give a statement and go. Let him not get involved in anything henceforth.' I mentioned this to Rai.

Rai returned to Bangalore. The lawyer Sambamurthy and I

went along with Rai to Ashoknagar police station, where the case was booked. Bachchan and Dadi Puttaswamy came along in another car. Initially we thought of sending Puttaswamy to Kemapaiah in case of any trouble. Although he had given us an assurance that nothing would happen, we were not completely convinced. Rai and Sambamurthy went into the station, leaving me sitting in the car. I sat there, tense, waiting for Rai to come back out. After an hour, I saw him. He said he'd given his statement and that there had been no problem.

After this, our days settled into a routine. It was four months before Kini, Sudheer Prabhu, Willy and the others were released. They said they had no problems in jail. It's always so: in jail, the group that is 'active' gets the most respect. However, Rai's group had committed a big mistake in jail—they had attacked Koli Fayaz over a small issue. They had also tried to assault Manibharathi, who was with Fayaz, but he had escaped.

The news that Rai's gang had assaulted Koli Fayaz spread outside jail. His boys were angry and Tanveer and Srirampura Sakkare went to the gate of the jail and made a big noise. They challenged Rai's gang to come out and face them 'if they had courage'.

We were also angry that they had attacked Koli Fayaz. Fayaz was an expert in straight fights. If Rai's boys had attacked one at a time, and not as as a group, he would have been strong enough to face every one of them and win. Further, Fayaz was very affectionate and humble with the Hindu underworld boys. Rai's boys attacking him in jail to show their supremacy had hurt all of us.

Rai told me about the attack with a lot of pride. When I expressed my shock, Rai changed his stand and agreed it was a mistake to insult someone who had made a big name in the underworld.

Rai invited Dadi Puttaswamy, whom he had only spoken to on the phone, to his home. Puttaswamy, who at one time had seen better times with Jayaraj and M.D. Nataraj and who always talked about his past glory, now got a new lease of life after coming in contact with Rai.

He was a little reserved in the beginning, but began to loosen up after a few pegs. He started giving Rai a lecture on how to tame the police. 'Hire a nice big bungalow and give it to me. Give me one boy who can arrange everything, none of you must come there; supply drinks and attractive girls—I will see that Kempaiah does not interfere with you anymore.'

I was absolutely furious. 'Look Puttaswamy, you should not ask such things of people who are in this field. We are fighters, not pimps.'

'Sreedhar, you keep quiet, you won't know anything,' Rai said, and then, turning to Puttaswamy, 'You tell me Sir, I will arrange anything you ask for. I will arrange for a house and give the key to you.'

I had not previously known of any instance in Bangalore where an underworld don had agreed to supply girls like this. I was furious that, along with the title of boss, the tag of pimp would be added to his name. I ignored Rai's words and told Puttaswamy, 'What Puttaswamy! Maybe you don't know, but Kempaiah is not the kind to accept such invitations.'

Puttaswamy, who is usually serious, laughed aloud at this. His plan was very simple. If it was not possible to invite Kempaiah himself, perhaps his close friends would come. And however efficient he was, he would listen to his close friends at some time, wouldn't he?

Rai was in agreement.

However, the plan did not materialise, or rather, we prevented it from materialising. From the day he brought up this plan with Rai, we, who were the mediators between the two, took precautions to keep them apart. Puttaswamy did call Rai on his own a couple of times, but Rai was always very busy and did not respond. Rai asked us about arranging a house a few times in the beginning, but the plan died a natural death.

Once Rai said he would make a safe house for us to hide in case of an emergency. We were elated. We also felt we needed shelter of that sort. Rai assured us he would arrange one for us and one for Balaram as well. I thought he was expressing his gratitude to Balaram for the concern shown during his 'no entry' days—the days when he could not stay at home for fear of being arrested. I told him Balaram had places of his own, and no one knew where they were.

'Whatever it is, isn't there a difference in staying at our own place? All facilities, with a cook and—'

I cut him short and said, 'Look, when Balaram is in hiding, he does not go to any place known to others. He does not come even if we call him . . . there is no need for you to arrange for a house for him . . . But we don't have such a place.'

'But why such a place only for you, Sreedhar?' Rai asked with a frown. 'Why would the police search for you? You don't do anything like that . . . I really want to make a place for Balaram.'

Rai's weakness was that he was not able to hide his feelings. The way he said this made me realise what he had in mind—he was planning to kill Balaram. I remained deadpan though; I told him again that Balaram would never agree to stay in any place that was given to him, and Rai's face fell.

After we left, Bachchan and I discussed in detail Rai's strategy. I remembered what he had said a long time before, right after Oil Kumar's murder. We had gone to his place and he had organised a cockfight for us. He had explained how fighter cocks want to take revenge till the last minute of their life. I felt he had still not forgiven Balaram for attacking his boy at the pub.

'At least fighter cocks fight straight until death . . . but this man, he makes devious plans.'

It was probably from that day that we became discontented with Rai. Until then, although we were unhappy about his way of working, we never had any reason to feel annoyed or frustrated with him.

By then Kini and the others were out of jail and they would share their jail experiences with us. We would listen carefully to pick up any note of dissent against Balaram, but none of them ever mentioned him.

During those days, Rai landed a courier company deal. I had earlier resolved a problem for them; Balaram, Kalapathar and Anil had also been involved. The management of the company was determined to suspend an employee of theirs, a boy called Neil Joseph who was a close friend of all our boys. The workers supported him. I made the management and the workers sit together. Neil had retained some parcels that had come for the company: I made him give them back, and I forced the company not to suspend Neil. After a year the problem had recurred and this time the management approached Rai and not me.

When the management was explaining the situation to Rai, I was sitting in another room in his house. Rai would come in several times to ask for my suggestions and then go out to continue the discussion. Finally he agreed that Neil should be suspended and assured them that he would make him give back the parcels he had with him. This made Balaram, Kalapathar and Anil angry with Rai. Neil had given the parcels to Kalapathar and Anil. I was not happy with Rai for supporting the moneyed and not the workers. I told Balaram that Rai was behaving like someone from the Bombay underworld; they always supported the rich. I persuaded him to get the parcels and give them to Rai.

Kalapathar and Anil resisted and Balaram had heated arguments about this. Rai asked the lawyer Santosh, a friend of his, to speak to Kalapathar. By then, however, Kalapathar had handed over the parcel, and there was no need for Santosh to talk to him. When Rai spoke to him, he asked Kalapathar, 'What did I hear . . . it seems there was an argument between Balaram and you? Did Balaram shout at you?'

Kalapathar reported this to Balaram, who in turn told me about it and expressed his suspicion that Rai would create trouble between the Bangalore boys if there was an opportunity. We had not told Balaram about Rai's idea for a safe house for him. Now the way Rai had spoken to Kalapathar confirmed our suspicion. Rai was raging to finish Balaram.

I later asked Rai what he'd said to Kalapathar, but he brushed it off. 'Why would I talk to him, Sreedhar? He himself spoke to me through Santosh. I never mentioned Balaram to him. Kalapathar said that instead of asking for the parcel through Balaram, if I had asked him directly he would have given it to me.'

It was evident that Rai was lying. Kalapathar was not smart enough to have made up the conversation.

After this incident, we realised that we had to find out how serious Rai was about killing Balaram. We had two ways before us: one was to talk to those in his gang who were unhappy. The other was to speak to Pushpa and Rajendra.

Both were seriously risky.

By then our relationship with Pushpa and Rajendra had improved considerably. We had met them only once without Rai, during a wrestling match at Kanteerava Stadium which had been organised by the legislator Devaraj.

Earlier, I'd suggested to Rai that we get all the boys together to resolve the differences between them. We were nervous that one day Balaram and Rajendra would fight. Rai wasn't in agreement, so we had been waiting for an opportunity to talk to Rajendra. We got the chance on that occasion. Devaraj had not only organised the meet but was also the chief guest. We found out about it from Jayanna and obtained three tickets and went to see it. As expected, Pushpa and Rajendra were there. As soon as his boys saw us, they informed Pushpa and Rajendra and immediately they came and sat with us. For about one-and-a-half hours we spoke affectionately. They were both careful when talking about Rai. Rajendra was not very interested in talking about Balaram, but Pushpa mentioned him. He said he was satisfied now that Balaram was with us, otherwise by now there would be serious conflicts.

'Henceforth we should not fight amongst ourselves, don't you think?' I said and looked at Rajendra meaningfully.

'That I have understood. He should also understand it, that's all,' Rajendra answered.

I'd heard that Balaram had mentioned several times that if he decided to finish Rajendra, Rai would support him. I understood that Rajendra was referring to this indirectly.

The next day I mentioned to Rai that we had met Rajendra and Pushpa. For a minute his face fell but immediately he managed to say casually, 'I see! What did you speak about?'

I said they both liked him.

Meanwhile, this development: We had become close to S. Ramesh who was in the Bangarappa cabinet. Ramesh was young and popular. We'd met him through Jayanna and Venkataswamy Reddy and had soon become friends. We started being seen with him at public functions.

Once I had taken Jayanth, Kini, William, Rajan and the entire Rai gang for a function at Jalahalli. At some level, the underworld depends heavily on powerful politicians. Of course, when a crime really takes place, no amount of influence can save you; but knowing the right people can help you avoid false cases and trouble from the police.

Rai was not happy that we were becoming close to Ramesh. 'Pushpa and Rajendra are going with Devaraj and you are becoming close to Ramesh . . . How can you be in rowdyism then?' he asked.

'Aren't they also doing the same thing?' we brushed it off.

Ramesh was interested in producing films in those days. He backed projects in Kannada and Tamil, and had once taken Jayanna, Venkataswamy Reddy and me to Madras. When we reached that city, we called Rai and asked him to join us. Rai had driven there in the morning in his friend's car. He was keen to meet Ramesh, so he came over. Within ten minutes of meeting Ramesh, he relaxed. From eleven in the morning to four in the evening we played cards. I did not usually play cards, but that day I not only played but won. Rai left the same night and we returned the next day.

It was when Ramesh was at his peak politically, that the infamous bypoll incident occurred at Kunigal, seventy-five kilometres from Bangalore. Y.K. Ramaiah contested the election from the Janata Dal and Muddahanume Gowda from the Congress. For former Prime Minister H.D. Deve Gowda, the election had become a matter of personal prestige. Rumour spread that there would be trouble on poll day—there were reports that a large number of Deve Gowda's supporters were coming from Hassan and Mandya. Two days before the election, Ramesh called me and said I had to be ready and take at least six hundred boys on that day to Kunigal.

I said, 'No, don't give any opportunity for violence in the election.'

Ramesh agreed but said, 'Let us not fight for any reason Sreedhar, but to prevent violence we have to show our strength.'

We collected two hundred boys. Balaram was very excited. He was always excited about such assignments. We bedded down at the Turf Club guesthouse in Kunigal a day before polling was to take place. The entire cabinet, except Bangarappa, had gathered in Kunigal. Kagod Thimmappa, Naseer Ahmed, D.K. Shivakumar along with party president Krishna Rao were there. Legislators Revanna and Devaraj too had their own groups and were busy campaigning.

The reports we'd heard were not false: Vokkaliga boys who had come from Hassan were cruising the streets on motorbikes and in jeeps in support of Y.K. Ramaiah.

The night before polling day, Ramesh threw a grand party and invited Shivakumar, Revanna, Naseer Ahmed and other small-time politicians. One of Ramesh's films under production at the time, starring Vishnuvardhan, featured a catchy number with the lyrics, '*Naane bere . . . nanna style bere . . .*' (I am different, my style is different). This song was played repeatedly at the party.

Shivakumar told Ramesh, 'Guru, after Devaraj Urs, it is you in Karnataka who is enjoying power of this sort . . .'

Everyone left late at night. Ramesh, Jayanna and I stayed back, talking. Ramesh asked my opinion about the people around him and his popularity. I answered him in all seriousness. 'You are making a mistake. . . . You swell up when someone compares you to Devaraj Urs. At such a young age, you should not dream of being so great—you must get success slowly and gradually.'

Ramesh looked at my face for a few minutes and then told Jayanna, 'Sreedhar is right, Jayanna; I should be more restrained.'

He understood my concern about him and decided to change his ways. But it was too late.

The Kunigal by-election incident shook the very foundation of the Bangarappa government. I remember the event clearly even though fourteen years have passed. Not because of the importance and gravity of the incident, but because of how a lie is recorded in history as truth; how a lie still remains in people's hearts as the truth. I had argued, fought, screamed with journalists, politicians, and friends till I went hoarse. My words—I was at the centre of the incident—and what was witnessed by thousands were twisted and presented as something completely different. Anything can happen in this country, it appears.

I refer to the Kunigal firing incident during the election.

We had a clear picture of the result—we knew Y.K. Ramaiah would win easily. We'd asked around, and Balaram and his boys had collected information from all over the town. Everyone, right from the women collecting water from tanks to auto drivers, everyone had spoken in favour of Ramaiah. We had informed Ramesh about this. He realised that it was difficult for the Congress to win. Revanna, who had travelled through many villages, had said that people were not even allowing Congress party workers to enter their villages.

Ramesh had told me and Jayanna that Bangarappa had said that if the Congress withdrew scared, then Deve Gowda would win and become powerful. I had told Balaram and the gang this.

On the day of polling, all of Kunigal had turned into a battleground. We set out in a group at ten in the morning, with Ramesh and Naseer Ahmed in the front. I was wearing a maroon T-shirt and a cap. Huge crowds surged everywhere and everyone was talking about how people from the Congress were being assaulted.

Balaram and his gang were waving Congress flags and raising slogans loudly. Some Janata Dal workers taunted us on the way. Balaram was about to hit them but I stopped him immediately. I calmed our group and also spoke to the Dal group. I advised both not to make the election a war ground. I then went ahead to join Ramesh and Naseer who had moved on. When I joined them I found another Janata Dal group surrounding the two of them and arguing. Ramesh was trying to calm them down. Just as I went there, a man who was totally drunk caught hold of Naseer's collar and taunted him vulgarly.

I'd just handled the previous group and my patience had run out. As soon as I saw the man pulling Naseer by his collar, I lost my temper. I charged and kicked the drunken man on his chest. Another man interfered and I punched him in the face. By then Balaram and his boys had covered me. Everyone was stunned and stood rooted to the spot. Ramesh was scared. 'No, no, stop it . . . they are all our people . . .' he said, and pulled me aside.

The Dal group saw that we were more in number and retreated. Ramesh then pacified everyone and sent them away.

As we proceeded, Naseer asked Ramesh in a whisper, 'Who is that guy? Like a military-trained fighter?'

Ramesh put his finger to his mouth and said, 'Shhh . . . Don't ask questions about him.'

Shortly after, Shivakumar and Revanna joined us. By twelve the news about our altercation and that I had kicked someone had spread all over Kunigal. Superintendent of Police Subhash Bharani told us that the atmosphere was very tense. And even a fool could make out that all the people supported the Janata Dal.

Ramesh made it clear that no more fights would be tolerated. After that we went to a few booths. Ramesh told people of both parties around the booths to maintain peace and casually asked the officials what percentage of voting had taken place. Those days, though Ramesh was just a state minister, everyone considered him to be Bangarappa's right-hand man, so the officers respected him.

At around one o'clock we received news that Congress supporters were not being allowed to vote in one village. We went there in four vehicles. When we reached the village, twenty people came to us and expressed their fury against the Dal. In the village of five hundred houses, no one except those twenty supported the Congress.

Ramesh spoke to the officials and said, 'Let everything be fair', but we knew that it was not possible. In elections, when the majority of the people favour one party it is inevitable that the officers will go with the tide.

On the way back, Ramesh said to me, 'That is why I asked you to get six hundred boys Sreedhar. We need not have hit anyone, but if some of the boys held bats and put up a "show", then all these voices would go silent.'

I said the more the number of boys, the more charged they would get, and in our camp, once the boys get into that mood it is very difficult to control them.

The road back to Kunigal was not good. It was not asphalted and was full of potholes. We reached a spot that was particularly bad and the vehicles had to go very slowly. Just when we slowed down, a jeep—carrying a banner that said Mandya District Janata Dal—came from the opposite side and stopped right across the road. Then several people came up on motorbikes and stopped, blocking the road. Every one of them looked tough and well-built, and all seemed extremely eager to fight.

We had four vehicles but one was filled with leaders. Only the other three carried boys.

Right from the morning I had a premonition that something bad would happen. Now it looked like that was about to come true. Balaram and the others got down from their cars and rushed in. They too were eager to fight. I did not want to fight at all.

First of all, this was an impersonal fight. There was no personal hatred or enmity. Secondly, fighting with villagers is entirely different from fighting in the city. You cannot just make a noise and get away. You can never predict to what level a fight can reach. At that point, our side had more men, but if a fight started, within minutes people from the surrounding villages would come and attack us.

When Balaram went to the jeep, the men inside said, 'Move your vehicle aside and give way.'

Balaram in his distinct style said, 'So . . . you want us to move our vehicle? We will . . . we will . . .'

Just then a senior man got down from the jeep. As soon as he saw him, Ramesh got down exclaiming, 'Oh, Manjunath!' He was former minister D. Manjunath from the Janata Dal.

Ramesh and Manjunath spoke to each other and the tension was diffused. We moved our vehicle and allowed them to pass.

We went to the guesthouse, had lunch and rested for a while. We could hear the noise being made by people on the road. In ten minutes Balaram and the others came in three vehicles and said the crowd was getting bigger and more restless. Some of Balaram's boys had mingled with the crowd and had heard what they were saying. They were all furious about the kick given by 'the man in a T-shirt and cap'. They knew I was staying at the Turf Club guesthouse and Balaram cautioned that they might all rush in.

I felt a little anxious. I changed out of the T-shirt and threw away the cap.

In a little while the crowd started getting closer to the guesthouse. We thought it would be safer to leave. Jayanna and I advised Ramesh to not just leave the guesthouse but to get out of Kunigal. Ramesh wasn't keen. He felt that if he left, the workers would be demoralised. We convinced him, however, and he finally got ready to go. But when we looked out at the road, we were shocked.

Thousands of people had gathered outside the guesthouse and were shouting slogans against 'Congress goondagiri'.

Luckily for us the watchman had locked the gate, otherwise the crowd would have barged in. Ramesh called some police officers and other Congress leaders. In ten minutes two jeeps arrived. We let the two jeeps go in front and Ramesh, Jayanna and I followed in the Ambassador. Balaram and his boys followed us in their cars. Ramesh had three bodyguards. One of them carried a sten gun. He held its nose out of the window and pointed it towards the crowd. We were anxious that the crowd would throw stones.

I had walked around with my chest out the whole morning like a hero, but now I sat huddled in the back in the car. No one could see me, so they continued shouting slogans. And since they could not recognise me, they did not follow us.

We reached the travellers' bungalow nearby, where a big gang of Congressmen was gathered. Some of them teased us because we were so anxious. It was three in the afternoon. After seeing them, Ramesh's mood improved and he postponed his departure to the evening. There was a big van in front of the TB and a police contingent sat guard in it. We also felt reassured by it.

Congress president Krishna Rao and all the other ministers were gathered there. Ramesh went in and joined them. We sat outside and started chatting.

The crowd that had gathered outside the guesthouse now started coming to the TB. They were shouting slogans against Ramesh. Since he had come out of the guesthouse with escorts, the crowd had decided that he was the brain behind the altercation in the morning. The presence of the tough boys who had followed our car seemed to confirm this.

As soon as I saw the crowd coming towards the TB, I went in and informed Ramesh. He and Shivakumar came out and saw the crowd but did not take it seriously. They went back in.

An angry crowd is extremely unpredictable. When some of the people in the crowd began to throw stones, those in the TB did not respond sensibly; instead they answered with violence. They threw stones back at the crowd, and Balaram's boys even held lathis and rushed towards the gathering.

We were around five hundred including our boys and the local workers. I did not know that Balaram, who understood the politics of small towns, had brought a hundred and fifty lathis in his car boot from Bangalore. Scared by the way our boys rushed in, the crowd scattered. Our boys came back shouting jubilantly.

Just then a car came into the TB. Without giving anyone an opportunity to get out, our boys broke the front and back glass.

It was actually a local Congress leader in the car!

The police requested us to remain calm no matter how the crowd outside behaved. 'If they hit us with stones, should we sacrifice our heads?' Balaram taunted.

The crowd came back in ten minutes with not just a few stones but hundreds. They started pelting the TB. The policemen sitting in the van looked helpless. We told them to fire in the air, but they would not listen.

The ministers and legislators came out to see what was happening. Our boys were excited to see them and, just to show them who was in charge, rushed again at the crowd with lathis. Even Shivakumar, who was then the prisons minister, held a lathi and ran into the crowd.

The entire scene was absurdly dramatic.

The other Congress leaders too joined Shivakumar, and about three hundred of us with lathis began chasing the crowd. People would run back half a furlong when we chased them but would return as we came back. We were lucky that there were not many stones left for the crowd to throw.

I went into the TB once in the middle of all the chaos, and Ramesh asked me anxiously if the crowd had reduced at least a little.

'What reduced . . . it is increasing,' I said.

'Is there no one pacifying them?' Krishna Rao asked me innocently.

I felt like laughing but controlled myself. 'Sir, it is better if you leave as soon as an opportunity arises,' I told Ramesh.

'I am trying to call Bharani, but I can't get him on any phone. We have to have security with us for at least some distance,' Ramesh said.

Since Bharani was the deputy inspector general of police, and the situation was volatile, it was difficult to find out where he was exactly.

The situation outside was getting more and more tense by the minute. The crowd began surrounding the TB from all sides—the numbers had surged to around five thousand now. It was only a matter of time before they would break into the TB. It was impossible to imagine the consequences if the enraged crowd rushed into the TB.

We called the police station but there was no one there. Finally a constable answered the phone and said, 'There is a rumour that Congress wallahs have abducted Y.K. Ramaiah and kept him in the TB. That's why all the people are there.'

Krishna Rao went up and tried, with folded hands, to appeal to the people. He was pelted with stones. He came back and sat down cross-legged, with his head in his hands.

As we began to realise the impossibility of containing the situation, we spotted Ramesh's bodyguards. There were three of them. One of them had a sten gun, the other two had revolvers. Jayanna and I had become quite friendly with them, and we asked them what could be done.

'Sir, no matter how many people barge in, we will not allow anyone to touch our sahib. If we open fire, with just one round at least ten bodies will fall . . . we have two hundred rounds,' they said.

We felt a little braver on hearing that.

The next hour and a half was spent in a similar manner, with the crowd gathering, and us trying to chase them away. By then it was getting to be six in the evening. Ramesh, Kagod Thimmappa, Naseer and Shivaram had called the director general of police in Bangalore, asking him to send some men, but no contingent had arrived.

The crowd was now very close to the TB. It seemed like they

could barge in any minute. We started asking the gunmen to fire at least one or two bullets at the crowd just to scare them away. They said they had to ask sahib's permission.

'If you ask him he will say no. Can't you see, if you wait any longer, many more people will fall dead,' I said.

The bodyguard did not want to, but he had no other option. He picked up the sten gun and fired six bullets.

There is a lot of difference between firing a .303 rifle and a sten or AK-47 gun. A rifle makes a big noise, but a sten gun is softer. Hence the crowd surged forward even though the bodyguard was firing.

No one was hit.

Now the crowd was just a hundred feet away. They were closing in slowly but surely.

Then a man in the front saw that the bodyguard was firing his gun. He became furious and immediately pulled down the zip of his pants, took out his penis, and started making obscene gestures.

The tragedy was that the bodyguard was not in uniform, and the man may have thought that it was a civilian shooting with his private gun. Also, because the crowd was so huge, he may have thought nobody would shoot to kill.

Just then it started raining.

The man looked up at the sky and continued his vulgar dance with more speed and vigour.

The crowd began to surge in with more force, in order to escape from the rain.

The bodyguard fired again.

I can still picture the scene.

A massive crowd, everybody shouting and screaming. In the front, a man dancing rhythmically, vulgarly, holding his penis in his hand. Shaking it. The crowd encouraging him, hooting for him. A hundred yards away, a bodyguard with a sten gun ready to fire. Raindrops creating a curtain of sorts, giving the entire scene a surrealistic feel.

The bodyguard fired and a bullet hit the dancing man.

Naturally, we did not see the bullet. But just as we heard the sound of the shots, we saw the dancing man fall dead.

Just a second before, he was dancing, and now he was dead. The crowd stood stunned. Everything went deadly silent.

The rain, as if waiting for a cue, began to come down very heavily. So heavily that one could not see anything even ten feet away.

In just two or three minutes the entire crowd dispersed. Though they were shocked that one of them had been shot dead, what really upset them was the rain.

I went in and saw Ramesh sitting with his head in his hands.

'What Sreedhar . . . why did this happen?'

'What can be done, Sir,' I tried to console him.

'Che . . . it was my bodyguard who fired, isn't that so, Sreedhar?'

I understood his anguish.

We had entered Kunigal the previous day full of life and spirit. Now, at around seven in the evening on polling day, we were leaving Kunigal with heavy hearts.

DIG Bharani's jeep arrived after a short while, along with two other jeeps. We left under their escort.

I sat with Satti—who used to be Kotwal's right-hand man and then became one of Bangarappa's close aides—in his car.

Around ten kilometres from Kunigal, it stopped raining completely. In one or two villages on the way we saw crowds gathered around, talking. The rumour that Y.K. Ramaiah had been abducted had spread to the entire taluk.

After Bharani and the other jeeps left us, we went straight to Bangarappa's house. Satti invited us in but we declined. We stood in a corner of the compound. We did not want Ramesh to feel bad if some policemen recognised us and told Bangarappa that we were responsible for the trouble in Kunigal.

Ramesh came out after half an hour. 'Sreedhar, you should have come in. I would have introduced you to the chief minister,' he said.

'No, Sir. In all this tension we thought he would be angry with you if he sees us with you . . .'

'Oh, you . . . I took you all only because he instructed me to.'

On our way back to Ramesh's house, I asked him how Bangarappa had reacted.

'What does it have to do with him? He has told us all not to say anything.'

'Okay, Sir, but what statement will he give to the media tomorrow?'

'What else? That a man is dead in police firing.'

I was shocked.

'Sir, no, he shouldn't do that. Hundreds of people saw your bodyguard firing the gun.'

'Sreedhar, let Bangarappa handle it any way he likes. No one will ask us. Even you people should not tell anyone that it was my bodyguard who fired. Tell all your men not to talk about this with anyone for any reason.'

But I was not convinced. 'Please don't be hasty . . . nothing that should not have happened has happened. But if you try to cover up by giving false information, things will take a different turn,' I argued.

'You are blowing it out of proportion, Sreedhar. All will be well by tomorrow evening,' he said, a little irritated.

The next morning all the newspapers carried a front-page report, which included a statement issued by Bangarappa, saying a man called Gangaiah had died in police firing during the election violence at Kunigal.

But will the press just listen to Bangarappa? In *Prajavani*, along with the main news, a small box also appeared that Dutta from the Janata Dal had issued a statement that it was not the police who had fired into the crowd, but Ramesh!

From the next day, all the reports seemed to have established that it was Ramesh who had fired the gun. Ravindra Reshme, a reporter with the *Lankesh Patrike*, stated with authority that it was Ramesh who had killed Gangaiah. He even gave the FIR number of the complaint registered at the Kunigal station, the bullet size and other technical details!

Ramesh had a large number of political enemies at that time.

B.K. Hariprasad, who was his staunch enemy in the Congress, exploited this episode to the fullest. Ramesh, who always walked around with pride, began to falter. Several times he said he regretted not listening to my advice.

In the beginning Bangarappa did not succumb to pressure from the Opposition and the media, but in a week's time, he got tired.

One evening Kagod Thimmappa came to Ramesh's house and spoke to him confidentially for an hour. We knew something was going wrong. After Kagod Thimmappa left, Ramesh came out looking very dull. He did not say anything, but began walking briskly with us. Finally I could not curtail my curiosity and asked him what had happened.

'I resigned,' he said. His voice broke. His eyes were filled with tears.

After two days, the media published reports that Ramesh had resigned and Bangarappa had accepted the resignation.

Shivakumar stayed with Ramesh the entire evening. He too felt very bad about the turn of events.

In one week we arranged a massive rally and a large public function at the Mahatma Gandhi statue in support of Ramesh. Bangarappa addressed the meeting. Muddahanume Gowda too spoke.

But it was of no use.

Ramesh's political career began to decline on that day, and it never recovered till his end.

Ramesh was not one of the best politicians the state had. He had several shortcomings: he had developed all sorts of vices and he wasn't particularly dynamic. So it was not that the state suffered greatly from the truncation of his political career. But I can never forget how an incident that a massive crowd of thousands witnessed was twisted so that an innocent man was made into a scapegoat. How a handful of politicians and journalists managed to prove an innocent man was guilty.

Those days, V. Shankar, who later served as the chairman of NGEF, a public sector undertaking, was a close friend of

Ramesh's rival in the Congress, Hariprasad. I met him a few days after the Kunigal incident and explained what happened in great detail.

'After all, you are close to Ramesh. It's your dharma to defend him, there is no mistake in that,' he declared!

I spoke harshly and asked him to tell the truth to Hariprasad. I shouted, 'Is it child's play to shoot from a sten gun?'

'I heard he shot with a revolver?'

'That's ridiculous. If he had shot with a revolver, Ramesh would have had to be outside. At least you could have alleged that somebody who was outside took the shot!'

Shankar also had close ties with *Lankesh Patrike*. The next week a detailed report appeared in that tabloid. It said, 'Many are saying that it is possible that someone from Ramesh's rowdy squad fired the shot,' and carried a cartoon that showed me standing on top of the TB terrace holding a revolver!

Instead of helping Ramesh, Shankar was trying to fix me as well.

The media is so powerful in modern times. Journalists in Karnataka conducted their own investigation of the Kunigal incident and pronounced the judgment that Ramesh was guilty! Even when the courts declared him to be innocent and acquitted him, the media did not agree with it: to this day.

S. Ramesh could not recover from this till the very end—he died of a heart attack in 2006.

Five

By the time Ramesh resigned, we were determined to sever connections with Rai. We had decided that, although Balaram was close to us, we did not want to reveal our discontent to him before reaching a decision and before talking to Rajendra and Pushpa. So one morning Bachchan and I went to Rajendra's house. Since we had informed him about our visit the previous night, he had asked Pushpa to come there as well.

We were worried about whether to mention Rai directly. If they said they supported Rai, all our plans would go haywire.

Rajendra and Pushpa were happy to see us. For some time we reminiscenced about our days together in jail. Then I brought up the British rule in India. 'Rajendra, the British were so intelligent—how well they ruled India for a hundred and fifty years by fomenting conflict between our kings . . .' I began, trying to delicately equate Rai with the British.

Rajendra became excited and stopped me halfway saying, 'Guru, I understand what you are trying to say, no need to go in a roundabout way. You are saying Rai is ruling Bangalore like the British. Is it not so?'

'So what do you think about it?'

'Guru, tell us the truth. How much can I trust you? Why are you really discontent with Rai? He has never spoken ill of you.'

I said that Rai's refusal to try and unite enemy groups in Bangalore hurt me. He was not allowing a compromise between Balaram and Rajendra, and that made his intentions clear to me, I said.

Then Rajendra told me how Rai had called him the morning after Balaram had attacked the pub owner's son. Rai had told us that Rajendra and Pushpa were waiting for him to talk against Balaram. But, apparently, he had called Rajendra and Pushpa that day and had asked for their help to finish Balaram within twenty-four hours. Pushpa, who was always very hasty, had agreed immediately. But although Rajendra felt strong hostility against Balaram, he had demurred. 'Guru, we will think about it for a week. Speak to Sreedhar also. In case your anger still persists then we can think about it. Such things are very common in the underworld,' Rajendra had said.

After telling us this in detail, Rajendra and Pushpa went out to confer. After five minutes they came back.

'Guru, we had to decide whether or not to tell you about something, that is why we went out,' Rajendra said and then came to the main point, 'Guru, shortly there will be an attack on Balaram.'

'How? And where?'

'Where he comes to see you sometimes . . . in your *adda*.'

'What Rajendra? What are you saying? He will be attacked when he comes to meet me? And I have no such *adda* . . .'

'Why are you hiding it from us, guru? Don't you meet often at a hotel near Jayanagar 4th Block?'

Rajendra was right. Balaram would come to meet us at La Casa, a restaurant in that area. It is a place where youngsters gather and it used to be packed in the evenings with boys and girls. Balaram was always an exhibitionist. He would tip waiters a hundred rupees. They all knew who we were so they paid special attention to us.

But just three days ago, there had been a problem. We used to meet Balaram and his gang there in the evening, and if we had to meet anyone during the day, I used to call them to La Casa. That day, at around noon, Jayanagar sub-inspector Lakshmipathi Gowda had come there on a motorbike.

I greeted him as I knew him. La Casa is at a height and the road is low. He sat on his bike and called me from there. I went down.

'How many boys do you have now?' he asked.

From the way he asked, I thought he was chasing some gang. It is usual for the police to take the help of other gangs in such circumstances.

'Only Bachchan and I are here. If you want more boys, I will call them,' I said.

By then Bachchan had come down and was standing next to me.

'Follow me, both of you,' he said and started his bike.

We got on our bike and followed him. But after a few metres, his bike turned right towards the police station and my heart lurched.

'Bachchan, stop him,' I said.

Bachchan went faster and caught up with Lakshmipathi. 'Saar, one minute saar.'

The sub-inspector stopped his bike and pulled over. We asked him, 'Sir, tell us the truth, where are you taking us?' I asked anxiously.

'Station.'

'Why Sir?'

'Somebody has complained to the DCP that every day you and your gang are threatening people in La Casa.'

I held his hand and pleaded, 'Sir, you saw for yourself. Somebody must have lied.'

He stared at my face for a minute and said, 'Okay, I will convince the DCP. But you should not be seen there anymore.'

We thanked him and left, having decided never to set foot in that restaurant again.

Later we found out that somebody had told the owner that young couples were scared to come there because of us. Also, that the waiters paid us so much attention, they were not attending to other customers. The owner had asked the sub-inspector to handle us.

Rajendar continued, 'Guru, it seems you have not gone there for three days now. You are being watched.'

'Tell me the truth Rajendra, don't hide anything. Who is watching me? Who is making them watch?'

'Chakre came here four days ago and said he would finish Balaram and insisted that I take him to Rai. We did not want that, but we thought that even if we said no, he may go on his own, so we took him to Rai. You know that petrol bunk in Indiranagar? We sat in a car near it and talked. Chakre told Rai, "This Balaram is becoming too much, I will finish him. What do you say?" Rai pointed at the two of us and said, "Apart from these two, finish anyone and I will not interfere".'

I could not believe that Rai had encouraged Chakre. I had thought that he would someday ask his Mangalore boys to finish Balaram, but I had never imagined that he would play a Bangalore rowdy against Balaram.

I asked Rajendra, 'Okay, if Balaram was attacked in La Casa, I too would have been there. Did he not mention me?'

'No guru, neither Chakre nor Rai mentioned your name. But if there had been an attack and if you had intervened, who can say what would have happened?'

(When I documented this incident in my autobiography, published as a series in my magazine *Agni*, Chakre called me and said, 'What you have documented—the talk between Muthappa Rai and me regarding Balaram—is true one hundred per cent. But I had not gone to meet Muthappa Rai on my own as you have written, Rai called me.')

Actually, until that minute, we were not totally convinced about the step we were taking against Rai. But now, we felt it was stupid of us not to have considered it earlier. We asked Rajendra what we should do next.

'Look, guru, first we must all unite. After we become one, then we should decide what to do with Rai,' he said.

'I will agree to encounter Rai straight on, but I won't plan to finish him while I'm in his gang.'

'Why should we talk about that now? First you speak with Balaram,' he said.

I said I would bring up the Chakre incident, and neither Rajendra nor Pushpa asked me not to; they only said that I should not reveal that I'd got the information from them. We decided to say that some Banasavadi boys had told us about Chakre. Agreeing to meet after one week and to keep in touch on the phone every day, we left.

The problem now was how to tell Balaram.

Balaram had no patience, and he was always ready to rush into a fight. He had assaulted Rai's friend just because he had not treated him well, and now if he found out that Rai was planning to finish him, he would definitely declare war. Whenever he got into a fight, he never worried about the result. Even if he thought he might suffer badly, he would still go ahead.

We had to plan our scheme to oppose Rai very carefully.

Though we were confident that Rajendra and Pushpa would stand by us, in the underworld, confidence is like a bubble. It can burst at any minute. Though they were cordial with us, we could not say what turn their relationship with Balaram might take. We could not declare war against Rai unless we had united the two groups and completely erased the possibility of a clash. If Balaram went against Rai before the compromise, then there was the possibility of Pushpa and Rajendra moving aside saying, 'It is good for us if either of the two is finished.' So we decided not to say anything to Balaram.

However, the day after we met Rajendra and Pushpa, Balaram came to me and asked curiously, 'Saar, it seems you went to meet Ghat yesterday?'

Rajendra's house was behind Harishchandra Ghat, the Hindu crematorium in Malleswaram, and Balaram referred to Rajendra as Ghat.

We had not told anyone about our meeting with Rajendra and Pushpa, and yet somehow he had got the information!

We decided then to tell him about our plans. We spoke for about three hours: we didn't once mention Chakre; we only focused on our decision to go against Rai.

First he showed surprise, 'Why Sir?'

We said we were unhappy about Rai being close to all the groups for his own benefit, but not trying to bring all the warring groups together.

He was not convinced.

'He must have spoken against you—or even me—with someone . . .'

Finally we told him that, after he'd assaulted the pub owner's son, Rai had called Rajendra and Pushpa and asked them to finish him.

'So what did Ghat say to that?' he asked curiously.

'Rajendra did not support—'

Before I could finish he cut me short, 'Why didn't he tell us that day and why is he mentioning it now, that Ghat? They must be having some trouble with Rai. That is why he is talking about it now. You should not trust them.'

It took all my patience and tact to convince him that Rajendra had not asked us to meet him; we had gone on our own.

Finally he said, 'Okay, now what should be done?'

'Now we, the Bangalore boys, should unite, Balaram. We have decided to separate from him.'

'For that why do you need that Ghat? You tell me, it's enough; I will finish that gojja nan maga.'

'It's no use finishing Rai, Balaram. Then we will have all the groups fighting each other. If the fights start, will the police be quiet? Now just listen to me, let us first unite,' I said affectionately.

'What are you saying, Sir?' he said with sadness and turned to Bachchan. 'Bachchan, you tell him, can I ever compromise with Ghat? Okay, let's do one thing, you stay in the background. Let Rai take Ghat also with him . . . we will fight . . .'

'You are ruining your life by indulging in fights, Balaram,' I yelled at him. I said I would not allow the Bangalore boys to fight each other on any account. I said he had to change his mind for our sake.

'Even if I agree, will the boys agree, Sir? Anil, Sudhi, Kisan—none of them will agree.'

'You first promise me that you will not oppose my decisions, we will convince the boys later,' I said firmly.

Balaram, who never feared anyone, would melt if I made a

long face. He could not displease me for any reason. He said he would talk to the boys the next day. Instead, he brought them all to me without having spoken to any of them about the issue.

In the beginning, Anil, Malayali Sridhar and Kisan voiced their opposition to Rajendra, but eventually, when I explained the seriousness of the issue, they agreed that it was right to unite and fight Rai.

'But one thing is certain Sir, if the fighting starts, we cannot fight depending upon *someone*,' they started hinting.

'If fighting starts, let us not depend on them. But they should not support Rai against us . . . isn't that right?'

Now they all gave in completely.

The very idea of a fight made Balaram's boys very excited. In that aspect, they were like their boss.

Time flew as we began to make our plans. In those days, there were several rowdy groups in Bangalore. Apart from the groups of Rajendra, Pushpa and Balaram, the other gangs were Kalapathar's, Tanveer's, Chakre's, Jedarahalli Krishnappa's and Tambu's. They were all quite active. Jedarahalli Krishnappa was in jail, and there were no indications of his early release. Big names like Kalasipalya Nagaraju, Narayana, Gedda and Koli Fayaz had retreated into the sidelines. Their names were very much in the news, but only in business matters. They had stepped out of the fighting ring.

We had to be extremely careful about coordinating enemy gangs. Except for us, all the other gangs had fought each other at one time or the other. Finally we decided that we should make a big gang comprising Rajendra, Pushpa, Kalapathar and Tanveer's gangs.

But who would be the leader?

Rajendra was sure he did not want to be called the boss. When I persisted, he said, 'Even if you insist, neither Balaram nor Kalapathar will accept me.'

I thought Pushpa was fit to be a don: he had the physique, he loved his followers and he was friendly with everyone. But Rajendra said—in front of Pushpa: 'I will not allow Pushpa to become boss.' Then he defended his stand, saying, 'He has a big family, he is the eldest, he has spent enough time in jail . . .'

Kalapathar and Tanveer were too young. And there was nothing I could say to Balaram: though I had not agreed, he had personally accepted me as his boss. Naturally, Bachchan and Krishnamurthy had given me the post. So though I did not desire it and I did not like it, all the dons came to a silent understanding that I would be the don after Rai.

Now discussions about how to convey our dissent to Rai started. One day, an incident occurred when we went with Balaram's gang to Airlines Hotel. We ordered coffee and Balaram went to the saloon behind for a shave, taking Malayali Sridhar with him. We were sitting in a Maruti van; there were boys in another car and three motorbikes as well.

Balaram was a bit of a dandy. I used to teasingly call him 'Sogasugara (Stylish) Puttaswamy'. He was always well dressed in fresh clothes, was always clean-shaven and wafting after-shave. He had shaved that morning, but as soon as he saw the saloon, he went to get another shave. We were joking about this, when Balaram and Sridhar rushed back from the saloon. They both looked tense.

'Sir, Satish and that other boy are in the saloon,' Balaram said. My heart missed a beat. Both boys were close to Rai. They were from Mangalore. Satish had acted in a Hindi film with Roopa Ganguli, who had acted as Draupadi in the television serial *Mahabharat*. The film was a flop. After that he had joined Rai. Naveen had recently come out on bail in the Oil Kumar case. Both had some regard for me.

'Saar, shall we pick them up?' Balaram asked with a twinkle in his eyes.

His boys heard him and immediately they were alert, ready for action in a second.

'Balaram, let us not do anything now,' I said.

'You don't have to do anything, Sir. You call them without getting down from the car. We will bundle them into the car, then you go away and we will take care of the rest.'

'Balaram, no—' Before I could finish, Satish and Naveen walked out of the saloon.

The boys stood in position.

Immediately I got out of the car. When they saw me they both smiled, but still seemed tense.

Our decision about Rai was not yet public, so there was no need for them to feel tense on seeing Balaram's gang. But in the pub incident, Satish had spoken harshly about Balaram. Also, it was possible that they knew about the talk Rai had with Chakre. More importantly, they knew about Balaram troubling Mangalore boys in the Mangalore jail. On the whole, they were scared.

To ease the situation, I touched Naveen lightly on his shoulder and asked, 'So what brings you here?'

'Oh, we came for a haircut.'

'I see. How is Muthappanna?'

'We spoke to him in the morning. You are not seen these days . . .?'

By now they had gained confidence. They felt Balaram would not try anything.

'I was a little busy . . . I will come soon,' I said and asked, 'How have you come? Will you stay?'

As if waiting for the question, they said no quickly, rushed to their car and drove away.

After they left, Balaram said unhappily, 'Why did you do this, Sir?'

'You have to use your brains . . . what use is it if we trouble them?' I said.

He turned to Bachchan, fuming, 'Listen to him—he doesn't say or do anything when their gang beats up our people. . . . I don't like your kind of rowdyism.'

Our stand on Rai was not yet known outside and, even among the groups that had agreed to unite, there was no consensus about him. I tried to convince Balaram that, under such circumstances, assaulting Rai's gang would be more problematic than beneficial.

'Okay, but once we have agreed to oppose him, it is not possible to sit waiting. Our boys now know that we have separated—declare it openly soon,' he urged.

That evening Balaram brought Kalapathar and Tanveer to meet me. Kalapathar had never liked the fact that a Mangalorean had become Bangalore's don. He happily agreed to be with us.

Tanveer had a personal grudge against Rai because his boys had assaulted his guru Koli Fayaz in jail. 'If all of you say yes, I will finish Rai alone,' he declared. Tanveer was a show-off. I cautioned him not to talk about finishing Rai anywhere.

The night after Kalapathar and Tanveer agreed to join us, I got a call from Rai.

I had not met him for a week; I had not even spoken to him over the phone. Except for his trip to Dubai after Oil Kumar's murder, it was the first time I had not met him for such a long time since the beginning of our association.

'What Sreedhar, not to be seen? No phone calls too?' his voice was normal.

Without deliberating about it, I simply said, 'Nothing . . . I am unhappy.'

'Why?' Now he was curious.

'You have spoken about Balaram with Chakre . . . you did not take me into confidence.'

Now curiosity turned into panic. 'What are you saying, Sreedhar? Who told you?'

'He has spoken here and there.'

Silence.

'Do one thing Sreedhar, come to my house at ten in the morning. Nothing has happened like you are imagining,' he said.

After the phone call, Bachchan, Krishnamurthy and I sat together and discussed how to confront Rai the next day. Krishnamurthy did not want to take on Rai at all. 'If we don't like him, let us just go away. Why take him on, *anna*.'

I convinced him that I would see how Rai behaved the next day and then take a decision.

As agreed, the next day Krishnamurthy and I went to Rai's house in Indiranagar. Bachchan waited along with some boys at the office of Zakaria, a car dealer we knew. His office was near Rai's place.

As soon as I went in, Rai welcomed me in his usual cordial way. Kini, Jayanth, Naveen, Satish, Rajan and all his favourite boys were there. They were all ready to go out, yet Rai sat down for a talk.

I started off straight away. I said that although I was ready to take such risks for him, he had spoken to Chakre without taking me into confidence, and this had hurt me.

'Sreedhar, where is Balaram and where is Chakre? I spoke to him only because Rajendra and Pushpa forced me to. Ask Jayanth what I said when we were returning . . . these people cannot take away anything from Balaram, they only talk. If I say yes, they have planned to fleece money from me, that's all,' he said.

'Look, you are Bangalore's boss. Is it right for you to talk so loosely?'

'What Sreedhar? We were so close . . . somebody is trying to poison your mind. You know I have regard for you. Balaram is like family to me. Pushpa and Rajendra are not important to me . . .'

I looked sadly at Jayanth and Kini, and then told Rai, 'I like you a lot Muthappanna, but you lack stability. In this field it is not enough if you are good, you have to be firm too.'

'No Sreedhar, I am stable . . . you are mistaken.'

Jayanth and Kini had told me the same thing several times. Hence I was talking confidently.

Just then, the phone rang. Rai picked it up, listened and said, 'Sreedhar, it's for you.'

It was Bachchan, 'Sreedhar, still not done? Are you all right? Are things okay?'

'Bachchan, just five more minutes. I will come . . . everything is all right.'

Rai was stunned. His face lost colour.

'What is this, Sreedhar? When you are sitting in my house Bachchan calls you and asks if everything is all right? What does this mean? How did this happen? *Che* ... why did it happen?' He stood up shaking his head as if he could not believe it.

His boys also stood up, and so did we.

'Sreedhar, come with us. Satish is opening a hotel in Gangenahalli and we are going for the inauguration. You also come with us,' Rai said.

It was hard for me to say no when he was inviting me so affectionately, yet I forced myself. 'No, Muthappanna, Bachchan is waiting. You go; I will come some other time.'

'Please come,' he insisted.

'Not this time, some other time.'

Rai stood at the door, looked at me and sighed. 'You used to like me so much. We also like you more than anyone else in Bangalore. Just see what kind of people there are ...'

'Forget it, nobody can spoil our cordiality,' I said, but I did not have faith in what I was saying. It was something I said as a formality. Not just formality, but out my personal affection for Rai.

I felt somehow that this would be our last meeting. I was neither happy nor excited, I felt strangely sad. I was also upset with Balaram. I was angry that because of his thoughtlessness he had spoilt a good friendship.

Bachchan asked me in detail every word I had exchanged with Rai. Finally he said, 'Rai will not have any bitter feelings ... but what could we have done? We cannot give up Balaram either.'

Krishnamurthy said, 'Even now if you make up your mind things can be set right, *anna*. I will speak to Rai. Kini and Jayanth also like us.'

This is how we felt till that evening—it all changed after we spoke with Rajendra.

Those days there were no cell phones. We called Rajendra from a public phone booth that evening. I wanted to tell him about our discussion. Before I could say anything though, he said, 'Guru, where are you? I don't know which phone you are available on ... Rai called—it seems you spoke to him? He said Chakre has made the conversation public. He said, "Rajendra, what can people like him execute? I have convinced Sreedhar that the issue is not serious. Tell Chakre not to talk anymore." What exactly did you say, Guru?'

It was not possible for anyone else to tell Rajendra about the conversation I'd had with Rai. The minute he said it, my mood from the morning changed and I explained to Rajendra what had happened.

'What shall we do next?' he asked.

'What else? We have to declare war, that's all.'

'We are ready whenever you call us,' said Rajendra.

After talking to Rajendra, Bachchan's and my resolve strengthened. Krishnamurthy kept saying we should not rush into anything.

That night at eight o'clock we ran into Balaram. We told him that we had met Rai. We did not tell him about the plot that Rai and Chakre had hatched, but we said we would come out in the open with our decision to oppose Rai in a couple of days.

'You just keep saying this, Sir, but you don't do anything. Why did you have to go meet him today? If you meet him one more time then there will be a compromise.'

'Come tomorrow or the day after, Balaram. Let us finalise everything. Then we will lay our hands on all their income sources,' I said.

Balaram knew many rowdies from Mangalore, who were all against Rai. After he had joined Rai, he had promised that he would no longer be in contact with any of them, but he had continued the association. He had never mentioned it, though.

Now he said, 'How could I disconnect from the Mangalore boys, Sir? Of course I am in touch with them. Let us do one thing—we will oppose Rai here and set them against Rai in Mangalore. Amar Alva will also give us total support.'

I forbid him from getting the Mangalore boys involved in

this. It was not for us to interfere between Rai and Alva. At first Balaram grumbled but eventually he agreed. We decided to meet Rajendra and Pushpa the next evening and make final plans.

That night, at around eleven-thirty, I got a phone call.

I picked up the receiver and said, 'Hello?'

It was Rai on the other end. 'Sreedhar, it's me. Amar Alva has been murdered in Mangalore! I need you to do one thing, where can we meet?'

When I heard that Amar Alva had been murdered, I went blank for a minute. The saying, 'an enemy's enemy is a friend' applies to the underworld more than any other field. Though we had decided not to involve the Mangalore boys, we were very aware that Amar Alva would play an important role. Rai could not have withstood the Bangalore underworld on one side and the Mangalore underworld on the other.

I was sure Rai had grasped, by the way our conversation in the morning had gone, that I would not be made happy by the news of his enemy's death. I was surprised he had called me with the information.

'Oh really? When?' I asked.

'Now . . . I think nine o'clock. My boys were trying to reach me but they couldn't get through. Sreedhar, I need a favour.'

'What?'

'Look, although I am not involved directly, his men will lodge a complaint against me. Is it possible for you to arrange for me to get arrested and locked in a police station for the night?'

He wanted an alibi to prove that he was not in Mangalore at the time of Alva's murder.

'I will speak to a couple of officers. Call me after five minutes,' I said.

I called some officers I knew. I said I wanted them to arrest a man who had a criminal record for a night as an alibi.

'That's all? Where did the trouble occur?'

'Udupi.'

Though Alva was murdered in Mangalore, I did not want to tell him that. He would have inquired with an officer in Mangalore and refused after realising the risk involved.

'Let's do one thing. You need an alibi, right? Why should he be arrested? Let him come to register a complaint. We will have it registered; that will prove he was in Bangalore.'

'What can he complain about?'

'Is that a problem? Let him complain that someone hit him in a bar.'

I thought this was more sensible. 'Okay, Sir, shall I bring him there in half an hour?'

'Yes, bring him. Who is it?'

'Rai . . . Muthappa Rai.'

'Who! Muthappa Rai?'

'Yes.'

The officer was shocked. 'What are you saying? If Rai gives a complaint like that will our senior agree? No.'

Without waiting for even a second, he cut me off.

Rai called after two minutes. I told him no one was willing to arrest him.

'But something has to be done Sreedhar. I cannot think of anything.'

I said instantly, 'We will go to a government hospital and get an x-ray or some tests done . . .'

'Which hospital will be open at this time? I wish we could meet.'

'Okay, where shall I come?'

'You tell me.'

'I will come near Puttanna Theatre in the Jayanagar shopping complex in ten minutes. Come there.'

'Okay, I will get there as fast as possible.'

How strange are human relationships! On the one hand I was preparing to oppose Rai and, on the other, Rai was asking an important favour from someone who was discontent with him. If I had made one phone call to Kempaiah, he would have immediately arrested Rai on charges of having conspired to kill

Amar Alva. After that it would have been a cakewalk for us to crush him. However, at that particular moment I wanted to help Rai. Not just me, I am sure even you help people you are unhappy with at certain moments?

So I set aside my discontent with Rai.

Those days I had a Yamaha bike. I had taken it from Ramanna who had produced *Garuda Rekhe* and other successful Kannada films. Though I had given up riding it after my accident, I still kept it with me in case of an emergency.

It was a quarter to twelve when I reached Puttanna Theatre. Rai was there within ten minutes. Pomma and Jayanth were with him. Rai asked me what should be done.

'Let us go straight to Jayadeva cardiology hospital. Let us get an ECG done, saying you have chest pain. Naturally your name will be registered.'

He liked my idea. I gave my bike to Pomma and sat with Rai in the car.

Rai gave me the details on the way. At around half past eight that night, Amar Alva had gone to his brother-in-law Ranjan Poonja's house to invite him for his son's birthday party. The assassins had fired at him when he was outside the house. Poonja had fired at the assassins and one of them was injured in the leg.

'He knew he would be attacked . . . why didn't he take any precautions?'

'They've been saying they will finish him for the last two months. Even I didn't know it would happen till it did.'

'Your boys?'

'No, Ashokanna's boys.'

As I'd mentioned earlier, Rai and Alva were mere pawns in the shadow fight between the two big dons, Sharad Shetty and Ashok Shetty.

Jayanth Alva was a close relative of Amar Alva. Whenever Amar Alva was mentioned, Rai would tell Jayanth, 'In our field kinship and friendship does not matter one bit, Jayanth. They are eyeing you too.'

Now, Jayanth was showing a lot of excitement—perhaps he was being cautious because his reaction was being watched as he was a relative.

On the way Rai said casually, 'I spoke to Rajendra about Chakre. I told him Chakre is coming to us saying he will finish Balaram and goes around telling everyone that I have asked him to finish Balaram . . .'

His words had no impact on me.

It was twelve when we reached Jayadeva hospital. We went to the outpatient department. The way Rai was holding his chest and writhing, I started to wonder if he really had a pain in his chest.

We took an ECG. The technician asked questions about Rai's habits and made notes. Rai clutched his heart and acted really well. I told the clerk how Rai smoked four packets of cigarettes a day.

Rai signed in the register. They said it would take twenty minutes to give the report. We made Rai sit there and Jayanth and I came out. Jayanth started telling me about the repercussions of Amar Alva's murder. He said Alva's associates would run away from Mangalore. Ramesh Pujari and Francis Cutinho would hesitate to even talk about Rai, he said. 'For the next four or five years no one will challenge us, what do you say?' He gave me a look. He knew about the fallout between Rai and me in the morning. Perhaps he thought I would never again show my discontent so readily.

But Amar Alva's murder did not make me tense. I was used to being part of a larger scheme and indirectly affected by murders that had to be committed due to circumstances.

I did not answer Jayanth. He changed the topic and said since carbine had been used for the first time in Karnataka, the police would take the case seriously.

'What is carbine?' I asked. I really did not know.

'Big guns are called that. Sten gun, AK-47 . . .'

'Did they use an AK-47?'

'No, sten gun . . .'

He was eager to talk about the gory details of the murder, but my cold reaction stopped him. I was sure he did not care much for Rai, but there was the possibility that if I spoke against Rai, he would not have liked it. They had no other name but Rai in Bangalore.

It was past midnight when they gave us the reports. The ECG was clear.

'That was a good suggestion, Sreedhar,' Rai said. 'If I am questioned, I will say I was waiting from ten o'clock and got the ECG done at eleven. I am leaving Bangalore tomorrow for a couple of weeks. I will see what developments take place and then decide when to return. Jayanth or I will call you.'

We shook hands. I looked into his eyes and said, 'Take care.'

'I will be careful.' Then he put his hand on my shoulder and said affectionately, 'You must not worry about Chakre and all that. I will come back and set everything right. There will be no problem in the future.'

But I was certain we would not meet again. It was very clear that the friendship of three years had come to an end. It was neither Chakre nor Amar Alva's murder that was bothering me at that minute. It was the end of a friendship that disturbed me.

That was the last day of May 1992.

I have not seen Muthappa Rai since.

PART V

One

The next day the papers were full of sensational reports about Amar Alva's murder. Only the assassin who was hit on the leg had been arrested so far. There was no mention of Rai. Instead of the Mangalore police, the Bangalore police began to search for Rai.

Our men were stunned to hear that I had met Rai the previous night. Balaram said, 'You don't know rowdyism, Sir. You could have given a message to any one of us.'

But Bachchan and Krishnamurthy did not agree. When I said in an uncomfortable tone, 'What do we have personally against Rai, Balaram?' he kept quiet.

From the way we had spoken the previous night, Rai had got a clue that the Bangalore underworld would protest against him, but he was expecting that everybody would be shocked by Amar Alva's murder. But it had no effect on the Bangalore boys.

At the moment, before publicly opposing Rai, I knew that I had to bring about a compromise between Balaram and Rajendra. Even at that minute, Balaram was not as angry with Rai as he was with Rajendra. Of the two, Rajendra had realised the inevitability of uniting. Also he was mature enough to understand what he was told. But Balaram was not like that. Even after explaining everything to him the whole day, he would still reject the idea.

Everybody said that there would be trouble if Balaram and Rajendra met face-to-face. I was largely confident that Balaram would not behave badly in my presence, but there remained a small niggling doubt.

One day I called everyone to a lodge next to Nalanda Theatre on Mysore Road. Balaram, Rajendra, Pushpa, Kalapathar, Mahadeva, Kalakar Kisan, Anil, Malayali Sridhar, Bruce Lee Naga, Kulla Narayana and Kutti—they all came. Outside the hotel there was a huge crowd of boys.

Bachchan, Krishnamurthy and I were the bridge between the gangs.

Although Rajendra spoke to him in a friendly manner, Balaram was a little stiff. With Pushpa, though, he was relaxed.

After everyone settled down, we started talking about how to tackle Rai.

'Guru, what if we finish him?' Rajendra shot out.

Balaram, who had been his sworn enemy till a second before, immediately agreed with him and said, 'Yes Sir, let us do that. Then all will be well.'

I looked at them both and asked, 'How do we finish him?'

'He will not know that we are opposing him to this extent. Let us continue to be like we were before. Soon after he returns to Bangalore, we will finish him,' Rajendra said.

The rest of them agreed, but I said this would not happen on any account.

'Why not?' Rajendra asked.

'Rajendra, you don't understand. We should not finish him just because we are together,' I said categorically.

'I know why you are saying this. You are scared that you will get a bad name, that people will say you killed Kotwal after being with him and did the same to Rai, isn't it? This is rowdyism. Here only one thing counts—who finished whom. Didn't Rai finish Oil Kumar even though he was a friend? Although they had reached a compromise, didn't Shetty finish Amar Alva? If we don't finish him now then it will be an eternal headache,' Rajendra said as Balaram kept nodding in agreement.

I spoke slowly, weighing every word, hoping they would

absorb all of it. 'Look, our first step is to oppose Rai. But that is not the last step. If he has to retaliate, he must first attempt to break our unity. So, what I say is that let us not think about what trouble he might bring us and be united till the end. If Rai is alive, it will be a motivation for us to be united. If he is not alive, we will not stay united even for two months.'

Rajendra was silent for some time, and then he agreed. Balaram kept grumbling. Finally everyone agreed.

We decided that we should call a meeting of all the 'para-underworld'—people who were indirectly involved—over the next ten days and inform them about our decision. It was also decided that the information of all the Bangalore boys coming together to oppose Rai should be made known to Kempaiah. They all gave this responsibility to me.

There were two reasons behind letting Kempaiah know of our decision. First, in case Rai's gang committed a grave crime, he should know that we had no hand in it. Second, as soon as the police find out that a group has split, they start hunting down members and we had to tell them that we had no guns with us.

The only police officer who agreed to take me to Kempaiah was Ishwar Prasad, then a sub-inspector, currently an ACP. He was my classmate when I was studying law. He was one of the people who were very unhappy about me being in the underworld. He is a very straightforward man.

When I met Ishwar Prasad and requested him to take me to Kempaiah, he said, 'It would be better if you give up this field and step into some other field . . . how long can you continue?'

I convinced him that after the disagreement with Rai came to an end, I would step out of the underworld. So one afternoon he took me to Kempaiah's chamber. Kempaiah did not remember me, but Ishwar Prasad had briefed him beforehand.

'Tell me, what can I do for you?' Kempaiah asked lightly. I had been apprehensive that he would be in an angry mood, but when I heard him talk in that tone, I was relieved.

I said I was in the underworld due to circumstances beyond

my control and I had come to him to give him some information. I was standing and talking. After three minutes he looked at Ishwar Prasad and said, 'My heart is telling me to ask him to sit down. How do you feel?'

'Sir, I am not saying this just because he was my classmate, but he is a well-read man and a good human being. He is caught in this field due to circumstances,' Ishwar Prasad said and agreed that I should sit down.

I thanked him, sat down, and spoke to him for about forty-five minutes. His words, like the white shirt on his back, were clean and straight and touched my heart. After listening to me, he explained why one should not be in the underworld, which came from his wisdom and experience.

'Can we live a thousand years, Sreedhar? If yes, then anything can be justified. At least making money would mean something then. For a life of sixty or seventy years, should we murder, threaten and earn money? Forget others, at least is what you are doing making you happy? And that Muthappa Rai—what does he say? He had come to me once. I advised him to give up criminal activities and lead a straight life. What does he say now? I don't think he has come out of it . . .'

I didn't know what to say. Here I was meeting him to inform him about the fall-out we'd had with Rai, and he wanted to know if it was possible to reform him.

Finally, with a great deal of effort, I told him that because of Muthappa Rai's passion for guns and his connections with the Dubai dons, we had decided to break away from him.

He was silent for a minute and then asked, 'If you separate from him, will you all lead a straight life?'

'Definitely. We will get out of the underworld . . . but we will stay united so that he does not trouble us.'

'Remember one thing: I am not an officer who supports one group to finish another. There are several police officers like that in Bangalore. But to me all are equal. I will not trouble you if you follow the law, but if you don't, I will not keep quiet.'

I convinced him that we would not do anything for any

reason and assured him that, within one week, I would get all the notorious people from the underworld to surrender to him.

'What does "all" mean?'

'Rajendra, Pushpa, Tanveer, Balaram, Kalapathar . . .'

'Will they all come if you call?'

'If you want them tomorrow, they will come tomorrow.'

'Okay, talk to all of them and tell Prasad,' he said.

All our men were very happy when I reported our conversation. After three days I went to the commissioner's office with Tanveer, Kalapathar, Rajendra and Pushpa. I had told Ishwar Prasad about it and he was waiting for us when we went. I made all of them stand aside and went up to him.

'Sreedhar, I told Kempaiah *sahebaru* about your coming. He said there is no need for all of them to talk to him. Let them not trouble anyone again. Maybe it is different talking to you alone and talking to all of them. Maybe he thought it would be a problem if they took it easy. Anyway, don't get involved in crime—all of you'

We were all very disappointed, but we could not do anything about it.

The news of my meeting with Kempaiah spread and strange rumours began to float. Muthappa Rai has said in several interviews and to this day believes that I convinced Kempaiah that Rai was planning to kill him and thus became close to Kempaiah. Kempaiah and Ishwar Prasad are amidst us to this day and Rai is in jail. I am very aware that if I say something that is untrue, they will deny it. Never did I mention anything like that to Kempaiah. I don't think Kempaiah would have believed me even if I had told him Rai was planning to kill him. He would have doubted my intentions and thought I was trying to suck up to him. Or he might have decided that I was part of the plan all along and now that we had fallen out, I was telling him about it. I have studied human psychology quite extensively and I am extremely careful when I talk to police officers.

Four days after I spoke to Kempaiah, the lawyer Santosh

Kumar called Kalapathar and gave him the message that Muthappa Rai wanted to see him. Kalapathar mentioned it to us. I suggested that Kalapathar meet Rai and find out what was on his mind. Balaram said that he and his boys would cover him, and if the opportunity arose, he would finish Rai.

I did not agree to that plan, but Balaram, Kalapathar and Tanveer refused to listen to me. Balaram said, 'If he has called Kalapathar, he must have got a clue about our uniting. If not now we will never get another chance.'

'Look, on no account will he trouble Kalapathar. Let us first see what Rai has to say, then we will decide.'

Finally they said they would not do anything, but I was aware that they were only pretending to have agreed to what I was saying. I was sure they would try and attack Rai.

In the underworld, one must learn to expect the unexpected, so we decided not to take the Rai-Kalapathar meeting lightly. I even informed a police officer known to me. Rai had sent word to Kalapathar to meet him next to the RTO office in Indiranagar. I requested the police inspector to be present at the spot. It is a well-known fact that, in the underworld, as soon as men spot a police jeep, they run half a kilometre away instantly.

On the designated day, Kalapathar was in a car at the spot from four in the evening, as was the inspector.

Bachchan, Krishnamurthy and I were in a car with dark windows, and Balaram was in another car with his boys. Balaram had told me that Tanveer had gone to Ramanagar and hence would not come. There were many boys loitering in the area, and it was not difficult for us to guess that they were Balaram's boys.

When Balaram saw the inspector's jeep he came to us and asked, 'Why have these people come here, Sir?'

'Somebody must have leaked the information,' I said.

'Who will leak, Sir?' he gave me a look of suspicion.

'Somebody from the Rai gang maybe,' I said casually and he went away.

At around four-thirty a car drove by and stopped near

Kalapathar's car. The men inside seemed like Mangloreans. Balaram seemed like he was about to go up to them, but I signalled him not to. The men in the car went up to Kalapathar, spoke to him and left. Kalapathar moved his car a little further.

After seeing this, the inspector thought Rai would not come and left. Ten minutes later, a Maruti van arrived and parked opposite Kalapathar's car. After two minutes Kalapathar got down from his car and went to the van. Thinking that Rai had come, I was all eyes. It looked like Rai had come after confirming that the inspector had left. I began to worry that Balaram and his gang would attack Rai, now that the inspector was no longer around.

Balaram went past the van and came up to me and said, 'Where is he, Sir? He has not come.'

'Who?'

'Rai . . .'

'Is that true?'

'There are two men sitting in front. Jayanth and Willy. There is nobody else.'

'Maybe he decided not to come after seeing the police jeep.'

He went away saying, '*Che.*'

Fifteen minutes after Kalapathar got into the van, a scooter arrived and stopped about a hundred feet away from it. The man riding it was hefty and wearing a helmet. He was staring at the van. The man sitting pillion looked scared.

'Tanveer!' Bachchan said.

It was definite now that they all had decided to attack without letting us know. Immediately we started the car and left, asking Tanveer to follow us. Balaram followed us as did Tanveer on the two-wheeler. We went straight to Zakaria's office on Airport Road. We had instructed Kalapathar to come there after the meeting.

Balaram and Tanveer joined us shortly. Tanveer said, 'Sir, there was an accident near Kengeri Gate, hence I got delayed. Why didn't you do anything? Didn't Rai come?'

'Who asked you to come? And why did you stand right opposite the van?' I asked. He looked questioningly at Balaram.

'No, Sir—to take a chance if Rai comes.'

Balaram stopped him and said, 'He doesn't know anything—keep quiet.'

I started yelling at them. 'Whatever decision we take should be after a discussion. If you had actually attacked, his boys would also attack. They would have definitely shot us if they had spotted us . . . we were not at all prepared.'

'No, Saar, do you think we would allow them to come near you? Do you know how many boys were there? One hundred and fifty!' Balaram said, smiling.

We were not at all happy.

By then Kalapathar arrived. 'What is this Sir, these people, they keep a revolver on the dashboard for all to see and then talk!' He seemed surprised at their craze for guns and added, 'Rai came. It seems he went away on seeing the jeep. Jayanth spoke to me—he spoke about Balaram and then you. He said, "Sreedhar said we asked somebody to finish Balaram—why should we attack him? Doesn't he have enough enemies in Bangalore? Isn't it?" They wanted to see how I would react. I just laughed it off.'

One afternoon a few days later, we all met at a hotel in Seshadripuram. Rajendra, Pushpa, Kalapathar, Balaram and the three of us—Bachchan, Krishnamurthy and I—were present.

There were four or five other men who wanted to support us. Though they were close to Rai, they had realised that they would have trouble from him sooner or later, and therefore decided to stand by us.

That day we were to announce openly our opposition to Rai. We started discussing how to go about it.

Balaram was irritated with the way we were deliberating. 'If you keep talking like this we will not come out in the open even after one year. We should go to all the clubs and tell them that we have nothing to do with him and ask them to deal with us directly. If it has to happen, let it happen today. Otherwise let us not talk about him,' he said curtly.

The manner in which he said it made it impossible for

anyone to refuse, so we went from there to the clubs in Majestic. Strangely, no one opposed us. 'We respected him only because you all were with him. We also want locals. Now we will not have any deals with him,' they assured us. 'If you need to say anything to us, call us, we will come,' they added, implying that it would not be beneficial to them if notorious rowdies like us visited their place.

I have not stepped into a club since.

It was evening by the time we completed our rounds of all the clubs.

We suspected by then that the news of our rebellion would have reached Rai, but we wanted to inform him directly. We had a reason for this: we had to bring to his notice that all the Bangalore gangs had united. We did not want him to play one group against the other.

We considered all those who were in contact with him and finally decided to send the information through the lawyer Santosh. Though the heat of Amar Alva's murder had died down, none of his boys were in Bangalore. We went to Santosh's office behind Ulsoor Gate police station. I was not very close to Santosh, but he was friendly with Kalapathar, Pushpa and Rajendra. He was stunned to see us there together. We told him that we had separated from Rai and that we would all oppose him if he tried to intervene in Bangalore deals.

Rajendra said, 'Rai may be your relative, but we are all closer to you,' and he couldn't refuse them.

'Rai is a distant relative . . . now what do you want me to do? You want me to give him the information?'

'Not just give him information, but also speak for us,' Rajendra said.

We wanted it known that we had nothing against Rai's relatives or associates. Santosh assured us that he would speak with Rai that night.

After this we went to Rajendra's house. Balaram and Pushpa's gangs left after a little while. We stayed behind. That night I could not sleep. It is not an easy task to challenge a don in the underworld. It requires a lot of preparation. Rai was not a street fighter in the traditional manner, but he had connections even in Dubai. Also, we had seen his weapon collection. Apart from this, a don usually has a large amount of money. Though we were all notorious in our own way, none of us had converted it into money.

We had another anxiety. If Rai closed his house and left, we would have had to struggle just to get his address. But we were all sitting ducks. The only hope we had was local support.

By the next evening, the news had spread all over Bangalore. An acquaintance in Krishnarajapura said, 'I heard that you and Rai have separated?' and by evening a former member of the underworld asked, 'Why did you oppose him? Now who is the boss?'

I said, 'The entire Bangalore underworld is the boss,' but he did not accept it.

'It is already well known that because of you Balaram and Rajendra have come together. There is no need to be so humble. You are the boss . . . please take care.'

For a few days everyone talked about it. Anyone who did not know about the new developments and who asked us, 'How is Muthappanna?' was confused when we replied, 'Which Muthappanna?'

'Didn't we see you with him just a month ago?' they would ask and we had to explain our stand.

Four days later, Tanveer, Kalapathar and Balaram came to see me at Banashankari complex. They were all in one car and in another car were some smart-looking boys.

'Sir, some friends have come from Mangalore . . . they want to see you,' Balaram said.

I was furious. 'Didn't I tell you not to have anything to do with them, Balaram? Why have you brought them to our spot?' I shouted.

'Sir, they cannot do anything here. Even if we do not support them, they will finish Rai someday. They have come to tell you that they will support us. If you say yes, they are ready to give us weapons.'

'We don't want their weapons or them,' I said tersely, but Balaram insisted that I should at least talk to them.

I finally agreed, but I spoke to them in an offhand manner, and did not mention Rai at all. Disappointed, they left.

The next morning, at around ten o'clock, Bachchan and I were in our Girinagar house, talking, when the phone rang.

I picked up the receiver and said, 'Hello?'

'Congratulations to Bangalore's present don from the ex-don!'

It was Muthappa Rai on the other side of the line.

My hair stood on end.

'What Sreedhar, am I not right? Former don congratulates current don?'

I did not answer. I did not know how to respond. The call was most unexpected and I was not prepared.

'Why Sreedhar, why are you not talking? Maybe you didn't think I would call?'

I thought then that if I did not talk, he may think I was afraid, so I said, 'Nothing, how are you?' the normalcy in my voice surprised even me.

'How am I?' he paused for a minute. I thought he was sighing. 'Why, Sreedhar? Why did you do this? I liked you so much . . .'

'Look, there is nothing personal in this. You are basically a good man, but you do not have the stability. I cautioned you several times. I had no other choice.'

Muthappa Rai must be the only don in the history of the underworld who engaged his rival in a decent conversation like this.

'But what was the need to insult me like this? You could have told me directly. Why did you have to go to all the clubs and warn them?'

'It was not my decision alone. How long was I to engage in shadow fighting? However, we have not spoken about you anywhere with contempt.'

'What do you mean you have not spoken with contempt? Haven't you said you have chased Rai out of Bangalore?'

We had not said that at any time; we had just said that Rai would not step into Bangalore again, and I told him this. I didn't think the people at the club would have made it up either; but we had noticed some of Rai's boys in one or two clubs and they may have said it to please him.

'Why? Why did you say I would not come to Bangalore? Am I not a Kannadiga? Don't I have the right to live in Bangalore?' Slowly, he was raising his voice.

'Look, Bangalore is not my father's property. But after every small little case, you left Bangalore for four or five months. I felt you would not return now.' I was also raising my voice.

Rai was silent for some time.

Then he said sadly, 'Okay, Sreedhar, you keep your Bangalore. I have had enough. But remember one thing Sreedhar, you cheated me. You never showed any interest in making money. You behaved like you were never interested in money. But now you got everyone to come together and made them go against me. Now you will get money, Sreedhar, but do you know what kind of tension the hand that counts the currency notes faces? Today you will not understand this. Some day you will understand. Then you will regret it. I could have called the club people and yelled at them and told them not to listen to you. Or I could have told the police and stopped everything, but I don't want all that Sreedhar.'

I had not addressed him by his name till then, but now his words moved me. His affection disturbed me. 'Muthappanna, please understand one thing, I did not oppose you with the intention to make money. We did not agree with your behaviour. You called Balaram part of your family. But you also called Pushpa and Rajendra that . . . you confused everything . . .'

'Oh, Pushpa, Rajendra! Sreedhar, how long do you think you will keep them together? I called them too.'

My ears pricked up. So he'd spoken to them before talking to me. They must have blamed me, I thought.

'What did they say?' I asked.

'What do they say? They are not taking my calls. They are hiding.'

I felt relieved. Also, I felt like consoling him. 'Look, Muthappanna, I liked you a lot. If we had met somewhere else, and not in the underworld, we would have been friends till the end. But in our world what counts is something else ... ask Jayanth, he will tell you what I used to say ...'

He was silent for some time. When he spoke again, his voice was very cold. 'Sreedhar, you have seen the weapons that we have, yet you dared to oppose me. How?'

It was an indirect threat. I had to answer categorically. 'Look, you have weapons, we have boys. If you don't have boys to use the weapons, they are worse than stones ...' I had spoken without addressing him as Muthappanna intentionally.

'So, you are ready to fight us?' It was more a challenge than a question.

'Anytime ... if it has to be today let it be today,' I said firmly. I had not said it casually. I was very aware that the Bangalore boys were eager for such a fight.

He had not expected me to accept his challenge so readily. After a few seconds he said, 'You are confident because you have Kempaiah.'

He wanted to believe that we were not capable of fighting him alone. I put my finger on his insecurity and said, 'Don't talk about the police. Call us anywhere in Bangalore—we are ready.'

'Okay Sreedhar, let it go. I don't want your friendship, neither do I want to fight with you, nor your Bangalore. But remember one thing. My boys were close to you ... don't trouble them because of me.' Again he was starting to sound sad.

'Definitely, no.'

'I am not talking about you, but about Balaram and his boys. He can't do anything, still he pounces.'

He was finding it difficult to request for the safety of his boys. I didn't want to make him say the words. 'I have told all the boys not to trouble any of your boys on any account, Muthappanna. I will not allow any accident, I promise.'

'Okay Sreedhar, then . . .?' it was a sign to end the conversation.

We had spoken for forty minutes. My heart felt heavy. I felt like asking him as I usually did, 'When can I come to see you?' But I did not. Instead, I said, 'When will you call again?'

'Let me see Sreedhar . . .' his voice was also heavy.

'Okay, all the best,' I said and replaced the receiver.

That day when Rai called, I had recognised his voice instantly. There was no need for me to think even for a second. But seven-and-a-half years later, in mid-January 2000, when he called me again in the quiet of night and said it was Rai speaking, I had repeatedly refuted it, saying, 'I cannot recognise the voice.'

His voice had changed.

Much had happened in those seven-and-a-half years.

The day he called me, we discussed in detail every word he had said. He had tried several times to talk to Pushpa. But, like he said, Pushpa had not taken his call. Every time he had called, Pushpa's younger brother had answered and said, '*Anna* is not at home.'

Finally Rai said dejectedly, 'Your *anna* has listened to someone else's words and gone against me. Please tell him to remember all the good I have done for them all.'

We thought his associates would fight us, though Rai may not have favoured it. But from my conversation with him, we felt he had no intention of fighting us. We decided, though, that we could not afford to be careless. We watched him and his associates for at least a year, although within a week or two we got definite indications that Rai was seriously considering leaving Bangalore. He and his boys were not seen anywhere. They had not tried to contact anyone who was in touch with us.

Then we took under our control the oil business, which was active at that time.

It is probably the only example of a smooth, bloodless handing over from one don to another in the history of the underworld anywhere. It is probably also one of the few times that the new don was so reluctant to take up the position. Although I had not desired it, rumour spread that I was the new don. Balaram's boys gave much strength to that rumour. I had observed, when I had been close to dons in the past, how they always had to be cautious and tackle highly complex situations, as well as deal with the anxiety of being a possible target. I had no desire whatsoever to undergo such tension. Whenever people asked me, 'So, you are the don now?' I denied it. But they would insist that it was true, and so my name as the new don of Bangalore stuck.

Having observed Jayaraj, Kotwal and Muthappa Rai closely, I had realised one thing very clearly: the don who gets his enemies killed by someone else is indebted to that associate. Kotwal had got several people killed or assaulted through rowdies close to him. By the time Kotwal died, they were all talking very disparagingly about him.

Kurubara Pete Raja (who wanted to kill Kotwal) would say slightingly, 'But for me, Jayaraj would have been killed,' and eventually became Jayaraj's enemy.

Oil Kumar got Jayaraj killed through Rai and soon Rai stopped respecting him. Rai also had doubts about those who killed Kumar.

Having seen all this, I decided never to get anyone killed or assaulted by anyone else. In case assault was inevitable, we decided that Bachchan, Krishnamurthy or I would carry it out with our own boys.

It may come as a surprise, then, that from the time I started opposing Rai to this day, I have not had anyone assaulted. Though there were several occasions when it seemed as if violence was inevitable, I resolved the issue with discussions.

Two

Though Rai had said that he would never attack me, I could not be incautious. So, after my conversation with him, I vacated my house in Girinagar and rented a house in ISRO Layout. Bachchan, Krishnamurthy and a few boys stayed with me at all times.

In order to prevent the neighbours from becoming suspicious, we put up a board reading, 'SM Associates, Land Developers', on the gate. SM stood for Sreedhar Murthy.

Our house was in a relatively undeveloped area. There were only three houses on our road. Our neighbour was a man called Shetty, and the house next to his was occupied by a Professor Lohitashwa.

We had lots of visitors coming in cars every day. Rajendra and Pushpa came once or twice every month and Balaram and Kalapathar came three or four times a week. There would be big gangs of boys with them when they visited.

Since Rai had left Bangalore, we started getting all sorts of deals, from as far as Bombay to a small interior village in north Karnataka.

Whoever came to visit us, we saw to it that our neighbours were not disturbed. The people in Shetty's home liked us. They felt secure because of us. Also, our boys ran small errands for them, like fixing a fuse or a dropping them in a vehicle. They did not know who we were; they just assumed we were some big businessmen. But our relationship with Lohitashwa was not very pleasant. He was always in a very troubled mood. If he was outside when any car came to our house, he would frown and look at it with contempt and suspicion.

Many years back, when I was working in Lankesh's films, a stage actor named Venkatesh Prasad had introduced me to Prof. Lohitashwa. We had met a couple of times. Prasad had told me then that he was a very arrogant man, so I had instructed the boys to be careful in front of his house.

One evening at around five o'clock, Balaram and Kalapathar came to visit me at home. Balaram was screaming angrily, 'Sir, I will do 307 to that mental!'

'307' means assault with a weapon. The man he was referring to as 'mental' was Lohitashwa.

As I've said before, Balaram was always eager for a fight. He would flare up if anyone spoke against him and he would make monumental even an insignificant issue. Rarely have rowdies been worked on by police like he was. Once, ACP Raviraj was after him in connection with a case. Anyone in Balaram's position would have tried to negotiate with Raviraj through mutual acquaintances. Or they would have gone for a legal solution. Instead, this is what Balaram did:

One day when he was on his bike, he saw a police constable taking Raviraj's children to school. He knew the constable, and so he stopped to chat. Balaram asked him whose children they were. The constable told him. Balaram asked him with a sly look, 'Okay, your boss is chasing me ... and now if I do something to his children?'

Naturally, the constable told his boss about this. Raviraj caught Balaram in a week's time and beat him to a pulp.

I asked Balaram how he could do such a senseless thing.

'What do I do, Sir? They took all my associates and put them on "aeroplane" (a form of torture). So I did it out of anger ...'

Usually Balaram listened to what I said and respected it. But sometimes he opposed me and irritated me. Once he had tried to get a man from the Congress called JP to become block president. He wanted me to bring pressure on S. Ramesh to do it. But Ramesh was unable to bring it about. There were several people vying for the post, and he had to give it to someone else.

Balaram got angry. 'You have to convince Ramesh to do it at any cost,' he insisted.

'That is not possible, Balaram. Look, he also has pressure from all sides. Also, we should not take such things seriously . . . are we politicians?' I tried to reason with him.

'I don't know all that, but if JP is not made block president I will not be quiet,' Balaram said, raising his voice.

I also got angry. 'If he says he cannot do it then what can be done?'

Balaram had not expected this. 'What did you say?! What can be done? Okay, you just stay silent . . . I will do whatever I have to do . . .'

'So what will you do? Kill him? Do you think he is a rowdy? He will shoot you . . . don't talk nonsense . . .'

We were on our way back from Mysore at the time, where we had gone on some work. Bachchan, Krishnamurthy, Balaram and I were in one car. Balaram's boys were ahead of us in another car.

'Ree Bachchan, drive a little fast and stop our car.'

'Ree Balaram, don't bother about it. Keep cool,' Bachchan said.

'Okay, I will be cool—you just stop the car,' Balaram said curtly.

I got really angry now. 'Okay, stop the car Bachchan. Let him go and attack anyone he wants. Did we oppose Rai just to kill and go to jail? At least if we kill someone from the field there will be some acceptance,' I started yelling.

By then Bachchan had overtaken the other car and signalled them to stop. Anil, Kisan and Malayali Sridhar were in the car. As soon as the car stopped, Balaram got out without saying anything and got into it.

That night I did not sleep. I was worried about what would happen if Balaram attempted to do what he'd threatened. Luckily nothing of the sort happened. JP himself, who had asked Balaram to get the post for him, had consoled and calmed him!

The next evening, Balaram came to see me. He was very embarrassed about his behaviour.

'Do I talk against you, Sir? You should make me understand! We went to Ramesh's house. He was not there. If he was there I don't know what would have happened. Then JP himself consoled me till midnight,' he said, as if he were doing me a great favour!

For about a week, I lectured to him for hours on end about how to be careful when using violence. He listened to me humbly, but later he told Bachchan, 'Can we really be like what he says, Bachchan? I listen to him so that he does not feel hurt.'

But I always said what I felt I had to say, irrespective of whether he listened or not. In the underworld, dons always look for boys with boundless courage. But in my case, it was the opposite! Balaram's boys had developed the same kind of daring he had, and it was like being surrounded by human dynamite all the time!

In those days, Ramanna, the producer of the blockbuster film *Garuda Rekhe*, was a close friend of mine. One night Balaram, his boys and I were sleeping in Ramanna's house. We had stayed there a few times before as well.

Ramanna, if he could not sleep, would get up and walk on the terrace. That night, he woke up at around two in the morning and decided to go up to the terrace. He was trying to open the door when Balaram's boy, Loki, who has very sharp ears, got up and caught hold of Ramanna's hands. A shocked Ramanna said, 'I am the owner of the house and I just want to walk for some time.'

'Nothing doing . . . just go and sleep quietly. *Doddavaru* is sleeping and I will not let you out.'

'Who is *Doddavaru*?'

'Sreedhar *sahebaru.*'

'He is my friend,' Ramanna began to say, but shut up when a razor appeared in Loki's hand.

Loki actually locked up Ramanna in a room that night.

The next day, when Ramanna told me what had happened, I asked Loki why he'd behaved like that.

Loki said, 'He may claim he is your friend, but what do I know? In our field, many people have stayed together and then been killed. I would not have allowed him out while you were sleeping.'

Balaram was one of the roughest men in the underworld. Rough does not mean strong. Usually strong men are not rough. Also, he had some sort of weird stubborn courage. I must narrate an incident here to explain this.

A contractor, who was very close to top politicians, died in a car crash. He had a son, based in the US, who came to India after his father's death. The father had property worth around two hundred crore rupees, as well as several benami properties. He had a factory worth fifty crore rupees in the name of one of his most trusted allies. Everybody knew about it, including the son.

The son wanted to transfer all the property to his name, pay all the taxes due and return to the US.

All the properties were transferred to his name without a problem, except for the one in the name of his father's trusted ally. The man would keep postponing it, till one day, he began avoiding the son completely and became very difficult to trace.

A legislator from Hassan district asked us to intervene and solve the problem, but he gave strict instructions that there should not be any violence. He just wanted us to find the man, get his signature on the relevant papers, and let him go.

I gave the job of getting him, without any violence, to Balaram.

The man was around fifty years old and very wealthy. He had two wives and two houses: one in Srirampura and one in Sadashivnagar. The first wife stayed in one house with their two children, and the second wife stayed in another house with their small baby.

Every morning, the man would go from his first house to his second house at around seven o'clock. He would return for lunch, leave again at four in the evening, and come back at eight o'clock. He rode a scooter.

Balaram and his gang waited for a week to get him. His second wife would accompany him to the first house, and Balaram thought that if they tried to catch him when she was around, it would lead to lot of commotion, so they decided to take him in the afternoon. Also, if a man goes missing in the afternoon, his people will not be immediately alerted as they are when he goes missing at night. Although the legislator had told us not to worry about the police, it was something we had to consider. If we were caught, it would be our legs that would be broken.

I had told Balaram that seven in the morning was better than the afternoon, but he would only wake up at two in the afternoon. For this job, he had agreed to get up and come at eleven in the morning, as if he were doing me a great favour.

From Sadashivnagar to Srirampura, there was absolutely no place where he could stop the man while he was on a scooter and drag him into another vehicle. The streets were always crowded in the afternoon. For about a week Balaram tried, but he was unable to grab the man.

One night, the contractor's son took us to the West End hotel. After a couple of pegs, he ran down the entire system. 'You know, I used to come to India once in two years and the man was so nice to me. How could he betray me like this? Okay, you have now agreed to sort out all issues, but it's getting delayed. In America, if such a deal were given to a mob, they would have finished it within twenty-four hours.'

Balaram became angry. He could not speak English, but understood what was being said.

Balaram cut the boy short, saying, 'This is not America. In America nobody bothers to interfere even if something is happening in front of their eyes. Here, even for a small accident, people from the next road will come running. We were not the ones who asked your father to register the property in that man's name and we have promised to get it back . . .'

Nobody had ever spoken to the man so rudely and he was shocked.

'Don't misunderstand me,' he started pleading. 'You see, I have committed to people all over the world. I didn't know there would be problems like these; this problem is threatening my personal relationships,' he said in a pathetic tone.

Balaram suddenly felt sorry for him and assured him that he would positively finish the job the next day.

The next morning, Balaram selected four boys to follow every move of the man and asked us to come to Srirampura Bridge at around noon, along with the son.

'Why Balaram?' I asked.

'You should know immediately if something goes wrong. Today I will definitely do the job. That man thinks we are useless, we must show who we are.'

I decided it was pointless to argue with him. I called the son at West End and he happily agreed to come with us.

We reached the bridge at around half past eleven. Balaram was waiting there with six motorbikes and two cars.

'He goes past this crossroad below. We will catch him here,' he said.

At around noon, we found out that the man had left his Sadashivnagar house. Balaram asked us to wait at the bridge and went down to the crossroad.

The NRI was very excited. 'Oh! Oh! What an adventure!' he screamed.

Exactly at half past twelve, the man came by on his scooter. There were a couple of Matador vans, three two-wheelers and a car and also a number of people on the road. It was not a good place to kidnap anyone.

The scooter slowed down when it approached the turn. Two boys who were waiting there stopped the scooter by catching hold of the handle bars. Balaram himself got down and tried to grab the man and pull him into the car.

Just then a small crowd gathered. Usually rowdies run when crowds gather, but Balaram and his boys took out swords.

'Bastard! He has taken money from us and is avoiding us. What if we take him? Is he your father?' Balaram yelled. Even as he was screaming, his boys had dragged the man into the car. The crowd dispersed. My heart was beating fast.

Just then a police jeep came. People stopped the jeep and told the police what was happening. Usually police who are out on some other work do not stop to attend to other matters. But that day they did. Seeing a police jeep, even tough rowdies scoot. We thought Balaram would push the man out and get away. But Balaram just started the car and drove away with the man!

The jeep started following the car. We were scared.

The NRI asked, 'Will there be a fantastic chase now?!'

We didn't bother to answer him but headed off to the previously designated house at Ramamurthynagar. When we went there Balaram was waiting for us with the man!

Surprised, I asked, 'How did you bring him?!'

'How could we let go? That American had run us down so badly. How long can the police jeep chase us?'

'What if they flashed the car number?'

'So what makes you think we use our car number?' Saying this, Balaram showed me their trick. They would change two digits in the number plate. If they had 8 they would paste a paper on it and write 3 or 7. Or they would paste a paper on the first or the last number. Balaram's method was so easy and simple. One of his boys would remove the paper in a few seconds and no one would recognise the car.

Finally the job given by the legislator was done. The man not only signed the papers in front of us but also transferred the property to the son's name.

Balaram accomplished several such daring acts that stunned us all. Once in front of the traffic signal at Chalukya Hotel, he opened the door of the car of a man trading in US dollars, pushed the driver aside and drove the car away.

Anil, Malayali Sridhar, Kisan, Huchche Gowda and his other boys did not lag behind when it came to daring. So when

Balaram, who was the leader of a gang of such boys, said he would do the 307 on Lohitashwa, I became anxious.

The main reason he was furious with Lohitashwa was—a dog!

The dog was always in front of Lohitashwa's house. It was a street dog, but he probably fed it, so it always hung about in front of his house and would bark at strangers. We never had any problems with it because we always drove in a van and kept the windows shut. But that day Balaram and Kalapathar had come on motorbike, and the dog had barked at them. What else would a dog do? But Balaram became angry. He stopped the bike and went to beat up the dog. Just then Lohitashwa came out and on seeing Balaram chasing the dog shouted at him.

Balaram too spoke roughly. 'You keep your dog in your house . . . is it right that it barks at all the passersby?'

Lohitashwa had not seen Balaram before, and he was enraged that he had shouted at him. Balaram and Kalapathar did not tell me what happened after that. They only said they would assault Lohitashwa.

'You want to assault someone just because a dog barked at you? Do you know who he is?' I asked.

'Who?' they asked in unison.

'Look, he is a big actor, also an English professor . . . he is known to all the writers. If you attack him things will turn serious.'

'What will happen? Will they hang us?' he replied in exactly the same tone as I was speaking in, to try and tease me. I started getting angry, but I could not show it. I was held back by the fear that they may then decide to go to Lohitashwa's house.

For about two hours we had a heated debate. I used all the arguments I could to convince him. I told him that Kotwal Ramachandra had tried to assault a Bangalore Development Authority official called Seetharam who was a relative of former police commissioner Garudachar, which is why the police force began to cut him to size.

'Keep quiet Sir . . . if you all had not finished him, he would still be around,' he said.

I said some auto drivers had made fun of Jayaraj a couple of times in front of us. We had gotten angry but Jayaraj had just laughed.

'Jayaraj was afraid of the police, Sir,' they said with contempt.

I tried to bring up Rai, but Balaram shut me up with his comment, 'You want to call Rai a fighter?!'

(Interestingly, in those days we had completely forgotten about Muthappa Rai. It was more than four to five months since we had separated and there was no sign of him in Bangalore. There were rumours that he had been in Madikeri for some time and then settled in Mysore, but no one knew his whereabouts. We had not bothered to find out.)

Finally, as if doing me a great favour, Balaram said, 'Okay, if I attack him now, people will know that someone coming to this house has done it. Then the police will chase us. In a week's time I will get somebody he doesn't know to attack him, then no one will suspect . . .'

'Is he a rowdy? Or is he engaged in any "number two" business? He is a lecturer! You must not treat him like this. Should he not question you if you try to hit his dog? This is why people hate rowdies.'

'Okay, let it be,' Balaram ended the discussion and left.

But I feared he would someday attack Lohitashwa.

I don't know if you will believe me, but I have never favoured violence. Even in circumstances where violence was justified, I have refrained from doing it as much as possible. Causeless and mindless violence is something I cannot tolerate.

In Lohitashwa's case, it was actually the police who came to my help to subdue Balaram!

In those days, Kumaraswamy Layout did not have a police station and the area came under Banashankari police station limits. Shareef was the inspector there. He naturally knew my history but since I did not engage in any illegal activities he did not trouble me. Sometimes, when on his rounds, he would come to my house and caution me not to let any active rowdy in the house.

He was very close to a Janata Dal leader.

At that time Balaram would come to meet me at least four evenings a week. Two days after Balaram ranted about Lohitashwa, I told the Janata Dal leader to bring Shareef and come to my house exactly at the time that Balaram would visit.

He came early and we spoke about our activities. Balaram who came and saw the police jeep outside stayed away. He waited till the jeep left and then came in ten minutes later.

'What, Sir? Police at this time . . .?' he asked.

'Balaram, someone has told him that you keep coming here often, that is why he came at this time,' I said seriously.

'But I don't have any case here Sir,' Balaram said, but with a shade of doubt.

'I told him that.'

'Sir, shall I stop coming here for some time?'

I felt that would be a little too much and said, 'No, no. I have convinced him that you are not involved in anything. But don't bring too many boys with you when you come; ask them to stay near Banashankari.'

No matter how big a rowdy gets, when he suspects that the police is chasing him, it unnerves him. Balaram was no different.

From that day Balaram did not mention Lohitashwa. Perhaps it would have come up at some point, but within four days of my telling him the police was trying to keep him under control, he really did get arrested and went to jail. This is what happened.

Balaram came to the house with Kalapathar, Kisan, his brother Chota Kalakar, Malayali Sridhar, Sudhi, Venkatesh and others. Only he, Kalapathar and Venkatesh came inside; the rest waited on the next lane. Balaram did not stay for long, but left after ten minutes.

That night, at around ten o'clock, Chota Kalakar came home. We were surprised to see him at that hour. As soon as the door opened, he started blabbering, 'Sir, please don't tell anyone that I came and gave you the news . . . Balaram barged into Blue Fox, he was dragging one man from there . . . police came and chased him . . . I escaped and came here to tell you.'

We could not understand what he was saying. We calmed him down and made him tell us everything slowly.

Apparently, after leaving our house, Balaram and his gang had gone straight to Victoria Hotel (where the Bangalore Central mall now stands) and stayed there till eight-thirty, drinking and eating to their heart's content. Balaram always liked to go to posh hotels. Though Victoria Hotel was expensive, the gang had drunk as if they were in a roadside dhaba.

While they were talking, the topic of Rai came up. One boy teased Balaram and Kalapathar, saying, 'You people only talk and don't act. Have you threatened at least one man from Rai's side?'

Balaram was not as rough as Kalapathar, but when he was drunk he would lose his balance. He asked the boy, 'Now who should we beat up?'

'Oh, you all make such claims,' the boy said provokingly. 'Don't you know that Blue Fox nearby is run by Rai's man? If anyone talks loudly there, they show revolvers.'

Blue Fox, on MG Road, was a joint with live music in those days.

'Okay, shall we go now?' Kalapathar asked.

'Why ask . . . let's go,' Balaram got up.

When the leaders are ready to fight, will their followers fall behind? They also were charged up.

One car and six bikes took them all to Blue Fox. When ten to twelve boys barged in flashing their swords, all the people there ran helter-skelter. The bouncers were kicked. The gang barged into the kitchen and ransacked the place.

Rai's boy Pomma was always there. We all knew him; he was a decent boy. The gang held a sword against his neck and dragged him. No one protested.

Chota Kalakar was also an active participant in the operation. When Balaram was dragging Pomma to his car and the boys were flashing swords on MG Road, two beat policemen saw them and asked, 'Who are you?' and began chasing them. Chota escaped, got into an auto-rickshaw and came to us.

This came as a shock to us. We had been careful not to allow any kind of problems in dealing with our enmity with Muthappa Rai. Also, as soon as we heard that the police were chasing Balaram, we were certain he would be arrested. And would the police stop at that? We were scared they would net us too, so we left Bangalore and went to a friend's farmhouse near Hoskote.

To be caught red-handed with weapons is the worst situation for a rowdy to be in. We could not sleep the entire night with the worry of the police working on all those arrested. The only consolation was that MG Road was not under the jurisdiction of Kempaiah! Although it was a rumour in the underworld that Kempaiah was close to us, only I knew the truth!

A decade ago, telephone connections were not as extensive as they are now, and there was no telephone anywhere near the farmhouse where we were staying.

We returned to Bangalore at around ten in the morning. First of all we had to find out whether Balaram had been arrested or not. If he hadn't, we had to take precautions to see that the news did not spread.

I called Rajendra. 'Guru, did you see the paper?' he asked.

'What happened?'

'Balaram is arrested . . .'

'Oh, really? Why? Which station?' I asked innocently.

'Cubbon Park station, guru . . .'

'They have not worked on him,' Rajendra told me. I felt relieved.

Usually when a notorious rowdy like Balaram is arrested red-handed, the police work on him. If Balaram was worked on, all our activities would come out, and though we were not involved in grave crimes, there was the possibility of the media exaggerating and playing up the issue.

There were two reasons why the police did not work on Balaram. One was that Venkatesh in Balaram's group had used his influence and got many powerful politicians to call police officers. He had even taken the then mayor Lakkanna at midnight to the police station and gotten him to make phone calls to all the officers for an hour!

Secondly, Pomma, instead of giving a statement against Balaram, had to struggle to save his own skin. He could not say he was Muthappa Rai's associate. If he had declared that, then the police would have started an inquiry into it. But if he did not declare it, then there was no substance to the accusation that Balaram was trying to kidnap him.

Police inquiries are very strange. Though Muthappa Rai was not active at the time, since he had a criminal record, they would start with, 'Muthappa Rai—oh you belong to his gang? Where is he?' and go on to, 'You must have done something for them to kidnap you; you must be a killer too. Tell us now,' and make his life miserable.

Hence Pomma had not given any serious statement against Balaram.

Balaram was sent to jail within a day.

For the next two days, newspapers carried strange reports. One paper even published a news item that said Balaram and his gang had found out that Muthappa Rai was in Blue Fox and hence had raided it to murder him!

Balaram was released after a week. The day he was released, I sat with him for two hours, trying to convince him not to commit such reckless acts unnecessarily.

Balaram listened to me most obediently and finally said, 'Sir, all this is common in rowdyism. We must give it to our enemies now and then and make them run around.'

The Blue Fox incident was forgotten in ten days, and everything went back to normal. Sometimes, however, cars would be parked behind our house at night. We suspected that Rai's associates must have found out about us. One night we went and surrounded one car. When the door was opened we found a middle-aged man with a young girl. He started sweating when he saw us. We warned them not to come to that road again and sent them away.

But cars did not stop parking there and we stopped taking note of them.

Three

The year 1993 had just begun.

To manage the underworld efficiently, it is absolutely necessary to maintain a meaningful relationship with the police. Of course, no don is able to get the entire force to support him. There is always that thirty per cent that will oppose him and plot to cut him down to size. Any don that is able to get the support of seventy-five per cent of the police starts behaving as if he owns the world. I have observed this in all dons. But what these dons failed to understand is that when the opposing twenty-five per cent pounce on them, the 'supportive' seventy-five per cent retreat into the background!

Since we were not acting tough with anyone at that time, the police were not very harsh with us. Except for four or five officers, the rest had a soft attitude towards us.

We were dependent on a politician from the Congress to keep our relationship with the police cordial. One day he brought us a piece of news: Muthappa Rai was at a farm forty kilometres from Mysore. He added: 'If you want to finish Rai, more information can be collected.'

Sometimes, the police themselves float such news to test how the enemy's mind works.

'If he is settled in such a place, he will not even turn his head towards Bangalore. Why take the risk of finishing him unnecessarily? Also, we never wanted to finish him. If we did, we could have done so when he was here. Besides, we really do not have such a strong hatred towards him,' I said.

Rai was actually facing more danger from Amar Alva's gang than from us. We had heard rumours about them planning to finish him in Mysore or Madikeri.

Rai had been wrong in thinking that Amar Alva's gang would wobble after his murder. Francis Cutinho, Ramesh Pujari and the others had made it their life's aim to finish Muthappa Rai.

In addition, after losing control over Bangalore, Rai had become weak in Mangalore too. My stand was that, in such a situation, there was no need to finish him.

Within fifteen days of that conversation, incidents occurred that led to great changes in the Bangalore underworld.

The media in Bangalore had recently developed a great deal of interest in the underworld. Until then, newspapers had published crime reports collected from the police, sometimes adding a few comments of their own. Now, however, they started giving the same kind of attention to crime and underworld issues as they had given politics and films. Bangalore journalists invented stories about the underworld, creating a parallel history. Most journalists had never met any don, but believed every word uttered by the police as if it were the ultimate truth. It seemed as if police officers were becoming addicted to praise by the media—they began playing up to journalists like never before. The more publicity they got, the stronger their political connections became.

During those days, the only magazine with a social concern was *Lankesh Patrike*. Tejasvini, who later became a TV anchor and then turned MP, was a reporter with that magazine. In February 1993, *Lankesh Patrike* published an interview with Muthappa Rai, by Tejasvini. The write-up glamorised Rai to a great extent. In that interview, Rai floated a lie in a very subtle manner. He claimed that Kempaiah had taken ten lakh rupees from him to favour him. Also, he accused the Bangalore rowdies of cheating him.

We later found out that Tejasvini had prepared the interview after a follower of Jeevaraj Alva, Prasad from Jalahalli, had arranged a meeting between him and Rai.

We asked Vale Manju, the Arakalgud MLA, to arrange a meeting with Tejasvini. Before it could take place, Rai was arrested. In those days, we did not have a phone connection, so we found out about his arrest only the next morning, through the newspapers. Apparently he was arrested at a farm near Gundlupet. The police had seized a pistol from him and sent him to the Mysore jail. The arrest received extensive publicity.

Swamy Anand of *Lankesh Patrike* interviewed Rai in jail. In the article, Rai expressed his anger towards one legislator. That legislator was R.V. Devaraj. It was a statement given specifically to demoralise Pushpa and Rajendra, as they were always seen with Devaraj.

After Rai was sent to jail, we became extremely cautious. Usually Bombay dons attempt murder under two circumstances: one when they are in jail or when they are abroad. We knew for sure that Rai would not choose a straight kill for which he'd have to go to jail—like Kotwal and Jayaraj. Rai's name had not figured at all in the Jayaraj murder case. When Kumar was murdered, Rai had been able to prove that he was in Dubai. So we suspected that he would try to kill one of us while he was in jail.

When such a suspicion occurs, there are two ways of handling it: one is to be extremely cautious, and the second, is to finish the enemy.

Everybody felt that the second option was better.

It had been difficult to trace Rai when he was outside jail. We never knew whether he was in Mangalore or Madikeri or Puttur or Gundlupet. Now we knew where he was, and it would be best to finish him while he was in jail, everyone said. But it would not be easy. There would, of course, always be policemen around. Also, since Rai was scared that he would be attacked, I was sure he would have alerted the jail staff. He would definitely be kept under strict security. They would bring him out only when he had to be presented in court or when someone came to visit him. It would be impossible to even go near him, I said, and brushed aside all their arguments.

I convinced them that it was easier to be cautious than to finish him.

They could not understand my anxiety. To me, Rai dead was more dangerous to the Bangalore underworld than Rai alive. I had absolutely no doubt that the Bangalore underworld would stay united as long as Rai was alive; they would fight and finish each other the minute he was no longer there.

Personally, I was more bothered that *Lankesh Patrike* seemed to be supporting Rai. The two interviews published within two weeks disturbed me. Lankesh had never considered the underworld seriously. Apart from Tejasvini, no other reporter had made comments on it.

We were finally able to meet Tejasvini through Vale Manju. She looked like our village girls, and was rough. Her conversation indicated that she was progressive. By supporting Rai, she did not want to make his opponents uncomfortable, she wanted to comment on the police system, she said. My anxieties were put to rest.

Within ten days, Rai's arrest started losing heat. We started hearing news of who had seen him while going to court and how he behaved, and so on. We heard he was brought to court in a big van with full security from Mysore. It was also rumoured that he wore a bullet-proof jacket while going to court. I had seen him wearing a jacket like this even when he was with us, and I was not surprised.

On one such visit to the court, Rai saw a boy known to both of us sitting with his head in his hands. Rai told him, 'Rowdies should not sit with their head in their hands. You should lift up your chest and sit confidently.'

Nowhere had Rai said anything against us.

Thirteen days after Rai was arrested, all of us met in our 'guesthouse' (which is what Balaram and gang had named my house).

Balaram usually woke up late, but that day he'd gotten up early and come at ten o'clock along with Kalapathar. Malayali Sridhar, Chota Kalakar, Sundra, Anil, Basava and others who belonged to his gang had also come with them. At around eleven o'clock, Pushpa and Rajendra came along with Mahadeva and Satya. Varada too was there. He rarely came to our guesthouse, but that day he dropped in to invite us for a function. Vijay Kumar, who worked with the Youth Congress, and Chandra, from the state transport corporation KSRTC, had also come. Together, we were more than twenty.

We got mutton to cook for everybody. We had a huge balcony and all of us sat there, relaxed and chatting about everything under the sun. A gentle breeze comforted us. The hills in the distance looked beautiful. Our conversation veered from Muthappa Rai to trees, hills and everything else. Time flew.

At around one o'clock, Chandru called us saying lunch was ready. Just as we were going down, an Ambassador passed in front of our house. Since there were only three houses on that road, cars were infrequent. We thought somebody must have lost their way and looked at the car with curiosity. The distance between us and the car was about fifty feet.

The car was about to turn at the corner—the guesthouse was at the end of the road—when it slowed and the people inside looked at us intensely. The car then braked and around five hefty guys got down screaming, and running towards us. Three of them had AK-47 guns with them, and the other two had revolvers. I still remember one of them. He wore black pants and a T-shirt with yellow stripes. His long thick hair was flying around because of the wind. His eyes looked cruel.

I thought they must be Bombay killers sent by a desperate Rai to kill us.

Just as they were coming in, Pushpa and Rajendra started shouting, 'Attack, attack, throw bomb, throw bomb . . .' This was only to scare the attackers: there were no bombs in the guesthouse.

I came down as quickly as I could and bolted the front and back doors and started telling the boys how we should counteract.

By then all the boys, except Pushpa, had come in and started preparing to defend ourselves. Pushpa came in last. He could not walk fast because of his bulky weight as well as a leg injury he'd suffered in an accident. He came straight to me and said, 'Sreedhar, they are not rowdies, but police—I saw Surendra Naik!'

Within a few seconds we realised that the police had surrounded us. We heard a knock on the door. 'Who is it?' I asked.

'Sreedhar, open the door, I am Inspector Shareef.'

I opened the door immediately.

Out of the six to seven officers who walked in, I knew only two—Shareef and Ishwar Prasad. I suspected the one in the T-shirt was Surendra Naik.

Within a couple of minutes I'd got them to relax. I said there was no need for AK-47s to raid us and they laughed. There was no complaint against any of us, but 'history-sheeters'—people with a criminal record—can be arrested without a complaint. Interestingly, none of the police officers knew why we were being raided. Apparently DCP Kempaiah had called them in the morning and asked them to raid the house. Somebody had called the police station saying all the notorious rowdies had met at one place.

I wanted to ask Shareef which of the officers was from our locality, but as soon as he got the door opened, he drove away in his jeep without waiting for a second. One of the officers speaking to me said Shareef had argued with the DCP about our arrest since neither I nor any of the others in the gang had caused problems anywhere. Kempaiah had curtly ordered him to take officers, show them the house and 'do what you are told'.

The police surrounded us at around one in the afternoon, but when they took us out, it was past ten-thirty in the night. Kempaiah and the commissioner were there too. A large contingent of media representatives were waiting outside the house. Everyone was shocked to see seventeen rowdies (three men had managed to escape) from the underworld in one place.

I still remember how *Kannada Prabha*'s Ranganath glanced at us and told Kempaiah in English, thinking we wouldn't understand, 'What if these people come across me in the street and bump me off?'

But Kempaiah, who knew I knew English, looked at me and replied to him, 'Nothing of that sort will happen.'

Then Kempaiah asked, 'What shall we do with them?'

All the other journalists were silent, but Ranganath said, 'Thrash them and break their limbs!'

Again Kempaiah gave me a look and then asked Ranganath, 'Thrash them . . .?'

Ranganath did not answer.

The media had a field day with the news—seventeen dreaded rowdies caught in a house in the outskirts of the city, with three kilos of cooked meat and four bottles of foreign liquor!

At this point of time, as I'm recording this, the cases against the seventeen of us registered are still pending in court, hence I cannot give details about them. I can only say that we were framed in two cases and sent to jail.

To this day we do not know who filed the complaints.

We were taken to Wilson Garden police station. Sub-inspector Shivaram was there specially to work on us.

Till midnight, the police worked on everyone else. Then I was called to the 'work room'.

Belliappa and Kumaraswamy, who were with Shivaram, said, 'No, no. Let us not work on him,' and sent me away.

Shivaram gave me a cruel look and said, 'Okay, I will work on you after they go . . . after all, this is my station.'

After all the officers left, around half an hour later, Shivaram came to the lock-up and looked at everyone's faces.

I asked him from behind bars, 'What Sir, you worked like this on everyone . . . will you work on me too?' I was very apprehensive that he would work on me.

Shivaram said with dejection, 'What have I done? DCP sent

me here especially to work on you . . . I don't know why you were all sent to my station.'

He did not work on me, but the next morning, at around ten, Kempaiah came to the station. Even as he stepped in, he asked, 'Why didn't you work on Sreedhar?'

I was called from the lock-up.

'I spoke to you because you are educated and you have used it as an NOC?' he asked fiercely.

'Sir, I have definitely not misused your name anywhere . . . someone has lied to you,' I pleaded.

But he was not in the mood to listen.

'Put him on the rope,' he said.

I've explained earlier in my story what 'putting on a rope' or 'aeroplane' is: it is the most inhumane technique the police has found to torture a person. Your hands are tied behind you with a rope that is then passed through a pulley on the ceiling. Four men will lift you up and the end of the rope is either tied to a window or some heavy object. The entire weight of your body is on your shoulders. However strong a man is, within seconds he will start screaming because of the unbearable pain. This was the method used in olden days to make a thief spill details of a theft. During Kotwal's time, they started to use it on criminals too.

Kempaiah had modified the punishment so that it was even more painful. He changed it so your hands were not pulled straight back but crossed across your chest and pulled from opposite sides and tied at the back. Just to understand how it feels, move your thumbs across your chest in opposite directions and try to meet them at the back. However much you try, you cannot touch them at the back. But four to six men will forcibly pull your hands and make them touch at the back and tie them tightly with a rope. By then your chest will be splitting and your body will go on the tips of your toes.

As soon as Kempaiah said, 'Put him on the rope,' police constables took me to the 'work room' and tied my hands in this new way. I thought they had made a mistake, and said, 'What? You have tied it wrong . . .!'

I actually knew four of the six constables there very well. One fellow told me softly, 'The old method is gone long ago . . . Don't worry, whatever Sahib says, we will get you down soon.'

Then Kempaiah entered.

'Lift,' he said.

They lifted me.

'Thrash,' he said.

The constables who had been talking to me softly till then started thrashing me. You would not have seen anyone thrashing a human being like that. I have not seen cattle being thrashed like that.

No one had complained against us; and we had not threatened anyone. Apart from Balaram's Blue Fox episode, none of us had shown any weapons to anyone. Yet, we were being tortured.

Looking back now, I think they had strung me up for five minutes, but at the time, it felt like hours. When I was brought down, Kempaiah's face had undergone a strange transformation. The angry eyes had turned soft with compassion!

As soon as I was brought down, I said, 'Water . . . water . . .'

Kempaiah said, sighing, 'No . . . no . . . you should not drink water for some time . . .'

Then they 'repaired' Balaram too. Krishnamurthy, Pushpa and Bachchan were also worked on, but no one else was put on the rope.

I don't know why, but Oil Kumar's wife Reeta's name was mentioned. Rajendra said he knew her house and would show it to them. I was scared that if I stayed back they would work on me again, so I said I also knew Reeta's house and saw to it that I went with Rajendra.

Shivaram and another sub-inspector took us both in a jeep. I can never forget the concern Shivaram showed towards me that day. I heard him tell his colleague, 'It would have been enough if he was given four thrashes on his legs and hands. Was there a need to put him on the rope? How can we work on those who are past thirty-five like this?'

They got me painkillers and tender coconut water. Then

Shivaram said, 'You don't need all this Sreedhar. After you've come out of jail, come to me. This is not for you . . .'

I was so tired I had trouble breathing; looking at me, Shivaram said he thought I should be sent to hospital.

Instead of going to Reeta's house, Shivaram took us back to the station. Kempaiah and the other officers had left. They decided to send not just me, but all of us, to Victoria Hospital.

We were seventeen rowdies and more than twice the number of policemen. The entire hospital came to look at us as if we were zoo animals.

Pushpa kept forcing me to ensure that the doctor's certificate was strongly worded. 'We have not done anything and they have thrashed us like this Sreedhar . . . we should not keep quiet. We should file a case . . .'

It was not just one officer who had tortured us. From the commissioner himself to the constables, everyone was involved in the violence. That is, the entire police system had participated in this human rights violation. I realised it was no use fighting the entire system.

At court, a huge gang of lawyers had assembled, including Sambamurthy and Partha. In those days, apart from Devadas, C.V. Nagesh, C.H. Hanumantharayappa and Sambamurthy were very famous. Sambamurthy was dear to all of us, but he had special affection for Pushpa and Rajendra. As soon as he saw us, even though he was at court, his eyes welled up.

You should have seen our faces. We were seventeen men standing in line, and all our faces had assumed weird shapes and sizes!

Sambamurthy presented his arguments very strongly. 'Your Honour, just look at their state. Are they human beings or animals? Have you ever seen anyone treating humans this cruelly? And for what crime? What have they done? Why have they been arrested?' For fifteen minutes he took the police to task.

The magistrate asked us if the police had troubled us. Pushpa, Rajendra and Balaram forced me to speak. Like Jayaraj, they also believed that if you spoke in English in court, you would be respected.

I explained how the police had tortured us without any reason.

We were remanded to judicial custody for two weeks.

Coming out of the court, I asked Sambamurthy on what complaint we were being sent to jail. He said the police were the complainants!

That case is still subjudice and hence I am not allowed to give more details of it. Everyone knows it takes a long time for cases to be cleared in our courts, but ours was delayed for various other reasons. It was a case in which all seventeen of us were presented as the accused. For the interrogation, all seventeen had to be present. Such a thing can happen only when the court issues a warrant. Even then, many do not come to court at all and lawyers keep taking dates. Also, even as the case was under inquiry, Balaram died and Malayali Sridhar left the country. Apart from this, all the main witnesses in that case were police officials. You know how busy they are—every day they are either in charge of some bandobast or some case. So they send the reasons for their absence to the court through a public prosecutor.

Even though the court remanded us to jail, the police did not take us there directly. They took us to the commissioner's office to take our fingerprints, photographs, etc. We were aware that officials would torture any accused who gave a statement against them in court. Though we were out of the police's control after being produced in court, till we were actually sent to jail, we were under their custody. They could do anything to us!

We prayed desperately that Kempaiah would not be there, but unfortunately, he was. Not only that, he sent for me, Bachchan, Pushpa and Rajendra.

First, Pushpa and Rajendra were called in. We stood at a distance. After about six or seven minutes they came out. They looked sad. Pushpa went towards the van without even glancing towards us. Rajendra looked at us out of the corner of his eyes.

Then Bachchan and I were called in. Kishore Chandra, another DCP, was with Kempaiah. Kempaiah first glanced at both of us and then fixed his stare on me.

His chin touched his chest and his eyebrows were raised, giving him a strangely cruel and dramatic look.

'So . . . you gave a statement in the court that the police beat you up?'

I had expected this. 'Sir, I didn't want to say anything, but Pushpa and Rajendra forced me.'

The cruelty in his eyes intensified as he clenched his jaws. By then I was certain they would not torture us.

'So they asked you to give a statement and you did? They said, "It is all Sreedhar's doing, we did not say anything". Also, you are telling me you listen to what they tell you?'

'Please understand me, Sir, everybody is very hurt. I could not say "no" when they all asked me to.'

Kempaiah smiled then, and said to Kishore Chandra, 'He is not an ordinary criminal; he is very brilliant. You know what he said this morning on the rope? He said, "What does Kalapathar know . . . he is still a small boy". See, all of Bangalore shivers at the mention of Kalapathar, and for him he is an ordinary boy! Then what must be his level?'

That morning when I was on the rope, Kempaiah had asked me about Kalapathar. Whatever he was to Bangalore, Kalapathar felt very shy to speak in front of me and I always treated him like a younger brother. Kempaiah had turned red, when I told him this.

'So . . . you don't care for Kalapathar and you listen to Pushpa and Rajendra?' he said, implying I was lying. Then he told Kishore Chandra, 'Somehow I like this boy Bachchan. This morning he said, "I am in the underworld for Sreedhar". Everyone has accepted him as the leader and see what he is doing . . .'

Kishore Chandra, who had sat there listening until then, gave his verdict. 'You are right, Sir. His face tells us he is a big criminal!'

'What have you decided for the future?' Kempaiah asked angrily.

Bachchan and I said in unison, 'We will not come out of jail till you tell us to, Sir.'

'We have not worked on you people much this time! If you come out of jail before I tell you to, I will work on you in such a way you will not be able to move in your life and then we will send you to jail under the Goonda Act . . .'

In that situation, if he had asked us to stay in jail for the rest of our lives, we would have said 'yes'!

After that warning we were sent out.

I felt bad for some time as Pushpa and Rajendra had put the blame on me. But when I saw them limping and looked at their swollen faces, I realised anybody in their place would have done the same.

From the commissioner's office we were taken to the jail. However, after seeing our physical condition, the jail superintendent refused to keep us there. Usually jail officials do not agree to take in accused who have been badly beaten up by the police; if the accused dies, then the jail officials will be held responsible.

We tried our best to convince the jailors that we were not that badly injured. We did not want to go anywhere other than Bangalore jail. There was a possibility of early bail as we were not accused of any serious crime. If they sent us to a jail outside the city, our lawyers would find it difficult.

Koli Fayaz, Tanveer and the others also tried to force the jail authorities to keep us in the Bangalore jail. But they refused. By then it was already past seven in the evening. If we were to be kept in any jail other than Bangalore Central Jail, they would have to send us to Gulbarga or Bellary, but the Reserve police did not have permission to take us outside the city. We were taken back to Wilson Garden police station.

This may be the only incident in the state where the accused were remanded to judicial custody but were brought back to the police station.

However, this time, we were not put in lock-up. They let us stay wherever we wanted in the station, including the central courtyard. The police were sure that none of us would try to escape.

I was feverish and Shivaram got me some tablets and bread. At around ten, Banashankari inspector Shareef and sub-inspector Ishwar Prasad came there. Shareef's eyes welled up with tears when he saw my state. 'God will take care, don't worry,' he assured me.

Ishwar Prasad is probably one of the most upright police officers Bangalore has seen. Usually, no police officer will defend even his own brother in front of senior officers and I was touched to hear that he had told the commissioner, additional commissioner and DCP, 'Sreedhar was a voracious reader in college . . . he has strayed into this field by mistake.'

Of the several legends about Kempaiah, one was that that he would go to any police station early in the morning and torture the arrested. We were all very worried that he would come back and torture us, not being satisfied with his morning's work. Nothing of that sort happened, fortunately.

Early the next morning, we were all taken to Bellary.

By then our arrest had become big news and a large crowd comprising our boys and friends had gathered outside the station. They had brought biscuits, cigarettes, towels, lungis and all sorts of other things.

None of us spoke on the way. We were all feeling a strange helplessness because of our physical pain.

Strangely, of the seventeen of us, only Malayali Sridhar had not been worked on. He was the most hardcore criminal in Jayaraj's gang, but when the police took him to the 'work room' he had said, 'Sir, a Congress corporator sent me to Sreedhar saying he would get me a job. I did not know that he is the leader of such a big gang; I am not from Bangalore.'

And the police believed him!

We reached Bellary at around six in the evening. It was the first time I was going to that city. It was already very hot, although it was just March. By seven in the evening, we had all been admitted into the jail hospital. Pushpa, Rajendra and Mahadeva had been in that jail before for about one-and-a-half years in connection with the Jayaraj case. For the rest, it was the first experience.

The heat in the jail and the numerous strange insects that came to life at night due to the heat cannot be described.

For a week, we remained in the jail hospital. Everything cost money there: from getting admitted into the hospital to drinking water. The jail staff had made fleecing their profession. Anyone coming to visit us would mean money paid, for both the visitor and us.

The jail superintendent, Gajendragad, had thought of a fantastic plan to make money: the construction of a temple for which he wanted our donations! He insisted that a temple was absolutely necessary for the transformation of criminals. There was no way we could argue with him. He was, after all, the chief of the jail. Since we did not know how long it would take before we would be bailed out, we had no option but to agree to everything he said.

We were all still suffering from our injuries, and we tried all kinds of ways to relieve our pain, from arrack to tablets. We cursed Kempaiah continuously. We were naturally very angry because he had arrested us and thrashed us mercilessly without any reason or complaint. One evening, when we were cursing Kempaiah, a policeman in the jail said, 'You are cursing Kempaiah so much, do you know what kind of a person he is?'

'We don't; if you do, kindly tell us,' we said sarcastically.

That policeman was from Bijapur. 'Before Kempaiah came to Bijapur as superintendent of police, the city was known for prostitution. Every road had a flesh market and Bijapur was known as the place of prostitutes and pimps. Kempaiah changed all that. He stopped prostitution by providing them all with alternative livelihoods. He organised bank loans so the pimps could purchase auto-rickshaws and the women could buy sewing machines. He helped their family members start shops and other professions. If not for him, even today we would be ashamed to say we were from Bijapur.'

We stopped cursing Kempaiah from that day. We consoled ourselves saying that someone must have instigated him against us!

We stayed at the jail hospital for fifteen days and were then shifted to the cells. Being in jail is a punishment, but to stay in Bellary jail is the greatest punishment. No one ate the food there then. We would get rice and other things from outside and cook our own meal. The jail staff looked the other way.

Srirampura Kitty came to the jail when we were there. He was notorious during Kotwal's time, but was now gradually losing his hold. Rajendra and I had a talk and decided we should get him to our side. However, Balaram, who was once attacked by him, would not agree to this on any account. He threatened that if we spoke to Kitty he would speak to Muthappa Rai, so we gave up the idea.

After we had been in jail for a month and a few days, the DIG came for jail inspection. Casually inquiring about our well-being, he said, 'It's a big headache to produce you all in court and bring you back safely.'

We said we had no enemies who would attack us.

'Just yesterday they attacked Muthappa Rai at the court premises. Couldn't they find any other spot to attack him?' he muttered.

We were shocked. Muthappa Rai attacked?

'Who, Sir? When?'

'Oh you don't know yet? Rai was shot . . . five or six bullets. He is in the hospital. We don't know if he will survive or not.'

We read newspapers only on Sundays in jail. After the DIG left we got all the papers. Rai had been attacked the previous day when he had been brought from Mysore and was being produced at a Bangalore court. A man dressed as a lawyer had shot him when Rai was getting down from the van. However, the man had been drunk and his hands were shaking, so he could not aim well: Rai was shot in his hand and thigh. He had managed to get under the van and thus escaped further bullets.

The man who had fired the shots, Saliyan, had been caught. Rai's lawyer Hanumantharayappa had alleged that DCP Kempaiah had a hand in the attack. Saliyan had given a statement that he had tried to shoot Rai to avenge Amar Alva's murder. Hospital sources said that Rai was out of danger.

That week, *Lankesh Patrike* published reports holding Kempaiah directly responsible for the attack on Rai. It also alleged that Kempaiah was corrupt. Coincidentally, within a week, the Lokayukta authorities raided Kempaiah's house. Lokayukta officials alleged that he had properties disproportionate to his income. Far from cooperating, Kempaiah treated the officials very badly and so, along with *Lankesh Patrike*, other papers also started attacking him.

The issue became too controversial for then chief minister Veerappa Moily to handle. The media were screaming that Kempaiah should be suspended. While they were thus engaged in bashing Kempaiah, in Bellary, the entire police system was hatching a plot to remove the jail superintendent, Gajendragad.

We often had visitors from Bangalore; they would bring food and other things for us. We were seventeen, belonging to five underworld gangs. Sometimes visitors from all gangs visited simultaneously and it would be a big gathering of people. It is impossible to describe the amount of things they brought for us. One such day, when around thirteen people had come to visit, the Bellary police raided the jail. The visitors ran in all directions and the police chased and caught them. The police shouted at all of us who were in the visitors' gallery.

The then Bellary deputy superintendent of police Gagandeep, who was a newly recruited IPS officer, behaved like a thug. He came into the room and kicked Balaram. Then, raising his hands and turning them in true filmy style, he screamed, 'Who? Who's there?' as if inviting a fight.

I have never seen a police officer like him in my life. What can you say to a man who puts up a show, like a film hero, in front of jail inmates who cannot retaliate?

By then the district commissioner and SP Praveen Sood

arrived. They suspected that our visitors were supplying drugs to us in jail, and believed that the jail superintendent was supporting this activity.

It was a strange farce.

The police started looking for proof of lapses that neither the jail officials nor we had committed. After the arrival of the DC, Gagandeep and the other officials who had unnecessarily been behaving cruelly towards the inmates kept quiet. The DC visited our cells and inspected them thoroughly. When he came to my cell he was surprised to see the English books that I had and started cajoling me in English, 'Please tell me if the jail superintendent is supplying drugs to you all . . . I will protect you.' Then he threatened me saying, 'You know, the Bellary police are known to put chilli powder up the arse.'

In fact, none of us was getting any drugs from outside. We only used ganja and the like and this was easily available within the jail itself. We did not have to depend on outside sources for that. Sometimes visitors would bring alcohol, but none of us in the gang were addicted to it. That day too, someone had brought a bottle of whisky, but the police were not looking for alcohol since they were expecting brown sugar, cocaine and other serious stuff. They went through all the stuff that had been brought by the visitors. Mahadeva, who belonged to Rajendra and Pushpa's gang, had brought a substance called 'raktabola', available in ayurveda shops. It was a red, hard substance, which, when heated and applied to any part of the body, would relieve pain.

The police decided that it must be a drug. We told them to check it at any ayurveda shop, but they did not agree. They even tried to make Mahadeva eat it. Finally, when Mahadeva heated it and poured the liquid on his thighs to demonstrate how it relieved pain, they kept quiet.

Still the police did not stop booking us in false cases. They arrested the visitors from Bangalore as well. Actually, all this had nothing to do with us. They only wanted to trouble the jail superintendent. Even the jail doctor was hand-in-glove with the police against the superintendent. They filed a case against the jail superintendent, saying that he was supplying drugs and drinks to the jail inmates and got him suspended from duty.

(Gajendragad fought the case in court and after a year returned to work.)

After that, Abbayi came to Bellary as the jail superintendent. He was known as an efficient officer. After he came, nothing eventful happened in jail. We would go to court in Bangalore every two weeks. Rai was still in Victoria Hospital at the time, and recouping. He had a thigh injury. But we were not worried about him. We were worried about what the police would do after we were bailed out.

It was at that time that we all took a decision to give up the underworld. We decided to get out of all the trappings of the underworld, except to unite and fight if Rai attacked again.

By then I was an expert in real estate dealings. Earlier, the underworld dons did not have any patience. They would solve any problem by simply taking a cut. These problems were often related to individuals and sometimes related to government institutions. I had enough knowledge about examining land documents and solving tough problems. Hence Bachchan, Bomb Krishnamurthy and I decided to give up underworld activities and get into the real estate business.

Another factor I have to mention here is that the day before Kempaiah arrested us, we had received twenty-five lakh rupees as an advance on some land we had invested in near Kengeri. I had informed Kempaiah about it.

'You are lying . . . if you were getting such big money, why would you be in the underworld?' he had screamed.

I gave serious thought to this in the Bellary jail. The question of why I was unnecessarily getting involved in all sorts of problems when I could really utilise my talents and connections and make enough money started haunting me.

Four

The year 1993 was when several notorious dons in Bangalore changed their ways.

It was two-and-a-half months before we were bailed out from Bellary jail. Varada, Viji and Chandru got out before us.

As soon as I came out, I went and met Ishwar Prasad and told him my decision to leave the underworld completely. He later repeated this to Kempaiah.

Kempaiah had not forgotten that we had assured him that we would not seek bail until he agreed to it. 'How can we trust these people? They have come out on bail without taking my permission. Anyway, tell them that if they are caught even in a small case, I will not spare them,' he told Ishwar Prasad.

Within a month of us being released, Kempaiah was transferred out of Bangalore. Commissioner Chandulal Kodandaramaiah was appointed in his place.

I moved from my old house. Apart from Bachchan and Krishnamurthy, I did not give my address to anyone. Meetings with Pushpa and Rajendra also became rare.

Krishnamurthy distanced himself not only from the underworld, but also from us. He became more active in the political field. He had close contacts with both Deve Gowda and J.H. Patel.

It was easy for us to get involved in real estate as we had no guilt, but killing time was our biggest problem! During this period, a man close to us called Lokanathan gave us a proposal— that of starting a fish business. We ridiculed him as soon as he mentioned it—from the underworld to a fishing business!

The business was to buy fish from boats in a coastal place called Nambudalai, around a hundred kilometres from Thiruchchi, and sell it in Kerala. The investment was not much, just two lakh rupees. Also, we had to be away from Bangalore for about fifteen days of the month. Finally, we agreed.

Nambudalai is not an interesting place, but the vast sea and great silence made me grow very fond of it. The village has around two thousand houses and the people there depend on fishing for their livelihood. People from all over south India come there to buy fish. Every day, hundreds of boats bring all sorts of fish. During the season we can get hundreds of tons of fish at two rupees per kilo. Transported to Bangalore, Madras and Kerala, it can fetch a handsome profit.

We would go once in two months and stay for fifteen days. Those were our travelling days. It was at that time that I got into the habit of visiting dargahs and ashrams. We visited Shimsha, Kaudalli, Nagur, Tiruvannamalai and Pondicherry several times.

During those days, I was so attracted to the fish trade that I would talk about starting a wholesale fish business in every locality in Bangalore, even with Balaram and his gang. They would laugh at me.

Whenever we were in Bangalore, we would meet Balaram at least twice a week. Once, he said Francis Cutinho and Ramesh Pujari from Mangalore wanted to meet me. At first I refused, but they insisted and I finally agreed to see them. So one afternoon, we met at The Club on Mysore Road.

Francis did not know Kannada, he only spoke in Hindi. He was tough. He had been framed in the attack on Rai in court (in fact, it was Kempaiah who was behind it). He was experienced and had not taken anticipatory bail like us, but always managed to escape from the police. He was in hiding.

By this time, Muthappa Rai was also out on bail and living in Madikeri. Francis and Ramesh wanted to finish him there. They wanted to avenge Amar Alva's murder, and they expected my support in this.

I said I was definitely not interested in finishing Rai. I said I was more interested in the fish trade than killing Rai. Since they had a good base in Dakshina Kannada, if they could send lorry-loads of fish from Malpe, I was ready to purchase the stock, I told them.

I tried my best to convince them that it would be good if they too gave up the underworld.

Francis was flabbergasted. 'I have seen several bhais in my life, but you are the only don who has advised someone who came asking for blood to give up the world of crime,' he said.

I don't know if he would have been able to kill Rai even if I had supported him. That was probably the last time we talked about Muthappa Rai in those days.

For some time, life went on without many ups and down. From the rented house in Banashankari, I shifted to another rented house in ISRO Layout. I moved to a quiet area so my mother, who was suffering from diabetes, could go for walks. Interestingly, Kempaiah had arrested us in the same area just a year before. Though it was a much-publicised incident, no one recognised us.

It was a time when no untoward incidents occurred, but *Lankesh Patrike*, for no real reason, directed the attention of the police toward us. It alleged that we were taking people to Best Club in Rajarajeshwarinagar, and were involved in all sorts of deals. It ridiculed the police for not intervening. The minute I read the report, I realised it had been instigated by a police officer just to trouble us.

The truth was, I had visited Best Club only four times, three times with my family at my daughter's insistence.

I did not take the report seriously. One reason was that I was not involved in any illegal activity, and the second was that we used to meet police officers freely as we were moving about openly. The officers assured us, 'Sreedhar, your names are even mentioned in the commissioner's meetings . . . if you can manage in the same way, within a year your name will be erased from the underworld.'

On the eighth day after the report was published, a police jeep came and stopped in front of my house at midnight. I was sleeping upstairs but awoke when I heard the sound of the jeep. I moved the window curtain and peeped out. It was inspector B.K. Shivaram.

I was surprised because, apart from Krishnamurthy and Bachchan, I had not shown my house to anyone. The man who had got me the house—Chandrappa—did not know anything about me. So who could have revealed where I lived to the police? Even in the middle of the tension of the fact that there were policemen outside my house, I was intrigued as to who had given out my address.

Shivaram and his staff came in and searched the compound, even moving the flowerpots, looking for weapons. After that they rang the bell. I opened the door. Sub-inspector Venkataswamy and three officers from the crime branch were also there with Shivaram. Since there were warrants against me, they could arrest me even without any complaints.

'What, Sir?' I asked.

'Nothing . . . come with me,' said Shivaram.

Since he knew me well, he did not handcuff me or tie my hands with a towel. After we went out, he asked me to show him Bachchan's house. It was useless to argue that I didn't know where he lived. I took them to Bachchan's house and I made him open the door. They forced Bachchan to show them Krishnamurthy's house. He said he did not know where it was. The crime branch police raised their lathis. I said I knew, and they took us out. We got into the jeep and I took them to Krishnamurthy's house, which was near my house in ISRO Layout. They made us sit inside the jeep and went in and got Krishnamurthy within five minutes.

They took us back to my house where they picked up my van. Shivaram drove the van with me in it. The rest followed in the jeep.

I asked him why we had been arrested.

'*Allappaa* . . . didn't you read the report in *Lankesh Patrike*?

Commissioner called us and ridiculed us saying we should all wear bangles. I looked for and found your house. You are not fit to be in the underworld—I found your house in just two days. Imagine what would happen if Muthappa Rai had found it,' he said.

I said I had decided to get out of the underworld and was planning to document my experiences.

'You will make me a villain in that, right?' laughed Shivaram.

'There will not be any hero or villain—only circumstances,' I said.

We were taken straight to Chikpet station and shoved into a cell upstairs. There was no one there but us. We talked about who could have shown my house to the police. This worried us more than the police raid. We thought of what might have happened if our enemies had found out where we live and decided not to spare the person who had revealed my address. Though we had distanced ourselves from the underworld, we could not make light of previous enmities. We knew that it could prove very costly for us.

We suspected that it was Chandrappa, the person who had got us the house. He must have talked about it when he was drunk, and the information must have reached the police, we thought.

Shivaram came in the morning and asked tauntingly, 'At least can you guess who showed your house?'

In the afternoon we slept on the floor of the lock-up. As soon as I got up, Krishnamurthy said, 'Anna . . . I know who showed the house.'

Bachchan and I looked at each other.

'*Anna* . . . it was me,' he said, distraught, holding my hand.

I thought something must have happened to him. Just the previous night I had shown his house to Shivaram. And I'd had some difficulty finding it. Though Krishnamurthy also stayed in ISRO Layout, I had not visited his house often, and it was difficult for me to remember where it was. Also, it is confusing to locate a house at night when you have only seen it in broad daylight. Added to this was the fact that I was with the police. I had taken them to a street thinking it was the right one. Several students stayed there and there were many motorbikes parked outside a house. Shivaram thought they must be my boys' bikes and stopped the jeep in front of the house. After I convinced him they were students, he kept quiet. I was not able to locate Krishnamurthy's house at all. Bachchan whispered in my ears, 'Next cross', and I took them there.

When they brought Krishnamurthy out, his face was swollen with sleep. So when did he tell them where I lived?

'*Anna*, they did not know where you lived. They brought our Viji to my house and pressurised me to show them your house. For some time I acted as if I did not know, but they knew that I knew, so they forced me . . . finally I had to show.'

I laughed at his innocence. 'Why didn't you tell me that immediately?'

'No, *Anna* . . . you were so tense, I felt odd to tell you.'

'Don't you know that with the police you should not make them force you? Didn't I agree to show yours and Bachchan's houses in a minute?' I consoled him.

Shivaram did not realise that we had shared his information amongst ourselves. (Perhaps he will know only after reading this. Sorry Sir!) So time and again he would try to scare me with, 'Just see, if I can find your house, I will know all your movements.'

I also reacted appropriately! 'Sir, please tell me who showed my house to you . . . please. I will not have the courage to stay there,' I would plead!

Krishnamurthy went one step ahead. He would beg, 'Sir, please don't tell them I showed the house—they will both make me go "missing". Please Sir, don't ever reveal it.' And he would come and tell us what he'd said!

But we could not overlook what Shivaram's police mind had guessed.

Shivaram was getting to know the underworld when Kotwal was at his peak. Kotwal never allowed anyone who told the police about him to live peacefully. He would torture that person in all sorts of ways. This type of behaviour had entrenched itself in Shivaram's mind. He had not understood or grasped the changed and delicate dynamics of the new underworld.

Shivaram kept us in the station for fourteen days and then produced us in court. Yes, fourteen days. Don't raise your eyebrows or bring up the law that says any accused should not be kept in a police station for more than twenty-four hours without informing the court. It's a common thing in our country to violate the law.

Shivaram had no complaints to lodge against us and produce us before the court. He could have fixed us in a false case like so many policemen did, but he did not do that. He sent me to court in connection with a warrant for a case in which I had not appeared at court. I appealed to the magistrate that I would appear before the court without fail in the future and he released me on the spot. Bachchan and Krishnamurthy were sent to jail on another warrant.

The day I was released is the most significant day in my life.

By the time I was free, everyone knew my house. For the last eight years—ever since I'd entered the underworld, from 1986— I had kept where I lived a secret. Rarely would more than one or two people know where I lived. During my acquaintance with Muthappa Rai, a few people did know my house; that was for a year. After that I was again secretive.

After being released from Shivaram's custody, I decided that I would not go underground under any circumstances. I gave my address to all my friends and acquaintances and invited everyone home. I was surprised when Balaram's gang, whom we met near the lawyer's office, approved of my decision. I still remember what Malayali Sridhar said, 'Sir, you are not suited to this field anyway. You should either be a businessman or open a factory. This "no entry" and hiding does not suit you.'

But Balaram said with concern, 'Careful Sir, at least till Bachchan comes out, be very careful.'

However, it was not an easy task to shake off the underworld tag and come out in the open. When you decide to change your path and join the mainstream, the police system still suspects you. It believes that it is impossible for a rowdy to change paths while the connections are still green. But I was not scared. Neither did I go to any influential person for help. I prepared a letter addressed to the police commissioner, Kodandaramaiah. I described how I was interested in literature, art and philosophy. I documented how I was forced into the crime world because of circumstances. I explained how I had decided to come out of that world and take a path within the accepted norms of society. I stressed how it was necessary to have the support of police officers and needed encouragement, and then I finally appealed for cooperation.

I waited for an hour but Kodandaramaiah could not meet me because of work pressures. I waited for him to come out of his office and held out my letter.

Maybe he was hungry—he started screaming, 'What is this? Don't you know you should not disturb people like this? What do you want?'

'No Sir, this is very urgent . . .' I continued to hold out the letter.

He took it and read it, and still in a foul mood, he asked, 'So what should be done?'

'You must tell the DCPs, Sir,' I said.

I had mentioned in the letter that I was submitting copies to all the three DCPs.

'Okay, go and see them, I will tell them.'

That was enough for me.

Even before he could talk to them I went to each DCP and said the police commissioner had asked me to meet them and gave them a copy of the letter.

DCP (West) Ramakrishna said, 'I don't agree with you when you say you are a victim of circumstances. You are too intelligent to become a victim of circumstances. Anyway, since you have decided to give up that world, I will definitely support you.'

Central DCP Bekal said, 'Sreedhar, I know Rai's gang too . . . you all should not fight for any reason. If needed I will set things right.'

South DCP Motiram, in whose jurisdiction I was living, was on leave for two days. When I finally met him, he neither lifted his head to look at me nor did he read my letter. He just grunted, 'If you do anything within my limits, I will not be quiet.'

~

It was during this time that, over twenty days, Balaram and his boys cajoled and pleaded with me to meet a journalist. I refused to give in initially, but the boys finally succeeded in making me meet him. The very first time I met him, I realised that he was a fake and an opportunist.

Sometimes life takes a different course than the one we intend. Hence circumstances brought us together and I had to tolerate a man who I would normally never have dealt with even for a few hours.

I am speaking of Ravi Belagere.

Rajendra had once told me in court that Ravi Belagere wanted to meet me; I had refused. He was writing about rowdies in *Karmaveera*, a weekly of which he was editor. I had not read what he wrote, but had heard about it. It was about the time it became fashionable to write about rowdies. But it was not Ravi Belagere who started it in Kannada, as many like to believe, but Tejasvini in *Lankesh Patrike*. Even when I was with Jayaraj, I had realised that newspaper write-ups would create—whether by criticising or by glamorising—unnecessary conflicts. The titles of Ravi Belagere's write-ups in *Karmaveera* were indication enough that they were highly glamorised reports. Hence, I had refused to meet him when Rajendra asked me.

Also, Bachchan, who was in jail, had sent word that I should not meet Ravi because he had no trace of discipline in him. Bachchan has this habit of noticing a person's footwear. If a man is wearing torn or worn-out shoes, it means he has no discipline, according to Bachchan! Ravi Belagere's chappals were badly torn, and Bachchan, who had noticed it, had not even bothered to talk to him. (Ravi also knows this.)

But when Balaram, whom I loved dearly, insisted that I should meet Ravi, I had to give in.

'I have told him all that there is to tell about you. I have said you read books that cost five hundred rupees! He is nothing in front of you. I have warned him that he should not talk too much in front of you, and that he should not write about you and all that . . .' He was so earnest I could not say no to him.

I met Ravi Belagere on 22 September 1994.

I asked him to be brought to the house of a friend, Hemanth, along with Balaram, Malayali Sridhar, Giri, Venkatesh and some other boys. Just as Bachchan had said, this man had no discipline in his dress or talk.

'I have heard a lot about you, Sir,' he started.

During those days, any conversation with a journalist would invariably lead to police officer B.K. Shivaram. The journalists known to me had decided (on their own) that the best way to get anything they wanted from me, including information, was by talking against Shivaram.

I was naturally angry with Shivaram for keeping me in lock-up for fourteen days without any reason, but it was by no means an obsessive hatred. I was also extremely aware that he had not behaved inhumanly with me. So whenever someone mentioned him, I would try to identify the reason behind it.

Ravi said he had come to meet me at the lock-up along with D.R. Nagaraj, a critic and scholar and an old friend of mine, but they'd left without seeing me.

'I don't know you at all, but DR is an old friend . . . he could have spoken to me,' I said, expressing my displeasure.

'Actually we came to speak to you, but we met Shivaram who said, "He is not the old Sreedhar that you know . . . now every evening he drinks arrack and sleeps", and prevented DR from meeting you. See how the man lies—do you ever touch arrack?' Ravi said with pretend compassion.

I doubted for a minute whether Shivaram would tell such a blatant lie, but Ravi said it with such conviction that I believed him.

I said that whatever the police officer had said, DR should have come to meet me. Ravi agreed immediately.

I realised right at the beginning of our friendship that Ravi could convince anyone of anything by his glibness.

As we continued talking, he mentioned names of several police officers and said all of them had a good opinion about me. After talking about police officers, when we discussed writers and finally moved to Naxalite leader Kondapalli Seetharamaiah, I felt I could chat with him for a while. Balaram and his friends who were watching to see whether I would approve of him or not relaxed when they saw that I had loosened up and immediately poured drinks. Ravi, before finishing his second peg, had replaced 'Sir' with 'Sreedhar'. By the time he was past four pegs, instead of *'neevu'* (the respectful plural), he was addressing me as *'neenu'* (singular), 'brother' and 'guru'.

He shifted from the chair on which he was sitting to the floor next to my chair and started pleading, 'Guru, I will become your voice . . . The only other man who impressed me like this was Kondapalli Seetharamaiah. I will write your autobiography, I will do anything for you . . .'

He was completely drunk.

I was unhappy about some news that had been published in *Lankesh Patrike*. We spoke about this and Ravi picked it up. 'Our management encourages any fight against Lankesh. I will not change a single word that you say . . . be it about Lankesh or any officer . . .'

I did not like his over-enthusiasm, and the fact that within a few hours of meeting me, he changed from 'Sir' to 'guru'. It's a habit from my childhood that I take time to get comfortable in any relationship.

It was a Friday. I said I would see him again on Sunday and asked him to leave. But he was so drunk that he was unable to ride his bike. I finally asked our boy Mehmood to follow on Ravi's bike and I drove him in my van (I rarely drive) and dropped him at his house in Padmanabhanagar.

All through the drive he kept blabbering, 'Sreedhar . . . hey brother . . . please give me ten thousand rupees. I want to publish *Paapigala Lokadalli*.'

Finally I lost my patience and snapped, 'First learn some discipline Ravi . . . we will talk about it later.'

After dropping him home, I decided never to see him again. I felt that a man who could ask for ten thousand rupees just three hours after meeting me could demand anything after three months.

The next day, I told Balaram firmly never to bring Ravi to me. He agreed.

That wasn't to be.

Bachchan and Krishnamurthy were released from jail after two months. When they came out, elections were approaching. A strong anti-Congress wave was taking over the state. No one had any doubts about the Hegde-Deve Gowda combine coming to power.

Usually we did not take active part in the elections, but Balaram forced us. He was very fond of the politician Binnipet Somanna. Some of Balaram's boys, like Huchche Gowda, were like family to Somanna. Also, he liked Somanna's friendly manner.

Although I was reluctant, Balaram arranged a meeting between me and Somanna at a farmhouse in Bannerghatta forest. I am normally allergic to politicians, but even I liked Somanna.

'Sir, Somanna will definitely win even without our support, but if we support him, it will be a thundering win,' Balaram said.

Balaram also liked R.V. Harish. When Balaram was with us in jail in connection with the Kotwal murder case, Harish was also jailed as an accused in the Diwakar Hegde murder case. Even though Jeevaraj Alva, who was the de facto chief minister in Ramakrishna Hegde's government, had issued a public statement that at the time of Diwakar Hegde's murder Harish was with him, he was fixed in that case. He was released after two months, on bail.

As the elections approached, many other candidates contacted us. Naturally, since S. Ramesh was a friend, we had to do our best for him. We organised everyone and divided responsibilities, and just one week before the elections, Bachchan and I admitted ourselves into the Vivekananda Yogashram near Anekal. At the ashram, all the inmates were assigned specific activities from four in the morning to ten at night, and had no time to think of anything else. After breakfast, they allowed us to make phone calls between nine and ten o'clock. At this time, we would call and give instructions to Balaram and the others.

The big problem during elections is that of funds. The boys have to be provided some money to take care of their barest daily needs.

People think elections are a money-making feast for the underworld, but this is a myth. Candidates usually have small-time local rowdies with them and they plead with dons for money and alcohol. Since we know many people who are in the wholesale liquor business, politicians will take their *mamool* quota and for any 'extra' quota they will contact us. It is the politicians who play a very important role in the underworld. A winning legislator, if he belongs to the ruling party, will get a police officer of his choice appointed to his constituency. In a police system, it is not the commissioner's office or DG's office that is most important, but the police stations. This is because in any incident it is the officers from the local police station who play a crucial role. Hence, the local small-time rowdies support politicians.

On the day of polling, only half the decent population comes out to vote, and in pre-poll preparations, apart from seasoned politicians, it is the jobless boys who get busy. It is the members of the underworld who take care of these boys in a systematic way. In the 1994 elections, it was Balaram who moved like lightning in Bangalore. For the sake of a couple of politicians, he kidnapped about twenty small-time politicians and kept them in his custody for three days.

I usually agreed with everything he did, but not kidnapping. I shouted at him when he first kidnapped a couple of politicians, so he started doing it without telling me. The boys who would inform me about it would beg me not to let Balaram know that they had informed me, so I acted as if I didn't know.

Just three days before the elections, Jayanth, Muthappa Rai's right-hand man, was murdered in Puttur. I was sad when I heard the news. Jayanth was the strongest in Muthappa Rai's gang and was very dignified. He never spoke disparagingly about anyone. Even after we had fallen out with Muthappa Rai, we had not heard him say anything negative about us anywhere. After Rai settled in Madikeri, Jayanth had gone to Puttur and it was there that one of Francis Cutinho's boys had shot him.

We left the ashram the night before the election results. The next day, when the results were declared and the Janata Dal won, we were all very happy. Luckily for Balaram, all the candidates he supported, except for Harish, won.

Ironically, though I had not even seen Deve Gowda till then, there were rumours everywhere that I was close to him. Since this benefited me, I did not deny it.

The day after the poll results, Somanna started working hard to make Deve Gowda the chief minister. Though all the papers reported that Varade Gowda and Deve Gowda's son Revanna were creating a ruckus and gathering people, it was actually Somanna who was responsible for collecting masses of people and demonstrating for Deve Gowda to become the chief minister.

The tragedy is that during Deve Gowda's term as chief minister, Somanna did not even get a post.

After the Dal came to power, my interaction with politicians increased. Now that I was staying at home and had not gone underground, there were more opportunities to make contacts.

It was at that time that I came in contact with B.C. Patil, a police officer. I met him through Ravishankar, a supporter of K.H. Ranganath. B.C. Patil was a daredevil who was suited to be a policeman, but was fonder of acting. By then his film *Nishkarsha* had been released and he had been received well by audiences, so he was even more interested in acting in films.

I tried my best to convince him that being a policeman was better than being part of the film industry, but he did not agree with me. When *Nishkarsha* received an award, he forced me to go with him to the awards function in Hassan. Balaram was also with us. Deve Gowda was also going to be at the function. It was the first time he was going to Hassan after becoming chief minister, and his supporters wanted to show their strength. Lakhs of people gathered there.

In Hassan, I was introduced to everyone except Deve Gowda. I met many legislators, including Revanna. That night there was a party and I met old acquaintances like S.R. Govindu, Nanjunde Gowda and others after nearly ten years.

On our way back, we visited Balaram's birthplace near Sravanabelgola. He was very happy that we had travelled with B.C. Patil, and when we were back in Bangalore, he said he had decided that even he would not engage in any work that would force us to go underground.

I said, 'We will definitely not indulge in such things, unless you do it.'

Balaram rarely drank in front of me, but he'd had a few pegs that day; hence, he spoke from his heart.

'Sir, before coming to you I had no interest in life. Now I know several leaders. On no account can we go underground; we will not have any respect if we do that. Also, even if it is we who commit the crime, you will get the blame . . . Somanna is also forcing me these days to quit all these activities and be with him. What do you think about my getting a house in Vijayanagar?'

As I listened to him, my mind soared and I felt relieved. But, the same Balaram shattered my wishes.

I usually do not attend functions like weddings and thread ceremonies, even to this day. However, in those days, I would attend weddings in families of those who were with us in jail. One such wedding I was forced to attend was that of the niece of a boy called Venkatesh, who was accused in the murder of M.C. Prakash, Kotwal's right-hand man. He had been very affectionate to me when I was in jail.

His elder brother Seetharam was the president of the Karnataka Kabaddi Association. I knew him as well, and he insisted that I attend the wedding and the 'beegara oota' (the non-vegetarian lunch hosted by the groom's family the day after the wedding). Venkatesh was close to Balaram too, and he and his boys wanted to attend the lunch, so we decided to go.

It was like a village fair at the venue. Since Venkatesh was active in the Janata Dal, he had a huge gang of boys with him. Police officers, kabaddi players, traders—all had assembled in large numbers. In addition to this, the underworld was in conspicuous attendance.

Within ten minutes I began to feel I'd made a mistake by going there. Apart from Muthappa Rai and his gang, we did not have any enmity with anybody else, but it was not the same with Balaram. He had participated in innumerable fights, and he had as many enemies as he had friends.

Balaram, Hemanth, Bachchan, Krishnamurthy, the producer Ramanna and I were sitting in one corner, all the boys around us.

Just then, Sriramapura Kitty walked in.

Five

Kitty had terrorised all of Bangalore during Kotwal's days. Although he had mellowed somewhat after Kotwal's death, he had attacked Balaram even when Jayaraj was alive. After this, he had distanced himself from the underworld.

Seeing Kitty, Ramanna's face fell.

Ramanna had been very close to Kitty till a couple of years before. After becoming close to Balaram, he had distanced himself from Kitty. Now, seeing Kitty face-to-face, he did not know how to react.

I had not seen Kitty since 1987, so I did not even recognise him. However, I could sense that Balaram was beginning to get very angry after seeing the man who had just walked in. He never crossed his legs in my presence, but now he suddenly crossed his legs and started shaking them. I knew something was wrong and asked Krishnamurthy, who was sitting next to me, who the man was who had just arrived.

'Srirampura Kitty,' he said.

If Kitty had gone straight into the dining hall, nothing would have happened, but he gave Ramanna a sharp look and said sarcastically, 'Hey, what happened, Rama? You said we would meet and I never saw you after that?'

Ramanna gave Kitty a sheepish grin. Balaram was furious that Kitty had spoken like this.

Just then, three policemen from the crime branch walked in.

I realised that things were getting out of hand, so I told Balaram, 'Looks like a lot of police personnel are present here. Why don't you and your boys have lunch somewhere else?'

As if waiting for some excuse, Balaram immediately said, 'Okay Sir, we will eat out and meet you at five o'clock at the Cosmopolitan Club,' and left with his boys.

The tension in the air diffused, and we had our lunch peacefully.

Since we did not have enmity with anyone there, everyone came and greeted us and shook hands with us. Kitty too was relieved after Balaram left. However, he left soon after lunch.

We stayed till four-thirty in the evening, chatting with everyone. The programme was at the Maratha Hostel in Gandhi Bazaar. From there we went straight to the Cosmopolitan Club in 4th Block Jayanagar. Ten minutes after we reached, Balaram and Huchche Gowda arrived. Balaram said he would have a wash and went to the toilet. Huchche Gowda came up to the car we were sitting in and said, 'He gave us the slip . . . he escaped, Sir.'

I didn't understand what he was saying. 'Who escaped?' I asked.

'Kitty, Sir,' he said.

'What happened?'

'Didn't Balaram tell you, Sir? We were waiting outside there for Kitty—to do a "307" on him—but since there were too many policemen, we decided not to do anything there and followed him after he came out. At Kohinoor Ground near Hanumanthanagar, guru (Balaram) flashed his long from the car, but Kitty escaped and ran into a hotel. When we went in he was crouching in a corner with a wok on his head and screaming. We gave it to him nicely,' he said, as if they were at war.

By then Balaram had returned.

'What Balaram, why did you do such a thing?' I asked angrily.

'Sir, you saw how arrogant he was while talking to Ramanna. If he can be so arrogant . . .'

'No, Balaram . . . he will think I sent you.'

'He is not a child, Sir. He knows I am his enemy.'

'No, Balaram. Earlier when Jedarahalli Krishnappa attacked

him, he had blamed Jayaraj. How do you know Kitty will not name me in his police complaint now?' I asked, annoyed.

Balaram was also irritated. 'Till what time you were in the chowltry?'

'Till four-thirty, why?'

'We attacked him at three-thirty. If he names you, there are enough people to say you were in the chowltry till four-thirty. Also, the police themselves have seen you there, and the hotel people can identify the people who attacked . . .' he started arguing.

Finally, I asked him, 'Balaram, today Kitty's name has been removed from the underworld. You said just yesterday that we should not get involved in any crime. We are now out in the open. And so soon you disturb everything?'

Balaram was silent for a few minutes and then said, 'Sir, I will call you in the morning. By then we will know what his complaint is.'

He left with Huchche Gowda.

I was restless. We decided not to talk about the attack on Kitty to anybody. Some of my friends advised me not to stay at home that night, but I did not listen. I convinced them that, in case we were named in his complaint, it was better to face the police rather than run away.

I stayed awake till one in the morning, listening for the sound of a police jeep. But no jeep came. Finally, I slept.

In the morning my wife woke me up, saying anxiously, '*Ree* . . . what is this—your name . . .' and handed me the Kannada newspaper *Prajavani*. I knew I'd been named in the complaint. I thought this would be page-two news, but right in the middle of the front page was the headline, 'Street fight of underworld dons.'

Now, there are two types of journalists: the first writes lies knowing full well that what he is writing is untrue. Even God cannot change him. Whatever you say, he will always argue that the lie is the ultimate truth.

The second type neither has the patience nor intelligence to find out what the truth is. If he finds out that what he has written is false, he will be polite enough to change his opinion, but until then he strongly believes that what he thinks is the truth must be the truth.

Now, the person who wrote the report in *Prajavani*, a certain Nanjundegowda, belonged to the second category. I don't know who had given him the information, but he believed I was the one who attacked Kitty. In his article, he said that Balaram, two of his friends and I had come in a Maruti car and attacked Kitty and his associate when they were on a motorbike.

No other newspaper carried the report.

Immediately after reading the newspaper, I called a police officer I knew and explained that I was completely innocent. He assured me that he would talk to the concerned official.

However, the next day, all the evening newspapers published the very same report.

Some lawyers and police officials of my acquaintance suggested that I take anticipatory bail, but I refused. Instead, I went to meet Kitty.

Oddly, although we had both been housed in the same jail for a year-and-a-half, we had never met. He had been a kabaddi player once and played for the state—we had actually met through kabaddi. Within five minutes of talking to him, he softened.

'The way you talk, no one can think you are in rowdyism . . . It was not me who mentioned your name: the man who was with me said all that. Now I will do whatever you tell me to,' he said.

We called a press meet at Jayanagar Cosmopolitan Club and Kitty clarified that I was not involved in the attack. When some reporters tried to interrupt Kitty, the reporter from the *Indian Express*, Daniel George, cleverly silenced them by saying that even a rowdy had the right to make a statement.

It was now five days since the incident.

More English newspapers than Kannada newspapers carried Kitty's statement. Instead of publishing Kitty's statement,

Nanjundegowda of *Prajavani* published another write-up questioning why I had not been arrested yet. But the most interesting report was published in *Lankesh Patrike*. It said I had threatened Kitty and forced him to hold a press conference!

However, the police said they could not remove my name from the complaint solely based on Kitty's statement to the media.

Now I had only one route—to surrender to the police. The police had concluded, based on their own investigation, that I had no role to play in the attack on Kitty, so they were not looking for me. However, I could not take it easy—I had to clear my name.

I knew the inspector general of police, intelligence, through B.C. Patil. I met him and explained my situation. He immediately spoke to the then commissioner of police Srinivasulu and said he would fix a meeting for me with him the next day. He believed I was innocent, and that I should, therefore, be helped.

I took Hemanth, Ramesh and Seetharam—who had been with me till late evening on the day of attack—with me when I went to meet the commissioner. Srinivasulu heard me out with patience and then called the then additional commissioner Kokkatanoor, explained my situation to him and asked him to handle it. Kokkatanoor immediately called the Hanumanthanagar inspector and asked him to take me with him!

'No, Sir, if I am taken to the station I will be framed in the case. Instead, can you not investigate here?' I pleaded.

'No one will be framed like that. He knows the details of the case and if you are innocent you don't have to be afraid,' he said curtly.

I kept quiet. I began to feel I had made a mistake in going there. But what other option did I have?

I stood outside and waited for the Hanumanthanagar police to arrive. By then it was past three o'clock and crime reporters had started assembling there. Some of them must have recognised me. *Indian Express*' Daniel and another reporter approached me.

Daniel asked me directly, 'Tell me the truth Mr Sreedhar, were you really not involved in the attack on Kitty?'

I said no. By then I was feeling helpless.

'Then why are they taking you?'

'Mr Daniel, I am telling the truth. I am innocent, but the police don't believe me—they don't even believe Kitty.'

The jeep from Hanumanthanagar station arrived then and I was taken to the station. Suresh Naidu was the inspector there. He had come to Bangalore recently from north Karnataka and did not know anything about the Bangalore underworld. He took down my statement and said he would go as per the decision of the higher officials.

By then it was getting dark and I started suspecting they would frame me in this case. Lawyers Udaya, Partha and Ramesh Kumar came to the station and spoke to me. Partha said Krishnamurthy had gone to the then deputy chief minister J.H. Patel's house to request him to talk to officials.

Every half hour I kept pleading with the inspector to take a just and ethical decision. He kept assuring me that the ACP would come and speak with me and a decision would be made then.

The suspense continued till eleven o'clock. Then they asked me to go to the lock-up, and now I was certain they would frame me in this case. I screamed, 'If truth has no value, why have you hung the photo of Mahatma Gandhi!' I said they were betraying my trust in them. They did not respond to anything I said, but put me in lock-up. I could not sleep the whole night. I sat in a corner, thinking. I was deeply sad that I had been arrested for a crime that I did not commit. However, I was not angry with the system. There are several actions that go unpunished for a man from the underworld, and this was true in my case as well. So I consoled myself that to suffer punishment for a crime that I hadn't committed was poetic justice for all my crimes that went unpunished.

At midnight a senior official in civilian clothes came to see me and spoke to me in a friendly manner. He tried to explain the attitude of the police department: in the case of a person without any previous crime record they would take utmost care to prove his innocence. But no one wants to take a risk when it comes to a history-sheeter.

'But Sir, Kitty himself has given a statement that it was not me who attacked him,' I tried to argue.

He asked, 'What if the same Kitty declares that you forced him to say so, what happens to us?'

His question was logical, and I had no answer to it.

'Anyway, don't lose heart. And you must try to get out of this world of rowdyism,' he said and left.

None of the constables there knew who he was, so to this day I have no idea who the man was.

The next morning, at around nine o'clock, the inspector took me in a jeep to my house and to the place of crime. This is required of the First Information Report. When we returned to the station, I saw that all the newspapers had carried the news that I'd surrendered to the commissioner. The reports said that the police would produce me in court by four o'clock.

By noon, ACP 'Benki' Muniyappa came to the station. 'Benki' means 'fire'; he was literally a terror to all the criminals in the state, and hence had that nickname.

As soon as he arrived he shouted at me, 'Why did you have to surrender and eat our heads if you are innocent? Did we come to arrest you?' He then called the inspector and sub-inspector and said, 'Do one thing for me, call Kitty and ask him. Let us see what he says in this man's presence. If we are convinced that he is innocent then we will release him, otherwise we will send him to jail.'

A police constable was sent to fetch Kitty.

I was afraid the police would threaten Kitty and force him to give a statement against me before bringing him there. However powerful a rowdy, when the police threatens, it is difficult to refuse them.

Kitty walked in wide-eyed. He glanced at me from the corner of his eyes and went to stand in front of ACP Muniyappa.

He and I were standing at opposite ends of the table. The ACP was sitting in front, with the sub-inspector and inspector sitting to his left and right.

Muniyappa stared at Kitty for a few minutes and then said, 'Look Kitty, I am not like the others. This Sreedhar here, I have nothing to do with him. I want truth and justice. You don't be scared of anybody. If he has threatened you through someone, you can tell us that also . . .'

Kitty nodded his head and kept saying, 'Yes Sir, yes Sir.'

For a full five minutes the ACP reassured him and promised to support him, and then, staring at him, asked, 'Now tell me the truth. When the attack on you took place, was this man (pointing at me) present or not?'

I listened nervously for Kitty's answer. He said, in a straightforward manner, 'No Sir, I swear on my children, this man was not there.'

ACP looked at the other officers and said, 'Then there is no point in keeping him here anymore . . . what do you say?'

The officers who had been sympathetic towards me since the previous evening said, 'Let us release him, Sir.'

The ACP first sent Kitty away and then turned towards me and said firmly, 'Go. Let any higher officer say whatever they want . . . you go.'

I walked to the main road, got into an auto-rickshaw and went home.

By then Bachchan and others had gone to the court thinking the police would produce me there. I called a shop near the court and told the boy to inform them all that I had been sent home. In five minutes all of them started calling me. They were all very happy that I had been released.

But Nanjundegowda, the reporter, was not convinced.

After two days, a write-up appeared at the bottom of the front page of *Prajavani*, alleging that the police had given in to political pressure and released me. It also accused me of creating a ruckus at the station. It quoted a police officer, who did not want to identify himself, who said that the underworld was ruling Bangalore and if the higher officials would support him, he had the ability to totally eradicate the underworld in the city.

We all discussed the report and decided that the police official quoted must be B.K. Shivaram.

The police did not let me live in peace after this though. They started pressurising me to get Balaram. Incredibly, although Balaram had been part of the underworld for the last fourteen years, the police had never been able to trace his house or the places he frequented. ACP Muniyappa finally discovered his birthplace and brought his elder and younger brothers to Bangalore. Balaram was stunned.

Huchche Gowda had shown Balaram's family home to the police.

Balaram pleaded with the minister Somanna and got his brothers, who were absolutely innocent, released. They were not even aware of Balaram's activities in Bangalore.

However, within ten days, the police went to their place and threatened them again.

Balaram, who never got scared, started having mild shivers.

Muniyappa called me again and started pressurising me to show him Balaram's house in Bangalore. 'I released you because you were innocent but you must now show me Balaram's house. You must,' he insisted.

I said I really did not know where Balaram lived, which was true.

'Okay, let me know when you meet him,' he said.

I said I could not do that. Doing that and shooting myself would be one and the same thing, I said. But I would try to get him to surrender.

Muniyappa did not agree. He became angry and said that if the department came to know of it, he would lose respect. Muniyappa had never chased rowdies, so he did not know what surrender meant. I explained to him that, in several cases, officers had gotten rowdies to surrender but then informed the media that they had caught the men with great difficulty. I even gave him several examples. I also told him that it was not wrong to use any strategy possible to arrest a rowdy who had 'escaped'.

He said he would need a couple of days to think about it and left.

In the underworld, when the police do not agree to let a man surrender, it raises serious doubts about their intentions. At that time Balaram was notorious; also, the attack on Kitty had gained enormous attention. So everyone thought the police was planning to finish Balaram in an encounter.

When I spoke with Balaram, he refused point-blank to surrender. 'Sir, whatever you say I will not surrender. In a couple of months, after everything cools down, I will take anticipatory bail,' he said.

However when Muniyappa brought his elder brother in again, Balaram's confidence was shaken.

Finally, through some officials who were close to Muniyappa, we came to an understanding. I was to show the police where they could catch Balaram. They would arrest him, but on no account would he be tortured. Muniyappa must have been tired of searching for him, for he agreed to our terms.

One day, when Balaram was driving his car on Bannerghatta Road, the police chased and caught him.

The police kept their word: they did not torture Balaram. He was sent to jail after two days at the station. Once there, Balaram expressed his appreciation for Muniyappa to the boys who went to see him. He praised him and said that no other officer had spoken like him and asked him to change his ways.

Mysore Ganesh was in the same jail as Balaram. He told Balaram about a couple of schemes—or 'sketches' as rowdies would say—and that Muthappa Rai had planned to finish me. He expressed his wish to meet me after being released from jail.

I refused.

In those days it was a strategy among rowdies to use Muthappa Rai's name to get close to me. I did not fall for it.

After Balaram was jailed, things calmed down.

It was at this time that Ravi Belagere wrote a three-part series about a young boy Soma, who had recently entered the underworld. The report's description of Soma was completely untrue—Bangalore has never seen a rowdy like the one in the article. Belagere wrote that Soma had a monthly income of about five lakh rupees, when in fact he struggled to get the ten thousand rupees he needed for bail.

Soma's gang and that of Pushpa's were always clashing. Soma had killed two of Pushpa's boys. The gang war was at a peak, at the time Balaram attacked Kitty. Pushpa, who had lost interest in the underworld, was in a way forced to get back into it. Within ten days of the attack on Kitty, Pushpa and his boys killed Bidda, one of Soma's favourite boys.

Soma, who was in jail at the time, sent a large number of his boys to kill Pushpa. By the time Balaram went to jail, Soma had been released, but some of his boys were still in jail. Though Balaram and Soma had no personal enmity, since Balaram was Pushpa's friend, it was possible that Soma felt some hostility towards Balaram.

The gangs that opposed Muthappa Rai may have been confused about who the don of Bangalore was, but no such confusion existed about who the general—dalapathi—was. Everybody knew it was Balaram. Also, everybody, even the police, knew that Pushpa, Rajendra and I did not want to fight. Only Balaram was always hungry for fights. So we were very worried that someone would finish Balaram in jail.

Also, he had decided that, after his release from jail, he would set up a house in Vijayanagar, which was Somanna's constituency, and live peacefully. We all were very happy with his decision, but usually, when underworld dons decide to come out in the open, they make a common mistake: they neglect to take precautions to ensure their safety. We were anxious that Balaram too would make the same mistake. We always sent word with whoever went to visit him to be extremely careful.

We were happy that Loki—a boy close to Balaram's heart—

was with him in jail. Loki was very alert and he loved Balaram dearly.

But soon Balaram got Loki bailed out. I called Loki and expressed my ire.

'What can I do, Sir, he got angry. He said, "If all sit inside who is going to take care of outside jobs", and sent me out on bail. I said, "No guru . . . ", but he shouted at me to just shut up and listen,' Loki said.

Another worrying thing for us was that Krishna, whose nickname was Korangu, was also inside the same jail as Balaram. There was a time when Korangu had considered Balaram his guru, but later his behaviour was not right and even Balaram had heard of it. Balaram was such a fool though, that when his close friend Jedarahalli Krishnappa alerted him about Korangu's ill-intentions, Balaram had innocently said, 'Oh, is it so? He has a "sketch" on me? Wait, I will call him here, let us ask him straight out!'

He didn't even make an effort to find out what the reality was.

Korangu was more of an expert in robbery than rowdyism. I've seen that robbery requires more daring. The transformation of those coming from robbery into rowdyism is mind-blowing. Kotwal Ramachandra and Jayaraj were two examples. That was the reason they were able to rule at that level. Dons who understand the cold-blooded cruelty of robbery do not let any robber get close to them.

It was Balaram who initially brought Korangu from robbery into the underworld. So although Balaram was confident that Korangu would not go against him, it was stupid to take it for granted.

One day, when in the jail 'entry room', Korangu, scratching his head, had tried to talk to Balaram. But Balaram, who was very crude when it came to human relations, had insulted him in front of everyone.

When Loki told me about it, I had sent a message to Balaram asking him not to be rude to anybody in jail and to be careful.

But Balaram had never been in the habit of taking any advice from anyone.

That day is still etched in my mind, crystal clear.

We had stayed the previous night at the farm of a friend on Old Madras Road and returned to Bangalore in the morning. On the way into the city, we met the lawyer Venkatesh. He said he had met Balaram the previous day in jail. Balaram wanted to get bail and come out. It had been nearly a month since he had gone to jail. He had initially said he would stay in jail for at least three months and I thought it was a good sign that he had shown an interest in getting bail.

Many notorious rowdies do not hesitate to take risks when they are in jail. They know that because they are in jail, they cannot be framed in any case. Which is why serious attacks are planned by dons when they are in jail. I'd had my suspicions about why Balaram had sent Loki out on bail and not kept anyone near him. I was worried he was planning something serious. Whatever action Balaram took would have a direct impact on us. So when Venkatesh said Balaram wished to get bail, I was relieved.

I put my hand in my pocket and took out whatever money I had, maybe a couple of thousand rupees, gave it to Venkatesh, and said we would arrange for bail within a week.

Then I went to a public booth and called home and asked whether there had been any calls for me. I was told that a police officer close to me had called in the morning and asked me to call back.

I called him.

'You still don't know the news?' he asked anxiously.

'No Sir, what's the news?' I asked, trying to be calm. The underworld had taught me to keep control of my voice under any circumstance.

However, the news he gave me not only made me lose control over my voice, but over my mind as well.

'In jail—Balaram . . .'

The officer I had called liked Balaram very much. He had

liked the fact that Balaram was straightforward despite his crudeness.

'In jail—Balaram . . .' he stopped mid-way and asked, 'you must have found out by now . . .'

'No, Sir . . . what happened, Sir?'

He drew a heavy breath. 'You don't know yet? They . . . finished Balaram.'

I remember that moment even now.

My mind became empty. My body went weak. Everything around me vanished. I almost dropped the receiver.

I struggled to gain control of myself and asked, 'When Sir? And who?'

Usually no one goes to the extent of murder in jail, so I thought Balaram must have fought with the police there and things had gotten out of hand.

'A few small-time boys have attacked. It is not yet known who is behind this,' he said.

I remained silent.

He continued, 'Sreedhar . . . your field is very uncertain, isn't it? You take care. Whatever has happened has happened. Maybe Rai has had a hand in this, so be very careful.'

It is impossible to explain the grief I felt that day.

Balaram had hurt a number of people, had attacked without any reason. More than anything else he had enjoyed torturing others. But after he came in contact with me he had undergone a change. Earlier he used to say, 'Our life is nothing but to kill and finally one day get killed, that's all,' but later his attitude changed and he began to feel violence should be used only as a last resort.

More than anything else, he had finally made the decision to lead a normal life after getting out of jail. But time did not give him the chance.

By that evening, the news spread everywhere that either Rai's or Soma's boys must have killed Balaram. He had been killed by three robbery boys.

One of those boys had taken a loan of five hundred rupees

from Balaram. Usually nobody returns loan in jail. But that day, as soon as Balaram's cell door was opened, the boy had come in and told the still sleeping Balaram, 'Guru, here is the money, take.'

It was Balaram's habit to look at a god's photograph as soon as he opened his eyes first thing in the morning, so he didn't open his eyes when the boy spoke to him. He simply replied, 'Keep it there and go.'

The three boys had then attacked Balaram with knives and razors, stabbing him in his neck and stomach.

Balaram died without so much as attempting to defend himself.

Six

The police did not have to make a great effort to search for the killers as the murder had occurred in prison. They caught the killers and handed them over to Upparpet police.

But inspector B.K. Shivaram raided every house from Bekkinakanu Rajendra's to Srirampura Kitty's. This was despite the fact that both the underworld and the police department were very sure that neither Rajendra nor Kitty had any hand in the murder.

Rajendra managed to escape, but Kitty, who had no clue that there were plans to kill Balaram, was caught by the police and framed in the case.

We later found out that Korangu was behind Balaram's murder.

Neither B.K. Shivaram nor any other policeman took the trouble of inquiring into this. The jail police did not keep quiet, though. They beat him up and made him spill the details of the plot. The police just turned the other way and remained silent.

We all knew that Balaram had not been treating Korangu well in the jail, even though he was once Balaram's favourite boy. We had even sent word to Balaram warning him that anyone in Korangu's place would take revenge. But Balaram 'yaamaarida', as we say in rowdy language—he was fooled.

Apart from our sorrow for Balaram's death, we felt terrible that the police intentionally framed Kitty in the case, despite knowing that Korangu was responsible. At that point of time, I had no weapon to use to expose the truth. I did not have my newspaper *Agni* yet. I did not know any crime reporter, other than Daniel of the *Indian Express*. The *Lankesh Patrike* had decided that whatever Shivaram said was the truth, and I held Nanjundegowda of *Prajavani* responsible for Balaram's incarceration and eventual murder, as it was he who had built up the attack on Kitty into something it wasn't. He even wrote a detailed article speculating about who had gotten Balaram to surrender. It was very clear that the person who had made him write that article wanted to get me framed.

I was also very sure that, even if we went to court, justice would not be done. And we feared that the police would bring pressure on those going to court.

One thing that disturbed me a lot was that one of the accused in Balaram's murder had been arrested and sent to jail from Banashankari police station—the same police station at which my younger brother was a crime sub-inspector. We heard that Shivaram was talking about this in a way that seemed to hint that I might have had an indirect hand in Balaram's murder!

Not a single police officer paid any heed to Shivaram's hints, but some reporters were heard discussing it.

At the same time, the special squad that was set up to look into Balaram's murder came to my house in search of me. I had not expected this.

Those were the days of police squads. When there was a disturbance of any sort, a squad comprising inspectors and sub-inspectors would be formed. The chief of the squad would submit investigation reports directly to the commissioner, and hence there was no room for 'influence'. However, officers in the squad would compete against each other and sometimes trouble innocent people who were in no way connected with the crimes, but were connected to criminals. Also, several officers would be sympathetic to one or the other don, and they would chase the rivals of that don.

The squad that was formed after Balaram's murder consisted of powerful inspectors like Sangram Singh, K.V.K. Reddy,

Ashok Kumar, Bheemaiah, Azeem and Shivaram. I made a phone call to Ashok Kumar who was in the squad. He pressurised me to issue a statement to the police. I said I was out of station and would meet him after my return in three days.

Bachchan made a phone call to Shivaram as I stood next to him. Shivaram said, 'You see, they say Sreedhar sent a killer through Banashankari station to jail. I don't know what decision to take.'

Bachchan does not think and talk like I do; he tends to blurt out whatever comes to his mind. He started innocently, 'Sir, everyone is saying that it was you who got Korangu to kill Balaram,' and continued to pour out all his anguish for the next twenty minutes without giving any opportunity for Shivaram to talk. 'Sir, what did we do to you that you are doing this injustice to us?'

'Okay, if you have faith in me, you come and meet me, I will make everything right,' he said.

But we did not have faith in him.

It is not easy to describe my mental state those days. One part of me was trying to deal with the loss of Balaram—my grief was boundless. The fact that the police never allow the associates of a dead rowdy to conduct the last rites did not help.

The other part of me was overcome with anxiety because of the possibility of being blamed for Balaram's murder. When the police start chasing you, the entire world becomes a jail. Several police officials warned me that Shivaram was trying to fix me in the Balaram murder case by using media pressure, so I had no choice but to take the help of all my connections.

People close to Nanjundegowda of *Prajavani* had assured me that, though he had mentioned me unnecessarily in the attack on Kitty, he was not stupid enough to claim that I was behind Balaram's murder. However, I had no such confidence when it came to *Lankesh Patrike*. I knew the police would give more attention to reports in the weeklies than daily newspapers, as the weeklies reported events in greater detail.

But through whom could I send word to Lankesh? I thought of all my writer friends, from Shudra Srinivas to D.R. Nagaraj. I knew Lankesh's character very well. If he believed in something, no one in the world would succeed in changing his mind. Also, he was very moody. If someone tried to recommend me and if his mood was not good at that moment, he would not only shout at the person but also continue to carry his bad feelings even after his mood became all right.

Hence I decided to go and meet Lankesh directly. I had reservations about my decision though, and it was Bachchan who encouraged me.

'Sreedhar, what's the worst Meshtru (as Lankesh was called) can do? He may shout at you. After all, he is a big man and he cares for you. Go with the expectation that he will shout at you and don't take offence. But you must tell him your problem,' he said.

So one afternoon he drove me there in the car and parked by the gate.

It had been fifteen years since I'd last seen Lankesh. The last time I had spoken to him was in 1979. Once, in 1990, we had gone to see a film in Plaza and I saw Lankesh, Siddappa and three other friends seated three rows away from us. I pointed him out to Bachchan and, worried that he would see us during the interval, I moved to a corner and started drinking coffee.

Whatever differences one had with Lankesh, to all those who knew him, he was like a moral conscience. Even if he did not see us, we felt he would condemn us in case we made any mistakes. I was notorious after the Kotwal murder at that point, and I felt he would scorn me.

I told Bachchan that we would leave five minutes before the film ended. Bachchan, who had heard all my stories about Lankesh, was also scared of him. He agreed. I went to the toilet, and as I was leaving, I bumped into Lankesh at the door.

Lankesh had the habit of looking straight into your eyes. He saw me just for a fraction of a second and, instead of going into the toilet, he walked away quickly and disappeared.

When I'd seen him in front of me my heart felt like it would explode, but when he walked away, I felt a deep sense of disappointment. It was actually fun to have him shout at me.

Funnily, Lankesh had a deep fear of dons. I decided that he walked away because he was scared that I would attack him. He was always criticising me in his paper at that time, and I had also climbed to a high level in the underworld.

I had a mental fear of him and he was scared of me doing him physical harm.

One evening in 1992, when Varada and I were driving in a jeep, we saw a Maruti car coming from the opposite direction. It was a one-way street. Varada, though he had been jailed in a murder case, is a strict disciplinarian and would not tolerate such flouting of the law.

He stopped the jeep next to the car and asked loudly, 'Don't you know this is a one-way road?'

The man at the wheel made a gesture indicating, 'What's your problem?'

I knew Varada would become dogged in such situations, so I got down from the jeep to tell the man it was wrong to drive the car the wrong way on a one-way street.

As I stepped closer, I recognised the man—it was Lankesh.

I immediately walked back to the jeep quickly and told Varada, 'Hey, it is Meshtru, Meshtru . . . let's go.'

But by then Lankesh had recognised me and he drove away very fast.

Except for those brief encounters, we had not come face-to-face at all.

When I went to his office, Lankesh was in his chamber. I sent word through a staff member that I had come to see him.

I heard him say, 'Send him in, send him in.'

When I went in, I saw that he was eating lunch.

'Hey, here, take my hand,' he said with affection and stretched out his left hand.

By his behaviour, I understood that he knew that I was in trouble and had come to him for help.

'Sir, I am in trouble, it is suffocating.'

'Sreedhar, don't worry, I am here for you, we will set everything right. It's so long since I saw you; you have remained the same. Look at you—you have maintained yourself very well.'

In a matter of minutes I felt relieved.

Lankesh looked out of the window. He could see Bachchan sitting in the car. We had asked our boys to park four furlongs away from the office! Bachchan could not make out that Lankesh was looking at him, but since the car was parked right in front of Lankesh's office, he was sitting in a decorous manner.

Lankesh looked at him for some time and then turned to me and asked, 'Is he with you?'

I said yes.

'Looks decent.'

Perhaps he was expecting me to be surrounded by rough-looking boys . . .

He inquired about Narayanaswamy, who we used to know during our walking days. I had forgotten him and I praised Lankesh's memory.

Finally I told him about Shivaram. How he was making use of the media and troubling me. Lankesh heard me out patiently.

'Sreedhar, I won't ask what you are doing to earn your livelihood. But one must learn to live in a balanced manner. For no reason should one go to the extreme. It's not important if I like your ways or not, but it is important that they should be acceptable to people surrounding me.'

He then called Basavaraj who was working for him and said, 'This is Sreedhar, my boy. Make a note of what he says.'

Basavaraj took me upstairs. He pulled out a notebook and pen and asked me to talk.

I started explaining the conspiracy behind Balaram's murder, but I could see that he did not know anything about the Bangalore underworld. Just then someone called him and, excusing himself, he went down and returned after some time saying, 'Sir, Ravi Belagere is here.'

I was surprised. I had not heard from him for about six months since my last talk with him. Also, in our previous meeting, he had said that he would publish anything against Lankesh in his weekly *Karmaveera*.

'Is Ravi working here?' I asked.

'Yes Sir, for the last three weeks.'

'But he is in *Karmaveera* . . .?'

'He has left *Karmaveera* and is with us now. It would be better if you talk to him.'

'Please no, I don't have confidence in him . . . please, you take down the notes,' I pleaded.

'Sir, I told him you are here and he wants to meet you. He is writing about crime. You talk to him first. If you are not happy then I will talk to you again,' he said.

I immediately understood that he was simply not interested in writing a crime story.

I knew that, after Lankesh, it was Basavaraj who took decisions about write-ups in *Lankesh Patrike*. I decided that in case I was not confident about Ravi, I would talk to Basavaraj about it. I asked him to call Ravi, though I was not at all enthusiastic about meeting him again.

Ravi came up.

'Hello Sreedhar,' he said and shook hands. As he glanced at the notes that Basavaraj had made, he lit a cigarette. His face was swollen. His eyes betrayed that he had been drunk the previous night and had not slept well.

'So what is your version about Balaram's murder? There is a rumour that you got some Backdive Raja arrested in Banashankari station and sent to jail?'

'Ravi, if not others, at least you know the Bangalore underworld. Can you even imagine I would get Balaram killed?'

'No, no . . . I know that. But I want to know what you have to say about it,' Ravi said.

Basavaraj was sitting with us till then; assuming that our conversation was going smoothly, he got up and left.

The minute he went down the stairs, Ravi's face changed. He relaxed.

'What Sreedhar ... not to be seen. Thought we would meet ...?' he started in a strange tone.

I said I had been busy with one thing or the other.

Glancing towards the stairs to check if someone was coming, he asked in a low voice 'Okay, when can we meet, Sreedhar?'

I did not want to meet him, but thinking that he may have improved now that he was with *Lankesh Patrike*, I said reluctantly, 'This evening.'

'Where?' he asked.

I mentioned a spot in 4th Block Jayanagar and said we could meet there at seven o'clock. Then he relaxed totally. He said it was Shivaram who was floating the rumour that I was behind Balaram's murder.

'If I had not been here, what would you have written?' I asked.

'Yes, if you had not come here to speak, what other choice would we have had but to write that it could be true,' he said.

'But you know all Balaram's boys, you could have asked any one of them.'

'Forget all that ... now that you have spoken to Lankesh, nobody can influence us to write against you,' he assured me.

But by the way he behaved it was evident that he was not respected there. I stayed in the office for about forty minutes, came down, and since Lankesh was taking a nap, said goodbye to Basavaraj and left.

At seven o'clock, Bachchan and I reached the spot I had decided on. In two minutes, Ravi came up and parked his bike near our car. Perhaps he had already arrived and was keeping an eye on us.

I sat in the back seat, told him to sit next to me and asked why he had quit *Karmaveera*.

He said the chief editor, Shyama Rao, had fired him over some difference of opinion.

'All for good; now that you are with Lankesh, it's a different status,' I said.

But he had not been made permanent, he said. It would happen eventually, I said reassuringly.

'There is a chance of that,' he said, although I could sense that he didn't quite believe it. Nobody could be certain about anything when it came to Lankesh, as he was very moody.

I asked him about the article he was preparing on me.

'Read it tomorrow,' he said. By his tone I thought he had taken my information seriously.

Then I asked him directly, 'What do you want from me?'

He just stared at me for a long time. His eyes were wide open and looked like they were filled with the grief of the world. As he stared at me, I remembered several painful moments in my life and, finally breaking the silence, I touched his hand and assured him, 'Don't worry Ravi, all will be well.'

The media, which had always lingered at the borders of the underworld, stepped fully into it at that moment.

The information given by me was prominently placed in the next day's edition of *Lankesh Patrike*. That evening, Ravi arranged for me to meet Dwarakanath and Tyagaraj, both from *Lankesh Patrike*. We all met at a bar in Jayanagar. Dwarakanath said he had been writing against me, having believed the information provided by the police. But he said Lankesh praised me in private meetings.

The next afternoon, Ravi took me to meet Ranganath of *Kannada Prabha*. In the corridor, we bumped into YNK (Y.N. Krishnamurthy), who was the editor. He had seen me with Lankesh when I acted in *Anurupa*, which Lankesh directed. When he asked very affectionately, 'What's happening, you are not to be seen of late. Are you still with Lankesh?' I didn't know what to say.

Ravi was very impressed by the way YNK spoke to me.

Ranganath and I spoke for a long time.

The next day Ravi called me to meet another journalist— Sathya of *Ee Sanje*—in Jayanagar. However, we went there and waited, but Ravi did not turn up. Despite this, I knew that Ravi Belagere was trying his best to have me meet a large section of the press corps and convince them that I was not a bad person. He would talk to anyone who refused to meet me, trying to get them to change their opinion. In those days, Bachchan and I were in 'no entry', meaning we would not stay at home, but at the house of a friend, Sundararaman, since his family was away in Tamil Nadu.

I mentioned to Ravi that we had told Ashok Kumar we would go meet him. Ravi called him and extended the deadline by two more days and Ashok Kumar agreed.

Ravi told me one day that he would bring Daniel of the *Indian Express* to meet me. I didn't tell him that I knew Danny. I had told Danny that Ravi had concluded that he was the best choice to resolve the police problem and he said, 'I will meet you along with Ravi, don't let him know that we know each other. In case he starts any loose talk we can take care. After a couple of pegs at night, Ravi starts "singing".'

I agreed.

Ravi brought Daniel on the afternoon of the day before the deadline given by Ashok Kumar.

'Hello Sreedhar, nice meeting you,' Danny said and shook hands.

Then we discussed how to deal with the police. There were no cases against us: the police were looking for us as a 'routine matter' and not for any specific crime. Hence we decided that we would meet Ashok Kumar the next day somewhere outside and send Bachchan with him. Ravi and Danny would go wherever Ashok Kumar was interrogating Bachchan.

Ravi Belagere was known to several police officers, but he did not command the respect that Danny did. Ravi would plead with officers to get him a drink. He himself had confessed that, after getting him drunk, Shivaram would try mining him for information, asking him, 'Where is Kalapathar?', 'Where could Balaram be?' and so on.

Ravi spoke to Ashok Kumar and told him that he would get Bachchan and me to surrender and brought him to a place near Nanda Theatre in Jayanagar. When we met Ashok Kumar, he wanted to know the reason behind the personal hatred between Shivaram and us. I explained in detail how Shivaram, who was our 'protector' at one point of time, had changed his stand after Muthappa Rai entered the scene.

Ashok Kumar said he would talk to Shivaram, took Bachchan with him, and left after assuring us that he would keep him under his supervision.

We received news that Bachchan was being interrogated at Seshadripuram station. Ravi and Daniel went there, met Bachchan and spoke to him. K.V.K. Reddy and Bheemaiah were interrogating Bachchan. The former was a strict officer, but we were not afraid as we were not named in any crime.

Since only Ravi knew where I was staying, I asked him to stay with me till Bachchan was released. He agreed. Two other boys, Sardar and Shakeel, were also there with me.

I remember the night Ravi stayed with us. A TV channel was telecasting an offbeat film titled *Chakra*, based on a story about the Bombay underworld. It was about an innocent man who is drawn into a life of crime and when he attempts to get out of it, he is killed. Ravi was drunk and droned on that he would do anything to support me and in return wanted me to help him. By the time the film ended, Ravi had gone to sleep. I was very disturbed by the film.

I did not like Ravi Belagere in the beginning, but gradually because of the commitment he showed towards me, I warmed to him. He very quickly realised that I did not like cheap comments about women, vulgar gestures and loose talk of any sort, and he started behaving very respectably in my presence. After he discovered that I liked ghazals, he would talk about a lot about singers like Jagjit Singh and Ghulam Ali.

While talking about the police, he tried to convince me that since I had Lankesh's support, they would not trouble me so easily.

That night, watching Ravi sleep after having drunk half a bottle, I felt sad that even a journalist as sensitive as he had become entangled in the underworld.

The police kept Bachchan with them for four days.

Strangely, although the police officers initially interrogated him about the underworld, they gradually shifted focus and began asking questions about their own officer, B.K. Shivaram. The first two days neither Ravi nor Daniel could figure out what was happening, but on the third day, after a talk with Bachchan, they realised that the interrogation was about Shivaram. They had mentally tortured Bachchan to find out details about Shivaram's connections with the underworld and also his possible activities. All Bachchan's statements had been recorded.

That evening Daniel called me and Ravi later told me in person a surprising piece of news: they were to produce Bachchan in front of the commissioner and make him give a statement against Shivaram.

By then I had already collected more information about the enquiries that the police department was making against Shivaram. Even before taking Bachchan, they had spoken to Bekkinakanu Rajendra. He had not only given a statement against Shivaram but had also declared that he would stand by it in front of any higher police official. His statement was recorded as well.

One piece of information in Rajendra's statement had drawn the attention of the entire police department.

About a year earlier, Shivaram had gone to Rajendra's house with three jeeps full of policemen. The people in the neighbourhood had recognised that the occupants of one jeep were not policemen. They sported long hair, thick gold chains and bracelets and the people had told Rajendra, who was not at home when Shivaram had gone there, about this.

Rajendra had guessed that they were Muthappa Rai's boys from Mangalore. He had realised that if he had been at home that day, he would have been finished in an 'encounter'.

On the very same day, after consuming two pegs, he had called Shivaram and expressed his anger and helplessness. When Shivaram confessed that if Rajendra had been home he would have been killed in an 'encounter', Rajendra had screamed that he would call a press meet and expose him. Shivaram, who was very careful about his public image, had gone silent after that.

This information had been recorded in Rajendra's statement.

The entire police department was stunned that one of their own was indulging in underworld activities. So the squad formed to control rowdyism had decided to fight an officer and a colleague.

Ravi was thrilled the day Bachchan was being taken in front of the commissioner. He was happy that, within a few days of becoming close to us, he was able to nab an opponent who had been troubling us.

However, I was more anxious than happy. It is never good to be either a friend or a foe of the police. I was very aware that no one can predict when the department will decide to finish a person, and that it is not possible for any one person or gang to break down the system. It was impossible for me to forget how Jayaraj had met his end after fighting with DCP Narayan. It would not surprise me if the same officers who were opposing Shivaram turned the tables on us and developed sympathy towards him.

On the day Bachchan was being taken to the commissioner, Ravi Belagere stayed put at the station. Every hour, from eleven in the morning to three in the afternoon, he called me on the phone and informed me of what was happening. By three o'clock, Bachchan had had a bath and worn the fresh set of clothes that I'd sent with Ravi.

By four o'clock, everything was called off.

To this day nobody will say clearly what happened. Strings were pulled, the commissioner was pressured, and the plan abandoned.

By five o'clock, a very disappointed squad sent Bachchan back home.

That night Bachchan told us about the strange way in which he had been interrogated. The first day, when he had attempted to explain about the underworld activities of Bangalore, they had shouted and stopped him saying, 'Don't tell us what we already know.'

Bachchan was confused and said desperately, 'What do you want me to tell you, Sir, I am not hiding anything.'

When a police officer had threatened him saying, 'What do you know about the Jayaraj murder?' Bachchan immediately understood what was happening. He reasoned that if the police were asking about a murder that had been committed five years ago, there must be something to it. Though Pushpa, Rajendra and others had served a jail term in connection with the Jayaraj murder, everybody in the police department knew that Muthappa Rai was the brain behind it. Also, it was common knowledge that Shivaram had supported Rai. However, it was not recorded anywhere officially.

Bachchan had realised that when he spoke about Shivaram, the officials relaxed, and so he had given out all details about him. When the officials asked him to 'go slow and tell all' and started noting down every detail, not even allowing officials of lower ranks to hear what he was saying, Bachchan realised the seriousness of it.

'I did not really want to reveal everything, but once I started talking I decided it was immaterial whether I told them or not and gave them every detail,' Bachchan said, sharing his anxiety.

We were not disappointed that the disciplinary action against Shivaram had been called off. If that had happened, it would have got enormous publicity and I would have inevitably been a part of it. In those days, I was terrified of publicity.

'Look at the paradox Sreedhar—Shivaram tried to kill two birds with one stone but instead spoilt his reputation. He will never look at you again,' said Ravi, as if hiding his disappointment.

In fact, our actions against Shivaram meant that he naturally tried to curb us. But at that time our real headache was Jayanagar ACP Jayaram.

There are three kinds of police officers.

The first are corrupt officers. For them nothing is more important than their own self-interest. They are not interested in preventing criminal activities. They are not inspired to nab criminals. Their focus is only on the money they can make in each case. They are not prepared to even glance at a case that gives them no opportunity to make money.

The second are officers who are not very corrupt, but will not refuse money if it comes their way. For them money is not everything. They are honest and sincere. They make an effort to safeguard the health of the society and are very humane in nature.

The third are the most sincere and honest. They don't take bribes. They won't even take a cup of coffee from others. They believe that corruption is evil and live an ordinary life. These officers elicit ridicule from one section of society, and great respect from another.

The third category can be further divided into two. One, honest men who practise honesty like they breathe air and don't make a show of their honesty. They don't ridicule corrupt men; instead, they decide it is not their business. Their honesty lies in the foundation of humanitarian considerations.

Opposite to this group are the officers who are honest but who use this honesty to torture others. They constantly announce their honesty and never let anyone forget it. By doing this they try to create an inferiority complex among the corrupt people around them. They are the power corrupt. Since they believe that they are honest, they think it is their birthright to torture others who they think are not honest. They are more cruel than the most corrupt. Their honesty is more dangerous to society than the corrupt.

Jayaram, who was ACP Jayanagar, belonged to the second group.

He had taken charge of the Jayanagar police station much before Balaram's murder and had paid us no attention—we had not committed any crime for him to take notice of us. But after Balaram's murder, though we were in no way connected to it, he started sending his staff to our house without any reason.

In the police department, the lowest cadre is the one that

does all the work and is in touch with things at the grassroot level, but when a crime is solved, the higher officials get all the praise. These lower cadre officers are always well informed about all criminals who are active. Jayaram, however, was not in the state of mind to consult any of his lower grade officers. Anyone speaking up for me in his presence would be reprimanded with his usual question, 'How much money has Sreedhar given you to say this?' For this reason, lower grade policemen who were well-versed with our activities did not bother to tell him anything about us.

However, they would not let us live in peace. Any time of the day and night someone would come and gruffly say, 'ACP is calling,' and leave.

One day I said I had to attend court and hence could not go to meet the ACP. He was furious. After this, whenever he sent word for me to go to the station, I did not go.

But I did not stay at home.

Since Sundaraman's family had returned, we could not stay in his house and we chose to stay at the house of Shafaqat, a boy known to us whose family had gone to Dubai. Ravi Belagere stayed with us—Bachchan, Sardar, Shakeeb and I— there for fifteen days. Every Monday, he would go to the *Lankesh Patrike* office and give them his article. He would gather through others what Lankesh had said about me and report it to me. However, since I was not talking to anybody, I did not know how much of what he said was true and how much was false.

One day, returning from office, he said Lankesh had told Basavaraj that if I wrote about my experiences in the underworld, he would be interested in publishing it. He had also said, 'Sreedhar will not have time to write; it would be good if someone talks to him and writes it for him.'

We both knew that the 'someone' referred to was Ravi.

At the time, I longed to tell my story, but I was caught up with several anxieties and pressures and it was difficult for me to get the mental stability to sit down and write. Though I was always reading, writing was another matter totally. Hence I said that if Ravi Belagere was writing my story, I would agree.

Ravi was always with us and he would take notes when I spoke, write them out in detail and then bring them to me to check. However I said I did not want to read anything till it had reached a certain stage.

All of us knew fairly early on that Ravi was in the habit of praising and playing up to a person when he was in front of him. In my presence, Ravi would be dignified, talking about literature and music, but as soon as I was out of sight, he would turn into a joker. He would begin drinking in the afternoon and tell so many stories that for rowdies in 'no entry', an entertainer like Ravi would be enough. In Shafaqat's house, I would often go upstairs and spend time alone exercising or practising yoga and I would hear Ravi talking to the others downstairs. Though Bachchan was not interested, he would talk at length about the Urdu language. He would refer to Bachchan as Hazarat—the honorific Arabic title. Whenever he had a peg and started talking, everyone would listen enthralled. When he was not around, they would mimic him and have fun.

Ravi was very interested in telling stories about rowdies to rowdies. He would often narrate stories of his days spent with the Bellary rowdies, embellishing facts with his imagination. We could always differentiate between the two, though.

He never spoke about women in my presence, but I knew that he would talk a lot about girls when I wasn't around. He would often take money from me, but never more than what he needed, and every time he asked, it was with a lot of hesitation.

Once I heard him very late in the night, drunk and roaring with laughter.

The next morning, I was sitting on a sofa after I had finished exercising. He came up to me and said he would go home as it was his wedding anniversary. His face was totally swollen.

I got very angry. I said he should behave with some dignity if he was with me. If he continued in the same careless manner, the underworld would treat him like a joker, I shouted. Most importantly, if he did not give up drinking, he could no longer stay with me, I warned.

Ravi stared at me with his eyes wide open.

He said, 'Take out a currency note from your pocket.'

I put my hand in my pocket and took out a fifty-rupee note.

'Write today's date and sign on it,' he said. I did. He took it from me and kept it in his wallet. 'From this minute, I will not drink for any reason—this note is my witness.'

Nobody except me believed that he would give up drinking. That evening, he refused the drink offered to him.

The next day, Ravi and Daniel took me to meet Srinivasulu, the commissioner.

Danny introduced Ravi to the commissioner. Ravi spoke to him in Telugu and within ten minutes had gained his trust. He reminded Srinivasulu about my meeting with him after the attack on Kitty and how my name was dragged into that matter. He also told him that although I was keeping away from underworld activities, the police continued to trouble me.

Immediately Srinivasulu asked, 'Who? B.K. Shivaram?'

Even the police commissioner was of the opinion that Shivaram was troubling me unnecessarily!

I said, 'Not him, but Jayanagar ACP Jayaram.'

He asked why Jayaram was doing this, and I said that my name had been linked with Balaram's murder, after which he had been chasing me.

The commissioner said, 'Sreedhar, I can understand your feelings. I know the drawbacks of this system. However, as a commissioner, I have different priorities and I am restricted by my office. You must understand that. But you must assure me that you will not get involved in any criminal activities. I will talk to Jayaram.' He also said I should meet him in case I had any problem.

From that day, I began to confine myself to the house.

The next day, Jayaram called me and spoke sympathetically, 'We are here to solve your problems. No need to go to senior officials. I had sent my staff to take care of you and not to trouble you,' he said.

However, I knew that if I had not gone to the commissioner, he would not have spoken in such a conciliatory way.

During those days, Kasturirangan was the additional commissioner of Bangalore. He was power hungry to some extent. He had decided that I was an inhuman criminal and stubbornly believed this to be the truth. He found out that Ravi was talking in my favour everywhere and all his attention shifted from me to Ravi. He started telling his officers to investigate Ravi. The lower cadre officers told us about this.

One morning, unable to tolerate the harassment, Ravi went straight to Kasturirangan's office and demanded, 'Why are you investigating me? What have I done?'

Kasturirangan had not expected this. He was totally flustered and, offering water to Ravi, pacified him and asked him to remain calm. He said he had inquired about Ravi as part of a routine check-up about criminals and people associated with them.

When Ravi told me about the meeting, I was upset that he had to face this trouble because of me.

'Ravi, your life would go on even without our friendship. Don't you think you are taking an unnecessary risk?' I asked.

'Just before entering Kasturirangan's office, the thought did cross my mind. I felt I should not have gotten so involved with the underworld.'

'What do you feel now?'

'When I am with you, I feel the risk is nothing,' he said warmly.

In those days, it was as if Ravi forgot the world outside of us. He had even cut off contact with Shivaram, whom he used to meet regularly before. 'I don't ever want to meet him in my life,' he said. All our friends had become his friends and our enemies his enemies.

One day, Shivaram sent two crime branch policemen to talk to me. They asked me to meet them near Nanda Theatre. Ravi accompanied us but sat in the car. The policemen, Honnaiah and Shivalingaiah, made attempts to convince me that Shivaram had no ill feelings towards me. Since Soma's men (Ravi used to refer to him as Deadly Soma) were active, it was very important for me to have Shivaram's support, they said. They insisted that I should speak to Shivaram on the phone. While Honnaiah was talking to me, I noticed that Shivalingaiah was whispering to Bachchan.

I said it was not right for me to speak to Shivaram on the phone and assured them that I would go and meet him in person.

When we were returning, Bachchan said Shivalingaiah had told him to think carefully before taking any decision. 'Tell Sreedhar to be careful. He is intelligent and not hasty. You be very alert,' he had said.

After listening to this, Ravi said, 'Let us not talk to Shivaram at all.' He had included himself in the 'us'.

We developed close ties with him as well. Bachchan, who is never emotional, had bought Ravi two pairs of shoes and taken me with him to buy clothes for Ravi. He also spent eight thousand rupees and had Ravi's motorbike repaired.

Once, when Ravi did not repay the loan he had taken from *Karmaveera*, Shyam Rao, the chief editor, sent people to throw his stuff out of his house, because the company had paid the advance for it.

Ravi appealed to me for help.

Expecting that he would only spend the money if I gave it to him, I paid the advance to the owner directly. Ravi had borrowed money from rowdies before, but whenever he took money from me, his eyes would well up and he would hold my hand emotionally.

One day, I received word that Soma had been killed in an encounter with the police.

Just before he was murdered, we'd heard from our enemies that Soma saw himself as our enemy. However, Ravi had some contact with Soma and his boys, and he said they had never discussed me. However he cautioned me, saying that small boys who craved notoriety would do anything. Since we had never seen Soma, we did not react to his death. We thought it would silence those who were saying that he was our enemy.

Ravi called the *Lankesh Patrike* office and asked Basavaraj to get photos of Soma's body for his article. He wrote the article on Sunday and sent it to *Lankesh Patrike*, which was published every Tuesday.

However, *Ee Vaara*, another weekly, published an article on Soma that had been written by Ravi for *Karmaveera* a long time before. They did not ask Ravi's permission to reprint it. *Ee Vaara* came out on Monday, and when Ravi saw his article in the paper, he was stunned and felt scared that Lankesh would think he had gotten it published.

I consoled him, saying the article was old and Lankesh would know he had not done it deliberately.

On Tuesday, not only was Ravi's article missing in *Lankesh Patrike*, but there was an editorial by Lankesh criticising Ravi. Lankesh had one weakness: when he decided something was true, he never consulted anyone or discussed it with anyone to confirm that it was in fact the truth. Lankesh not only said bad things about Ravi, but also attacked me indirectly. 'Those who are close to rowdies are as dirty as the rowdies ... I have rejected an article written by a dirty fellow ...' and so on.

Ravi collapsed after reading the editorial. He said that he was now completely cut off from *Lankesh Patrike*. I felt very bad for him and I suggested that he write for *Ee Vaara*. He met the publisher, Satyamurthy Ananduru, and explained the situation. They agreed to let him write for their paper.

Amidst all these problems, my younger brother, who is a sub-inspector, was suspended in a case that he was not even aware of. Those were days filled with anxiety for me. Balaram had been murdered; Lankesh, who I thought would support me, had deserted us; and my brother was suspended from work. All these things kept me on my toes. However, I did not lose courage. I tried to face everything with patience.

Ravi started writing for *Ee Vaara*. In one edition, he wrote a very demeaning article about BJP MLA Suresh Kumar's wife.

He had written quite overtly about a possible relationship between Suresh Kumar's wife and Bekkinakanu Rajendra.

Daniel immediately called me. Nobody would take a derogatory article written about one's wife lightly, and Suresh Kumar would hit back at Ravi, he said. And since everybody knew that Ravi was with me, all those opposing him would attack me, he pointed out.

I did not like Ravi's article. I knew that it was through Suresh Kumar's wife, who was an employee of the Kannada daily *Samyukta Karnataka*, that Ravi had met Rajendra. Ravi was quite friendly with Rajendra too. To demean Suresh Kumar's wife, just because she was with *Samyukta Karnataka*, was wrong, I felt.

That evening I met Ravi near lawyer C.V. Nagesh's office. We had come to meet Nagesh as he was handling my brother's case. I am usually calm, but as soon as I saw Ravi I got very angry and started shouting.

'Forget Suresh; what did Nagesh say?' Ravi asked casually. I said his article was more important than that.

All of a sudden Ravi's demeanour changed. Both anger and helplessness played simultaneously on his face.

'Okay, I say,' he said and sped away on his motorbike.

I did not calm down even after he left; I continued to shout. But Bachchan was very worried by the way Ravi had sped away.

'Now Ravi will start drinking again, and you will never be able to control him anymore,' he said.

I had not thought of that. Ravi had not had a drink even during a seminar with writers, and that had made me believe he would never relapse. But after hearing Bachchan's words, I became worried, and we decided to look for Ravi.

From South End Circle where lawyer Nagesh's office was situated, we went to the wine store near his house and waited. After about ten minutes, Ravi came there. He parked his motorbike near our car, came up to me and put his hand on my shoulder through the window.

'Hey, Sreedhar,' he started to talk but could not as his eyes had welled up. He couldn't continue. I also felt emotional.

Controlling myself I said, 'They said you would go and drink . . .'

Ravi said, 'You are like my elder brother, Sreedhar. Who else but you can scold me?'

~

For some unknown reason, *Ee Vaara* stopped accepting Ravi's articles and he was once again without a job. He applied for a position with *Prajavani*. The process would take a while, and so Ravi began spending more time with us.

Meanwhile, Koli Fayaz was killed in Shivajinagar. It had no effect on us. Life had assumed a steady routine.

One day Ashwath, a Youth Congress man, told me that Ravi was planning to start a weekly. I laughed at first; we thought it was a joke. We even told him so.

The next day, we went to see Ravi. We sat on a stone bench near his house and chatted for a long time. He did not mention any plans to start a weekly.

Finally, I asked him, 'What . . . I heard that you want to start a paper?'

He laughed and said, 'Just thinking . . . what if I start a tabloid called "Hello Bangalore"?'

I was not at all agreeable to the idea. Dozens of weeklies had started and died after *Lankesh Patrike* came into existence. Also, by then it had been established that he was a member of our gang. I knew that whoever he criticised would turn on us. More importantly, he did not have the finances for the venture. I had been to his house. When we went there, I sat on the one broken chair there. Ravi spread a mat for Bachchan to sit on, but since Ravi himself had nowhere to sit, Bachchan stood and drank his tea. The minute I entered that house, I realised that the children were the real sufferers. Ravi could have given them a good life through his talent, but his drinking habit had made their life miserable.

We left and within an hour's time bought some chairs and a TV for his children. When we took them there, Ravi cried and I had to console him.

In such a situation, how could he start a paper?

'Are you mad?' I shouted. 'Is it a joke to run a weekly? Can you reach a circulation of ten thousand a week? Who gave you this idea?'

'I know why you are saying this, Sreedhar. I know whatever I do will reflect on you. You stay out of this from the beginning . . .' he said seriously.

I stopped talking and let him and Bachchan speak. I realised that he was very serious about this idea, and it was useless to argue with him.

Finally I said, 'Okay Ravi, but be very careful.'

Now Ravi relaxed, 'You don't know, Sreedhar. Even if I reach five thousand it's enough. You don't know the power of a newspaper.'

I suggested he use writers who were not close to Lankesh. He agreed. He was planning to take a loan from his friends and, 'If that is not enough, you are there.'

I said, 'Of course.'

At that time, Ravi collected funds from people I'd introduced him to. Those who gave him money would tell me about it within hours. Ravi never informed me about it and I never asked him.

Next, he started looking for a name. Someone had already registered 'Hello Bangalore'. We could not locate that person.

Finally I said, 'Why not "Hi"?'

He immediately agreed and started looking into it. He got it without any problem.

He then converted a room near his house into an office.

At one stage he said he would take advertisements. I said I didn't think that was a good idea. Whenever he got into trouble, I would help him, I assured him.

The weekly *Hi Bangalore* was launched without any fanfare. Ravi worked day and night. Seethanadi Surendra, Nivedita,

Satish and Tulasiram joined him. For the first five weeks it made a soft entry into the market. Slowly, it began growing.

People thought it was my weekly and Ravi was only running it. B.K. Shivaram even told his staff sarcastically, 'See, Sreedhar finally started his own paper . . . now society will definitely improve.'

The first week, Ravi did not take money from me. From the second week he started taking money for printing. When I was not at home, he would take money from my wife. I felt it was my moral duty to give him money as I had closed all other doors for him, but I did not want to get more involved than that. I knew that whoever he criticised would complain to me.

After eight weeks, he asked me if I could arrange for security for a bank loan so that he could procure newsprint wholesale and work comfortably for several months. I asked him how much money he needed. He said two lakh rupees. The very next day I received some money from the sale of land I had invested in. I gave two lakh rupees from this to Ravi.

After this, there was no need for him to ask me for money again. Even a year-and-a-half after starting the weekly, Ravi took money from me only on two occasions: once when purchasing a Maruti car, and the second time to give to serial killer Ravindra Prasad as he wanted to write about him.

Once, he expressed his wish to return my money but I refused. Three months after starting the paper, he shifted his office to the *Sangathi* office, which belonged to a friend of mine called Venkatesh. By then his weekly was well established and had a good circulation.

Ravi then embarked on a method to increase circulation that I would not tolerate. I felt disgusted with him for the first time. Before *Hi Bangalore* completed a year, news of Ravi's roll call, or extortion, began to circulate. For me, who had spent a decade in the underworld, roll call was not shocking, but when I heard the rumour that it was for my safety, I felt disgusted.

There was a reason for such a rumour to spread.

Ravi often heard news of threats being made against him

when he targeted someone in his weekly. We tried to pacify him saying that they were only rumours, but he was still scared. Once he had written against Balagangadharanatha Swamy and two weeks later called me to say that he'd heard Shekhar Swamiji, Kulla Shantha, Venkatesh and two others from the mutt were plotting to kill him. I dismissed these stories as exaggerations, but he wasn't convinced and would not calm down. Finally I called Kulla Shantha and arranged a meeting with Ravi at the Cosmopolitan Club. On the phone, Shantha said that although none of them liked Ravi's way of writing, they were not thinking of killing him. But he hinted that there were others who were ready to do the job.

'Ravi is like my younger brother . . . I will not tolerate any harm done to him,' I said gruffly.

However, when Nanje Gowda expressed his displeasure with Ravi, I could not speak in the same tone.

Nanje Gowda was one of the toughest politicians our country has seen. In Parliament, he had said to Rajiv Gandhi's face, 'You came to power in front of your mother's dead body,' and resigned.

When Ravi wrote about him disrespectfully and criticised him, it angered him no end. He called Ravi, but he had asked his daughter to tell the politician that he was not at home. An angry Nanje Gowda screamed, 'To which brothel has he gone so early in the morning? I know he is at home and he is scared to come to the phone . . . you tell him everything I am telling you now. After reading what your father has written about me, hundreds of people have come from Hassan and are asking me to get ready a bier to take a body home . . .'

Upon receiving such threats, Ravi would rush to my house. I was angry that Nanje Gowda had conveyed all this through Ravi's daughter. Also, I felt it was not proper for him to issue a death threat. I knew many who were close to Nanje Gowda and I expressed my irritation through them.

I don't know what his reaction was, and Ravi too did not write about him again, but the threatening calls from swamis, politicians and several unidentified persons continued. He became paranoid. He often requested my help and I became tired of consoling him.

I called Rajendra and spoke with him about this. He cut me short. 'Guru, he called me ten minutes ago. Nobody is threatening him, he is obsessed with it. You don't worry about it,' he said.

The one good thing that happened after Ravi started the paper was that inspector B.K. Shivaram stopped troubling me. Ravi would say, 'Whether it is Shivaram or anybody else, if anyone troubles you, I will not keep quiet. I will catch them by the collar.'

Once there was a shootout involving a jockey in front of Race Course. Everybody knew that Muthappa Rai had no hand in it, but Ravi wrote an article putting the blame on him. I had not read the article—I never read *Hi Bangalore*; I only found out when Ravi brought the paper to me and showed the report to me.

I was alarmed. 'No Ravi, everybody knows that Rai has no hand in it, why did you write this?' I asked.

'We have to somehow nab him through the police,' Ravi said.

'Ravi, never attempt anything like that—I didn't even know you had written this. Rai will think that I got it written through you. He cannot do anything to me, but you are a sitting target. For no reason should it become public that you belong to my gang; otherwise it becomes a problem for me to protect you.'

The next day, he got a call from Muthappa Rai. According to what Ravi told me, Rai had challenged him saying, 'Sreedhar has made you write that article. You should not have written it without confirming anything. If I tell you what Sreedhar is doing, will you write about that?'

After this incident, Ravi did not attempt to criticise either Rai or any other rival of mine. In a way, a mutual protection equation had developed between us.

However, when Ravi started targeting call girls to increase his circulation, I felt disgusted.

It is not easy to run a magazine. One has to constantly search for interesting topics to lure readers. Ravi started using a community that had already lost its voice. This not only angered me, but also all people with a conscience. What especially sickened me was the way he toyed with the lives of prostitutes. He would not only write about them but would have their places raided by the police. On the one hand, the paper was titillating young boys with sensational write-ups about prostitutes, and on the other, police raided their places. Those were the most troublesome days for Bangalore's prostitutes.

Ravi once wrote about a raid that he and a police officer had conducted on one such house in Yeshwanthpur as if it were a great victory. I was furious. I went to his office immediately. I met writer-journalist Prathibha Nandakumar there for the first time. As soon as we were introduced, she touched my feet and said, 'Thanks for saving Ravi.' I felt embarrassed.

After having tea with them I took Ravi out and spoke to him in the car. 'What are you doing, Ravi?' I asked.

He started boasting about what he'd done, not realising I was angry.

I shouted at him. 'What . . . are you becoming an informer? Your job is to report, not to take the police with you and threaten people . . .'

Ravi assured me he would not do such a thing again. But he never stopped writing about prostitutes. He would befriend people in the racket, get information about others and write sensational reports. It was rumoured that filmstar Tara was informing him about extras in films who were involved in this business.

Along with this, rumours of his roll call also started spreading far and wide.

I have never been to a prostitute in my life but many of my acquaintances were not really like Sriramachandra. From them, I started getting news about Ravi's roll call activities.

By then I had already heard that Ravi was taking money from politicians. He had sought money from former chief minister and Deve Gowda's son H.D. Kumaraswamy to celebrate the first anniversary of the weekly in style. Kumaraswamy initially said he would give the money but later reneged on his promise.

I was not bothered about this, but when I heard that he was destroying the lives of prostitutes, I was shocked. When I questioned him about it a couple of times, he flatly denied it. However, when the prostitutes who paid up started complaining to me, I felt very bad. I expressed my inability to tackle Ravi as it was a very delicate matter.

By then *Lankesh Patrike* had published articles for two weeks running, strongly criticising how Ravi was running his paper based on stories about prostitutes. Though Ravi published some write-ups in retaliation, he never bothered to deny the allegations. Instead, he reported how sales of *Lankesh Patrike* had gone down after his weekly started. (To this day he equals right and wrong with sales!)

Around that time, an incident took place that disturbed Ravi for some time. His younger daughter, who was studying in the seventh standard at the time, went missing after school hours. The school authorities said she had left the premises in the afternoon. Naturally all sorts of rumours spread and Ravi believed that four people had kidnapped her in a car.

'I heard the prostitutes were saying that people would not let go of me . . . maybe they are capable of doing anything . . .' he said, terribly worried.

I consoled him and asked our boys to search for her. Ravi did not want to lodge a police complaint. He was afraid that instead of finding her they would publicise the issue and get sadistic pleasure from it.

At half past seven that evening, his daughter called me on the phone. She had gone to Nelamangala with two of her friends, she said. She was calling from the bus stand. I asked Loki to get them.

The reason why Ravi felt the police would not help him was because he was severely critical of them in his paper. Once he wrote against police commissioner Shankar Bidri and I started getting calls from everywhere. He wrote that Bidri had raped a twelve-year-old girl when he was on the hunt for Veerappan. Officers who respected Bidri were outraged. Once, inspector B.C. Patil called me at midnight and warned me saying, 'Everyone thinks it is your paper Sreedhar, you will have to pay for all this.'

I was very upset with Ravi and warned him not to exaggerate in his paper. Finally Ravi agreed to meet Shankar Bidri through Patil. I organised the meeting at Patil's house, but I was not present. Ravi, who had been off alcohol till then, drank that day. I was worried that he would start drinking again, but he promised me he would not.

Despite all the problems, for the first two years of the weekly, I was relieved because the police stayed off my back. I started making trips to dargahs and ashrams, places I'd been attracted to since my younger days. I'd always been strongly drawn towards the lives of sufis and sanths.

At this time, I told Ravi that we should meet Shivaram and make peace with him. He agreed. We met him in the beginning of 1997. He spoke to us affectionately and suggested that we get out of the underworld. About Muthappa Rai, he said, 'You be careful, but I will see to it that you come to no harm from him.'

We trusted Shivaram's words, but it would be something that we would end up regretting. Rai had moved a long way ahead and was beyond listening to Shivaram. We believed that he would not act against Shivaram's orders, but how wrong we were.

Seven

It was the first of July, 1997.

In those days, Bachchan stayed at 6th Phase, JP Nagar. He would come to my house every day at ten in the morning, and leave at five-thirty in the evening. He had a reason for this precise, government official-type timing. Neither the owner of his rented house nor his neighbours knew who he was. He had told them he had a real estate office in Basavanagudi. So he would leave home at nine-thirty in the morning. If his neighbours discovered who he was, naturally the police would come to know and they would force him to leave their station limits. That is a mistake police make. They should instead keep track of rowdies in their area; it makes it easy for policemen to tackle them when the need arises.

That day too, Bachchan came exactly at ten o'clock. He had to go to court. In those days, I had a Maruti Esteem. Bachchan always drove and I sat to his left. I didn't trust anyone else in the driver's seat. Bachchan and I were co-accused in most cases, but there were a few in which only he was charged. That day, one such case was to be heard.

It has an interesting history.

In 1993, Shivaram had arrested Bachchan in front of Airlines Hotel. There were no warrants or complaints against him, but he was kept in lock-up for three days while the police tried to figure out what to charge him with. A case had been registered in Frazer Town station about a forgery. Several boys including Kalapathar, Tanveer, Kalakar Balakrishna and others were named in it. This word 'others' is very useful. When it suits them, the police may categorise anyone they see fit under 'others'.

Shivaram slid Bachchan into this grouping in the forgery case and sent him to jail. But on the day of the crime, Bachchan had actually been arrested in another case at the Central Station and a chargesheet had also been submitted in court. But not a single lawyer or judge or senior police official bothered to question how a man arrested and put in lock-up could be one of the 'others' accused in a crime that had happened outside. When I brought it up, I got responses like, 'So what? ... Bachchan is fitted in so many false cases and this is one such ... never mind!'

Anyway, that day when Bachchan came home, he said he would go to the court in connection with this case. Usually no one but Bachchan drove that car, but when I went out and informed him it was time for him to go to court, Bachchan was smoking. A new recruit, Srinivas, or Seena as he was known, without waiting for him to react, said, 'You smoke and I will drive.' He took the keys and started the car.

Seena had joined us about six months before. He came from a rich family but had lost a lot of money as a result of his wasteful habits. When he came to me in search of a job through my friend Krishnamurthy, I had flatly refused to employ him because of his ways.

He had then written me a long letter. I can never forget some lines from it. '*Anna*, I know there are boys with you who are stronger than me. I am neither stronger nor more courageous than them. But if on any occasion you are in danger, I will give my life and save you ...'

I yielded. I felt bad for this boy who had seen better days. I took him in and though we never treated him like an employee, he would do the job of a driver.

Mehmood, another one of our boys, joined them. Seena sat in the driver's seat, Bachchan in the place I usually took and Mehmood behind him.

In those days Bachchan and I would roam the streets freely. In fact when we went to Ravi's housewarming, Rajendra had warned us not to be so careless. But we believed that after the talk with Shivaram, Rai would not harm us in any way.

I was not a good mood that day. The previous night I had had an argument with a close associate and when I raised my voice in anger, that person cried and cut the call. When I tried to call back, I found that my phone was out of order. I could not sleep that night. When I checked in the morning, the phone was still out of order. I was so worked up that I went to my neighbour's house and asked to use their phone, and they obliged. I consoled my friend and returned home.

Just as I was climbing the steps to go up to my room, I heard an auto-rickshaw stop in front of our gate and bent down to see who it was. Then I heard someone banging on the door, 'Sreedhar, open the door, quick . . .'

It was Bachchan's voice.

I immediately knew something was wrong. It had been only ten minutes since he'd left for court.

I opened the door and Bachchan rushed in, his clothes soaked in blood. 'Sreedhar . . . don't get tense . . . attacked . . .' His distress evident on his face, he said, 'Seena out.'

'Seena is dead?' I asked, half hoping that Bachchan was mistaken.

'He was driving and as soon as a bullet pierced his head he fell forward on the steering wheel . . .' he said, and described everything to me.

Within ten minutes of leaving home, near Kadirenahalli Main Road, a Maruti van had driven up next to them. Mehmood, who was sitting behind, first noticed it and saw that the door was slightly open. Immediately he said, 'Maam . . . danger . . .' and put his head down. Bachchan in a flash slid to the floor of the car and told Seena, 'Seena, don't panic, drive fast.'

But Seena made an amateurish mistake. He turned and looked at the van. If he had just stepped on the accelerator, he could have lived.

But the minute he turned to look, a bullet flashed from that car and went through his head. Just by the sound of the gun, Bachchan could tell that it was not only a bullet but also gun powder. Seena's entire face was blasted to pieces and his body collapsed on the steering wheel.

The Maruti van had stopped around ten feet from the Esteem. Two men began pumping bullets into the car. About eleven shots were fired at the seat I usually occupied. Bachchan was shielded as he had slid to the floor. The men assumed that the person sitting next to the driver had been killed. They got down from their car and started walking toward our vehicle.

Bachchan and Mehmood, who were waiting for the second when the firing would stop, opened the door and jumped out of the car. The shooters were taken aback.

Bachchan hid behind a house under construction and Mehmood screamed and ran in the direction of the attackers' van and into the PST Hostel compound.

The attackers fired bullets at both of them. Mehmood was hit in the back. Perhaps since he was screaming the shooters could aim at him.

Bachchan was more angry than scared. Earlier, when he carried arms—bombs and longs—we were not attacked. And now, barely a month after talking to Shivaram, they had been attacked. He was fuming.

But he didn't have anything with which to strike back. Besides, the shooters had guns. He picked up bricks and stones from the construction site and hurled them in the direction of the van.

Since the area in which they were attacked was home to many of our boys, Bachchan was emboldened. The building behind which he stood was actually being constructed by an associate of ours, Anwar. He was standing on top, checking something, when he heard the sound of bullets being fired and looked down. First he couldn't fathom what was happening, but when he saw Bachchan and Mehmood run, he knew. He shouted for help. Within seconds a large crowd gathered.

All this happened in a matter of two minutes.

When an attacker realises that the situation is out of his control, he tries to escape. The assailants ran away.

Bachchan then came to the car. Seena was dead. Mehmood joined him, limping and with blood flowing down his back.

Most of the people had not grasped what had happened. Many thought a film was being shot. When they saw Seena, they were shocked.

Bachchan showed presence of mind even in such a situation. He put Mehmood in an auto-rickshaw and asked him to go to a nursing home. He then asked a bystander to take him to the police station on his bike. That man was so shocked that he requested Bachchan to ride.

The station was on the way to our house. Bachchan wanted to alert me first before going to the police—he had realised, by the way they had fired at the side where I usually sat, that the attackers wanted to target me. But when he rode the bike past the station, the man started screaming and asking where he was taking him. So Bachchan had to stop the bike; he thanked him and then took an auto-rickshaw to my house.

Bachchan recounted all these details in three minutes. By then the Kumaraswamy Layout police came in a jeep to our house and took Bachchan to the station to record his statement. Before going Bachchan warned, 'They will know by now that you are safe. Take care—call the boys . . .'

The phone, which had been dead till then, rang that very minute. A boy known to us, who was working in the telephone exchange, had seen the attack and had tried to inform me. When he realised that the phone was dead, he had set it right and then called.

The next call was from my younger brother. He was very upset. I consoled him. Another police officer called and said, 'Sreedhar, they think they have finished you. They may attack your home. Don't worry about the police, keep a gun or bomb or whatever . . .'

I was shaking with anger and helplessness. My wife Latha let our two dogs loose and came to me and, although fear filled her eyes, said, 'Calm yourself . . . it should not have happened, but it has . . .'

I heard a car turning with great speed on to our road. I went up. The vehicle stopped in front of our house and Ravi Belagere got down.

As he came in asking questions, another Maruti van came and stopped in front. It was Bachchan. I was surprised that Bachchan had returned from the station within ten minutes.

'Sreedhar, I was standing in front of the station. The way Ravi was driving his car shocked me . . . I thought something must have happened and I jumped into a van of a friend who was passing by and came here.'

'I heard Sreedhar was attacked and one spot death . . . how else can I come?' Ravi asked, shocked.

Then Inspector Siddappa came rushing in a jeep since Bachchan had fled without even telling him what had happened, and he took Bachchan back with him.

Talking to Ravi, I let out my anger that I had controlled till then and I started screaming that I would destroy the entire Rai gang and if Shivaram came between us I would not take it anymore.

Ravi was equally angry.

By then the news had spread and boys began to gather. All of Bangalore, including the police, thought I had been attacked. Even the police control room announced that two people had escaped and I had been killed on the spot. It took about twenty minutes for the police to discover that it was not I who had been killed. By then the police had ordered *nakabandi* in four places.

Journalists who rang me were confused when I answered. Daniel called and said, 'Thank god! I got the news you were dead.'

By eleven o'clock hundreds of boys had gathered in front of my house.

Half an hour later, Revanasiddaiah, who had recently taken

charge as commissioner, arrived at Kumaraswamy Layout station and sent for me. DCP Jayaprakash and inspector Ashok Kumar were also present. When they asked who had attacked the car, I said, 'Muthappa Rai's gang.'

'Reason?'

'Old rivalry.'

But the officials were not willing to believe this. If I'd had differences with Rai in 1992, would he wait for five years to take revenge?

I reasoned, 'It is only six to seven months since he has moved to Dubai. If he had not left India, he definitely would not have attacked.'

'You mean if he was in Madikeri and had attacked you, you would have retaliated, and he knew this?'

'No Sir, in that case he would not have escaped the police, isn't it?' I tried explaining.

But Revanasiddaiah and Jayaprakash were convinced the attack was because of a deal gone sour. They asked me to give details of deals in which we'd had differences, but there had never been any friction between Rai and me in any case. Finally, Ashok Kumar, who was well informed about the Bangalore underworld, convinced them that it was true.

'Now where to look for them?' Revanasiddaiah asked Ashok Kumar. He turned to me.

I said, 'If the shooters are from Bombay, they would have left in a car by now.'

'What about by flight?' asked the commissioner.

'There is less chance of that.'

He looked at Ashok Kumar and said, 'Search is on everywhere . . . keep an eye on the railway station, airport—'

I interrupted him. 'Sir, I don't think they will go by train.'

'That is exactly why I said we should look there. They know that you're acquainted with their methods since you were with them. So they will use a tactic that you will not anticipate.'

I realised then that he had gained great expertise during his stint at the CBI.

After the attack, I had to face two kinds of disturbances. One, I had to take a stand on how to react to the attack, and second, I had to deal with the police.

Just because he had left the country did not mean Rai was not active through the police. Till he left the country, his name was not registered in a single case. But within fifteen days of his departure, he figured in a crime—the murder of timber merchant DeSilva in Madikeri.

In fact, we had anticipated that Rai would attempt an attack on us as well. We had heard earlier that he was talking of attacking us even before he left the country, but we had not bothered much about it. We would gruffly retort that we too would bomb and destroy him. So we had anticipated that he would attack, and we were actually prepared to counterattack. Even when he left the country, we were extremely cautious. It was only after our conversation with Shivaram that we relaxed. Though Shivaram had cautioned us and told us to be careful, we firmly believed that Rai would not attack without his consent. Even after the attack, we held a faint suspicion that Shivaram might support Rai, but we knew he'd had no hand in the attack.

Later in the day, some boys and I, along with Ravi, went to Seena's house and informed his family of what had happened. Even four hours after his death, his family members were not aware of it. By the time I could make them understand what had happened, I felt I would totally collapse.

When I returned, the Bangalore boys were already preparing a counterattack. 'Saar, there are two singing joints frequented by the Mangalore boys . . . we are setting them on fire tonight,' they said.

Tanveer had been brought from Mysore jail by the police that same day because he too had a case coming up in court. He had heard that the Rai gang wanted to finish him too. He called me on the phone and said, 'Saar, now we cannot keep quiet. I will tell my boys to attack a hotel on Brigade Road (belonging to a Rai associate) and destroy it.'

Everyone was waiting for my order.

Whenever there is an attack in the underworld, three kinds of pressures build up.

One is from associates. The underworld survives on propaganda. Every don depends on it to boost his power and persona. Those who crave to be dons intentionally fuel such propaganda. For instance, once a newspaper had published a report that Kotwal Ramachandra had raised his machete at the then chief minister Ramakrishna Hegde. Of course, it was an absolute lie, but Kotwal never once denied it. Not just that, he would even dramatically enact how Hegde had raised his hands and got scared! Boys of such dons narrate hundreds of stories about their boss. When such a don does not react to an attack on his life, people get disillusioned. Hence dons retaliate after an attack and the stronger the counterattack, the more his image grows.

The second pressure is from rivals. When an attack fails, the rivals are stunned. An attack requires financial backing and several months of planning. More than the rival don, those who benefit from an attack are people who are dependent on him. Hence, when an attack fails, the don immediately makes another attempt in order to maintain his image. Also, he creates a wave of negative publicity about the rival who has escaped. Within four to five hours of the attack on me, the Rai gang spread the rumour that I had decided to flee Bangalore!

The third pressure comes from the police.

For the police, neither Sreedhar nor Rai is important; maintaining law and order is what is important. On a personal level, some policemen may identify themselves with a gang, but when an attack happens, a close vigil is kept on both gangs. Commissioner Revanasiddaiah had warned me through Bachchan: 'If you retaliate, I will attack you.'

I discussed my options with some of my police officer friends. They all felt that since Rai was in Dubai, and nobody in the department, except for a few, had any sympathy for him, it was not wise to attempt an attack and draw police attention towards me.

Only one officer said angrily: 'Don't just sit there, take a couple of sten guns and shoot and kill a couple of his men!'

The problem was: who to attack? Though we had no doubt that it was Rai who had arranged the attack, neither the police nor I had any clue about who had carried it out. If Bachchan had given a statement that he could not identify any of the attackers, it would have weakened the case, so he had named some of Rai's followers in Bangalore. But even Bachchan was doubtful about how many of them had actually participated in the attack. There was no other way out: whether they were party to it or not, we had to crush Rai's backbone in Bangalore. The police started chasing the men Bachchan had named, and also those he had not mentioned.

In such a situation, I did not want to retaliate, but the boys disagreed. Finally we all came to a conclusion. We decided not to trouble innocent men just because they were known to Rai, but to catch hold of anyone who may have been a participant in the attack, 'repair' them first, and then hand them over to the police. However, I warned all the boys that we should not shift the police heat from Rai to us.

Then we discussed whether I should remain at home or shift. Even Ravi did not want me to stay at home. He had just then purchased a house next to his rented home, and he suggested I stay in the big room upstairs. I refused. Even if I had left home for a week, my enemies could capitalise on that and start a negative campaign. When I had confronted Muthappa Rai, I had said he had only guns, whereas I had boys. When it was time for me put my words to the test, I thought it was incorrect to step aside.

Though they didn't like the idea, all the boys agreed.

However, given that I was in the habit of trusting people easily, Bachchan decided to stay with me. Bachchan has committed to the decision he took that day. If he hadn't, things would have turned out totally different. More than him, the way his family accepted his decision surprises and makes me feel proud too. It's only in such critical situations that the strength or feebleness of a relationship is revealed. Though Bachchan was always dear to me, the way he has set aside his own interests for someone else and stood by his commitment is extraordinary.

Of course, there is a huge gang of boys who are willing to give their life for me to this day.

For two months, though I did not like it much, we had to torture a few people. A man, Bannaje Raja, whose name I had never heard, had called a newspaper office and claimed that he was responsible for the attack. We thought it was a strategy Rai had adopted to turn the police's attention away from his boys.

After reading about this in the newspaper, some boys used Bannaje Raja's name and attempted to threaten members of our gang. We chased them. I personally participated in one such chase. On one occasion we caught three men. Though I had given strict instructions that they should not be hurt, Bachchan, Layout Manja and others beat up two of them badly.

I finally decided it was not correct to act in this manner and put an end to it.

Within three months of the attack, the police arrested and chargesheeted about fifteen men connected with Rai in one way or the other. They included lawyer Santosh Kumar, Kini, Sudheer Prabhu, Satish and others, some of whom I had not even heard of. However, the police had not 'fitted' them without reason. All of them had supported the attack in one way or the other. Though some were hesitant to carry out the plan, when Sharad Shetty of Bombay himself gave the order, they could not refuse.

I should record here the state of the city's underworld after the failed attack.

Dons Pushpa and Kalapathar never mentioned the attack to me, not even once. Whenever I called them for anything they would speak to the point and then cut the call as quickly as possible. Tanveer was with us, but he was in jail and hence of no use. Bekkinakanu Rajendra called every morning. He was willing to risk anything for us, but I didn't want to use him as he was extricating himself from the underworld. Bomb Krishnamurthy, although not always in our midst, would appear within minutes of a phone call. Layout Manja, Loki and Kantha stood by us. And with them came a battalion of boys.'

After about two months, things returned to normal. Most of Rai's boys were in jail and we turned to our daily routine.

At the time, there was a great rivalry between Layout Manja and Krishnappa, and it was intensifying. I tried to make peace between them. Though initially opposed to the idea, Manja agreed, but Krishnappa initially refused to even meet him. Eventually, they both agreed to meet.

One day, at around eleven o'clock in the morning, Manja came home and we waited for Krishnappa's call. After half an hour, Krishnappa called and said he was ready to meet.

'Where shall we meet?' I asked him.

'Where else? We will come to your house,' he said.

By then Manja was a regular figure in our house. I didn't want Krishnappa to feel awkward, so I said, 'Let us meet in Ravi Belagere's office. We will go first and you come later.' He agreed.

I called Ravi and told him about our meeting in his office and asked him to call Krishnappa and fix the time.

Two minutes later Ravi called me and said, 'What's this Sreedhar? Krishnappa is backtracking from what he said earlier? He is asking, "Why is Sreedhar interested in making peace between us? Why should we bother about it, let's keep quiet".'

I got angry. After several rounds of discussions, Krishnappa had agreed to meet and was now backing out. I didn't like it. However I didn't want to create more trouble between Manja and Krishnappa either. I asked Ravi to be patient.

Two weeks later, Loki and Manja came to meet me after they had visited Ravi's office. Manja had a strange look on his face. Loki told me about their conversation with Ravi. According to him, Ravi had said, 'Sreedhar does not like fighting, that's why he is asking you to compromise. But you are in every way stronger than Krishnappa . . . I know that. He is hiding because of you; if you finish him, it will be good for you and Sreedhar as well. Right now, he is forever a danger.'

When Manja had expressed his helplessness saying, 'Whatever I do I am not able to catch him', Ravi had assured him, 'Leave it to me, he comes where I ask him to come, I will arrange that . . .'

I was furious. Now I realised why Krishnappa had changed his stand after his assurances to me. The possibility of Krishnappa deciding against the peace meeting because of Ravi was more likely.

Ravi had once written against Krishnappa. Wanting to retaliate, Krishnappa had arranged, through Muniratnam, for Ravi to be taken to the Best Club. Before he could tackle Ravi, however, Krishnappa had got into a fight with the club people and Ravi was saved. I realised Ravi was taking revenge on Krishnappa for this.

But none of us in the underworld wanted any fight between the Bangalore boys. We were worried that it would give Rai hope that he could get active again.

I called Ravi and shouted at him. I said it was wrong to talk to young boys about fighting.

Ravi brushed me off. 'Krishnappa must go . . . it will be good for you,' he said.

Realising it was useless talking to him, I warned Manja, Loki and the others never to step into Ravi's office again. They had to agree to it.

In the clash between me and Rai, the Bangalore police naturally supported me. Since I was available 24x7, they felt I was less dangerous. If Rai were to become powerful again in Bangalore, they would not be able to arrest him since he was out of the country, and the situation would be volatile. They felt I could not attempt any crime as they were keeping a strict vigil on me.

In a way, it was true.

Ravi once again organised a meeting between Shivaram and us at his office and helped clear some doubts. Though we were not cordial like before, at least some differences were sorted out.

After the attack on us, Shivaram had arrested Sudheer Prabhu and his gang. But we knew that Sudheer Prabhu was always drunk, and there was no possibility of him having participated in the attack on us. It was not just us—the entire police department knew Shivaram had made that arrest only to prevent the police from focusing on others from the Rai gang who actually were active.

Sudheer Prabhu's arrest was very dramatic. He was arrested while in the company of women in a retreat on the Bangalore-Mysore highway. But what I learnt later was that the day before his arrest, Sudheer Prabhu along with his lawyer, Santosh Kumar, had met and discussed with officials how his arrest should take place! The officials had assured him they would release him after recording his statement and so Sudheer Prabhu had volunteered to get entangled in the situation. However, later the officials who were investigating the attack on us did not release him.

When we discussed this with Shivaram, he was stunned. He criticised the officials who had taken him to the resort and agreed that my doubts were correct.

Exactly one year after the failed attack on me, I decided to start a weekly. But it was not a spur of the moment decision. I'd wanted to start a paper from when I was twenty. Even when I was writing my law exams, I was not interested in becoming a lawyer. I wrote my IAS exam when I was doing my final year law. Since I had not done well in two papers, I had to interview for the IPS. Though I scored well in these interviews, I decided to apply for the IAS again. But I never got the chance to do the exam again.

I was then twenty-two.

I decided to start a four-page weekly when I was twenty-three. I still remember my friend Agrahara Krishnamurthy saying, 'It's not important to be a success, it's okay if you are, but do start a paper . . .'

It was Lankesh who stopped me from taking such a step and suggested I get into business. Before I could take a decision on this, I had entered the underworld. But Lankesh started his weekly and made history.

While I was with Jayaraj, we did discuss starting a paper, but nothing came of those plans.

When Ravi started *Hi Bangalore*, I felt there was no need for me to start another paper of my own, but within two years it had become impossible for me to even look at his weekly—the journalism practised in it went so totally against my beliefs.

I began to feel again that I wanted to start my own paper. If there had been no attack on me, I would have started a paper at the end of 1997. But seeing Ravi's emotional reaction to the attack, I again felt there was no need for me to do so. When I was attacked, Ravi had written about it under the title, 'My friend shall come back from the ashes like a phoenix'.

It is ironic that I decided to call my weekly *Agni*.

Here I must tell you an interesting incident that occurred during the time when the attack on me took place in 1997. I have explained how Ravi was at my house within half an hour.

Bomb Krishnamurthy had said, '*Anna*, now the police will start coming often. Let us send away all the important papers like land documents.'

I knew the police would not trust even the most legal of documents, or that we had not committed any crime so I agreed. Krishnamurthy started sorting out all the papers that were on the teapoy. He found one paper that was an application for the registration of a weekly. He showed it to Ravi and asked him, 'Ravi, see what this is?'

As Ravi reached out for it, I snatched it and tore it.

Later one night I asked Ravi's opinion about launching a labour-relations' weekly that a friend was planning. Ravi had realised that I was suggesting I would start a paper, and immediately he said, 'It is of no use, Sreedhar, I was in union activities before, but it is a thankless job.'

I did not continue the conversation.

Both of us knew that if I started my paper, we would take totally different stands. But I had no choice. I was fed up of his articles glorifying the underworld. He would give boys titles like 'Tiger' and 'Cheetah'. He would write as if the don Sadhu Shetty was the greatest hero the nation had seen. Then, while describing the Mangalore gang that was against Sadhu Shetty, he would call him a small-time guy.

He wrote about a police officer in Mangalore, Jayanth Shetty, saying he was a replica of Shivaram and Ashok Kumar, but when I had an interaction with Shetty, Ravi had cautioned me, saying, 'He is a Sharad Shetty guy.'

He could never understand the turmoil in me during such situations. He never realised that his closeness to a police officer who was friendly with my enemy troubled me.

So I started to seriously consider starting a weekly in July 1998.

In those days, writer-journalist Prathibha Nandakumar used to meet me often to chat. She started doing the running around for me. But she was so innocent, she would say, 'Ravi will be very happy if you start your own weekly.'

Bachchan, who knew nothing about journalism, understood exactly how much it would embarrass Ravi if we started a weekly, but Prathibha—who knew the media so well—hadn't a clue.

In the first week of August 1998, I had the name *Agni* registered.

Why did I choose a name like that, a name so Brahminical, especially when I was so fiercely against Brahminism? Agni— the fire—existed much before the vaidiks claimed it as their god. Fire existed much before life on earth. More than that, I like the two qualities of the sun: its burning energy and its giving light.

We began preparations to start the paper. But how would I tell Ravi about it? Abhimani Venkatesh agreed to print it in his press. Prathibha Nandakumar was all set to bring good writers on board. All this news would definitely leak. Ravi would call me sometimes but he did not ask about it, and I too did not tell him anything.

At this time, an unexpected incident occurred.

Bachchan had gone to court one day. Tanveer too had a case the same day. Rizwan and his gang, who had participated in the killing of Koli Fayaz, had started to become strong in Shivajinagar. Bachchan had been close to Koli Fayaz and since Tanveer was also close to us, that gang was against us.

We heard a rumour that they were trying to contact Muthappa Rai through a lawyer. Bachchan anticipated that if that happened, the fights would not be limited to only Shivajinagar, but extend to us as well. So he called Rizwan and his gang through a *hazrat* and spoke to them, and convinced them to make peace with the Tanveer gang.

When Bachchan was waiting for Tanveer at the court to talk to him, a small altercation occurred and the police arrested Bachchan and took him to the station.

I sent word through somebody that Bachchan was innocent.

The next day, Ravi called. 'Sreedhar, why didn't you tell me about Bachchan's arrest? Are you suspicious of me?'

I tried to change the subject.

Then he said, 'Sreedhar, I heard a joke that you are launching a weekly! I said I am not so stupid to believe such jokes.'

'No Ravi . . . it's not a lie. It is true.'

'Why, Sreedhar? Why one more paper? You don't think *Hi Bangalore* is your paper?'

I sighed, and he did too, and said, 'Sreedhar, I will come and see you tomorrow.'

The day Ravi came to speak to me he had published an article about Muthappa Rai, in which he said there was no connection between Rai and Dawood Ibrahim. He had written that Muthappa Rai had told him over the phone that he was not stupid enough to have any connection with a traitor like Dawood.

There was a strong reason for him to publish that report.

An evening paper had been writing for the last six or seven days that the CBI was seriously looking into the Rai-Dawood connection. The paper had also published a report that B.K. Shivaram, who was close to Rai, had interrogated Khaleel Ur Rehman, who was said to be close to Dawood, for an entire day and sent him back.

Actually, there was no such investigation being conducted. Neither the paper nor its readers bothered to find out how reliable that news was.

But Ravi was desperate to show Rai that he was willing to help him, and hence, instead of limiting his article to say that the eveninger was wrong, he struggled to establish that Rai and Dawood had no connection at all.

As soon as that edition hit the market, Rajendra and some others asked me about the report. They asked if an article supporting Rai should be published in 'our' paper.

Though I had been unhappy about Ravi's ways for a while, I had never shown it to the outside world. That day, I talked to Ravi about it. He asked me straight out, 'Why Sreedhar . . . is my paper not yours?'

I mentioned the article about Rai and asked him, 'Is this a write-up to be published in "our" paper?'

He stared at me.

'Ravi, did I ever ask you to consider my enemies as yours? Did I not tell you never to attack my enemies? Did I not say you should not get caught in the crossfire? Did you think about what I would feel if you published something like this?'

Ravi heard me out fully and then said, 'I was threatened and forced to write the article, Sreedhar.'

Anybody could tell this was a blatant lie. 'Who threatened you?'

'Rai.'

'What?'

'He said if I didn't write and clarify the rumours about him he would finish me . . . I yielded, Sreedhar, for the first time I yielded to threats,' he said very dramatically, even choking.

I behaved as if I believed him; but we both knew it was a charade.

Just look at the paradox: both of us did not want to hurt the other, but both had gone too far ahead to return. He was trying to pretend that a lie was the truth, and I was acting as if I believed it.

'When did he threaten you?' I asked.

'Two days ago.'

'Why didn't you tell me?'

'He said if I told you, he would shoot me.'

'So you got scared?'

'Yes, Sreedhar.'

I caught on to that firmly and asked, 'Today he may threaten you to write in his favour, tomorrow he may threaten you to write against me—what will you do then?'

'No, not possible . . . there is a limit to my fear also.'

'No, Ravi. The only solution is to launch my own paper. I can write what I have to say about Rai, Shivaram . . .'

He could not reply.

Later, after a long time, after many arguments, differences of opinion and a final reconciliation, the first question he asked was this: 'You've written sometimes about Rai, but what about Shivaram? Why have you not written anything? Didn't you start the paper for that?'

I laughed. Society is always like that: it fixes a person in a category. A person is fixed as a writer, a politician, a rowdy. It's a prison. A prison accepted by all. And the one who wants to get out of the prison suffers.

To tell the truth, being part of the underworld had never created any inferiority complex in me. Whatever they said behind my back, in my presence they treated me well. But it was I who did not want to remain within the boundaries of that image. I was always driven by the urge to write.

Isn't life defined by such urges?

I was surprised by the reactions of people when I started the paper. One person from the elite said, 'If you think by starting a paper the police will be scared to touch you, you are wrong.' Another said, 'Who will write your editorial?' Another tried to pull me down by asking, 'So, you want to start a magazine like M.P. Jayaraj's *Garibi Hatao*?'

All these people knew well my interest in literature.

By then Ajay Kumar Singh had become the joint commissioner of police. He wanted to collect information and make a data file on all criminals, just like the fashion was in the West. Computers had just made an entry into the police department and they wanted to 'feed' them. But one thing Ajay Singh overlooked was the fact that developed countries closely watch all criminals and thus collect information about their habits and routines. But in India, they called the criminals in and asked them questions about themselves!

Although after 1992 not a single case was filed against us, they called us and showed us a paper with twenty-five questions typed on it. We had to answer them. It started with our names, the school and colleges we went to, where we worked and continued with:

– Which brothel do you go to?
– How often do you go?
– To which bar do you go to drink?
– Where do you get your hair cut?

Now, forget a rowdy, which man will tell you to which brothel he goes?

Exactly three weeks before *Agni* was launched, they called me and got my answers. By then the news of me launching a paper had spread.

'So even in the paper you want to do rowdyism?'

I said there was no connection between the newspaper and rowdyism. 'Then why did you call it *Agni*? You are out to give a message that you will burn anyone opposing you.'

An extremely sleepy inspector was asking these questions and I was very irritated, but somehow answered him with patience.

Agni was finally launched. In it I specifically explained why I started the paper and also my stand. It was evident I would go against Brahmins. Many were in a dilemma and did not know if it was me writing, or I was having it ghostwritten. By the end of four weeks, many who had identified themselves with pro-people movements came to work for me.

The police department watched me carefully.

Those I criticised tried to threaten me. When Nanje Gowda spoke against Justice Saldanha in the Cubbon Park issue, I supported Saldanha. A friend called me and said, 'Gowda will cut you to size through the DCP. Be careful.'

When we wrote about Khaleed, Roshan Baig's personal secretary, an inspector called me and argued, 'You have written without knowing anything about him. He is a very good human being.'

'What am I to do Sir,' I replied. 'Our informant has given documents to prove his allegation.'

He was not satisfied and said, 'Do one thing, just call him and say you are sorry, that you wrote without finding out the truth.'

I very humbly rejected his advice.

When another official tried to interfere, I said, 'I respect you, not your bosses.'

Most police officers were happy that I had launched the weekly. They were surprised that a person they had identified only with the underworld had social concerns, and so they encouraged me and provided information when it was needed. But there were officers who were only waiting for the opportunity to bring me to order. They were full of suspicion. More than suspicion, it was a sort of resentment that their word was not being given any value.

After the Rupini episode, it was established that *Agni* would go to any lengths to prove the truth.

Ravi had written in his weekly that the actress Rupini had died of AIDS. We found out she was alive and well and living in Bombay. We brought her to Bangalore and held a press meet where she declared—'I am not dead.' It got huge publicity.

Then we published an article about the former police commissioner Kodandaramaiah. After reading it, JCP Ajay Singh spoke to Prathibha Nandakumar and expressed his displeasure. Though she explained at length that it was about a particular individual and not a blanket insult to the police department, he didn't believe her.

After a month, we published a report on how IAS and IPS officials from outside the state function in Karnataka. Since Ajay Singh is not from Karnataka, he took it as criticism against him, said a couple of journalists.

I was not scared.

Meanwhile, Tanveer, who had escaped from jail, was caught again and it was said that he had given a statement that he escaped from jail because he feared me. Maybe he was made to give such a statement.

Ten months after the launch of the weekly, a case was registered against me. I learnt later that some journalists who did not want me to be a media person had complained to Ajay Singh and he had taken action.

Ajay Singh had decided that I was the most dangerous criminal in Bangalore, and he thought nobody would come forward to complain against such a man. So he got his staff to find anybody who had spoken to me in the last three years, take them to the station and interrogate them from six in the morning to nine at night. They were forced to write complaints against me.

When that was not sufficient, he got three persons who had never seen me, nor I them, to lodge a complaint against me. He did all this within a month.

The cases he had 'fitted' were so feeble that I got a stay within a month. They chargesheeted me in four cases within two months. It is a record in the Bangalore city police that, while thousands of cases remain pending for two to three years before being chargesheeted, I was chargesheeted within two months!

To this day I don't know why Ajay Singh behaved in that

manner. He was an honest officer and the only reason I can come up with is that he was power-hungry. It was more important to him to get publicity than to find out the truth—to prove that he had tamed an ex-don, a current journalist.

The truth is, people are scared to complain against a don only when he is not visible. Nobody would come forward to complain against Kotwal or Rai. They naturally reason that if he can escape the police, he will not leave them alone. But what about a person who is visible 24x7 throughout the year? Ajay Singh never thought about that. Revanasiddaiah, the commissioner at that time, was very clear that I was innocent, but he hesitated to give Ajay Singh an order. The entire police department was stunned. It is one of the mysteries of my life why Revanasiddaiah, who never feared anybody, hesitated to order Ajay Singh not to frame me in false cases.

I must share with you an interesting incident that occurred during that time.

One day, when I was in Frazer Town station, Ajay Singh came there at around one o'clock in the morning. My interrogation started. I looked him straight in the eye and asked him, 'Are you happy now that you have fitted me in false cases?'

'If people come and complain, what can we do?' he waved his hand.

ACP Ganapathi and inspector Pratap Singh were with him.

Singh asked, 'When did you go to Nepal?'

In 1997, five friends and I had gone to Kolkata and then to Tara Peeth, Siliguri and touched the Nepal border. We had bought cheap shirts and shoes. I told him this.

'You purchased dry fruits there, didn't you?' Singh asked me.

I was taken aback. I am very fond of dry fruits, but I could not remember buying any in Siliguri or Nepal. 'Sir, I didn't see many dry fruits there . . . I may have bought some and eaten them there, I don't remember,' I answered truthfully.

He smiled. 'You ate them there and also brought some here!'

'Sir, we went there to explore the silk business and also to see Tara Peeth. I am interested in the Tantric cult . . .'

'So you definitely did not bring dry fruits from there?'

I laughed. 'Sir, if I had brought dry fruits, why would I be scared to tell you so? It is not a banned item anyway.'

'Ravikanth Patil had come with you right?' he changed tracks.

Ravikanth Patil is a politician who is sometimes in the news for non-political reasons. Though I know him, he had neither come with me to Nepal nor met me anywhere outside Bangalore. I could not understand why the police were mentioning him now.

'No Sir, he did not come with us.'

'Try and remember. He had come with you and you both purchased dry fruits?'

I found this extremely funny. 'Sir, he did not come with me and even if he did, would we be purchasing dry fruits and chatting?'

He said 'Okay' and left it at that.

The entire night Ravikanth Patil and the dry fruits troubled me.

Only the next morning, when a lower cadre officer explained it to me, did I understand.

'Well . . . do you really not understand what dry fruit means?'

'No.'

'Bullets, bullets! Somebody has told our joint commissioner that you had gone with Ravikanth Patil to Nepal to purchase bullets!' he clarified.

Usually I don't disclose who my friends are, or talk about the places where I have travelled or am going to travel. My friendship with Ravikanth Patil and the fact that I had stepped into Nepal was known only to one person apart from Bachchan—Ravi Belagere.

Now I understood the basis for Ajay Singh's question.

~

When we were in Bellary jail for these cases, Ravindra Prasad (Ravi Belagere's serial killer hero) came to visit me with someone he said was his friend from Goa, Eric. I was not there at the meeting.

Bachchan and our boys in jail could easily figure out that he was a supari killer. When the boys offered to kill him, Bachchan had said no, and asked them to be quiet.

Eric was killed by ACP Bawa in an encounter.

Later, when Ravindra Prasad was interrogated, he gave a statement that Muthappa Rai had introduced him to Eric through Ravi Belagere, and had sent him to kill me. However, the police were not willing to interrogate Ravi Belagere based only on his statement.

Commissioner Revanasiddaiah sent word through Prathibha Nandakumar that he would take action only if I lodged a complaint.

I refused.

One week after Eric was killed in the encounter, I got a phone call at midnight. When I answered the phone, the voice on the other side said, 'I am Muthappa Rai.'

It had been more than seven years since I'd heard his voice, and I could not recognise it. Finally he had to narrate an incident that only the two of us knew to establish his identity!

We spoke till four in the morning.

After an initial ten minutes spent accusing and scolding each other, the rest of the conversation was cordial. We spoke about each other's life, Ravi Belagere, dons of Dubai, children, family and many other topics.

'You don't be careless. Once I will organise a conference call with other dons, Sharad Shetty and Chota Shakeel . . . you will know in what high esteem they hold you,' said Rai, and strangely the past cordiality that we had shared returned to my heart.

To tell the truth, the night Rai called, the little interest that I had remaining in *dadagiri* melted away. Rai did not sound fake. There was no need for him to please me. Also, it was not challenging to fight or kill others after having fought face-to-face with a person like Rai.